Robert Payne

The Marshall Story

A Biography of General George C. Marshall

Brick Tower Press
Habent Sua Fata Libelli

Brick Tower Press
Manhanset House
Dering Harbor, New York 11965-0342
Tel: 212-427-7139
bricktower@aol.com • www.BrickTowerPress.com

All rights reserved under the International and Pan-American Copyright Conventions.
Printed in the United States by J. T. Colby & Company, Inc., New York.
No part of this publication may be reproduced, stored in a retrieval system, or transmitted in any form or by any means, electronic, or otherwise, without the prior written permission of the copyright holder.
The Brick Tower Press colophon is a registered trademark of
J. T. Colby & Company, Inc.

Library of Congress Cataloging-in-Publication Data
Payne, Robert
The Marshall Story, A Biography of General George C. Marshall
Includes biographical references, index, and photos.
ISBN 978-1-883283-94-0

1. Payne, Robert— 2. Biography—George C. Marshall 3. Military History 4. World War II 5. Robert Payne Library, Volume 7.

Copyright © 1951 by Robert Payne
Originally published by Prentice-Hall, 1952

First Trade Paper Printing, January 2015
The Marshall Story
—*A Biography of General George C. Marshall*

Robert Payne

The Marshall Story

A Biography of General George C. Marshall

Also by Robert Payne

By Me, William Shakespeare
The Great Charlie, A Biography of the Tramp
Leonardo
Gershwin
The Life and Death of Mahatma Gandhi
The Great Man, Winston Churchill
The Life and Death of Adolf Hitler
The Christian Centuries from Christ to Dante
The World of Art

SONG FOR THE OLD GENERAL

When he was fifteen or twenty years old
He snatched a wild pony's bridle, then rode away.
In the mountains he killed a tiger with a white forehead:
Once with his sword he stopped a million men.
Swift as the blaze of lightning were his troops.
Today his left elbow is knotted like willows,
And by the roadside he sells ripe melons.
Dark green are the ancient trees beside his house,
And the winter hills shine on his window.
See, he still polishes his armor till it shines like snow,
And brandishes his jewelled sword like a flashing star.
Do not think lightly of the old general
Who still may fight a battle to keep his laurel green.

—WANG WEI (about 740 A.D.)

ACKNOWLEDGMENT

The photographs in this book have been made available through the courtesy of the United States Army.

CONTENTS

	ACKNOWLEDGMENT	vi
	INTRODUCTION	ix
I.	THE ANCESTORS	3
II.	THE SHADOW ON THE WALL	12
III.	THE FIRST ENCOUNTERS	25
IV.	PREPARING FOR WAR	40
V.	CANTIGNY	60
VI.	ST. MIHIEL AND SEDAN	71
VII.	TOWARDS OBSCURITY	93
VIII.	THE DANGEROUS YEARS	100
IX.	THE VOLCANO	121
X.	THE MORNING OF PEARL	152
XI.	THE FIRST GROPINGS	163
XII.	THE RAGE FOR VICTORY	191
XIII.	THE WINNING OF THE WAR	221
XIV.	DEBACLE IN CHINA	255
XV.	MR. SECRETARY	289
XVI.	PORTRAIT	324

INTRODUCTION

This book is more concerned with the mind of General Marshall than with a recital of his day by day activities, and though the general form of a biography has been followed, it is not in the strict sense a biography at all. I have attempted to discover what kind of man he is, why he developed in the way he did, and how he became a legend. The examination of legends presents obvious difficulties, for legends acquire forces over which men have little or no control, and we are tempted to bow before legends when we would refuse to bow before men. The historian concerned with great historical figures must perpetually ask himself: Where does the legend end? Where does the man begin? Unfortunately, there are no easy answers to these questions, and historical characters themselves are often confounded by their own legends.

I imagine that the pathways of the mind are a little like the terrible roads of the Pentagon. These roads seem to have been designed for the special purpose of ensuring that men lose themselves in a maze. Bays, rings, corridors, ramps, stairs, a profusion of colored pillars, conflicting direction signs, passages which seem endless and others which end abruptly, these are the things we may expect to find in the mind of a modern general. The difficulty is to find where the mind's core is. General Marshall, more complex than most American generals, and far more subtle, tends to disappear in the heart of the maze. Sometimes a mirror flashes; sometimes we catch a glimpse of him, but not for long. He eludes us, as perhaps he eludes himself. His real power is something that can be felt rather than described.

There are dangers in writing a study of a modern general: the same kind of dangers which confront those who deal with high explosives. The modern general is a new species. Nothing quite like him has ever existed before. He wields such vast and deadly forces that he becomes more than human, removed from the preoccupations of ordinary mortals. Catastrophe or triumph are at his command: he can not only defeat, but he can annihilate whole populations in a moment of time. He can lay waste whole areas of the earth, sink islands below the level of the seas, sweep centuries of history away with an order dictated calmly over the telephone, and simply because he possesses these powers, he is continually tempted to use them. By 1945 the powers of a general had become so prodigious that the game of war was hardly worth the playing; war itself had reached a crisis, and was in danger of becoming something else altogether. A new vocabulary was needed to describe the stresses and strains operating on the minds of men who wield such incalculable powers. In the absence of a new vocabulary, it should be realized that in the chapters concerning Marshall's direction of the war, the ordinary words sometimes fail to convey the requisite meaning. Marshall likes to use the word "tremendous." The Fathers of the Western Church spoke of the *tremendum Dei,* the earth-shattering terror which is a portion of the mercy of God. Sometimes, when Marshall uses the word "tremendous," it would be wise to remember the medieval meaning.

If the modern general is almost superhuman, he is also—far more often than he suspects—less than human. The historian concerned with the career of Marshall inevitably finds himself reading the autobiographies of the lesser generals. They are not always pleasant reading. Too often the military autobiographers suffer from the first of the seven deadly sins, which is pride; they ascribe their successes to their superb intelligence, their occasional failures to the unkindly fates. They speak of the soldiers under their command as one might speak of robots, and they very rarely speak of the soldiers. They forget that the mistakes of generals are never small. General Bradley boasted frankly of his successes, but he had little to say about the disaster in the Ardennes which resulted in fifty-nine thousand American casualties, a disaster which was due to his own failure in tactics. (He noted that the command sometimes makes mistakes.) Humility is not a characteristic of generals, but it is reasonable to suggest that generals should in future be examined for their humility, for fear that their overweening pride lead them to errors and a mental disturbance which is not far removed from madness. General Eisenhower once remarked that the occupational disease of generals is an exalted belief in their own importance. This is a belief which is rarely shared by the soldiers, who do not die to glorify their generals, but in the hope that their deaths will help their country to live.

We live in a sacrificial age, and generals are the executioners. Even the best of them by the very nature of their profession are tainted with guilt, for no man has the right to traffic with the lives of human beings. So there can be no end to war until there is an end to the officer caste, and no peace as long as the military virtues of cunning and ruthlessness are acclaimed. General Marshall wrote somewhere that the historians have failed in their task: they should have been able to discover and reveal the causes of war and make war impossible. It is more likely that wars arise because ruthlessness, cunning, and the desire for power over their fellow men, the qualities which are indispensible in a general, are still regarded as conventionally desirable. To find the causes of war we should dissect the minds of generals.

Mercifully, General Marshall provides an admirable case history of a general in possession of a superb intelligence, a man who was oppressed by war and yet strove to bring himself to a pitch of mechanical perfection in the art of war, a man who is humane and humble and not very proud, and who knows more about war than anyone else in his generation. It would seem that the scientific historian, embarking on a study of General Marshall, would be able to find the clue to the problem "What brings wars about?" without any great difficulty.

Unfortunately, the problem is not so easily solved, if only because General Marshall is the least typical of generals. More and more as we enter into his story we shall see that he has little in common with contemporary generals and less with the generals of the past, and very often he gives the impression of being a general against the grain. What is remarkable in him is the mind working relentlessly to assume responsibilities, as though seeking to expiate an ancient crime, a fastidious and beautifully balanced mind thinking in terms of the dignity and integrity of the country which gave him birth, and almost in no other terms.

I have tried to dissociate him from his legend. It has not always been easy, partly because some of the legends seem to be inextricably woven into the fabric of the man. Twice, when he committed errors of vast and tragic dimensions, I have thought it necessary to enquire into the reasons for his failure; but those who believe that General Marshall is an agent of an enemy power will find no comfort in the chapters which explore his errors. For the rest, this is the study of a gallant, gentle and tormented man who worked wonderfully to revive the ancient American virtues of fortitude and mercy at a time when those virtues were more than ever necessary.

ROBERT PAYNE

THE MARSHALL STORY

CHAPTER ONE

The Ancestors

The Pilgrim Fathers came late to America. Fourteen years before they sailed from the barbican at Plymouth, three ships, the *Susan Constant,* the *Pinnace* and the *God Speed* sailed from London, and the adventurers who sailed in them established a colony on a strip of coast which came to be known as the Tidewater of Virginia. They were the forerunners of the American adventure. The new colony was English to the core, conserved the English traditions, became a repository of the English character and the English habits of mind, until the subtle processes of transplantation made the Virginians more English than the English, their faults and their virtues increasing as under a magnifying glass. Among these blue misty hills, among the shaded rivers and the groves of wild strawberries and forests of cedar and scented boxwood, there grew up a race of tall, vigorous and determined men, many of them royalist refugees from a puritan England; and long after the establishment of the Republic there were men like John Randolph who spoke of "going home to England."

The planters and the great landowners made Virginia, and left their stamp on her. A Georgian graciousness settled on the old Tidewater houses with their porticos and shaded carriage roads. Gradually the Tidewater lost its significance. Jamestown and Williamsburg fell into decay; and eventually the obscure city of Richmond became the capital of a state lopped of its former magnificence—until, in time, it became the capital of the Confederacy. Some with ancestral memories may have remembered that the War between the States had its origins in England, for once more the baffled Cavaliers were at war with the Roundheads; and in the disastrous illusion of war the Confederacy saw the expiring gesture of chivalry.

It could hardly have been otherwise. Virginia, the old Dominion, became the battleground: the place where the armies grappled, the place where ideas fought one another to an embattled standstill. The imperial domain became, by the accidents of geography and settlement, the heart of the Republic, at the mercy of all the forces which arose during the two great revolutions which have occurred on American soil. It was no accident that Virginia became the battleground in the War between the States. Nor was it an accident that a Jefferson of Virginia drafted the Declaration of Independence, that a Washington of Virginia led the army and became the first President, that a Madison of Virginia fathered the Federal Constitution, that a Marshall of Virginia became the greatest American jurist, and that a Henry of Virginia uttered the most resounding phrase of the Revolution. These men were larger than life. They had to be. They were hard, choleric men, disputatious by instinct, aristocratic and austere by tradition, free men by choice, with a streak of wildness and chivalry and romance running through them: they possessed the gift of leadership, and never made their peace with slavery. When Jefferson said that "the whole commerce between master and slave is a perpetual exercise of the most boisterous passions," he was offering a rebuke. He implied that passions, boisterous passions, were unworthy of Virginians, who should be passionless and austere: he chose an austere and indefinable happiness, rather than pleasure, as man's birthright.

The Marshalls were Virginians. They belonged to the class known in Virginia as "good people," a label which distinguished them from the aristocratic estate of "good families." Their origins were humble. If later there were some who claimed descent from William le Mareschal who fought at the Battle of Hastings and was rewarded with an estate on the borders of Wales, there were others like Captain John Marshall of the Forest, the grandson of the first settler, who remembered only that his grandfather came from Wales. There are family legends which say that the first settler fought for the King at Edgehill as a captain of cavalry, but no one knows for certain whether he did. It is more likely that he came as an indentured servant, serving his master for five years and at the end of this period receiving his freedom and a free gift of fifty acres of land according to the ordinances of the government of colonial Virginia. Beyond the statement that the first Captain John Marshall came from Wales there are no clues. Long before 1650, when he is supposed to have arrived in Virginia, there was a Robert Marshall who owned property at Goose Hill in Jamestown, and there were other Marshalls in the interior.

We know almost nothing about the original Captain John Marshall or of his son Thomas, a carpenter in King and Queen County. With John Marshall of the Forest the family emerges from obscurity. Born in 1700, he became a large planter, married the daughter of the sheriff of Westmoreland County, and sired nine children. In 1728, six years after his marriage to Elizabeth Markham, he acquired from John Washington and Thomas Pope some two hundred acres of uninviting land, which grew eventually to twelve hundred acres. He planted well, cut down the underbrush, bought slaves, and became a captain of militia—Campbell in his history of Virginia gives him credit for the successful termination of the Indian wars. He was a man of substance, and owed much to his wife's connections—Elizabeth Markham's grandfather, who formerly kept tavern at Nomini, acquired from another John Washington the lease of a plantation—but he owed more to his own strong arm. He was on speaking terms with the Washingtons, whose children played with his children, a stern man, given to rebuke, the first of the patriarchs who from time to time came to rule over the Marshall clans. When he died he left his wife the main portion of his estate together with "one Gray mair named beauty and side saddle also six hogs," while to his third son William he left "one negro woman named sall and one negro boy named Hanable to remain in the possession of his mother until he comes to the age of twenty years." From this third son George Catlett Marshall Jr. is descended.

William began life as a rakehell. He was handsome, well-built, a good swordsman and a good card-player, who fought duels and rode to hounds, until, wearying of the artificial life on a colonial plantation, he took to the excitement of revealed religion. He became a Baptist preacher of such vehemence that people doubted his sanity. He delighted in the ceremonies of baptism, and once baptized fifty-three people in a single day in Shenandoah. Once he fell from his horse and broke a leg. The accident did not put an end to his preaching. He demanded to be taken to the pulpit. Propped up, he delivered to an open-mouthed audience a raging sermon full of brimstone and hellfire, his eyes flashing and his arms wheeling. In time he was thought to be deranged, and was locked up. He was released from prison on the intervention of his brother Thomas Marshall. Thomas knew the Washingtons well and fought with George Washington in Braddock's ill-fated expedition; he became high sheriff of the county, a member of the House of Burgesses and of the council which asserted Virginia's independence, and had a horse shot under him at Brandywine. Afterwards, when the wars were over, he set out for Kentucky as surveyor-general of the lands beyond the mountains. He was the father of Chief Justice Marshall through his marriage with Mary Randolph Keith: the marriage brought him into family relationship with the first families of Virginia, for Mary Keith descended from the Randolphs of Turkey Island. He was the accomplished soldier-politician, rich, generous and brave, and he had little in common with his brother William, the spendthrift preacher who cared nothing for worldly accomplishments.

But if Thomas was a leader of men, so was William in his own way. In 1781, at the age of forty-six, fourteen years after his marriage to Mary Anne Pickett, he was a pastor in the Upper Spotsylvania Baptist Church, sharing his duties with another pastor called Lewis Craig. On September 12, he delivered a sermon before his congregation calling upon them to abandon their evil ways and march out like the Israelites of old to the new land of Canaan. He believed that Canaan was situated in the Blue Grass region of Kentucky, and spoke so vehemently and so convincingly that the whole congregation to the number of two hundred, together with three hundred more people from the surrounding districts, set out the next day for Kentucky, moved by a sudden spiritual fervor. At Fort Chiswell they abandoned their wagons and continued the journey on foot. There were rumors of Indians in the neighborhood. Frightened, they clustered together for protection; and there were more rumors of Indian outrages when they reached Wolf Hills, where they received news of Cornwallis's surrender. So they journeyed on, singing hymns, baptizing as they went, full of visions of a land flowing with milk and honey. They formed the largest body that had ever set out from Kentucky at one time. They reached Lexington on the third Sunday of December, having journeyed for more than two months mostly on foot; and on the day they arrived, Lewis Craig and William Marshall delivered more fiery sermons which lasted well into the night.

Of the direct ancestors of George Catlett Marshall two at least were leaders of men: one fought the Indians, and the other led his flock over the mountains to a promised land. The first died in the odor of respectability, leaving a small fortune. William Marshall came to own property in Kentucky, but was so desultory a landlord and possessed so little interest in his holdings that his children lost nearly the whole of their inheritance, partly because their father had forgotten to legalize his holdings.

There appears to be a law of descent by which children make up for the deficiencies of their fathers. William's son Martin became a lawyer who spent his life among land titles, and did uncommonly well from his office in Augusta. Reticent and dignified, with no pronounced interest in religion, a man with a distinguished bearing, he married Matilda Battaile Taliaferro, a marriage which linked him with the fabulous fortunes of the descendants of "King" Carter of Corotoman. One of his sons, Thomas Alexander, became a judge. Another, William Champe, became a lawyer. Thomas Alexander's son Martin was the first Marshall to enter the Virginia Military Institute. As a cadet private he fought at the battle of New Market, helping to throw General Sigel's forces back across the Shenandoah River. In the battle ten cadets were killed or mortally wounded, and fifteen severely wounded. Part of Martin's knee was shot away. A handsome and eager youth, his name was recorded in the battle honors. He had wanted to be a soldier; instead, he was compelled to follow his father's trade. He became a lawyer, but to the end of his life he complained against the fortune which made him a lawyer when he would have preferred a regiment. He died at the comparatively early age of forty-nine. It was said that his early death was due to his wound.

Martin belonged to the legendary Marshalls, the men with dash and brio, like the Colonel Thomas Marshall who fought at Valley Forge, and like Louis, the brother of the Chief Justice, who wandered off to France, where he witnessed the massacre of the Swiss Guards and the fall of the Bastille and took part in duels with students in the Latin Quarter. There is a story that he was arrested and condemned to death by the Revolutionary Tribunal, and was rescued just in time. He became the first president of Washington University until he resigned in disgust over a matter of principle. Of this Louis Marshall, the rough-riding General Basil Duke said, in words which were appropriate to a whole series of Marshalls: "His opinions were frequently inaccurate, for they were much controlled by his prejudices, but were often profound, always striking and original."

No one ever accused William Champe Marshall of either profundity or originality. He conformed to the rules, a pure Kentucky lawyer with a flair for politics. He became a member of the Kentucky legislature and mayor of Augusta. He married the daughter of an Augusta merchant and produced nine children. With him the fire of one line of Marshalls seemed to have died out. Colorless, precise, conventional, he dominated the life of the growing city, and he had nothing in common with his distant relative, Colonel Charles Marshall, the grandson of the Chief Justice, who was Lee's *alter ego*. It was Colonel Charles Marshall who prepared Lee's farewell address. Dressed impeccably in a new uniform, Colonel Charles Marshall was present at McClean's farmhouse on the day when Grant walked in swordless and wearing a private's coat to confront a defeated general who wore gold epaulettes and a tasseled sword. William Champe Marshall took no part in the war; nor apparently did his fifth son, George Catlett Marshall.

There was no sudden decline in the family spirit. It had come slowly over the centuries. More than anyone else William Marshall had been responsible for the fall. Now the Marshalls were becoming urbanized, losing their wilfulness and their claims to fame, immersed among legal briefs or their small businesses, at a world's remove from the fiery Colonel who hacked his way through a forest with a company of Virginia troops in a despairing effort to rescue Braddock from an Indian ambuscade. It seemed as though the Marshall virtue perished the further the Marshalls left their native Virginia.

George Catlett Marshall became a coal and wood dealer in Uniontown, Pennsylvania, prosperous in a small way, a Mason and a

Democrat. He was a man who dreamed of the past with some bitterness; he was vain and litigious, and at the same time he had a reputation for being good company, a vestryman who took his church duties seriously and brought up his children to be devout Episcopalians. He liked to spend hours surveying the family tree, and he liked to talk especially of the extraordinary Chief Justice who had been ambassador to France under Washington and Secretary of State under John Adams. He had a surgeon's delicacy when it came to carving a Thanksgiving turkey, but his finesse failed in business, for he sold out his coke companies to the combines without making any singular profit. There were twenty-three serious strikes in the coal-bearing regions of the Alleghenies between 1880 and 1900. All these affected his industry. Once, one of his factory managers was killed by a striker. On another occasion he was shot at in the dark, the striker aiming at the red glow of his cigar. It was the time of the "Molly Maguires," the secret organization of Irish roughs in the Pennsylvania anthracite country, who answered the mineowners' brutality with more brutality. In an effort to break the strikes the coal operators imported laborers from Poland and Germany. Years later, when General Marshall spoke of the sons of these immigrants who came to Uniontown in his childhood, he remembered how their fathers had been strange, gaunt men, utterly unlike the Pennsylvanians; but their sons looked like Americans. Meanwhile the satanic mills were grinding. Uniontown was caught up in the flood of a harsh, intolerant industrialism.

The town, given over to coke factories, was ugly. But then, it had never been beautiful. As long ago as 1784 General Ephraim Douglas wrote: "This Uniontown is the most obscure spot on the face of the globe. The town and its appurtenances consist of a courthouse and schoolhouse in one, a mill four taverns, three smith shops, five retail shops, two tanyards, one saddler's shop, two hatters' shops, one mason, one cake woman, two widows and some reputed maids." There was also, the general added with a final snort of disgust, only a single distillery. With its wild setting at the foot of the Alleghenies, the town deserved better. It possessed however a few laurels. Lafayette had visited it; so had Washington; Albert Gallahn's log cabin, the beginning of New Geneva, was nearby; Whitman visited the place on a memorable occasion; Jenny Lind spent a night there and breakfasted on speckled trout fresh from a mountain stream. Here, in a house perched eerily on a mountainside, among the smokestacks and clouds of sulphur-laden smoke, George Catlett Marshall Jr. was born on December 31, 1880.

There flowed in his veins the blood of the Taliaferros, the Catletts, the Pendletons, the Markhams, the Picketts and the Carters, and all of these are names which appear among the first settlers of Virginia. The name Catlett was derived from the Elizabeth Catlett who married the eldest son of Robert Taliaferro, who came to Virginia in 1650, and from her father, Colonel John Catlett, a Kentishman who settled in Essex County around 1650. He became a colonel of the militia, a magistrate and justice of the peace; he was commissioned to settle the border dispute between Maryland and Virginia, and he accompanied John Lederer on his famous expedition through the country west of the Blue Ridge. Catlett was therefore a name to be held in honor, serving to remind him that he was a Virginian in exile. The name Marshall might mean no more than that an ancestor had been a blacksmith, the word coming from the Old High German *marahscalc,* meaning horse-servant; but the name bore a reputable ancestry. There was no need to search for Marshalls in English history, among the Cavaliers and the Earls of Pembroke. Their noblest claim was that they were Virginians, rooted deep in Virginian soil, and their proud boast was that they had kept faith not so much with England as with the transplanted values of courtesy, chivalry and saintliness, which had been the characteristics of the Cavaliers.

"A Virginian," said the Marquis de Chastelux, "never resembles a European peasant. He is by birth a freeman who partakes in the government." He might have added that it was one of the traits of the Virginians that they remembered the past, were themselves a part of the past, lived according to ancient rituals, and were never happy unless they saw the shape of the past in the present. They believed in privilege. How could they avoid it, since the traditions of the Cavaliers were so insistent? And if they desired that all men should partake of privilege, this too arose from their sense of duty, their knowledge of a harm done long ago, of a king who was violated, a sin to be punished by the ritual dethronement of still another king. Ironically, the founders of the American Republic were largely the descendants of the enemies of the Roundheads. There is some significance in the year 1650, which saw the coming to America of so many of the Virginian patriarchs: on a cold January morning of the previous year Charles had been killed with a single slice of an ax wielded by an unknown executioner who wore a mask and concealed the lower part of his face with a horsehair beard. And while Cromwell ruled over the Republic of England, Virginia was still royalist to the core.

There are mysteries here, as elsewhere. A strange, dispassionate, nervous and handsome race came to birth in Virginia. You recognized them by their long faces, the delicacy of their bones, the subtle quarrels in their blood, the panoply and the glory which surrounded them, though they pretended not to be aware of it themselves. They called themselves gentlemen, but they were given to sudden violence, and they had a lust for self-sacrifice. "The first hostile forces sent out were Virginians, and the first blood was shed by Virginians," wrote Governor Dinwiddie of a war against France; and so it was throughout the long history of Virginia. They held their honor high, and never forgot their hurts.

As the story of General Marshall unfolds, we see behind him another Marshall larger than life, compounded of the "good families" and the "good people" of Virginia. Hard-riding landowners among Corinthian pillars, women in starched crinolines, young bloods in scarlet coats and linen ruffles, in knee-breeches of watered silk and with immense blue bows on their painted slippers: somewhere behind them is the smoke of war and the bloody scalps dangling from the hickory branches. To forget his ancestors is to forget the man; for more than any other modern American he belongs to another age, so that sometimes the General seems to disappear altogether: he becomes John of the Forest, mad William, the patriarchal Thomas and the plodding Kentucky lawyer by turns. He is all these, and more. The fire of the Taliaferros burns in him; he inherited the physical beauty of the Pendletons, the courage of the Catletts and the fierce waywardness of the Markhams, who attracted legends to themselves, inventing piratical ancestors for the pure pleasure of invention; but none of these were so important as his Virginian birthright, the knowledge that he was an appointed guardian of the new land of promise which Drayton called "Earth's only Paradise."

CHAPTER TWO

The Shadow on the Wall

It was the time of the marble fireplaces, the ormolu clocks, the velvet plush, and the bowls of fruit made of colored glass, of antimacassars and soft carpets and men with waxen moustaches and women in whalebone corsets, of heavy mahogany tables and great displays of silver plate in the evening gaslight, before electricity came in to give a cold pinpoint glow to the industrial revolution, a world of great joints of meat at twelve cents a pound and heavy Sunday meals and all the ornate comforts designed to deaden the roar of furnaces and coke-ovens and the incongruous voices of the multitudes of foreign-born workers. The year was 1882, with America in the full tide of industrial expansion. It was the year when the Standard Oil Company emerged as the first great trust, when the young Edison set up the first generating and distributing station in New York, and the Anaconda mine was being opened, and the Noble Order of the Knights of Labor was beginning to exert its strength. The crust was breaking. There was a beginning to the long series of savage strikes which broke out in the Pennsylvania coal fields; and like a seismograph the Marshall household registered the shocks and motions of industrial earthquakes.

George Catlett Marshall had begun well enough by setting up the Dunbar Manufacturing Company, producers of firebrick, and afterwards he had leased mining and coking businesses, acquiring coal properties and firebrick manufacturing rights, until by 1880 he was in full or partial control of more than two hundred coke ovens, only to sell them all shortly afterwards to H. C. Frick's expanding empire. Then his mind turned inevitably to Virginia. Characteristically—for he was an expansive man, and for years he had lived with the thought of leaving Uniontown forever—he thought of acquiring a hotel. He chose one at Luray Caverns in the Shenandoah Valley, not far from where his ancestors had settled. When it came to signing the document, he simply wrote down his signature, forgetting to add the word "President" which would have ensured collective responsibility if the venture failed. The venture did fail. He was never to return to Virginia. He grew old rapidly, growing more and more religious, never sullen, delighting in the small ways of a provincial town, having foresworn the idea of launching his own industrial empire over Pennsylvania, looking after his three children with the air of a man who refused to be enmeshed in their pursuits while marveling at their grace. There was Marie, and Stuart Bradford, and now there was the two-year old George Catlett Jr. On one day in the year 1882 the baby was taken to be photographed.

It is a strange and revealing photograph. The cheeks are puffy and the hair has been combed smoothly down the forehead and he wears his elder sister's laced dress under a velvet coat sprinkled with mother-of-pearl buttons and an immense lace collar, but he stands even then with an air of authority. The lace collar gives him something of the look of a Cavalier princeling. One elbow rests on a stone balcony, the bright eyes look straight at the camera. Underneath the lace collar there can be seen a polka-dot ribbon tied in a bow, put there for no reason that can be discovered, unless it was that an adoring mother was determined to relieve the monotony of lace with a splash of color.

As he grew up, pug-nosed and freckled and with sandy hair, he lost his air of childish authority. He could hardly be distinguished from the other boys of the place. He kept pets, but most of them were boarded out: only the dogs were allowed in the house in Main Street by his father. His friends whispered that he kept a caged wildcat in some remote recess of the house. It may have been true, for he had a passion for all kinds of animals, and he was not afraid of his father's ordinances. He owned a share in the favorite stock of Pennsylvania children: gamecocks, which fought to the death in remote cockpits in the hills. Long afterwards he remembered the contentment which came to him on Saturday afternoons when he ventured out to a secret rendezvous, remembering the passwords and the secret handshakes of the conspirators who brought their wicker baskets to the hills and sometimes wept when they were compelled to bury a gamecock where it fell. He read riotously, exhausting his father's small library with its morocco-bound histories of Virginia and Kentucky, but more often he was deeply immersed in the adventures of Diamond Dick and Nick Carter. Nick Carter caused one downfall. Serving as organ-pumper at St. Peter's Church, he sat goggled-eyed over a Nick Carter romance and failed, at a solemn moment, to supply the organ with air. On another occasion he ducked into an alley on his way to school and spent the day in a blacksmith's shop learning the trade, only to be discovered in the evening by his sister, who was sent out to fetch him home. His father gave him a beating: it was the only beating he is known to have received. But there was something odd in his choice of a blacksmith's trade: it was as though ancestral memories were working again.

The boy was hardly in his teens when he determined to be a soldier. His sister Marie could never remember a time when he was not dreaming of entering the Virginia Military Institute. He was ten when his brother entered the Institute, and there were Stuart Bradford's letters home to remind him of the glories of the place, and there were the family traditions and all of Virginian history to tempt him towards the college at Lexington. He imagined battles when he was young, himself a commander of invisible armies in the garden behind his house, where he threw up a military tent, made from a blanket thrown over the branches of an apple tree; but in all this he differed hardly at all from the other boys of Uniontown, who took part in imaginary wars against imaginary French and Indians on imaginary western frontiers: Braddock's red-coated regulars had marched to battle not far away, though the battlefield on the banks of the Monongahela River was now unrecognizable: Andrew Carnegie had built his steel mills on the very place where Braddock fought. Where Thomas Marshall had nearly died and only thirty Virginians had lived to tell the tale, industrialism was rampant.

Industrialism claimed George's elder brother, for after graduating from Virginia Military Institute, Stuart Bradford took no more interest in military affairs. He became a blast furnace assayer in the United Verde Copper Company, then head chemist and later manager of the Dunbar Furnace Company, then manager of the American Manganese Manufacturing Company. It is at least possible that George's devotion to a military career was a reaction against the empires of the Carnegies and the Schwabs.

He was growing into a tall, handsome youth with clear blue eyes, a sensitive mouth and freckles all over his face. The nickname Flicker clung to him, perhaps from the German *Flecke,* which can mean freckles. He was sensitive of his pug-nose and timid in the presence of young women, saying afterwards that he lost his nerve with women at the age of ten when his childhood sweetheart at a kermess said: "You make me sick." But he acquired a reputation of being an unusually sensible and sensitive boy, dull at school but bright outside, who liked climbing trees and staging shows in Thompson's stable and coasting on Gilmore's Hill. And he had a passionate fondness for animals, his greatest tragedy being that no one would give him a pony, and he never had enough money to buy one. Also, in an odd boyish way, he was deeply religious, with a pronounced objection to sin in all its forms. There was nothing vulgar in his desire to be superlatively good: it was simply that he had absorbed from his mother and from his father's library the formal code of a Virginian; and though he had been exiled from the pump-blower's position at St. Peter's Church, he attended church regularly and read the Bible every night before saying his prayers and leaping into bed. He followed the religious code of his time, being baptized at St. Peter's on June 5, 1881, and being confirmed there on February 7, 1896. In the following year he entered the Virginia Military Institute.

All that he had desired to do, all that he ever hoped to do seemed now on the point of fulfillment. Long ago, at some time in his childhood, he had determined to be a soldier. The name of Martin Marshall was spoken in the family as one might speak of a canonized saint. The name of General Scott-Shipp was spoken in the same breathless manner, and it was this general, then known as Colonel Shipp, who had led the two hundred and fifty cadets of the Institute to New Market during Grant's Wilderness Campaign. It was Colonel Shipp who marched at the head of the long column which raced out of Lexington, and who had given orders for the famous charge; and now, already an old man, bluff and vigorous still, he was superintendent of the college, a straight-backed disciplinarian who stood no nonsense and seemed determined that though Virginia had been defeated in the war, she would show by the courage of her cadets that she was still an example to the world. The War between the States was still a living issue at the college. On the staff there were men who remembered vividly the details of Lee's campaigns. Above all, there was the memory of "Tom Fool" Jackson, who was Professor of Natural and Experimental Philosophy and Artillery Tactics at the college until he joined the Confederate Army and earned the name of "Stonewall" Jackson.

At V.M.I, the cult of Jackson was celebrated in an atmosphere of asceticism which would have pleased that wild-eyed general, who once taught optics, mechanics and astronomy, drilled the cadets and instructed them in the art of gunnery, saying that he could always keep a day or two ahead of his students, though he knew hardly more theory than they did. Here they still guarded Jackson's desk in the old recitation hall, and interminable solemn speeches were dedicated to his honor. Three months before young Marshall's coming in September, old Dr. Hunter McGuire had addressed the students with memories of Jackson. He told how President Davis had ridden up at Manassas and stopped his horse in the middle of a little stream, having heard from stragglers that the Confederate Army was defeated. The President stood up in his stirrups, showing the palest, sternest face the doctor had ever seen, and then shouted to the soldiers: "I am President Davis—follow me back to the field." Jackson was nearby, having a wound in his hand attended to by the doctor. He was a little deaf and had not caught the impact of the President's words, but when the President came nearer, Jackson removed his cap and said: "We have whipped them—they ran like sheep. Give me ten thousand men and I will take Washington City tomorrow." The old doctor told a fistful of similar stories. Once he had asked Jackson what he thought about the first time he was under fire. Jackson answered: "I was afraid the fire would not be hot enough for me to distinguish myself." It was a typical remark, to be repeated and commented upon endlessly by the cadets, who could weary of the constant adulation of Jackson without ever wearying of the resourceful fighter.

The Virginia Military Institute was not one of the great military academies. It was one of those civilian schools, called "tin colleges," like the Citadel at Charleston, the Virginia Polytechnic Institute and the Agricultural and Mechanical College of Texas, which were specially favored by the War Department for their strict military training. With its two crenelated towers, it looked from a distance like a medieval Scottish castle. There were relics of the War between the States everywhere: cannon and cannon balls on the grass, a militant statue of Jackson standing in front of the barracks archway, and not far away the bodies of the cadets killed at New Market. "I wish you could see our Institute," Jackson wrote from Lexington to his sister in the summer of 1852, "for I consider that it is the most tasty edifice in the state." It was still tasty, and little changed since Jackson's day.

Marshall arrived late at the college when it opened in September, 1897. One of his classmates said he was "a clumsy unpromising recruit, ill-looked-upon by the exacting faculty of the ancient institution." General Johnson Hagood, who came to know Marshall first some years later in the Philippines, heard a similar story. He told how Marshall entered the Institute "as a long, a lean and a gawky cadet, sensitive and shy; a Pennsylvania Yankee in a Southern School at a time when the Blue and the Grey had not yet been welded in the fires of the Spanish war.... He landed in the awkward squad, and he stayed there, on and on. He could not drill. He could not march. All he could do was sweat, look uncomfortable and be embarrassed whenever he was spoken to." It was not a very fair description, for "Rat" Marshall was hardly a Pennsylvania Yankee, and with any encouragement at all he would have been able to demonstrate his Southern sympathies. There was something in that ridiculously gangling youth which looked Yankee; he suffered for it, and was never quite sure why he was suffering.

As the most junior and the most unnecessary person at the college he was given a quarter share in a room on the Third Stoop. This meant that he had to run the gantlet of any Second or Third Class tormentors who chose to waylay him on his way to his distant cell. It was a barren and monkish cell, with no ornament, no running water, no suggestion of what is nowadays called, with some effrontery, "civilized living." There was a large wooden wardrobe with open shelves, gunracks where the guns stood vertically, a shoebox below the guns, chairs, a washstand, a slop bucket and a water bucket. Cots were stacked each day. Water was drawn from two hydrants in the courtyard: to reach them it was necessary to run the gantlet. It was bitterly cold in winter. There were small steam radiators; to warm their bath water some cadets boot-legged a petcock on a radiator with a strip of rubber hose—the steam could then be shot into a water basin. To do this was strictly against the rules. Mechanical obedience was demanded not only by the teachers but by the upper classmen, who invented obscure punishments for "Rats" who did not hold themselves up like ramrods. "Rats" were regarded as the scum of the earth. They must not speak unless spoken to. They must jump at the flick of the whip. They were continually employed as "dykes" or fags by their seniors, and every indignity was heaped on them, including the indignity of changing their names. Marshall, who had been known as Flicker in Uniontown, found himself to his horror bearing the name of Pug, a word which unhappily described his small nose. Years later, without knowing anything about the former name, President Roosevelt decided to call his Chief of Staff "Plog." It amused the President to give the war leaders code names based on the names of his own servants at Hyde Park: so Churchill was called Moses Smith after a tenant on Roosevelt's estate, and Marshall was named after William Plog, the superintendent at Hyde Park. An odd fate had decreed that a great soldier should advance from Pug to Plog.

When Marshall came to the Institute he had overgrown his strength, and he was nearly six foot tall. He had no experience of discipline, and little intellectual equipment. He blushed easily and nervously. An upperclassman, flinging a glass to the Rat without even troubling to order that the glass should be refilled (for it was assumed that the Rat would obey the lift of an eyelid) might readily come to the conlusion that this was the most useless student who had ever attended the Institute. Mercifully for Marshall, he made friends with Leonard Kimball Nicholson, a boy from New Orleans who had no intention of studying and who was perfectly prepared to assume the demerits which Marshall should have received. Nicholson was short, mild-mannered and frivolous, and he was to become Marshall's constant companion and to wield over him an extraordinary humanizing influence.

"Rat" Marshall had attended the Institute less than a month when it was decided to punish his gangling awkwardness. The ferocious discipline known as "hazing" is still remarkably severe at V.M.I.; in the nineties it was in its heyday. It was decided that Marshall deserved the ultimate in tortures. A bayonet was stuck in the floor, point up, and he was ordered to squat over it. In this torture a tall boy is at a disadvantage. Inevitably he begins to sway, cramp sets in and eventually he loses consciousness. Straining his muscles, Marshall remained rigid by an act of will power, while sweat dripped from his face and his eyes became glazed. He knew, or guessed, he was as near death as he had ever been. If he stayed there a little longer, he might hope for mercy, a sudden acquittal, a pat on the shoulder, some kind of acknowledgement that he possessed some physical courage in spite of his awkwardness, but twenty minutes passed and they were still jeering at him. Then the blood drained from his face and he reeled over. There was a deep gash in his buttock. If the point of the bayonet had entered his flesh an inch away, he would have died. He limped off to the post surgeon, refusing to inform on his tormentors. Awed by his courage and his silence, the Third Class cadets promised there would be no more hazing in the cell which Marshall occupied, but they went on blithely hazing all the other Rats at the college.

During the next month Marshall saw something of the panoply which surrounds the cadets at a military college. With enormous plumes to their shakos, with chin straps, crossed belts and dangling swords, the cadets took train for the Nashville exposition grounds. They were on parade, a part of the exposition, showing their finery like peacocks, taking part in mock battles with blank cartridges in the rain, while the band played "Dixie" and the Tennessee belles smiled approvingly. They were not always on parade. They were given free tickets to the exposition grounds, paid tribute to the bearded lady and the plaster model of the Parthenon, returning at midnight to their tents. It was such a taste of freedom as he was rarely to have again; and when the cadets took train at last for Lexington, weary of the long week's holiday, they had added enough store of anecdotes to keep them busy through the winter.

Gradually Marshall's shyness vanished. He grew accustomed

to a harsh routine, becoming a part of the machine. He rose at six twenty a.m. winter and summer, breakfasted at seven, attended his first classes at eight, worked through the day with an interval for lunch until four and then attended an hour of drill. After supper there were more classes until taps were sounded at ten.

In this remorseless mechanical life he was determined to succeed, but though he inched his way gradually from thirty-fifth to fifteenth place, he never showed any remarkable facility for his lessons. Unable to shine in his lessons, he showed a genius for shining in other ways. Looking round his bare cell his eyes alighted on the shoe box conveniently located under the stacked guns. He determined to polish his shoes so brightly that he would be the envy of his comrades. His fastidious taste in shoe polish extended to his clothes. He would dress so smartly that no one would ever find fault with his uniform. He pressed his uniforms with exquisite care, polished his rifle stock till it shone with a blinding light, cleaned his shoes till they resembled patent leather—indeed, on one occasion he was asked on the parade ground why he was wearing patent leather pumps and was compelled to explain that he had used polish and elbow grease beyond the call of duty. Towering among his brother Rats, he had no alternative but to present the appearance of a precision machine. In the end he was elected senior officer of his class and First Captain of the Corps of Cadets: these were tributes not to his brains but to his prowess as a precision machine. He did not like the Institute. He honored it because it taught him discipline and loyalty. "I hear army men say their happiest days were at West Point," wrote General Grant in old age. "I never had that experience. The most trying days of my life were those I spent there and I never recall them with pleasure." Marshall could have said much the same, but he would have added that there came a time when he half-enjoyed the rigorous discipline, and there were odd moments during his career at the Institute which gave him a curious feeling of identity with all the Virginian soldiers of the past. Such moments occurred during the evening parades when the sun was sinking over the roof of House Mountain and purple shadows fell over Brushy Hills, or on the solemn anniversary of the battle of New Market, when the cadets presented themselves at the small cemetery which contained the bones of the dead youths, and the muster roll of the dead was answered at an early morning reveille by cadets who stepped out of ranks, saluted and shouted: "Died on the field of honor!" Red roses were scattered on the graves, the minute guns sounded, the battalion fired three volleys and a bugler sounded taps. Forty years later, when Marshall returned to attend a Commencement Day at the Institute, he said: "This institution gave me not only a standard for my daily conduct among men, but it endowed me with a military heritage of honor and self-sacrifice." The words, taken out of their context, look almost inhuman. They were, however, no more than the truth.

The anniversary of the battle of New Market, which fell on May 15, was also the anniversary of the burial of "Stonewall" Jackson. Sometime in his first or second year Marshall discovered Jackson. He had, of course, known the name since he could remember, and it had been repeatedly drummed into him at the Institute that a cadet could do no better than follow in Jackson's footsteps. But suddenly and almost unaccountably it came to him that Jackson was a strange and wonderful genius, to be copied and worshiped. Jackson haunted him. The young General who had swept up and down the Shenandoah Valley with 17,000 men, marching his army 170 miles in 14 days, routing 12,000 of the enemy, taking 3,000 prisoners and 250,000 dollars worth of supplies was a man to be reckoned with, a fit champion for a young soldier entering upon his career. Imitating Napoleon, who put great value on being able to focus on objects in the mind for a long time without growing tired, Jackson had prodigiously exercised his powers of concentration. He would hold up his left hand to the level of his small weak eyes with the palm turned to the front as he tried in that strange, wild and impassioned head of his to visualize every detail of what he had so suddenly contrived to put out of sight. Jackson, the mystic of war, seeing patterns of forces, the trembling power lines between the chessmen on the board, reducing the art of war to a mathematical guessing game in which the proper guesses were arrived at by the ferocity of calculated logic: here at last was a man who demanded homage, and Marshall was prepared to give him homage to the utmost. The man who said: "Rather than wilfully violate the known will of God I would forfeit my life. Such a resolution I have taken, and I will by it abide" had something in him of Marshall's deeply religious ancestors. Two days after receiving his commission, Jackson had written to his wife wondering whether he had made a mistake—perhaps it would have been better after all if he had become a parson. There was warmth and humanity in this tortured man with the flashing deep-set eyes who laughed silently and roared curses on his enemies, and Marshall studied the Shenandoah Valley campaign feverishly, until he knew more about it than anyone else at the college and could say exactly what Jackson was doing or saying at any moment of those magical fourteen days. With the same desperate earnestness he studied the New Market campaign and the battles of the Revolution, until he became a kind of plague, forever cross-questioning his friends, asking impossible questions and supplying answers concerning the tactical details of these battles from the heights of his contrived knowledge.

He could be a plague in other ways. One day he invited his classmates to accompany him on a leisurely hike. There was something faintly sinister in the suggestion of a leisurely hike from someone who did not know the meaning of leisure. It was President Jefferson Davis's birthday, one of the rare holidays at the Institute. In the end, only Leonard Kimball Nicholson, always loyal to Marshall, and one other cadet agreed to go with him. Some time after they started they learned that the leisurely hike was a thirty-mile march to the summit of House Mountain at a parade ground pace and without a single moment of rest. By threats and cajoling Marshall succeeded in preventing his companions from becoming mutineers.

In his third year Marshall developed a passionate interest in football. Though he was very light in spite of his height, he played tackle against a 250-pound guard, pitting tactics against brawn. Afterwards, when he was asked how he felt, he said: "I didn't feel any too happy about the outlook, but after two or three plays I found I could out-think him. Since that day size has never bothered me." He had powerful shoulders and long legs: he could out-race most of his opponents and butt in with his shoulders. He played on the team which fought against Washington and Lee University at nearby Lexington, trouncing the "minks" with a crushing 39-0 defeat. The match was played in October, 1899, but immediately afterwards an epidemic of typhoid broke out and the entire corps of cadets was furloughed until after Thanksgiving Day. There was a six weeks' holiday which none of the cadets enjoyed: for three of the cadets died of the epidemic and no one knew where the blow would fall next. Old General Scott-Shipp felt an oppressive sense of guilt. On September 27, a cadet had been sent to hospital with typhoid: it was nearly three weeks before he gave orders to close the Institute. But there was football again the following year. This time Washington and Lee University was trounced with a still more shattering defeat, 40-0, which did nothing to heal the wounds between the rival colleges. There were further victories to come, for on Thanksgiving Day, 1900, Virginia Military Institute sent its team to Roanoke to play against the Virginia Polytechnic Institute, which was another military academy, one of the famous eight "tin colleges" recognized by the War Department, renowned for its football team. V.M.I, defeated it 5-0. There were processions and parades when the heroes returned to Lexington. Such complete victories, in the favorite phrase of General Scott-Shipp, "lacked the elements of verisimilitude," yet they had undoubtedly happened and the college surrendered to a day's rejoicing. Marshall was particularly happy. He was now an all-Southern football tackle, and G. Marshall's behavior on the field was being noticed even in the newspapers.

He was coming to the end of his stay at V.M.I., and beginning to be worried about the Philippine Insurrection. He hoped there would still be some fighting to be done when he left the college. He wanted an appointment to the Army for many reasons. He had developed a taste for action, and little enough taste for scholarship. Like Jackson he was consumed with "an intense earthly ambition," and he was beginning to regard himself as a strategist on the basis of his studies of the New Market and Shenandoah Valley campaigns. Also he wanted to marry Elizabeth Carter Coles, the reigning belle of Lexington, and he could not even hope to support her unless he transferred to the Regular Army immediately after leaving college, when his salary as a second lieutenant would amount to no more than $116.67 a month. His commission, if he got it, would be the reward of his own dogged efforts. He need not have worried. As Cadet First Captain, first in military proficiency, he received from the President his formal appointment as a second lieutenant in the U.S. Army. The appointment however was not confirmed until after his twenty-first birthday, which occurred on December 31, 1901. There were still some weeks of waiting. On February 2, 1902, he was able to take up his commission. Nine days later he married Elizabeth Coles and went to Washington on his honeymoon. Within two months he was on his way to the Philippines, alone, with orders to join the Thirtieth Infantry.

The strange gangling youth who came to V.M.I, four years before had changed beyond recognition. He had progressed from an obscure Rat to become the acknowledged leader among the students at the Institute. He had been nervous and undecided, and he was now even-tempered and determined. He had absorbed what he came to call later the great virtues of the Institute: "development of character, integrity and responsibility to constituted authority." He, who had been so much younger than his age, was now older; there was something of an old man's reserve about the young Lieutenant who was to hold himself continually erect and disciplined throughout his life, rarely unbending, possessing even in his young manhood the mask of a grand inquisitor or of a judge. He looks deadly serious in the early photographs, the chin is thrust out, the eyes are steady, and on the face of the young Second Lieutenant there is already the look of a commander.

On moonlight nights, the statue of "Stonewall" Jackson at the Virginia Military Institute throws a furious shadow on a blank wall. Students have been known to haunt the place and to gaze for hours at that slowly changing shadow which seemed more alive than the statue itself. There was something about the shadow which suggested the alarming energy of the man, and also his greatness. Contemplating that shadow it was possible to guess at some of the terrible secrets of the art of war.

When Marshall left the Institute the shadow of Jackson lay over him, as it lay over George S. Patton, another student of the Institute. For the next fifty years he was to walk with this shadow perpetually by his side.

CHAPTER THREE

The First Encounters

When Marshall left America, the war in the Philippines was still raging and the *insurrectos* were still at large. By the time he arrived at Manila on May 13, 1902, the war had been over a week, and Miguel Malvar, who called himself Commander-in-Chief and Supreme Head of the Filipino Government had issued a manifesto calling upon the surrender of the army in the Batangas and admitting defeat "inasmuch as all my trusted officers and my general staff have been captured by the American army." Marshall's dreams of active service came to a sudden end. Instead of fighting, he was called upon to spend his years in the Philippines in the endless tasks of garrison duty, his chief enemies boredom, cholera and malaria, his chief occupation to keep a handful of enlisted men out of mischief.

In those days there were few attractions in garrison duty. Time weighed heavily. The tropical weather sapped men's strength. Mail was irregular, like the soldier's pay and like a man's temper. Sent to an obscure island, where nothing of importance had happened and nothing was ever likely to happen, Marshall could reflect that he had come to the most ill-favored of the overseas possessions of the United States. He was stationed at Calapan, the capital of the island of Mindoro, in command of a detachment of fifty men of Company G. Manuel Quezon, who practiced law on the island a year later, spoke of the place as "dreadful, infested with malaria." It was also infested with Asiatic cholera. One of his men died of the disease three weeks after Marshall's arrival. A heavy, sultry fate seemed to be hanging over the young Second Lieutenant: he had come to the end of the world, where no battles were being fought and no hopes of advancement were ever offered, a place of steaming jungles and houses on stilts and suspicious natives who accepted the presence of the Americans without enthusiasm. Men in such circumstances have been known to kill themselves from boredom.

If Calapan was bad, Mangarin which lay at the head of Mangarin Bay was worse. This cluster of native huts surrounded by malarial swamps had become the headquarters of Company G, and a few weeks later Marshall was sent there to take command. The only reason for the existence of this encampment was the presence of some *Recoleto* friars in the monastery of San José, some three miles to the north; the friars had asked for protection from the wrath of the *insurrectos,* and now that the war was over they demanded protection from the *ladrones,* the bands of wandering robbers who moved secretly around the island. The principal wealth of the friars lay in cattle; the American troops were therefore cattle guards. Marshall had dreamed of taking part in the campaigns in the Philippines, but his military activity was reduced to an occasional pursuit of bands of *ladrones,* a long trail over forest paths in search of enemies who faded into the jungle, the weary and empty-handed return, reveille and retreat, the little details of a company command in the broiling heat which debilitated and sometimes demoralized officers and men, the endless reports about nothing at all; and all the time there was the knowledge that nothing of value could be accomplished. Men fell sick of malaria, and some died. The sun burned through the thatched roofs of nippa palms in the small encampments where they lived. One day, if one was very lucky, it might be permissible to escape.

The misery of the place was like the misery of the early days at V.M.I. In this dead end a good soldier would stand up and take his punishment; and Marshall, remembering the traditions of the Institute, was perfectly prepared to regard his stay in the malarial swamps as an essay in self-control and responsibility. He possessed the confidence of a recent cadet officer. He would address his men as though they were on a parade ground in the United States. He knew his drill, and if he knew very little about cooks and kitchen police, these were, after all, things which could be learned by experience. It pleased him that the sword he carried at company formations was the same sword which he had worn as a cadet officer, but he now carried a Colt revolver at his hip as well. Filing along the narrow mountain trails in pursuit of *ladrones,* he drew comfort from his new revolver. Gradually as the days passed he found himself more and more convinced that the training he had received at the Institute possessed the peculiar property of exorcising the devils of Mindoro; he would think of evening parade at Lexington and the sun setting over House Mountain with a sense of unappeasable longing to return to Virginia, but at the same time he derived strength from his memory of the Institute, where he had learned his trade, his austerity and his calm.

Austere, a little remote, uttering commands in a crisp voice, always immaculately dressed and always strict in his regard for military duty, the young officer was curiously unlike the general run of officers. He neither drank nor smoked. He refused to be demoralized by the weather, by sickness, or by boredom. He learned Tagalog well enough to speak the language with his native *muchacho,* he went hunting after alligators and cranes in the swamps, and he was concerned that his men should have enough to do: he took them on hunting trips, insisted that they learn the language of the place and interested them in local customs. Beyond that, and a few excursions to neighboring islands where the presence of the *ladrones* had been reported, there was little for them to do. It was heartbreaking work, but Marshall was determined not to be heartbroken, even when the men's pay was four months late in arriving. There came a time when the men had exhausted all the books and all the games at company headquarters, when they were faced with the prospect of remaining interminably on this desolate coastal swamp where the rain fell in torrents or else the sun blinded them out of a cloudless sky, and they had to remain there without mail, with no ice to cool them, with none of the morale-building services which came into the Army later, with no telegraph by which they could send off an appeal for help, and all this because the transport which was supposed to come to provision them each month had failed to arrive. When the transport did arrive at last, Marshall's duties, which included the guarding of monastic cattle, were widened to include coaling. To save expense, the Quartermaster Department at Manila had come to the conclusion that soldiers should be used as common laborers: the crew were protected from handling the coal until it was delivered on the deck of the transport. This meant that the soldiers, who earned thirteen dollars a month, were required to sack the coal from the coal pile on the edge of the jungle, slide it down chutes to the beach, haul it onto the one and only flat-bottom boat, then row through three quarters of a mile of heavy surf to the transport and laboriously transfer the coal to the deck. In the sweltering heat of a Philippine summer, such duties frayed men's tempers to the uttermost. Marshall remembered these days with a bitter relish, and forty years later, addressing the House of Representatives Committee on Military Affairs, he returned to one incident which occurred during his first year of foreign service. He said:

> One day while working in a torrential rain, a tall, lanky soldier from the mountains of Kentucky paused in the middle of his shoveling job, with this comment: "I didn't see nothing like this on that damned recruiting circular." My old first sergeant suppressed a laugh, and flashed back the order to "Keep your mouth shut and shovel coal; that's your job." That gave me a lasting impression of the Regular Army; what discipline meant, what dependability meant in times of difficulty.

As usual, Marshall was learning his lessons the hard way, and when he went on to say that the business of a soldier, as he had found it, involved mud, extreme heat, and irritating dust, long marches in bad weather with insects and all manner of discomforts, he was evidently remembering the Philippines. But the miserable period at Mangarin came to an end; his company was ordered to Manila in December and there they stayed until the following November, while the *Alphabetic List of Officers Serving in the Division of the Philippines* continued to list the name of Marshall, George C., Jr., 2nd Lieutenant, Santa Mesa (Thirtieth Infantry), with monotonous regularity. Santa Mesa was a garrison encampment three miles east of Manila. Mangarin had been boring and hard, and demanding of Marshall's patience; Santa Mesa was boring and soft, and demanding of nothing more than a quiet passion for tennis and reasonable care with mosquito nets. There were no insurrections to be put down, and though there was a sudden murderous attack by *ladrones* at Calapan during this period, Manila was quiet, and the worst that happened was a plague of grasshoppers. He had time to lead a considerable social life and study the military history of the Philippine war; he studied the guerrilla tactics of the *insurrectos* with the same care with which he had studied the Shenandoah Valley campaign. He may have come across the notes prepared by Major M. J. R. Taylor, who was present throughout the greater part of the war and who wrote: "Aguinaldo's was a force which could disintegrate, but could not surrender. Only armies can do that. Forces over which their leaders have lost all except nominal control when beaten do not surrender. They disintegrate by passing through the stages of guerrilla warfare, of armed bands of highwaymen, of sturdy beggars who at opportune moments resort to petty larceny." He had himself seen how the war had degenerated into a kind of stalemate between the garrisons and the *ladrones,* the raiders who were the relics of the vast armies which Aguinaldo once commanded; and forty-five years later he was to see the same disintegration occurring in China.

On November 12, 1903, G Company of the Thirtieth Infantry sailed out of Manila Harbor for a period of duty in the United States. Marshall went with his company, and found himself transferred to Fort Reno, Oklahoma Territory. Once again there was garrison duty, no better and no worse than garrison duty at Santa Mesa, and just as boring; and here he remained with a brief interval spent in map making in the desolate Big Bend area of Texas until June, 1906. The period at Big Bend left its traces on him. In that weird wild country, which resembled brightly colored lava, his only companion was a grizzled sergeant of regulars. Together they worked on their map making, and for four months they saw only a few Indians in their secluded encampments, but they returned with maps which are still standard in the Army. Marshall then reported to his new superior officer, a young captain of cavalry called Malin Craig.

Though Marshall could hardly have realized it at the time, the fates were beginning to spin their slow web. Four or five chance encounters were to alter the course of his life, and the first of them was this encounter with Captain Malin Craig, who was to become in time a bluff and extremely conservative Chief of Staff. But Malin Craig had observed the extraordinary air of military brilliance which Marshall took no pains to hide, and he came to the conclusion that the young Second Lieutenant would be better employed at the School of the Line at Fort Leavenworth, Kansas. Marshall was delighted to leave his garrison duties. He was to spend many more years in those small garrisons where soldiers are hermetically sealed from the outside world so that they come to resemble the military monks of the Middle Ages, but henceforth his chief interest was to lie in the theory and practice of the art of war as seen from the point of view of a highly educated specialist. Instead of rifle drill, his preoccupation was to be operations, the complex management of men in battle.

The School of the Line, which had been closed during the Philippine war, was revived immediately after the war by General J. Franklin Bell, the second of those who subtly altered the course of Marshall's life. General Bell had entered the Philippine war with the rank of first lieutenant and had come out with the rank of brigadier-general; he was responsible for the capture of some ten thousand rebels; and he was soon to become Commanding General of the United States Army Forces in the Philippines. He was quite easily the most brilliant of the Americans who had taken part in the Philippine campaigns. At Fort Leavenworth he surrounded himself with a nucleus of young, hand-picked Army officers. He removed them from garrison duty and put them through a hard course of strategy, tactics, military history, fortifications, map making and logistics. Immediately under him, acting as Senior Instructor in Military Art and Assistant Commandant in the Leavenworth Schools, was Major John F. Morrison, an exacting taskmaster and an inspiring lecturer who shaped his pupils and left on the best of them the imprint of his quiet intelligence. Among his students were John L. DeWitt, who would probably have been the wartime Chief of Staff if Marshall had not secured the position, and Stephen O. Fuqua, whom Marshall came to admire during the course of the First World War. On March 7, 1907, Marshall was promoted to first lieutenant, and three months later he came out first in his class at the School of the Line. He was still first a year later when the Academic Board met to survey the results of the year. Their report, which was twice as long as that for any other officer in the class, read like a universal hymn of praise:

Has shown marked proficiency in Field Fortifications, Topographical Surveying and Sketching. Has exhibited qualities which would appear to fit him especially well for the following professional employments: Topographical officer on marches, expeditions and explorations. Aide-de-Camp. Inspector General. Pay Department. Military Attaché. Quartermaster's Department. Ordnance Department. Adjutant General. Subsistence Department. Signal Corps. College Detail. Recruiting Officer. Organizing and commanding native troops. Staff Officer with volunteer troops. Duty with organized militia (Governor's Staff). Line Officer with volunteer troops, with advanced rank. Assistant Instructor, Army School of the Line, Military Art, Engineering. Chief of Staff in time of war for large tactical units. Duty with organized militia (special detail conducting field exercises in summer camps).

Appears well fitted for the following professional employments: Post Engineer Officer. Acting Judge Advocate of Department. Especially recommended for War College Detail.

This was the first time that the Marshall legend had been written down at length. No one else ever received at Fort Leavenworth a comparable report. To be well-fitted for so many employments was the mark of a purely military mind dedicated to all the departments of war, and Marshall was showing himself to be the officer *in excelsis*. He was twenty-seven, still reserved and a little remote, but intense and excitable, with a brooding determination to reach the heights; and if the journey to the heights had not been mathematically marked out by seniority tables, it was evident that he would reach them before he was forty. He was not given any of the high positions suggested in the report. Instead he was given the comparatively lowly position of Instructor in the Engineering Department at Fort Leavenworth, where he continued his work on map making, helped to write a small manual on cordage and tackle, and acted as associate editor and Fort Leavenworth correspondent of the *Infantry Journal,* a position he occupied from July 1, 1909, to June 30, 1910.

The *Infantry Journal* was a remarkably forthright semi-official journal which took a determined stand on Army politics and occasionally contained dull articles on military map making. One of the dullest was written by Marshall and appeared in the January, 1910, issue. It was called "A Record of Military Mapping," and described an exploration undertaken the previous summer near the town of Nevada, Missouri. Written in a deliberately dry military style, it reads a little like a schoolboy's diary of a summer hike:

> The class left Fort Leavenworth by rail on the evening of June 19 and arrived in the town of Nevada at 7:00 o'clock the next morning. Breakfast was served at the station, and at 7:30 a.m. the officers drove off in six vehicles to the site of the encampment. The western border of the area was reached at 8:30 a.m. . . . and the deployment of the sketchers at once began. The last man did not reach his place on the line of deployment until 9:30 a.m. At this hour all had started sketching. None of the sketchers had ever seen this terrain until the moment he started work.
>
> At 3:30 p.m. the last sketcher had finished his work and the strips of celluloid, containing the sketch of the entire area, were put together on the ground.
>
> The following is a resumé of just what had been accomplished: In seven hours 24 men had completely sketched an area of 27 square miles on a scale of 6 inches equal one mile, with 10-foot contours and all roads, fences, crops, woods, telegraph lines, houses, and even the plan of the camp water pipe-line shown. At the close of this period the work was ready for immediate blue-printing.

There is a great deal more of it, and the final map is reproduced in the pages of the *Infantry Journal*. The same kind of colorless military writing appears in *Notes on Cordage and Tackle,* which he wrote with Captain C. O. Sherrill, who was also an instructor in the Engineering Department. The pamphlet, which is bound in blue paper, appeared in the same year as the article on map making. It consists of twenty-five pages of text and seven plates, and does not claim to be anything more than a resumé of existing manuals. The manual begins with the definition of a rope:

> A rope is composed of three or more strands of fibrous material, iron or steel twisted together. It is usually designated by its circumference, occasionally by its diameter, is sold commercially by the pound, and, up to the size of five inches circumference measure, the fibrous ropes come in coils of 1,200 feet length.

There follows a discussion of knots, splicings, lashings, slings, blocks and tackles, which are reproduced in steel engravings. There is something a little apologetic in the nature of the manual, for rope fastenings were already going out of favor in the Army and there was not very much excuse for the existence of the manual. The authors admitted that nails had almost won the victory over rope:

> Rope fastenings will probably not be used in the field in the future as much as they have been in the past; the amount of hardware, especially nails, bolts and wires, has vastly increased in the last thirty years, and this material will ordinarily be as easily obtainable as rope, if not more so. Rope, however, is of great value in many cases, and almost indispensable in some, and every officer ought to know such fastenings as will enable him to get full service from it.

This manual, the second of Marshall's published works, bore the *imprimatur* of the Commandant of the School: "Adopted by Direction of the Commandant for Use in the Army Service Schools at Fort Leavenworth." It was a strange production, for it was the last thing one would expect from a man who had received such high praise from his superior officers, but it was characteristic of the man that he should interest himself in humble details. There were excellent traditions for preoccupation with minor details, and Grant, who was forever writing about mules and wagons, and shoes for his soldiers, was only one of the great soldiers who saw that the army was composed of details, and every one of them were of superlative importance. The wooden and graceless style was also characteristic of the man who only learned to write well towards the end of the Second World War, when he produced in a swift, clear and altogether admirable style his third Biennial Report on the course of the war.

One of Marshall's duties at this time was to join a small committee of four officers assigned to study the question of producing a single promotion list. Such a list had never been attempted before, for it meant cutting across the prerogatives of the chiefs of the arms of the Army. Marshall was assigned the task of collecting data for the experiment. One of the officers concerned was John McAuley Palmer, one of Marshall's students, later to become a bitter critic of the policies of General Peyton C. March after World War I, and still later to become Marshall's Special Assistant to the Chief of Staff, in World War II.

Marshall remained at Fort Leavenworth until the summer of 1910, when he attended the first of the National Guard camps which were to be his preoccupation for the next two years. He attended the National Rifle Matches at Camp Perry, Ohio, and developed a fondness for this camp which led him to return several times later. There followed a period of duty as inspector-instructor of the Massachusetts National Guard, and a brief service with the Fourth Infantry in Arkansas and Texas, which lasted until the summer of 1913. He had now spent more than nine years of duty in the United States, and was due for service abroad. His name was near the top of the foreign service roster; Mrs. Marshall was ill, and he was beginning to hope he would be able to avoid another tour of duty in the Philippines, where the climate was always forbidding. He asked to be transferred to any one of the foreign duty areas—Hawaii, Alaska, China, or Panama. All these were refused. With a heavy heart he learned that he would be sent once more to the Philippines, and it would be necessary to leave his wife in America. In July, 1913, he sailed for Manila, where General J. Franklin Bell was the department commander.

Marshall was still an inconspicuous and almost unknown first lieutenant. There were to his credit a number of magnificent testimonials, an article on map making, a little blue book on ropes and cordage, and something of a reputation as an excellent instructor at the Engineering Department of the service schools at Fort Leavenworth. He was known by reputation to General Bell, but he had been only one of many brilliant students at Fort Leavenworth, and the General did not of course seek him out the moment he arrived. Marshall's reputation grew slowly. Legends began to cluster round him. They were a little like the small preliminary miracles of a saint. He had the detective's eye, a relentlessly logical mind, and a gift for improvisation. One day in the Philippines he made a bet with his fellow lieutenant that he could name three trivial faults the inspecting officer would find when he inspected the men on parade. Furthermore, Marshall proposed to bet that during field exercises he would commit three grave errors in tactics which would pass unobserved. The bet was accepted. Marshall wrote down the three errors, and sealed his list in an envelope. When the time came for the inspection the three trivial faults were noticed by the inspecting officer—they concerned buttons misplaced, a soldier who had not shaved for two days and another who had come on parade without a bayonet. The errors listed in the envelope showed a greater daring on Marshall's part. They were (1) the company was marched in columns of four straight up a hill towards the enemy, instead of being dispersed; (2) a corporal was sent out on patrol without any instructions whatsoever; (3) the attacking force would be sent up the sheer face of a hill in full view of the enemy when a convenient ravine would have offered protection, and given them a flanking position. Having committed these errors, Marshall observed quietly that no one saw anything amiss, and he thereupon collected his bet. The story is illuminating. It suggests an almost insolent contempt for the ignorance of his superiors and a tragic inadequacy in the umpires of the field exercises; and some of that insolence and daring were to remain.

These were preliminary miracles. The story of the bet, which has been recounted in many different forms, told nothing of Marshall's real capability. The story of his work as chief of staff of Detachment No. I during the maneuvers which began in January, 1914, is considerably more authentic and more revealing. The maneuvers involved the defense of Manila, and Marshall was given the comparatively lowly position of assistant to the adjutant in the routine administration. Captain Jens Bugge, a recent graduate of the School of the Line at Fort Leavenworth, was appointed chief of staff, but he fell ill and was taken to hospital while the maneuvers were already going on and the enemy was almost in sight. General Bell was away in Manila, but his aide, Major . E. Booth, called for Marshall to take Captain Bugge's place. Major Johnson Hagood, who was also an aide to General Bell, and who was acting as one of the umpires, has left a record of what happened. Major Booth had ordered Marshall to be sent for.

> A tall, thin colorless lieutenant came out of a nearby tent. He was bareheaded and in his shirt-sleeves.
> "Lieutenant," said the bewildered commander, "do you know how to draw up a field order?"
> "Yes," said Marshall, "I think I do."

"Very well," said the commander; "go ahead, and draw up one."

The umpires and observers stood aghast. Marshall had not been told whether to attack or retreat; whether to stand aside or hold his ground. But he did not lose any time. Sending for the regimental commanders and others, he asked them a running fire of questions. He had them indicate their positions on the map—the infantry, the cavalry, the medical troops, the supply trains and all the rest. The intelligence service had located the enemy, and he ordered an immediate attack.

He dictated the order very calmly, very deliberately, but without hesitation. Each of the commanders and staff officers concerned took down his instructions, verbatim, in longhand. Sentence by sentence, paragraph by paragraph, Marshall provided for every contingency. When he came to the end, he made no change, no correction, of a word or a comma. The whole thing was astounding to those who stood about.

While Marshall was working on these orders, an obscure lieutenant, known as "Hap" Arnold (the nickname which had been given to him at West Point continued to be used until the day of his retirement) came upon the group standing around Marshall as he lay in the shade of a bamboo clump with a map spread out before him. He heard some of Marshall's orders and took part in the attack Marshall ordered, and he made a mental note that the gangling lieutenant sprawled out on the ground would one day become Chief of Staff.

The incident did not end there. The chief umpire had pronounced that Marshall had carried out a difficult task with extraordinary success, but it was left to General Bell to provide the accolade. Some days later he invited his entire staff of some twenty-six officers to lunch at his quarters. No explanation was given, and the officers were in some perplexity about the kind of greeting they would receive. They need not have wondered. General Bell had taken it into his head to commend Lieutenant Marshall in front of his officers. Years later, when Major Johnson Hagood had become a general, he wrote down what he remembered of his commanding general's speech:

"Gentlemen," he said, "I have called you all together to tell you something remarkable. As you know I fought over all these islands in the early days, and I know them from end to end. After that I was Chief of Staff in Washington. And now I am the commanding general and responsible for their defense. I have seen a great many plans for the defense of Manila. Some of these I have drawn myself. Some were drawn by the Army War College. Some of the more recent ones were drawn under my direction by our local defense board. But the best plan that I have seen, the most complete, the most concise and the most effective, I hold in my hand. It was written in pencil and was dictated in the field by a lieutenant of infantry unexpectedly called from other duty.

Do you think, however, that this was the result of a sudden inspiration and that the author had never given the matter previous thought? On the contrary it shows deep study and thorough knowledge of the terrain around Manila. This lieutenant is one of those rare men who live and dream in their profession—a soldier who was not satisfied with daily routine superbly done. He looks forward to the time when he himself may bear the responsibility of high command, and he makes sure that he will be prepared to assume it.

Gentlemen, I know this young officer well. He greatly distinguished himself at the Army Staff College, both as student and as an instructor, when he was a very junior lieutenant among many officers of higher rank and much more experience. Keep your eyes on George Marshall. He is the greatest military genius of America since Stonewall Jackson."

The praise, though extravagant, was not undeserved, and from that moment the legend which had been gradually increasing in force—the legend of a quiet, reserved and rather colorless genius who could be relied upon in emergency—grew and expanded. There were to be reverses, long years spent in exile, strange passages of arms between himself and his superior officers, but the excellence of the soldier was now known, and before he left Manila the third of the men who violently altered the course of his life took Marshall under his wing. By January, 1916, General Bell had left the Philippines, and General Hunter Liggett now commanded the Department. For a few months Marshall served as Aide-de-Camp to Hunter Ligget, and then, his three year period of foreign duty over, he returned to the United States, becoming Aide-de-Camp to General J. Franklin Bell at his headquarters in the Presidio at San Francisco. The appointment pleased Marshall: he possessed a deep respect for General Bell, they had been close together in the Philippines after the Lieutenant's extraordinary success during the maneuvers organized for the defense of Corregidor and the Bataan Peninsula, and Bell was one of those gruff legendary generals, like Foch, and still more like Joffre, whose earthiness concealed an infatuation with military theory and a furious brilliance. Equally pleasant was the news which came six weeks after reaching America that he was promoted to captain of infantry. The long years of apprenticeship were over.

At that time the War Department, concerned as always with recruiting, had instituted business men's camps, and early in the summer of 1916, General Bell began to organize these camps in California and Utah. Lieutenant Colonel Johnson Hagood was placed in charge of the camp at Monterey. The camp had proved a failure, and a new camp was opened at Fort Douglas in Salt Lake City with Johnson Hagood in technical command, and with Marshall as his adjutant. The arrangement pleased Johnson Hagood, who had no illusions concerning his own brilliance. He genuinely admired Marshall and explained to General Bell that though Marshall would be acting as his adjutant, in fact Marshall would be the commander of the camp. General Bell nodded. He was concerned only that the camp should work well. It was two years since the famous incident at the maneuvers. The camp which opened in August continued through the late summer, and at the close Marshall's qualifications were once more reviewed. As usual, Johnson Hagood's opinion was forthright. He wrote: "This officer is well qualified to command a division, with the rank of major general, in time of war, and I would very much like to serve under his command." He noted that on the seniority lists he was separated from Marshall by over eighteen hundred files.

The war which the Germans and the Austrians had launched upon Europe was now drawing dangerously close to America. For a few more months Marshall served as Aide-de-Camp to General Bell, first at the Presidio and then at Governor's Island, New York; and when President Wilson proclaimed a state of war on April 6, 1917, Marshall was still a very junior captain with no experience of leading troops into battle, untried and inexperienced in the art of war. He pulled strings.

He clamored to be tried and to be given experience, and with General Bell's quiet help he was detailed to the General Staff Corps. On June 26 he sailed in the first convoy which left for the battlefields of France.

CHAPTER FOUR

Preparing for War

With the Americans in the war, the hopes of the Allies soared. Though the situation on the western front was acutely dangerous, and more than once the Germans had broken the Allied lines, it was believed that the vast man power and the huge mechanical resources of America· would redress the balance. The cry went up: "The Yanks are coming!" and the words themselves were like an incantation promising the end of the war. It seemed to many that simply because the Americans were coming the war was nearly over; by the spring of 1918 only the peasants would be watching the poppies growing in Flanders.

Marshall was not so sure. He had pored endlessly over the war maps and the war reports, and he came to believe that this war was unlike any previous war and the Americans were ill-prepared for it. Furious wars of maneuver had been characteristic of America. The War between the States, the war against the Philippine guerrillas, the skirmishes in Mexico, all had something of the aspect of border-raids: they had little in common with the positional war now being fought in Europe. There the giants grappled to a standstill while the trenches filled with blood—those trenches whose lines had remained virtually unchanged for eighteen months. The tradition of the war of maneuver was native to America, but there were no signs that this kind of war could be fought in Europe.

The American tradition is a complex one, with no single threads in evidence. A multiplicity of contraries have fused together in America, whose history is marked by a strange ambivalence, and nowhere more in evidence than in her military history. The War between the States could be seen as a brilliant, complex and neverending series of skirmishes, but it could also be seen as an ultimate vindication of superior organization. For four years Lincoln had pressed on, accumulating slowly and inexorably every kind of material resource, laboriously teaching the troops the very elements of their trade, never disturbed if he had to begin all over again, throwing out incompetent generals as a machine will discard the strips of metal which do not exactly fit the requirements of the machine: in the end, the Federal Army had won by sheer weight of organization. So it was again in 1870, when von Moltke plodded forward against the French with the same sure-footed stride as Grant, the same invincible sense of mechanical organization. The embattled Allies were looking to the smooth-running American machine for victory.

Marshall had hardly set foot on the ship which would take him to France before he realized that the smooth-running machine showed no signs of being in evidence. There was confusion everywhere. The U.S. Transport *Tenadores,* anchored in the Hudson River opposite Ninety-Sixth Street, was an almost perfect example of a machine in a state of disorganization. He noted an almost complete lack of medical supplies on the ship. This was a minor matter, for there was worse to come. The Commanding General and the General Staff, of which Marshall was a member, found to their horror that the ship's complement of soldiers consisted of untrained recruits who had received their rifles on the trains between the Mexican border and Hoboken. The troops charged with operating Stokes mortars and 37mm. cannon not only, for the most part, did not have these weapons but had never seen one: they had never even seen a model of one. Before they reached the ship, no tables of organization had been shown to the General Staff. When the tables were, at last produced, the officers discovered they were in command of units they had never heard of, and the organization of the troops was entirely new to them: there were four regiments of infantry in the Division instead of the nine they were accustomed to. There were no rolling kitchens and no automobiles, and the cargo was stevedored and manifested in such a way that it would be quite impossible to assemble it quickly when they disembarked. There was no literature on the war except for a single copy of a British pamphlet which the officers studied until it was dog-eared. When the S.S. *Tenadores* lifted anchor at four o'clock in the morning of June 14 and pushed its way down the North River, the heavy fog which descended was like an ironic commentary on the adventure. Here was the spearhead of the powerful American army which would sweep the Germans back to Berlin; and no army so ill-equipped or unprepared had ever left America, not even the fabulous army which left San Francisco for the Philippines in 1898, with only one hundred and fifty rounds per man. The fog continued. They anchored for several hours off Governor's Island, and then, escorted by the cruiser *Charleston* and three torpedo-boat destroyers, they headed out to sea.

Marshall was in his element. As a very junior captain on the General Staff, he was entrusted with keeping the records, and these he was to keep for some months with an amused bitterness and a slowly mounting horror against the improvisations he saw all round him. Everything was being improvised: even the name of the first contingent was improvised, for it left New York as the First Expeditionary Division, and two weeks after landing in France it became the First Division, A.E.F. The naval guns had been improvised at Hoboken, just before they sailed; charts and war maps were improvised; even the uniforms were often improvised. For obvious reasons they were compelled to radio silence, and the General Staff traveled three thousand miles across the ocean without being able to discover the names and the numbers of the units in other ships: they therefore improvised the orders they would issue on landing and drew up detailed plans for armies which were, for all they knew, totally imaginary. As Marshall records the events of the crossing, we become aware of a sense of desperate uneasiness. Of one thing he was certain: this was not the way the war should be begun.

The dullness of the journey across the Atlantic was pleasantly relieved by a torpedo attack. Exactly a week after they left Hoboken, at 10:30 at night, the men on watch saw the gleaming phosphorescent wake of a torpedo. Two alarm shots were fired, the *Tenadores* increased speed and changed course ninety degrees. There was no more excitement, and on June 26, in a deep fog, the convoy arrived at St. Nazaire. Other convoys followed later, but it was not until December 22 that the last unit of the First Division reached France. By that time most of its knots were untangled, and improvisation was giving place to the streamlined machine which the Allies had been praying for.

Meanwhile there were knots everywhere. Marshall noted at St. Nazaire the stalled trucks, the incessant congestion of traffic, the appalling difficulties in assembling equipage from the ships, which seemed to have been stevedored by malignant devils. There were other difficulties. He had the highest possible regard for the American soldier, but there were times when he wished that the doughboy was a little less casual. Headquarters were hastily established in a stubble field the day they landed. Almost immediately the French general in command of the military district came to pay his respects to the General Staff. Beautifully dressed, with rows of medals gleaming on his chest, he was calling as he thought, on the Regular Army. The guard saluted him. He was a tall, rangy, Tennesseean, and he did his best to salute, his blouse partly unbuttoned, his watch chain slung from one pocket to the other, and he had some difficulty in holding his rifle. The General commented upon the performance of the salute, whereupon the Tennesseean simply offered his rifle to the General and calmly sat down on a post to roll a cigarette. It was that kind of army, and though it was possible to have immense faith in the doughboys as human beings, there must have been moments when it was doubtful whether they would ever be successfully integrated into a military machine.

Order began to appear when, on July 8, the Division was commanded to move from St. Nazaire to billets at Gondrecourt, near the St. Mihiel salient, with one battalion of infantry making a detour through Paris. There they were greeted with open arms, flowers were thrown at them, bands played, speeches were made—here at last was evidence of the mighty spearhead, the dazzling power of America at the service of France, and hardly anyone realized that this army was untrained, so untrained that its leaders would not let them deploy in a battle until September 12, 1918, more than a year later.

Marshall's first task was to round up the contingents as they came ashore, discover how many men there were, what training they had, and what they knew about this new organization. Having now had some experience as a traffic manager at the port, he set out for Gondrecourt, where he was placed in charge of training, though it was only too evident that facilities for training were largely absent.

His memoranda at this time are full of complaints. He had lamented the absence of automobiles even when he was on the *Tenadores,* suspecting that someone would forget to send them, but on August 13 he was able to note that twelve seven-passenger Cadillacs had arrived, but he added that they came without extra tires, extra inner tubes and chains. Ten days later he noted that the food was good, but its arrival was uncertain; there was also insufficient lumber. On August 26 he complained that materials for mess halls, amusement rooms, kitchens, and quarters for the men were slow in arriving. The next day he boiled over, and wrote a solemn memorandum on quartermaster supplies. He announced that 100,000 board feet of lumber had disappeared except for a miserable 13,000 feet, and these were being used "for mangers and feed stalls required for animals without nose bags." There was therefore none in use for mess halls and amusement rooms. Thereupon he lists, one by one, in a mounting crescendo from matches and pickles to commanding officers, the things that have not arrived but *must* arrive if the training at Gondrecourt is to be continued.

This tragic and hilarious list should be quoted at some length, for it reveals his preoccupations at the time:

> Matches, soap and pickles have all failed to arrive; shipment was four crates short in baking powder. Twice sacks of beans weighing eighty-five pounds net were sent as weighing 100 pounds. Two cases of pumpkins were sent in place of tomatoes. There are also shortages in jam; apples, evaporated; vinegar; pickles and butter.
> There are shortages of tire tubes of all sizes and of lubricating oils.
> Shortages are also apparent in tobacco. The total of supplies received to date are as follows:
> 25,920
> packages (one ounce) Bull Durham
> 1,744
> lbs. chewing tobacco
> 411,160
> cigarettes
> 4,320
> two-ounce packages tobacco P.A.
> 864
> packages tobacco Tuxedo
> A limited supply of cigars
> There are only negligible quantities of ordnance for firing

practice. Finally, there is a shortage of field company officers in the command.

This memorandum was signed: "G. C. Marshall, Jr., Chief of Staff." The title, surprising in a document written in 1917, was his by right, for he was acting chief of staff for the Division during the absence of his superior. Towards the end of August, just before or after the famous memorandum on quartermaster supplies, he was promoted to the temporary rank of major. His duties changed. Operational notes begin to take the place of reports on lumber and tobacco, though his interest in the men's well-being continued, for on December 7 he recorded: "Men's rations short on onions, soap, candles and dried fruit." It was as though, after a long and decent interval, a forgotten melodic theme had returned to haunt a symphony.

The beginning of the American Army in France consisted of improvisations, sometimes comic, nearly always heart-rending. Now a new, more somber note begins to appear. The Germans knew of the presence of the American forces, and on September 4, German airplanes dropped bombs near St. Joire, the station of the Second Battalion, Twenty-Sixth Infantry. There were no casualties, Marshall noted; but the threat was clear. Then the infantry of the Division was reviewed by the President of the Republic, with General Pershing standing at his side; and the old "Tiger," Clemenceau, came to pay his respects to the Division: the preliminary period of training was coming to an end. On October 3 Pershing visited the Division and witnessed something more substantial than a review. He witnessed the solution of two battalion problems on the grounds.

At that time General Pershing had no great opinion of the American soldier. He spoke of rigorous training and the necessity of putting the American soldier through a hard regimen. He criticized the performance of the maneuvers, pointed out the defects of the men, and said pointedly that it would be a long time before they would be ready to make an effective contribution to the war. They did not obey orders with the alacrity desired. There were also defects in the tactical plans. Marshall spoke up. He said they had received warning of the General's arrival the previous day, and with the warning came the announcement that the maneuvers would be held.

"They should have had two weeks preparation for a complicated maneuver like this," he said.

Pershing's large eyes opened wide. He gazed at Major Marshall with the air of someone who was about to swallow hard, and then barked: "Yes, you're quite right." Shortly afterwards he disappeared from sight, and though Marshall was pleased, he was also aware that he had been thoroughly rebuked by the Commanding General.

By October 21, some battalions of the Division's artillery and infantry were thought to be sufficiently prepared to be moved into the line. They were still ragged, they did not yet resemble a spick-and-span army. As he watched them going into line, with half their uniforms and equipment begged, borrowed or stolen from the French, Marshall felt an odd pleasure at the sight of these irreverent men who had cut the rims off their campaign hats and wore nothing but the crowns, or wore headgear made from bath towels, or Belgian *képis*. The *képis* pleased them because there were gold tassels dangling in front. He said afterwards that it was a trying experience and a complicated affair to manage; it was particularly trying because some of the staff from G.H.Q. were present, and they could not fail to observe that the men had insufficient winter clothing.

The battalions went into line for ten days at a time, taking their places alongside the units of the French Eighteenth Division. Marshall had made a preliminary reconnaissance of the front with the Chief of Staff, Colonel Ely, and two officers from G.H.Q., Colonel Malone and Colonel Drum. They reported that the front had been quiet since 1914, but might flare up. That was on October 17. On November 3, the front facing the Sixteenth Infantry did flare up. The first news reached Divisional Headquarters at eight in the morning when Marshall telephoned from the headquarters of the French Eighteenth Division, saying that two men had been killed and two wounded in the Second Battalion, Sixteenth Infantry, during a bombardment which had broken out at three o'clock in the morning. There had been a German raid, and Marshall was off to discover exactly what had happened. Early in the afternoon he was able to send off by courier a connected account of what had happened:

> About 2:50 a.m., Nov. 3d, a heavy bombardment was delivered by the enemy on our line from Aero to the south,

including Bures. In the vicinity of the Artois salient it was extremely violent. It lasted about fifty minutes. Apparently the tip of the salient was only lightly bombarded with 77mms., as it was only slightly damaged.

The men generally sought shelter in their dugouts. Lieut. McLoughlin, commanding the platoon holding the salient, sought to get his men back to the doubling trench, but the latter was under the heaviest bombardment and he was knocked down several times by shell blasts. During this bombardment the enemy exploded long, gas pipe dynamite charges under the wire in front of each face of the tip of the salient.

When the bombardment lifted on the front trench about forty or fifty Germans rushed in from the two sides, killed or drove off the one or two soldiers who had come out of their dugouts, and carried off twelve of our men. Three soldiers of Co. F, 16th Infantry were killed. One had had his throat cut; one had been shot by a revolver as he stepped to the door of his dugout; and the third had had his head crushed in—whether by a club or by a piece of shell fragment I do not know. The man with the cut throat was found, I understand, on top of the parapet.

I have not yet had an opportunity to question the wounded and I now understand that a German was wounded by the German barrage and has come into our lines, stating that the raid was planned in August and 250 volunteers called for, and that fifty participated in the raid. Everything regarding the German prisoner is new to me and as yet unchecked. Practically all the other details I found out for myself.

In order to get this off by the courier I have written it the moment I reached Einville and it is therefore disconnected and hurried. I will make a rough sketch to enclose. I am sending with this the list of names of killed, wounded and missing.

This was an important document, for it described the first engagement with the enemy. The names of the first American soldiers killed in action were Corporal James B. Gresham, Private Thomas F. Enright and Private Merle D. Hay. They were not the first soldiers of the A.E.F. killed by the enemy, for an American lieutenant and three privates were killed when a British military hospital was bombed early in September, but they were the first to be included in the battle roll; and Marshall, writing a wooden and graceless account of the engagement, was reflecting his own horror of what he had seen. It was not the first time he had seen the effects of shots fired in anger. He had been under fire during a brief three-day visit to Verdun in August, when he had accompanied a French Moroccan division in an assault against the German lines. Two days after the incident in the Artois salient, Marshall was deeply moved when General Bordeaux in command of the French Eighteenth Division presided at the funeral ceremonies held at Bathelémont. Marshall wrote to General William M. Sibert, the Commanding General of the First Division:

> An altar was improvised and elaborately decorated in the village, and the chaplain of the French regiment conducted the church services . . . [Afterwards] the cortège proceeded to a field adjacent to the village and formed on three sides of a square, the bodies being placed in front of the graves on the fourth side. General Bordeaux arrived, the chaplain performed the religious ceremony and the General addressed the troops and then the dead. Afterwards the company of the 16th Infantry fired three volleys and its trumpeter sounded taps. All the troops were then marched by the graves, saluting as they passed. Throughout the ceremony at the graves French batteries from their positions fired minute guns over the village at the German trenches. . . .
> Later in the day I called formally on General Bordeaux and told him that if you had been present, I knew you would have expressed to him your appreciation of the honor he had paid to our first dead, and that your division, the entire American army and the American people would always feel grateful for this action.

No one reading this letter would suspect the element of poetry in him, which sometimes erupted through the savagely dry deserts of his military prose; the poetry was to come later. Writing on a bleak November day, with the rumble of the minute guns in his ears, the words have dull edges: "The cortège proceeded to a field adjacent to the village. . . ." He wrote no better when he described how deeply moved he had been. "The entire ceremony," he told General Sibert, "was one of the most impressive I have ever witnessed." Yet the style was indicative of the man, who was slowly fashioning himself into a superbly streamlined machine, the pent-up imagination at the mercy of logistics, while memories of the memorial ceremonies at the Virginia Military Institute gave added dignity to the funeral at Bathelémont until they seemed to belong to a single magical ritual; and years later, whenever he met French officers, he would talk simply and well about that desperate little engagement in the Lunéville sector and its sad aftermath.

The first brush with the enemy had done little to advance the credit of the American forces. They had been caught by surprise. A full investigation was ordered, and on the day he wrote the letter to General Sibert, Marshall was relieved from the post of divisional liaison officer with the headquarters of the French Eighteenth Division, a position which had been only temporary. He attended the court of enquiry and agreed with the verdict that the First Division was still insufficiently trained, and must be pulled out of line. It was a blow to the divisional commander, for the First Division was already known as "the nursery of the High Command." The original plan envisaged a three months work-out before they were sent up to the front: the first month spent in drill, the second month in training with the French, and the third month in training as a reassembled division; but the plan had proved a failure. Vast changes were needed; and among the most urgently needed was a change in the command. On December 14, General Robert L. Bullard took over the command. Immediately the change was felt. Until the end of the year the First Division was put through its paces: the training in the autumn had been bitter enough, but the training during the last weeks of the year was designed to create a mechanically efficient army, toughened by experience. There were long night marches; the men slept on the icy ground, or were made to stand about during long hours of waiting in the cold blustering wind and the drenching rains. Pershing had said: "We'll whip that bunch of recruits into shape and get them into action," and now out of that inchoate mass a real army was being formed. It had to be; for that terrible autumn had seen the Russian collapse and the disaster of Caporetto, and the available man power from America was still depressingly small.

Marshall took part in the training programs, setting up his own headquarters at the corps school, receiving distinguished visitors like Pershing, Colonel House and Lord Northcliffe without taking his eye from the main object: which was to see that the honor of the First Division should be upheld in war. Some short while previously Lieutenant Colonel Johnson Hagood took over command of the advance section of the Line of Communications, later to be called Services of Supply. He offered to take Marshall on his staff, and when he returned to G.H.Q. at Chaumont-en-Bassigny he asked that Marshall be promoted immediately to be temporary colonel and given to him as assistant.

"Marshall!" exclaimed the G.H.Q. spokesman. "Why, you can't have Marshall. Marshall is the First Division!"

"I agree with you," Hagood said, "that Marshall's place is at the front and not back with the services of supply. But if Marshall is the First Division, why do you not promote him to be major general and put him in command?"

"Oh, no," replied the spokesman. "Marshall is the First Division and cannot be spared; and he cannot be promoted now."

Hagood went away in a rage against officialdom, and with the certain feeling that the young major was not being used to the best of his capacity. In this, Hagood was probably wrong. There were good reasons for keeping Marshall at the front. One could discount the official restrictions imposed on promotion; one need not take too seriously the alarming effect a sudden promotion of an obscure temporary major would have on senior officers; but in his own place Marshall was performing a necessary function. There was a great need for staff officers who could measure exactly what was happening near the front and who were absorbed in problems of training, communication and supply.

The training period, which had begun on November 20, was now coming to an end. On January 15, during a storm, they began to move towards the front to relieve the French First Moroccan Division in the Ansauville sector north of Toul on the St. Mihiel front, which was then under the command of the French Sixty-Ninth Division, although no French units were in the line. Not all the Division went forward: the Second Infantry Brigade and some elements of the artillery and engineers were left behind at Gondrecourt to continue their training and to be available as reserves. There was nothing to reassure them in the positions they now occupied. The trenches were in low-lying ground, while the Germans occupied the heights of Montsec, close to the south face of the St. Mihiel salient. Montsec was defended by a complex system of trenches, machine-gun emplacements and barbed-wire entanglements; there were large underground shelters in the hill and observation posts on the crests. There was to be a great deal of fighting in this sector later in the year, but for the moment it was comparatively quiet, though the men suffered from the incessant rain, trenches collapsed, and what fighting there was took place in the biting cold. By February 5, General Bullard took over command from the French, and to celebrate the occasion he ordered an increase of activity on a front which threatened to be permanently quiet. Marshall, now assistant chief of staff, G-3, under Colonel Stephen O. Fuqua, described the day briefly in his report to G.H.Q.:

> It was a comparatively quiet day, with only three men of the 18th Infantry wounded, and no German airplanes in the air. The Americans dropped 26 shells on Richecourt, and two batteries fired on some German infantry marching along the edge of a wood: the effect was not observed. The Germans were more active than the Americans. They dropped 129 105's and 115 77's. Trenches are being repaired and drained.

The next day the situation remained roughly the same, though the German and American artillery were stepped up. The cleaning and repairing of the trenches went on, and Marshall noted that the only loss was one soldier who committed suicide. He had the detective's instinct for recording the most minute details in the hope that they might acquire significance. He noted, for example, that a sack containing an O.D. blouse without buttons, one pair of O.D. breeches and one canteen without cover were found concealed in the Bois de Rambucourt. No explanation for the mysterious sack is given, nor does he explain why it should have been hidden. He is content to record the discovery, and passes on to repair works, minor raids, all the drudgery of an army dug in during a deathly winter.

So it goes on, day after day. A small red balloon was seen crossing the American lines, a large column of smoke was observed, somewhere a dog barked, and somewhere else a dug-out opened and a gruff voice was heard saying *"fertig"* (ready)—everything is noted; and Bullard, reading these reports as they were sent to Divisional

Headquarters, passed them on to G.H.Q. in a suitably revised form. He sent telegrams to Pershing which read: "situation unchanged bullard."

By February 10, an air of excitement begins to appear in Marshall's notes. He observes the exceptional quietness of the German front lines, a few winged bombs are dropped, there are more illuminating flares than usual. Somewhere an electrified wire throws off mysterious sparks. Horses are seen near the gravel pits. Then quite suddenly there is the announcement: "At 1:45 a.m. a gas alarm from F/i was confirmed by telephone. A humming sound was heard and a few shells were fired. The gas had a smell similar to that of bananas." Even then Bullard reported that the situation was unchanged.

These reports make fascinating reading. Cold and precise, they are like the notes which a wanderer at the foot of Kafka's Castle might have written. The landscape is etched in. You are made aware of the trenches wandering between the lakes, the mud, the crumbling villages, the sprawling rain-drenched forests, while high above them all lies the dark hill of Montsec, ghostly and impregnable, its very name a rebuke to the sodden doughboys in the plain. Marshall still carefully observes the mysterious signs and portents. A pistol and four grenades are picked up: there is no explanation, no attempt at an explanation, and we are left in doubt whether the pistol was German, American or French. A dog has been heard growling at the approach of a patrol. Ten spherical bombs, about the size of a baseball, have fallen on H/3. Numerous red rockets are seen, some single and some in clusters. The mysterious details describe an atmosphere of menace. He noted on February 25 that the enemy was using a very powerful flame which was able to cross the Richecourt salient into the American wires; on the next day two men were dead after a gas attack, and nine were taken to hospital.

So far there has been no excitement in the reports. It is not, of course, his task to convey excitement. His task is to report meticulous and accurate details from which the atmosphere of the front lines can be gauged at Chaumont. Yet excitement creeps in, and he describes the effects of the heavy artillery attack on February 28 with ghastly brevity and precision:

The dug-outs were all blown in and the craters made by the bombardment are thirty feet wide and fifteen feet deep. Pieces of men have been found but an estimate of the number of men blown up is impossible for the fact that it cannot be ascertained whether or not these fragments are part of one man or two. Sixteen of our men were lost, and there were fifteen Germans hanging in our wire.

This attack, which occurred at night, was the heaviest they had encountered; it had extended into the French Sixty-Ninth Division, and Captain Hoover of the Eighteenth Infantry had been killed. Confused reports reached Marshall, but it was three days before he was able to produce a connected account. After this there was quiet for a few days. He mentions a piece of insulated wire which has been discovered running towards the enemy lines—again there are no explanations. Very occasionally there is a flash of wry humor, as when he wrote in the operations report for March 6, an account of the angry words of a German soldier who wanted only to live in peace. As Marshall related the incident:

A sentinel in a listening post heard the enemy opposite Center H indulge in the following conversation: (translation) "Come here, come here, Fritz. Take this pick and pry that loose stone. Take this shovel and throw that dirt out. Those—over there, we work all night to fix these trenches and they blow them to H—in the daytime."

The Ansauville sector continued quiet throughout March, with Bullard sending to headquarters the usual "situation unchanged" bulletins. Everyone knew that the Germans were about to launch their spring offensive, but no one knew from which direction it would come. Pershing had hoped to get his men out of the trenches; he could see no solution in trench warfare, and he had deliberately encouraged training in terms of open warfare. The training program was now designed in the proportions: two-thirds open warfare, one-third trench warfare. It was a wiser decision than he knew, for the Germans were already massing their forces for a war of movement.

During the previous year the Germans had evolved a method which enabled them to break out into a war of maneuver. Such a method had been practiced by General Von Hutier on the Russians near Riga. Instead of concentrating his troops on the front some days before an attack, with the result that they were nearly always detected by the enemy, he brought his troops along converging lines from all possible directions and arranged that they should arrive at the same time. The transportation system worked like clockwork and in secret: the armies moved mostly at night, then the sudden attack across the lines with the support of light artillery. By using the Riga method the Americans, with Marshall in charge of the complex problems of transport and supplies, were eventually to throw back the enemy. Meanwhile the Germans, using this method, were preparing their breakthrough.

The blow fell on March 21, when the Germans launched the first of the great offensives by which they hoped to win the war before the American army could take the field in force. The Germans broke through the British Fifth Army, driving a deep wedge at the junction of the British and French armies; in five days they had gone twenty-five miles to within artillery range of Amiens and the main railway behind the British lines. The position was desperate. Pershing had hoped all along to preserve the A.E.F. intact, but now the hope was temporarily abandoned, for the front had to be buttressed wherever it was weak. The Secretary of War, Newton D. Baker, was in France. At a conference in Paris, Baker and Pershing decided that a formal offer of the American army should be made to Foch. The difficulty was to find Foch, who was reported to be at Clermont-sur-Oise. Pershing motored out through roads blocked with trucks and supplies, learned at the headquarters of the French Third Army that no one knew where Foch was, but eventually the General was discovered in a small French farmhouse hidden among trees, with spring flowers growing in the garden and a cherry tree in bloom in the courtyards. He found Clemenceau, Foch and Pétain studying a map. Having a slight distrust of Pétain and a considerable wariness of politicians, he asked to see Foch alone. Then, speaking in French, Pershing announced the decision to turn over the American forces to Foch. "I have come," he said, "to tell you that the American people would consider it a great honor for our troops to be engaged in the present battle. Infantry, artillery, aviation, all that we have is yours. Use them as you wish. More will come, in numbers equal to requirements." It was now the late afternoon or evening of March 27.

At this moment there were four trained American divisions in France, hardly more than 100,000 combatant troops, with not a single American airplane: all the training of the fliers had taken place in French planes; but the Americans were now beginning to arrive at the rate of 250,000 a month, and the whole force of the First Division could be thrown against the sector where Foch anticipated the next blow. This was the Montdidier sector, then being held by the French First Army. On April 5 the Division was therefore pulled back to a region north of Paris, and prepared for a full-scale entry into the war. There were last minute exercises, and on April 14, Marshall ordered Lieutenant Colonel Erickson, Major Greely, Lieutenant Edgar and Mr. Tuley to attend these exercises. Characteristically, he made a precise list of all the things they must take with them. The list included:

> 1 folding table
> 2 folding chairs
> 1 typewriter
> necessary stationery
> field message books
> maps
> operations stamp

He added that the officers should come properly equipped with maps, notebooks and field glasses, and he arranged about who should go in which automobile. Lieutenant Colonels Marshall and Erickson and Major Greely would go in the Operations Cadillac, while Lieutenant Edgar, Mr. Tuley (evidently an aide) and all materials would go in the Operations Dodge. Such strict attention to protocol proved no more than that he was acting in character; he was, after all, the same man who had written the memorandum on quartermaster supplies, professional and precise, with a talent for minor ironies. Marshall's order was dated April 14. This was exactly two days after Douglas Haig issued his famous communiqué: "With our backs to the wall, and believing in the justice of our cause, each one of us must fight to the end."

The Americans were soon enough to be in the same straits. At midnight on April 20 the concentration of the First Division at

Montdidier, at the tip of the Somme salient, was completed and General Debeney of the French First Army assumed command. The Americans began to take over the line four days later, moving always at night, and elements of the French 162d and 45th Divisions were completely retired from the line within three days.

Just before the First Division had moved into the sector, Pershing summoned all the officers of the Division for a final brief-taking. Standing beside Major General Bullard, in the grounds of a French château, he declared he was well-satisfied with their training, and added a note of warning:

> Whatever your previous instruction may have been, you must learn in the actual experience of war, the practical application of the tactical principles that you have been taught during your preliminary training. Those principles are as absolute as they are immutable. Whatever may be the changing conditions of this war, those principles remain practically the same, and you should constantly bear them in mind.

But though Pershing could announce that the principles were unchanging, they were in fact continually shifting; and Marshall learned that the intricate and elaborate system of defense in depth which characterized the Ansauville sector was now to be modified as a result of the fighting on the Somme: against the Riga maneuvers it had been found wanting. A new system of trenches and emplacements, less than a quarter of a mile in width, were now regarded as essential. This meant heart-breaking work for the men who were coming into line, new maps, new problems of supply, and an increased burden on Marshall, who was also acting as liaison officer with the French while preparing operations reports and ordering himself on periodic missions to the front lines to observe the morale of the men.

How deeply Marshall was affected by the sudden change in tactics and in the methods of defense can be seen from a description he delivered in a speech addressed to the Army Ordnance Association meeting at Washington in October 1939, shortly after the Germans had completed their lightning advance into Poland. He told the story well (as he always does when he is talking of the men in the trenches) and with an urgency which showed that he was thinking in terms of the Riga maneuver adapted to modern warfare. The *blitzkrieg* was only an armored modification of the Riga maneuver, and the question which was uppermost in men's minds was how soon it would be waged against the British and French. Marshall's account is lengthy, but it should be given in his own words, because it is one of his finer pieces of prose:

> We had been there (on the Ansauville sector) but two or three weeks when there was received from the Intelligence Bureau of the French Army a description of an expected assault to be made by German forces, which had been heavily reinforced with divisions drawn from the collapsed Russian front. The reported nature of this new attack, termed a "maneuver of rupture," was such that it caused the French High Command to direct a complete reorganization of the defenses—from that of a shallow nature to one of considerable depth. This meant the complete change of a system which had existed for nearly three years. It meant, in brief, that a regiment which had occupied a deployed depth of about five or six hundred yards, would be disposed over a depth of a mile or more, and that the regiments, the companies, the individuals, could be much more widely dispersed; that a great many machine-gun emplacements, which had previously been located along the lines of trenches, would have to be relocated in staggered formation of great depth.
>
> To the First Division it meant a tremendous planning problem, and for the troops hard manual labor and much exposure to the weather of that bitter winter of 1917-1918. Snow was deep on the ground. Every move we made could be readily traced by the tracks of vehicles and of men on foot, as well as by the signs of extensive excavations. Construction was started and the men worked very, very hard. They suffered extreme hardships because of the inadequacy of the arrangements we could make for their shelter in the newly deployed positions in depth, but they did their work uncomplainingly. Then, when we were about half-way through with this program, the great German offensive of March 21, 1918, broke against the right of the British Army.
>
> The First Division was hurriedly withdrawn from that sector and sent to Picardy. As its trains were arriving northwest of Paris, I personally reported to the headquarters

of the group of French armies in which we were to serve. There I was informed that the system of organization in depth which we had just been carrying out on the St. Mihiel front, had since been greatly modified as a result of the experience of the recent heavy fighting. I was given the new method for taking up dispositions in depth which we were to follow as we went into the new sector, on ground but recently occupied and without trenches. We started work on the defenses under this new arrangement. Again the men worked in the cold and mud of early spring in northern France, but just as they had gotten well into it, another German offensive broke, this time down the Valley of the Lys. Two weeks later new instructions were received for a further modifying of the method of deployment in depth. Once more we were forced to abandon the results of work that had been laboriously accomplished.

The troops were very tired. They had had no relief since early January. They had endured the cold, the mud, and the snow or rain of that bitter winter. It is true that they had not been engaged in an active operation, but they had been under such heavy fire that about three or four thousand men were casualties. Nevertheless, every man set about this newest task of reorganization in a fine, soldierly spirit. And then we entered into the Cantigny operation, where we suffered heavy losses due to a series of desperate German counter-attacks and violent artillery reactions. Simultaneously with that fight came the German attack on the Chemin des Dames, which thundered down to Château-Thierry—to make it a historic ground for our Army. And then once more, two weeks later, we received a new set of instructions completely modifying the organization in depth that we were then in the process of completing.

I recall that in our reply to these new instructions we notified the French headquarters that we could do one of two things; we could fight or we could dig, but it was no longer possible for us to do both.

All these changes in the patterns of deployment and defense had arisen as the result of the new German tactics brought about to put an end to the sterile trench warfare of the time. Pershing welcomed the change.

In a letter to the Secretary of War, Pershing noted the

revolutionary tactics and the atmosphere of hope in the air: "On April 26, the First Division went into line in the Montdidier salient on the Picardy front battle. Tactics were revolutionized to those of open warfare; and our men, confident of the results of their training, were eager for the test."

From that time to the end of the war the American troops were engaged in open warfare. The First Division was well-trained for it: Marshall could look back on ten months of remorseless training in which every conceivable maneuver had been carefully worked out in advance. He was happy in his commander, Robert Lee Bullard, who resembled a Virginian aristocrat—with his strong sensitive face, fine hands and soft drawl, as became an Alabamian. Bullard spoke French well, suffered atrociously from neuritis which mysteriously disappeared at the beginning of a battle, and was so thin that he always seemed to be drowned in his heavy fur coat. Blue-eyed, tall, nearly always with a smile playing on his lips, he commanded instant obedience by a trick of personality which defied definition, for he possessed nothing of Hunter Liggett's majestic presence. His gentleness concealed a relentless devotion; and insofar as one man ever models himself on another, Marshall modeled himself on Bullard, who was known to complain that "in every army there are two kinds of soldiers: those who do things they are ordered to, and those who are always looking for things to do." Marshall belonged to the second kind. He had thirsted to show his capacity in battle, and now at long last the opportunity was at hand.

CHAPTER FIVE

Cantigny

The village of Cantigny lay on high ground, well-defended with machine guns, and behind it was a screen of woods where the Germans kept their reserves and artillery. It was a village like all the villages of Picardy, with slate-roofed houses and a small church facing the village square. Hardly a hundred people had lived there before the war. The village itself possessed no importance: much larger villages were to be fought over by American troops with an even greater loss of life, and most of them are forgotten. Cantigny is remembered because it was the first village to be taken by the Americans, and because here there was established a pattern which was to be followed until the end of the war.

The blood-letting began almost as soon as the First Division was in the line. Bullard assumed command of the sector at 10 a.m., April 27, putting two battalions in the front line and keeping one battalion in reserve. He had the French 152d Division to his left and the French 162d Division to his right, and he could use their artillery to support any attacks he ordered. He had excellent maps, close liaison with the French, and a definite objective—the capture of the village and the crest which dominated the valleys beyond. He was determined that the first major combat assignment given to American troops should be successful. Plans were laid carefully. As usual Marshall had his eyes on supplies and communications. On May 12, he issued a memorandum to the company officer, Eighteenth Infantry, on reconnaissance for supply officers: "Battalion supply officers of the 28th Infantry will join 18th Infantry Supply Trains at Bonvillers tonight and make reconnaissance at the front in reference to methods of supply." A stream of memoranda on reconnaissance followed. Other problems disturbed him. He was aware of the difficulties of giving warning signals, especially during a barrage, when an alarm given by advance posts would remain unheard in the rear. He wrote:

> During the recent German offensive there were instances when German infantry reached the line of resistance before the alarm was given. Patrols and advance posts will be instructed in several methods of giving the alarm quickly and effectively, despite the noise of bombardment. All front line troops will be similarly instructed. Whistle signals, rifle and revolver fire, "to arms" sounded on the bugle and any other available means will be employed to give the alarm to rear echelons in time to permit them to man the trenches.

The problem was one to be solved urgently, for the possibility of a German thrust in this sector was not to be discounted, and though the sector was relatively quiet there had appeared in the operations reports from the beginning of the month the monotonous inscription: "Heavy shelling." The losses were beginning to mount at a sickening pace: during the month which preceded the battle for Cantigny, the First Division lost in killed as many as they lost in the battle itself, and nearly two thousand were wounded.

By May 17 the complicated plans for the offensive by the Eighteenth Infantry had been worked out. Two days later Pershing arrived at Bullard's headquarters at Mesnil-St. Firmin for a last briefing of the Division staff, which took place the following morning. Afterwards Pershing held a conference with Marshall on tactical methods. It was not a long conference, for Pershing had already dealt directly with the Chief of Staff, but the plans had been very largely prepared by Marshall and he was interested in seeing the man who already possessed the reputation of being a tactical genius. He made a short speech to Marshall on the importance of the forthcoming battle, and then returned to Chantilly.

The original plan which Pershing approved with some slight emendations remained unaltered, though it became more detailed as time went on. The Division order was an incredibly lengthy document, neglecting no detail and leaving little to the initiative of subordinates. It had been carefully rehearsed behind the lines on terrain which roughly resembled the terrain of Cantigny, but whatever else it was, it was not an illustration of the open warfare on which Pershing had set his heart. As Marshall wrote some years later:

> The order for the Cantigny attack is an extreme example of the extent to which minute details may be prescribed in preliminary arrangements for combat. It illustrates the maximum authority a commander can exercise over a subordinate who leads a unit in combat. In war of movement, such an order would have been wholly impracticable, but it was well-suited to the special conditions of Cantigny. The troops were inexperienced; the objective was strictly limited; there were good maps; there was plenty of time. Therefore, the higher commander, having much at stake, exercised the maximum of authority.

How detailed these plans were can be seen from a quotation of only a small part of the long memorandum as it appears in the collection of documents gathered together by the First Division after the war:

Operation against Cantigny

Subject. Cooperation of adjacent divisions 152d D.I.

(A) *Before the attack and at the moment of the attack*
diversion in region of LA CHAPELLE ST. AIGNAN

(Note: The exact portion of the front for this diversion will be determined by the 152d D.I. who will notify the First Division)

H-2 hr. to H-1 hr.	Regulation fire of 75s, 155s and 220s.
H-1 hr. to H hr.	Regulation fire on points selected for diversions. Destruction fire by 155s & 220s. Combing fire for 75s.
H-15 mins. to H hr.	Simulated attack. Continuation of heavy artillery fire. Establishment of 75 barrage similar to that in zone of attack.
H hr. to *H plus 5 mins.*	Lengthening of range of 75 barrage. Bursts of machine-gun and rifle fire.

(B) During the attack.
Fire of interdiction, neutralization and blinding on the region of Bois de Lalval, Ferme de la Folie ridge southeast of la Chapelle St. Aignan

H hr. plus 5 mins. to H hr. 15 mins. The artillery (75s and 155s) will execute the following fires:

75s   I Group—Combing fire on ravine southwest of the Ferme de la Folie.
I Group—Neutralizing and blinding fire on the Bois de Lalval and region of coords. 30.30—38.26.
I Group—Neutralization and blinding fire on the plateau north of the Ferme de la Folie.
155s   Neutralization and blinding fire on the region of Ferme de la Folie—Bois de Lalval.

But if the plan of attack appeared complicated, it was basically simple. The plan comprised a rolling barrage moving forward at the rate of fifty meters a minute (which is roughly the rate at which a man would stroll leisurely across an open field), while protected by this barrage the First Division moved up with tanks and flamethrowers. After advancing one hundred meters the barrage would hold its fire for four minutes, to give the infantry time to get up, if it had fallen behind, and then it would roll forward again. Within forty-two minutes the barrage had covered two kilometers, with the infantry lagging only two minutes behind. The tremendous and merciless barrage cleared the path, and though there was heavy resistance beyond the town, chiefly from the woods on the other side of the crest, and artillery and machine-gun fire from the left flank, the German defenders were overcome, the village was occupied and the Twenty-Eighth Infantry passed over the crest and occupied the valley, where they built trenches, laid barbed wire and prepared strong points. Exactly twelve hours after the American rolling barrage had begun, the Germans also attacked behind a rolling barrage, but this was thrown back. By nightfall the Americans were securely in command of the line they had gained in a two-hour attack during the morning. Late that night Marshall sent his operations report to headquarters:

I. *General Characteristics of the Day.*
We successfully attacked and took Cantigny.

II. *American Activity:*
(a) *Infantry:*
After a heavy destructive fire by our artillery the 28th Infantry advanced and took Cantigny in accordance with Field Orders #18. All objectives were taken and the ground is now being consolidated. 175 prisoners, of whom 3 are officers, have been counted. It is impossible to estimate the enemy's losses in killed and wounded, but they were very heavy. Our casualties were estimated to be about 300. Details will be furnished later.
(b) *Artillery:*
No figures available.

On the same evening Marshall was visited by Thomas M. Johnson, the correspondent of the New York *Evening Sun,* who asked for an account of the battle and was rewarded with a detailed report—exactly the same kind of detailed report which Marshall was to give to amazed correspondents in the Second World War. Johnson evidently took down Marshall's report by shorthand, for he said afterwards that he reproduced Marshall's account "word for word" and Marshall's style is clearly evident in some of the paragraphs which were published in the *Evening Sun* under the date line of May 29, 1918. Occasionally Johnson has interpolated a passage of his own in which he discusses at some length "the pregnant darkness" and "the first rosy streaks of early dawn"—these passages can be easily detached from Marshall's words, which should be quoted at some length because they show for the first time his extraordinary sense of historical detail and his capacity to describe a battle tersely and accurately. Marshall said:

> The Americans have made their first real attack of the war, and it is a complete success. Advancing up a wooded slope behind French tanks and protected by a perfect and annihilating barrage from French and American guns, our infantry at 7 o'clock Tuesday morning, May 28, stormed and captured the village of Cantigny, northwest of Montdidier,

and the German defenses to the north and south, making an advance of a mile on a two-mile front.

This operation had been planned for weeks down to the minutest detail under the direction of the Superior French Command, and in the closest cooperation with the French, to whom must go a liberal measure of the credit for its success.

So far as its objects may be disclosed, they were the following: To reduce the enemy salient and capture its strong point and observation post. Cantigny was all those things. Jutting out from the German front, it gave the enemy an advantage in the field of fire, while, because of its strong cellars, which were linked up with an especially long tunnel under the château in the southern part of the village, which might be likened to its citadel, it was decidedly a strong post.

Perhaps most important of all, it gave the *Boche* a local advantage comparable to that of a man looking down a well. It commanded a sort of valley running back into our lines and permitted the enemy observers to see many things which went on there and so direct his artillery fire upon our back areas. For all of those reasons Cantigny was a prize of value altogether out of proportion to its size.

Marshall went on to talk about the preparations for the attack, the information gained by night patrols, the rehearsals and the dilemma which faced the American commanders when they learned that two American soldiers had been captured in a trench raid and might perhaps have revealed the plan of attack under a terrible Prussian grilling. The soldiers revealed nothing, and the attack went on as expected. In his characteristic fashion, Marshall discussed the order of attack with a kind of mathematical precision. He said:

> This is how the plan of attack was executed: The troops selected to make it entered the trenches in two shifts, the first on Sunday night and the second on Monday night, May 27. Special trenches had been constructed to accommodate a larger number of men than usual. Two hours before zero—that is to say, at 4:45 o'clock this morning—the men withdrew to supporting trenches, whence they went to the front line at zero, or 6:45.
>
> They were divided into three waves for the main attack,

with separate detachments to whom had been allotted the task of mopping up the Cantigny cellars. On the right and center the advance was made to the furthest objectives, while on the left, according to the plan, after mopping up the German trenches, our troops withdrew slightly to a better position, connecting with our old front line.

The troops went forward in extended order, preceded by the powerful tanks, all of which entered Cantigny and went some distance beyond. With the infantry went a detachment of flame throwers who were used against the cellars when the *Boche* refused to come out when ordered to do so. They were also accompanied by a strong detachment of engineers, signal corps men, and carrier pigeons, but the wires have remained intact.

The artillery fire was tremendous. The German batteries at the rear were also drenched by gas. A rolling barrage behind which the infantry advanced was laid by the field guns. The infantry went forward first at the rate of fifty yards per minute and then at twenty-five yards per minute. The moving barrage of fire stalked ahead of our men into Cantigny, keeping the *Boche* down until the infantry was upon him.

The time-table was adhered to perfectly. At 4:45 o'clock the artillery began a concentrated fire, swelling to a drum fire at 6:45, "zero," continuing thence onward to 7:20, when the infantry reached their final objectives. At 7:30 the infantry outlined their position with flares so as to enable the airplanes to signal back. Thus it will be seen that Cantigny was taken in less than thirty-five minutes, for the final objectives were beyond the village.

There were some tough nuts to crack besides Cantigny itself, such as the trench system protecting it on the south, also part of the Fontaine Wood, and some separate houses at the crossroads at the southeastern outskirts of the town, but all were reduced with bombs, bayonets, or rifles, while the machine-guns which went along with the infantry also aided.

Besides all this, a heavy smoke barrage was used, not only to screen our infantry from *Boche* observers, but to blind the *Boche* gunners. The tremendous effectiveness of the whole thing was shown by the fact that for nearly half an hour after the infantry went over the top, the German artillery was practically silenced. This was due especially to the accurate counter-battery work of the French heavies.

So the Americans in their first attack had the aid of every engine of modern warfare—tanks, gas, flame throwers, smoke barrage, numbers of airplanes, machine guns and automatic rifles, while some especially heavy trench mortars were also concentrated and hurled great bombs into the German trenches from close range. Reports all agree that the German defenses were completely leveled, and the smashed-up trenches look like a field plowed by a gigantic harrow. Our men walked into the trenches through great gaps torn in the barbed wire, but in many places there was no wire at all for great stretches. So much for the main outlines of the attack.

Marshall's operations report and the report which he gave to the correspondent of the New York *Evening Sun* were written when the fate of Cantigny was still in the balance. There were to be repeated counter-attacks by the Germans, beginning about noon on May 28 and continuing solidly for seventy-two hours. There were altogether seven unsuccessful German efforts to regain the village. All failed.

The victory had come just in time. On May 27, the Germans rushed across the Chemin des Dames behind waves of gas and artillery fire, scattered the French defenses and pushed on towards the river Vesle; within three days they were smashing against the outer defenses of Rheims. By the fourth day the Marne was in reach, and General Bliss, the Permanent Military Representative at the Supreme War Council, filled his trucks with files in case Paris should have to be abandoned. The Second and Third American divisions, one trained and the other not yet out of training, were thrust hurriedly into the Allied lines to help stem the German tide; and while the First Division at Cantigny provided the perfect example of the classical victory, the fate of the Second Division was to be dragged through the wheeling confusion of the times, sent on forced marches along roads clogged with refugees, coming into line without knowing where the line was, the regiments blundering into each other and losing themselves in the woods, until at Belleau Wood they fought at last the open war for which they had been trained.

On a small scale and in an unimportant sector, Cantigny had

been a prodigious success. An enemy stronghold had been reduced with the employment of a minimum of means and at the cost of a minimum number of casualties. And though the Germans were busily occupied elsewhere and paid scant attention to the loss of an obscure village (for they thought the conquest of the capital was almost in sight), the victory, as Hunter Liggett said later, "was the first cold foreboding to the German that this was not, as he had hoped, a rabble of amateurs approaching." As for the casualties, they were not negligible. Marshall's estimate of the casualties was hopelessly wrong: the total casualties suffered by the First Division that day amounted to 580, of whom 244 were killed or died later of their wounds. This was only the beginning: there were to be more than five thousand casualties before the Division left the sector in July. Many of these casualties were unnecessary. The soldiers were not yet skilled veterans and they showed a careless contempt for danger, walking round the village streets as though they were invisible and invulnerable. Bullard wrote in his telegraphic report: "The losses sustained, caused in part by lack of experience, will be a lesson which only personal experience could have given."

Honors fell thick on the Division. General Debeney, who retained titular command, reported that the operation was well-prepared and vigorously executed, and would "serve to give the Americans and others a realization of the offensive valor of our allies." General Pétain cited the regiment—the Twenty-Eighth Infantry—which had borne the brunt of the fighting. Colonel Hanson E. Ely, who had commanded the regiment, was marked out by Pershing to receive command of the Fifth Division, while Bullard himself was to command the Second Army when the A.E.F. was reorganized later in the year. Marshall's share in the victory was noted by Bullard, who recommended an immediate promotion to colonel. This was refused in obedience to the War Department precept which demanded that all officers should be promoted according to seniority. He had no time to be bitter. Small-scale German attacks had still to be faced. On June 18, in a memorandum on the defense of the Cantigny sector, Marshall urged that "in the event of a hostile local attack" there should be "immediate counter-attack by the support or the reserve platoons of the outpost company. If this is delivered quickly and intelligently, following a previously accepted plan, the enemy will not have had time to properly locate his light machine guns." Evidently, the work of consolidation was still going on. There were patrols, raids, short jabs at the enemy. There were occasional scares, as when on June 6 the entire Division occupied its battle positions in anticipation of a new German offensive against the sector, but though the Germans attacked between Montdidier and Noyon against the French First and Third Armies, there were no infantry attacks against the Division, though the bombardment continued, that long and relentless bombardment which was chiefly responsible for two thousand casualties between May 29 and July 13.

Marshall was now weary of Operations. He had always wanted to be assigned to duty with the troops. There was something terrifyingly cold-blooded in those large, intricate plans, the innumerable large-scale maps with the red boxes outlining the stages of a creeping barrage, the summary statements on gunfire and attack and patrol. He wanted to be among the men and to share their dangers. He wrote a brief message to Bullard:

> 1. Request that I be relieved from duty on the General Staff and assigned to duty with troops.
> 2. I have been on staff duty since February, 1915, and I am tired from the incessant strain of office work.

Bullard was bound by regulations to forward the message to the Adjutant General of the A.E.F., but since he was also bound to attach a covering letter with his own views, and since Pershing had complete faith in him, the decision remained in the division commander's hands. The covering letter was nearly as terse as the original request. It read:

> I cannot approve, because I know that Lieut. Col. Marshall's special fitness is for staff work and because I doubt that in this, whether it be teaching or practice, he has an equal in the Army today. But his experience and merit should find a wider field than the detailed labors of a division staff.

From that moment Marshall was doomed. There was not only Bullard's letter, which would inevitably come to the attention of Colonel Fox Conner, who was G-3 at General Headquarters at Chaumont, but there were other forces at work. Fox Conner had long had his eyes on Marshall. Major Robert Lewis, who was liaison officer with the French for Fox Conner, had come to know Marshall well, and he was continually sending messages to G.H.Q. in which Marshall's views were put forward. They talked French together. Though Lewis knew Marshall's desire to be assigned with troops, he was also perfectly aware that his friend's abilities lay elsewhere. On July 4 the Americans celebrated their independence by shelling the German positions. Then the artillery brigade put on a horse show in the woods behind the Château de Tartigny, and in the evening the officers attended dinner at the French Corps headquarters. Major Lewis had sent a stream of messages about Marshall to Colonel Fox Conner in the previous months, and did not neglect him now. On the following day, writing from the First Division headquarters, he told Fox Conner: "In the evening of July 4 Marshall and I and some other officers were invited over to the Corps for a big inter-allied dinner which went off very well. Marshall made a fine speech in French."

At the dinner the French and American officers bade farewell to one another. On the next day the First Division began to be pulled out of line—pieces of it were pulled out during four consecutive nights—and within a week they were to find themselves far in the rear, in the Dammartin-en-Goële area northeast of Paris. On the day when they reached their new training grounds Lieutenant Colonel Marshall was reporting for duty at General Headquarters in Chaumont. In front of him lay two more classic battles and a fiasco.

CHAPTER SIX

St. Mihiel and Sedan

The week following Marshall's appointment to G.H.Q. saw the turning of the tide. All along the front, from the Channel to the Swiss frontier, huge armies were rushed against the invaders, who wavered and stepped back and were gradually pushed into a rout. The Germans had expected Paris to fall by the end of the month. "We expected grave events in Paris for the end of July," wrote Chancellor von Hertling later. "But on the 18th the most optimistic among us understood that all was lost. The history of the world was played out in three days."

The history of the world was played out in those three days without the full employment of American combatant troops in France; but that was no fault of Pershing's. To throw the Germans back there was needed the menace of the American reserves, the knowledge that they could be thrown into combat wherever the German line threatened to stand. Inevitably there was confusion at the American headquarters—there was confusion in all headquarters. As the battle rolled along a 200-mile front, maps became antiquated overnight, directives lagged behind the march of events, the sudden turn and twist through a wood or a ravine, the breaching of a line. The divisions had secret code names, and the general staff at headquarters were demanding: "Where is Kitty? Where is Jenny?" They need not have worried. The First Division on the left, the First Moroccan Division (of which the Foreign Legion was one regiment) in the center, and the Second Division on the right had formed the spearhead of the attack of the French Tenth Army during the dawn of July 18. General Mangin, the "Butcher of Verdun," said of the Ill Corps, which comprised the First and Second Divisions: "They rushed into the fights as to a fête."

But if Mangin regarded the battle as a fête, there were some who thought otherwise. The successes were paid for at a costly price. A single day cost the First Division 3,000 casualties: when the Division came out of line it had lost more than 7,200 men, mostly in the infantry. The full complement of infantry in a division is 12,000. They attacked continually for five days after a long march; they had kept pace with the famous First Moroccan Division and stayed longer in the fight; they had advanced ten kilometers at a time when ten kilometers represented a prodigious assault through mine fields, barbed wire and creeping barrages. The Eighteenth Infantry, Marshall's favorite, had lost all its officers above the rank of captain except the commanding officers; the Twenty-Sixth had lost all its officers except a captain of less than two years experience. The Germans were being driven out of the Marne salient, but at a cost which made the readers of the casualty lists wince.

The General Staff was in turmoil. The reserves were coming to the end of their training, and vast new reserves were on their way— 313,410 Americans landed at the French ports in July, though the actual combat strength during the month was only in the region of 600,000. But where should the new forces be thrown? And under what conditions? Pershing wanted the American army to be under American control. Haig wanted the Americans fighting with him to remain, hinting that they had been trained in British ways and would be useless otherwise. Foch wanted the Americans to be used to plug the gaps, a vast roving army behind the lines, to be gathered piecemeal and thrown in when required. There were continual conferences. In the end Foch was able to split the American forces and use them in two widely separated sectors; some American units remained under Allied tactical direction; and a First American Army under Pershing's command was brought into being. This last decision was reached at a conference in Paris held on July 24. There Foch, Pétain, Haig and Pershing had sat in council, haggling among themselves for advantages, certain now of victory by the following spring. Haig wanted the Americans west of Verdun: it seemed to him that the most profitable field of investment was along the Channel. Foch wanted to keep the enemy rolling back along the whole line: the success of the thrust at Soissons must be followed up evenly, fiercely, without regard for any particular sector. It is possible that he was wrong: there was no need, at this late hour, to reduce the salients, and the whole German line could have been turned by an advance along the Channel. But Pershing played his cards well: he desired to have an army under American control, and he had long ago regarded the St. Mihiel salient as a balloon to be burst, a balloon which might reasonably be burst by his First Army. Oddly, the trump card was Murmansk, of all places. He brought to the conference the promise that the Americans would send three battalions of infantry and three companies of engineers to Murmansk, where Allied supplies which had accumulated during the war were in danger of falling into the hands of the Bolsheviks. An obscure town north of the Arctic Circle decided the issue. For Pershing the price was small. He returned to Chaumont to sign the order, effective August 10, for the creation of the First Army.

At Chaumont, seventy miles due south of Verdun, General Headquarters of the A.E.F. had previously been the Caserne Damremont, an immense U-shaped barracks, full of small cluttered rooms and squeaking staircases. Here Pershing, like a live stone image, had ruled the progress of the American armies with a curt "Yes" or "No," an astonished stare, a line drawn across a map, one of those maps where the Allies were shown in red and the Germans in blue and little crosses represented barbed wire and small squares represented the entrances to dugouts. From here the telegraph wires led to all American sectors, though often enough the wires were torn by the treads of French tanks. This was the brain center of American power in France, but it still resembled a barracks, and it looked more than ever like a barracks when Marshall reached the place, for the files were already being transported to a new General Headquarters at La Ferté-sous-Jouarre, not far from Maux, and some forty miles from Paris. It was at La Ferté that the British after the retreat from Mons had struck back at the Germans in the first battle of the Marne. At another time the small village had been the headquarters of the American I Corps. Then, three days later, Pershing gave orders to transfer the headquarters to Neufchâteau in the Vosges. They were at Neufchâteau less than two weeks. There followed three weeks at Ligny-en-Barrois, and then Pershing ordered another transfer to Souilly. In the famous *mairie* of Souilly the peripatetic G.H.Q. finally came to rest.

However often Marshall complained of life at G.H.Q., with its eternal improvisations, he was happy in his job. He even liked General Hugh A. Drum, who had worked out some of the strategical plans in the early days, in the Rue Constantine in Paris. General Drum was irascible and self-opinionated, and he detested the Air Service. He declared later: "I see no reason why the range of a military airplane should ever exceed three days march by the infantry. An independent air force, if adopted and maintained, can only contribute to disaster and defeat in war." He could, and did, make blunders, and he was more than once admonished by Pershing, but he was indispensible. General Drum was Chief of Staff. Marshall's immediate superior was Fox Conner, now a general and in charge of operations. Conner was tall, imperturbable and, like Pershing, he preferred to speak in monosyllables. He had spent a year with a French artillery regiment, and spoke French well. The relation between them became so close that they were generally referred to as a mutual admiration society. They worked continually together, and if Fox Conner deferred to Marshall's sharper intelligence, Marshall deferred to Fox Conner's riper wisdom.

They were not, of course, alone in preparing the plans for attack. Others who took part, either then or immediately afterwards, were Colonels Robert McCleare, Stephen O. Fuqua, Walter S. Grant and John L. DeWitt. Two majors, Lewis H. Watkins and Ralph Ward, also had their full share, while General Hirschauer of the staff of the French Second Army was continually suggesting changes based on his knowledge of the topography of the salient, and acting as liaison officer with the command. Most of the officers were young. Colonel Walter S. Grant, for example, was only two years older than Marshall, and Colonel John L. DeWitt, who later became General in command of the Fourth Army in charge of evacuating the Japanese from the West Coast, was exactly the same age. They were a young team, and they were determined to show their mettle. Nearly all of them were graduates of Fort Leavenworth, and regarded themselves as a class apart. They devised the tables of organization, and often wrote the orders signed by the Chief of Staff, which the divisional and corps generals and the generals of the Services of Supply had to obey. Frederick Palmer described them in *Our Greatest Battle* without malice when he said: "They thought of themselves as apostles, their voices unheard in a land saturated with pacificism and indifference, who, in fasting, prayer and industry, had studied the true gospel in their holy of holies. They alone had conned the pages of the sacred books behind the altar where the regular army kept the sacred fires burning." They were a small dedicated clique which believed ardently that "war was the greatest game on earth."

There were many reasons for the predominance of Fort Leavenworth graduates on the staff, and not the least of them was that they were especially educated for staff work. There were, of course, great dangers. They were sometimes too academic for the practical aspects of war; for them war was too often a chess game fought for incredible prizes; there was an air of mysticism about them, a sense of conscious superiority to the rest, a desire to make the Army a massive impersonal machine with the Regulars, the National Guard and the National Army harmonized until they resembled a colorless hammer, with the graduates as the gawdy mechanics of the new engine of destruction. Pershing prized them for their cold professional zeal, and he said repeatedly: "We would not have been able to win our battles without them."

On the day before the First Army came into being, Pershing reached an agreement with Foch by which the first task of the new army would be to reduce the St. Mihiel salient. Both were delighted with the choice. The Americans would avenge the wounds they had received when the First Division, in the early days of the year, had entered the Ansauville sector, which lay on the south face of the salient. The French would also taste revenge, for in the early days of the war they had fought bitter hand-to-hand combats in the region, waging a desolate, protracted underground war of mines and countermines at Les Éparges, Apremont and Bois-le-Prêtre—these names, in the French battle rolls, were as famous as Tahure, Vauquois and Verdun. There were other, more practical reasons for taking the salient. The salient was a nuisance. It interrupted traffic on the Paris-Nancy railroad and cut the Verdun-Toul railroad. Capture of the salient would mean a breakthrough of the Hindenburg Line (here called the *Michel Stellung*) and the possibility of a developing campaign which would threaten the fortress of Metz and the coal fields of Briey.

For the moment the sector was quiet. Behind the trenches, the concrete shelters and the barbed-wire entanglements, on a plateau from which they could direct an incessant plunging fire, were nine German divisions, perhaps ninety thousand men. Six out of these nine divisions were second- or third-class troops from the reserve, Landwehr and Austro-Hungarian regiments. Nevertheless, with an elaborate system of elastic defense, these wooded heights had been transformed into a field fortress, against which the French in the preceding years had battered in vain. Pershing's plan, as it was finally worked out, was to take advantage of a fairly level valley called the Rupt de Mad, to attack along this while at the same time hammering at Montsec with artillery and bombs. Montsec, shaped like a grey sinister half-moon, crowded with observers and artillery emplacements, must be made to burn.

From August 21 to September 12, American preparations for the attack went forward in the utmost secrecy. Suddenly, at the end of August, the French called a halt. On August 30, Pershing as Commander of the First Army took over the sector, and on the same day he was visited by Foch and Weygand, who urged an entirely new strategy. They argued that the St. Mihiel salient no longer possessed great importance. After all, the French had managed for four years to fight the war without relying on the Paris-Nancy railroad, and they could wait a little longer. The fortress was probably impregnable. There was the danger of a catastrophic defeat, and in any event the fate of the 1918 campaign would not be decided at St. Mihiel. There was also the danger that the mines in the Briey Basin would be devastated, and they hoped by a circling movement to capture them intact. Foch wanted the American divisions distributed between the French Second Army, the French Fourth Army on the Aisne and the existing sector on the Hindenburg Line at St. Mihiel, but he wanted this last reduced to a comparatively light holding attack on only one side of the salient. Pershing replied that it was too late. For more than a month the American Services of Supply had been directing their operations towards the St. Mihiel sector. The plans for the attack had already been made. He had now assumed command, and he refused any longer to let the American Army be scattered along the front. There were more conferences. Finally, on September 2, it was agreed that the St. Mihiel attack should be carried out with a strictly limited objective, so that the American Army could undertake another offensive ten days later between the Meuse River and the Argonne Forest. This meant that in twenty-four days, beginning fourteen days before the St. Mihiel battle, he must concentrate six hundred thousand men and twenty-seven hundred guns, together with a million tons of supplies, for a still greater operation. He was to carry on two operations at once: he must safeguard the St. Mihiel operation, and he must throw his whole fighting strength into the new field west of Verdun. This was the largest operation in which the American Armies had ever participated, and as he looked at the maps hanging in his small office at Ligny-en-Barrois, Pershing sighed with relief, for the test was about to come.

The changed decision of the High Command meant increased work for the General Staff, who slept in their clothes, took part in ten or twenty conferences a day and wondered feverishly whether two large battles could be won by the Americans in a single month, for the date of the attack on St. Mihiel was now set for September 12, and thirteen days later there would follow the Meuse-Argonne offensive.

Meanwhile, the enemy was aware of impending changes on the front, but did not know and could not guess the American plans. These plans appeared more mysterious when Pershing, who possessed considerable skill in planning ruses, decided that the time had come to hoodwink the enemy by pretending to prepare an attack at a place where no attack was in fact intended. He sent Colonel A. L. Conger, the battle expert in the intelligence section of his staff, down to Belfort, near the Swiss frontier. Colonel Conger wrote out some carefully faked corps orders and threw a sheet of carbon paper, on which the corps orders could be read without difficulty, into the wastepaper basket in his hotel room. Thereupon he decided to leave the room, walked round the corridors for five minutes, and returned to discover, as he suspected, that the sheet of carbon had disappeared. The faked plans were soon known to the enemy. They referred to operations in the neighborhood of Mulhouse. Such an operation was one known to have occupied the attention of the American General Staff earlier in the war. It was a possible, and even likely operation, and the Germans saw, or imagined, concentrated American forces preparing for a drive on Mulhouse, which might effectively turn the German flank. They removed some of their heavy artillery from the woods above St. Mihiel, and began to build heavy defenses in the south. There were blinds within blinds. The Americans leaving or entering the sector were sworn to secrecy, nearly all movements took place at night, but occasionally American movements were such that they were observed by balloons hanging above Montsec: the Germans began to believe that the American concentrations could only be explained as a feint, and when the attack came they were puzzled and dejected, having expected a smaller and altogether lighter attack.

The attack, when it came, surpassed American expectations. The bombardment of the German positions began at 1:00 a.m. on September 12. For four hours the bombardment was maintained, the whole landscape lit up with the flashes from the gun mouths and the spreading flashes of the bursting shells. It had rained hard during the night, there was mud everywhere, and when dawn broke a heavy mist was smeared over the ground, screening the movement of the American troops, who went over the top at 5:00 a.m. without the support of tanks, which came up too late to take part in the preliminary stages of the battle, but with the support of General William Mitchell's fourteen pursuit squadrons, fresh from the lessons they had learned at Château-Thierry. The infantry were equipped with colored panels with which to signal to the airplanes overhead, and the airplanes were ordered to signal back to headquarters the infantry positions. They failed in this: which was probably the reason for General Drum's lifelong aversion to the Air Service. But this was the only failure. The attack continued with clockwork precision, and before dawn on the following day the salient was closed, the defeats on the hills of Les Éparges had been avenged, and Montsec with its ravines and forests and countless acres of barbed wire were in American hands. Pershing reported the capture of 14,439 prisoners, 443 guns and over 200 square miles of territory at a cost of 7,000 casualties. The Paris-Nancy railroad was freed, and could be used to transport troops and supplies to the Meuse-Argonne. All that remained to be done was to correct the new line, so that it could be held after the First Army had taken up its position across the Meuse.

The capture of the St. Mihiel salient was a feat of organized skill involving 550,000 Americans and about 110,000 French, who were moved in at night and hidden in the woods according to prearranged and carefully drawn plans. Four hundred tanks, 1,481 airplanes and 3,000 artillery pieces were also involved. The airplanes, chiefly British and French, were in the largest numbers ever brought together up to that time. But if the problem of bringing these vast forces into line strained the General Staff to the utmost, it was to be still further strained by the fantastically large problems of the Meuse-Argonne offensive.

Within a week of the reduction of the St. Mihiel salient, new headquarters were established at Souilly on the road from Bar-le-Duc to Verdun, a road which came to be known as *la Voie Sacrée,* for it was along this road that millions of Frenchmen came into line in 1916 and 1917 and some hundreds of thousands of them never returned. Pershing had a little corner room in the *mairie* previously occupied by Pétain, who had announced his famous battle cry: *"Ils ne passeront pas!"* from the same shabby little town hall. Here, too, Nivelle had planned the recapture of Fort Douaumont. Marshall and Drum occupied a small front room cluttered with maps: there were orders that no one disturb them. Marshall, who was now beginning to be called "the wizard" for his success in planning the St. Mihiel offensive, kept going back and forth along the roads where the American forces were moving up. He had arranged a system of stationing officers at fixed points with orders to report and check on the movements of these forces: it was essential to the battle plan that the roads should be kept clear of everything except troops and supplies, and that there should be no breakdown and no entangling of these immense floods of trucks. About 220,000 Allied soldiers had to be moved out and some 600,000 Americans had to be moved in. There were fifteen divisions moving into the area. Mostly, they came in French trucks, twenty-four men to a truck, and since it takes about a thousand trucks to move an American division, without counting the baggage trains, it follows that one division occupied about four miles of road, and fifteen divisions occupied about sixty miles of road. In addition there were artillery, ammunition, supplies of all kinds to be accounted for. It was necessary to calculate the amount of traffic each road could bear, and each unit of the army received an exact schedule of the time it was allowed to spend on each road.

These schedules were not always followed. As Marshall explained in a memorandum drawn up shortly after the end of the war, it was impossible to provide ordinary march tables for the troops, because it was never possible to know twenty-four hours in advance what units would be available. There were endless difficulties. It happened sometimes that solid columns were placed on the road composed of elements of different divisions, different corps and different armies, all moving at the same time. Trucks broke down or were delayed; the horses bringing up the artillery were so worn down that they could go no further, with disastrous consequences to the entire schedule of movements. Some tractor artillery could move at eight kilometers an hour, while other tractor artillery moved at fifteen kilometers an hour. How to arrange that they should arrive at the same time? Altogether it was necessary to account for a million and a half men, and most of the movements had to be at night, in bitterly cold weather, without showing lights or fires, along roads which were in disrepair, using trucks which had been used all over the battlefields and were no longer reliable. The endless list of details to be moved included 93,000 horses and mules, 4,000 cannon, 40,000 tons of ammunition delivered at the rate of 13 trainloads a day, and 34 hospitals. There were nineteen railheads and 87 depots established for supply, 164 miles of light railway and 74 miles of standard gauge railway: for the most part these were rebuilt or entirely reconstructed. The change in plan decided on September 2 meant that all this had to be done in a period of about fourteen days, starting just before the St. Mihiel offensive.

The task was backbreaking, but it was accomplished successfully. There was relatively little confusion or congestion on the roads—those three pathetic roads running north and south, one up the Aire Valley, one from Esnes to Montfaucon, a very poor one, and one along the Meuse, which was under fire from German outposts on the other side of the river. Mostly, the railways brought up supplies and trucks brought up the men—the trucks carried 428,000 men, often with Annamites in the driving seat. The weight therefore fell on the roads, and it became necessary to establish elaborate plans to concentrate engineers and matériel along the roads to see that the traffic went through. There were nine American divisions to be moved up the line. The usual formula was: one road to a division, but there was no hope of such largesse. What was astonishing, at a time when spies were believed to be everywhere and the Germans were believed to have tapped telephone wires on the ground, was that the movement was accomplished with profound secrecy: to the very end the Germans thought the attack would be directed on Metz and the Briey Basin. What was still more astonishing was that the Americans were working only a short distance behind the front lines and German airplanes were overhead daily. It might have seemed impossible for the Germans not to observe what was happening. It was not only that the Germans failed to perceive what was happening, but they had no inkling that an offensive was being mounted, and General von Gallwitz in his memoirs admitted he completely failed to penetrate the American design.

When the time came to make up accounts, Pershing gave the credit for the successful withdrawal from St. Mihiel and the concentration along the 25-mile Meuse-Argonne battlefront to Marshall. He wrote:

> As in the concentration prior to St. Mihiel, the route and length of each day's march for each unit had to be prescribed in order to prevent road congestion and insure the necessary daily delivery of supplies. It was a stupendous task and a delicate one to move such numbers of troops in addition to the large quantities of supplies, ammunition and hospital equipment required.
>
> That it was carried out in the brief time available without arousing the suspicions of the enemy indicates the precision and smoothness with which it was calculated and accomplished. The battle of St. Mihiel followed the plan so closely, however, that it was possible to withdraw troops exactly as intended. It seldom happens in war that plans can be so precisely carried out as was possible in this instance.
>
> The details of the movements of troops connected with this concentration were worked out and their execution conducted under the able direction of Colonel George C.

Marshall, Jr., of the Operations Section of the General Staff, First Army.

Understandably, Marshall's own lengthy account of these troop movements, written from Souilly on November 19 and later published by the War Department in its historical survey of the war called *The United States Army in the World War 1917-1919*, ends in a note of triumph:

> Despite the haste with which all the movements had to be carried out, the inexperience of most of the commanders in movements of such density, the condition of the animals and the limitations as to roads, the entire movement was carried out without a single element failing to reach its place on the date scheduled, which was, I understand, one day earlier than Marshal Foch considered possible.

The battle, which began with an artillery barrage at 2:30 a.m. on September 26, was to last for forty-seven days. Once again there were networks of wires, thick fog, millions of shell craters, heavily defended heights to be taken. Once again there were troops who had taken no part in offensive combat before: of nine American divisions, four had no more experience than that which comes from occupying comparatively quiet sectors. The I Corps had two experienced divisions and one inexperienced; the V Corps on the center had three inexperienced divisions; and the III Corps had one untried division, one with a little experience and only one which had received a baptism of fire. All these were supported with French artillery and French tanks, though it was in the nature of things—there were deep ravines and dense woods—that the tanks should be nearly useless.

St. Mihiel had offered comparatively simple solutions, but the Argonne Forest, considered impregnable for four years, offered sterner material. The Argonne Forest resembled the Wilderness in Virginia: there was the same thick growth of woods and absence of roads. There was, however, one great difference: where the Wilderness was fairly level, the Forest was full of steep hills and ravines, and where it was easy to build roads in the Wilderness, it was mortally difficult in the Forest, with the result that attacks were frequently held back from a lack of supplies. The Germans were well-entrenched. They had three massive defense systems, all named after the ancient Germanic gods: the *Hagen Stellung*, which formed part of the Hindenburg Line, and beyond this lay the *Kriemhilde Stellung* and then the uncompleted *Freya*

Stellung. The Germans occupied heights they had occupied before, for in these thick forests they had fought in 1870, and here, too, Bismarck once hunted wild boar. Their defenses were so powerful that Pétain advised Pershing that the ridge of Montfaucon, the great whale-back dominating the whole region, was as far as he expected the Americans to advance before winter. In fact, Montfaucon, "the mountain of the falcon," once a thriving medieval town, now a battered village with only a few walls standing, was captured by two divisions of the V Corps under General Summerall by noon the next day.

The original plan had been to rush Montfaucon during the first day. The plan had been described by Pétain as "more than human," as indeed it was. But in two days an advance of only eight miles had been made, and on the third day the advance was only one and a half miles—the plans had called for entirely different rates of advance. The Americans moved too far in the first wave of attack—the troops outrunning their artillery support—and not far enough in the second wave. On September 29 Pershing called a halt, to reorganize the line and construct defensive positions. For the Germans, the position was becoming desperate. Fresh armies were about to be thrown into the battle by the Americans: if they could shatter the German positions in the Ardennes the fate of the war might be decided. On October 1 General von der Marwitz, in command of the German troops in the Ardennes, stated in his order of the day: "The fate of a large portion of the western front, perhaps of our nation, depends upon the firm holding of the Verdun front. The Fatherland believes that every commander and every soldier realizes the greatness of his task and that everyone will fulfill his duties to the utmost. If this is done the enemy's attack will be shattered." It was not done. Three days later Pershing ordered another pounding attack which continued unabated until the 12 th, the day when the American Second Army was formed. Then the attack was resumed on the 14th, and in three days the German third line of defense was gained. It was not gained easily. On October 15th Marshall wrote in his operations report: "The enemy is making a determined resistance, principally with machine-gun and artillery fire. He gives every indication of resisting our advance with all the means at his disposal." The next day the Americans appeared to be in no better case, for Marshall noted:

"The enemy continues to resist our advance stubbornly, depending primarily on machine-gun and artillery fire, including the plentiful use of gas." On October 17th Marshall wrote: "Our forces at present are not sufficiently strong to do other than work forward slowly and generally improve the line for an additional attack." But by now the worst was over, the *Kriemhilde Stellung* had been breached and there remained only the *Freya Stellung.* Marshall was still thinking in terms of a long battle. "It seems to be probable," he wrote on the 20th, "that the enemy is prepared to resist on the *Freya Stellung.*" The war, however, had only a few more days to run.

The fighting in the Meuse-Argonne was open warfare with a vengeance. It took place in unbelievably cold weather, among trackless forests where the thick fog settled on the trees, along the muddy banks of rivers and in deep valleys dominated by strong points. Half way through the battle, Pershing, during a temporary lull before the final all-out onslaught against the enemy, completed his arrangements for creating his Second Army. Bullard was placed in command of the First, and Hunter Liggett in command of the Second. On October 17, the day after these appointments were made, Hunter Liggett asked for Marshall as his chief of operations. Marshall remained at Souilly, in charge of the planning of the offensive which would produce the last American breakthrough, while at the same time producing his regular operations reports. These reports are quite exceptionally interesting. They provide in colorless and technical language, often at great length, a picture of the slow cracking of one sector of the German army. On the 18th, Marshall's estimate of the situation read: "Enemy still opposes us by an outpost zone skillfully covered by machine guns and artillery." On the 20th he wrote: "The enemy still prepared to resist future advance, but not aggressive." On the 22nd the battle flared up, with American advances along the line. The enemy gives orders for a withdrawal, then countermands the orders. Prisoners report that the Germans believe a massive American attack is imminent. Marshall notes towards the end of the month that German officers are beginning to talk about maintaining their lines only in the hope that this will favor the peace settlement. By November 1 he notes that the German will to fight is crumbling. German defenses now consist largely of machine-gun nests: the artillery is silent. Captured prisoners are "in poor condition, due to lack of nourishment, and all seem fatigued." Afterwards there is a rout.

Marshall's appointment to Hunter Liggett's staff was no surprise. He had been Hunter Liggett's aide-de-camp in the Philippines. They had both spent many years in the humdrum activities of regimental soldiering. The general was genial, thickset, powerfully built, over six feet tall, majestic and ponderous; he swelled out his uniform; he breathed an air of dignity; he had a brain like the cutting edge of an ax. In nearly every way he was the opposite of the scholarly Bullard who would never have bewailed, as Liggett constantly did, the absence of cavalry.

Pershing set October 28 as the date for the general attack; this was postponed to November 1 at the request of the French Fourth Army, which had not yet recovered from a severe mauling. The task of the First Army was to cut the Metz-Sedan-Mézières railroad. Pershing proposed that the American left should strike first, followed by attacks from the remaining corps all the way to the right. This meant battering at the wooded hills of Bois de Bourgogne due north of the Argonne, where the enemy was in force. Liggett and Marshall recast the tactics and the plan, preferring to drive a broad wedge to the center, so outflanking the dangerous Bois de Bourgogne: a very similar plan had been employed at St. Mihiel. There were other reasons for modifying Pershing's plan, including the necessity for speed and the need to conserve supplies, for Pershing had cabled the War Department earlier in the month: "Unless supplies are furnished when and as called for, our armies will cease to operate."

American reserves were assembling in their hundreds of thousands in France, but there were not enough officers, there was no place in the crowded lines where the reserves could be thrown in, and casualties were mounting—there were seventy-five thousand American casualties in October. There was need therefore for one last violent attack which would send the Germans reeling across their own frontiers; and with the British and French armies smashing through the German defenses, it was hoped that all the German lines would crumble.

By November 5 the end was already in sight. In those five days the colored pencil lines on Marshall's operations maps in the front room at the Souilly *mairie* moved forward furiously. Sleepless and grey of face, Marshall, surrounded by the admiring staff-officers, met the war correspondents and talked about the absolute inevitability of a German defeat, explaining that the line could only move forward, the worst was behind them, all that was needed now was one final dash to the railroad. He wrote in his operations report that day: "Enemy retreating with his infantry in confusion and his artillery actively employed. Situation favorable for pressing the pursuit."

Marshall was working in his office on the afternoon of November 5 when General Fox Conner came to see him. Fox Conner had received a telephone message from Pershing saying that he desired the First Army to enter Sedan, and this order was to be communicated to the I and V Corps, who were then believed to be close to Sedan. General Liggett was away; so was his Chief of Staff, General Drum; and it therefore fell upon Marshall to prepare the order. Marshall dictated the order, but he hesitated when Fox Conner asked him to send it at once. There were many reasons for his hesitation. If anything went wrong, the responsibility for publishing the order would fall on him. It was evidently an order which might result, probably would result in angering the French, who regarded the capture of Sedan by their own forces as a point of honor, for it was at Sedan that the thickset little Emperor Napoleon III, wearing a long black coat, red trousers and white kid gloves, had surrendered to von Moltke. Marshall also hesitated to publish the order in the absence of Liggett and Drum, who were his superior officers and might be in a position to suggest amendments or an entirely different deployment of forces. They discussed the matter for an hour—it was then 5:30 p.m.—and soon Fox Conner left the First Army headquarters to return to G.H.Q., taking with him a draft of the order as originally drawn, while Marshall kept another copy on his desk. It had been agreed that if neither Liggett nor Drum returned by six o'clock the order should be telephoned to the front.

The order as written by Marshall read:

Received 16:30 November 5, 1918

Memorandum for Commanding Generals, 1st Corps, 5th Corps.

Subject: Message from Commander-in-Chief.

1. General Pershing desires that the honor of entering Sedan should fall to the First American Army. He has every confidence that the troops of the 1st Corps, assisted on their right by the 5th Corps, will enable him to realize this desire.

2. In transmitting the foregoing message, your attention is invited to the favorable opportunity now existing for pressing an advance through the night.

By command of Lieutenant-General Liggett:

Official:
G. C. Marshall, Jr.,
A.C. of S, G-3

The irascible General Drum had been visiting the front, and he returned to the *mairie* at Souilly at six o'clock in no mood to deal with trifles. Shown the order, he approved it at once and added one blinding phrase which illuminated not only all his own sentiments, but it also illuminated some part of the tragic ethos of his nation. He wrote, or directed the addition of the following words at the end of the second paragraph: "Boundaries will not be considered as binding."

The order, with the addition of this phrase and the signature "H. A. Drum, Chief of Staff," was sent off by courier and telephoned direct to the headquarters of the I and V Corps. The telephone messages were received by both Army corps between 6:30 and 7 p.m., but nothing was done about the order during the night for patrol activity had flared up, the Eighteenth Infantry was advancing furiously with the Sixteenth Infantry on its left, and assault companies had reached the Meuse.

By noon on November 6, the position was stabilized, and General Summerall, returning to the headquarters of the First Division about two o'clock in the afternoon, saw the message for the first time and prepared to carry out his instructions. He then telephoned to Brigadier General Frank Parker and gave him orders to march immediately on Sedan with the mission "to cooperate and capture the town," Two field orders covering the operations were made, one giving the details of the march, the second prescribing the attack. The attack orders announced that the First Army was advancing on Sedan and the First Division would constitute the advance troops and seize the city. The plan called for an advance in five columns towards the hills which overlook Sedan from the southwest; the attack would take place at daybreak, November 7.

The race for Sedan, which ended in confusion and terror, was conceived in ignorance and carried out without regard for probability or the claims of the French. No one had any detailed information about the situation in the areas where the movements were to be carried out. The Division was sent out in five columns, and not in one, in order, according to the First Division's *Summary of Operations,* "to cover this territory as completely as possible." By ten o'clock at night the enemy troops opposite the First Division's positions had been withdrawn, and the race for Sedan could begin. By midnight all five columns were on the march.

The rich confusion which followed has rarely been excelled in war. Through thick woods and over marshy ground, on roads pitted with shell holes, in mud and rain the five columns blundered towards their objective in the dark, butting directly across the communication lines of the entire I Corps commanded by General Dickman, the armies heaped pell-mell one on top of another, the roads jammed with trucks which showed no lights—on the next day Pershing was to give orders that the trucks could show their lights—the communications tangled, and the American outposts occasionally fighting one another. Father Duffy, the famous padre of the 165th Infantry, afterwards swore that he saw the First Division advancing on him in waves, form a hollow square around him and take him prisoner. General Douglas MacArthur, who commanded one of the Rainbow Division brigades, was found by scouts of the Sixteenth Infantry poring over maps with his staff officers in a command post near his own front lines. His strange cap made him look like a German officer. The scouts captured him, and took him to the brigade headquarters of the First Division, where he was at last released. The incident occurred near Beaumeil Farm about 30 kilometers from Sedan. The fifth column, composed of the Twenty-Sixth Infantry, found itself under fire near Omicourt and learned that it was occupying a position where General Laiguelot, of the French Fortieth Division, wanted to lay a barrage. Asked to retire, the regimental commander, Colonel Theodore Roosevelt, Jr., refused, saying he had orders to reach Sedan. General Laigiielot thereupon discovered that the Americans were behaving with impropriety on two grounds, and he had as little sympathy with their desire to reach Sedan as with their desire to block the path of his barrage. He telephoned to Liggett at First Army headquarters, and explained the situation. Liggett exploded with rage. This was the first he had heard of the progress of the First Division during the night. He rode to the I Corps headquarters and began to curse vividly at General Dickman, only to discover that General Dickman knew nothing of the adventure. At that stage it looked as though the whole scheme might very well have been engineered by Dickman, who was known for his intransigent attitude towards limitations imposed upon him by a higher command. He possessed Patton's furious drive. (He had once wanted to attack Metz, saw no reason why he should not, and blamed Foch and his staff for a strategical blunder in failing to push the attack. Liggett, older and wiser, a heavy man with a clear mind, saw good reasons for holding the Americans in reins, for he knew the faults of his young army. "The possibility of taking Metz," he said, "existed only on the supposition that our Army was a well-oiled, fully coordinated machine, which it is not as yet.")

Meanwhile the confusion continued. The Rainbow Division was ordered to take command of all troops in its zone of action regardless of division, but no one knew for certain where the troops were. There were continual delays owing to the breakdown of communications. The situation became grave at 10.00 a.m. when the French notified the Rainbow Division, which was part of the V Corps and had therefore received the original order to seize Sedan, that they would fire on any troops obstructing their movement towards Sedan. The French warning was grim but courteous. Addressed to "our brave neighbor," it said simply: "I am obliged to use my artillery in that region." By eleven o'clock the First Army had given instructions to the V Corps to withdraw the First Division, but the First Division was still scattered, and it was two o'clock before the order was received, and dusk before they completed a movement to a new line. During the night of November 8-9 some patrols of the French Fourth Army and the Forty-Second Division entered Sedan, but the American patrols were quickly removed and the honor of entering Sedan was granted to the French.

The confusion had led to the disruption of the communications of a whole field army and a clash between the French and Americans. Neither of these was so serious as the fact that the Germans could have broken through the American line with comparative ease if they had learned of the confusion in time. The danger of a vast, violent and well-organized breakthrough, which would disrupt the whole Allied line, had existed for a period of twenty-four hours. All this seems to have been unknown to Brigadier General Frank Parker, who wrote on November 9, in answer to an enquiry by Marshall: "I visited the division headquarters of the 42nd and 77th Divisions and saw both of the Division commanders, who seemed a bit annoyed at the First Division's appearance in what they considered their sector, but I do not believe there was any serious feeling about the matter." This was bluster, and he knew it: some hours later in the day he wrote a further letter to Marshall, saying he had thought over the matter and had now come to the conclusion that they were very annoyed indeed. At 10:38 a.m. on the same day General Summerall reported to the Commanding General of the First Army: "First Division reports all elements back in V Corps area at 10 o'clock today." The damage however had been done. An enquiry was ordered, and the responsibility for leading the five disorderly columns naturally fell on General Parker. No court-martial was ever held, for the Armistice on November 11 soothed the ruffled generals and high officers, Pershing, Fox Conner, Marshall, Summerall and Parker, who in their different ways had contributed to the prize fiasco of the war.

On that day Marshall wrote his last operations report. He said nothing about the march on Sedan. He noted that during the night there was fairly heavy activity concentrated on the American front lines, and that the First Army attacked along the whole front. In his estimate of the situation, he said that "the line attained by our army at 11 hours is very favorable to possible future operations." Plans for the future were "to hold the front now attained while preparing for further advance. To cease hostilities until further orders." The morale of the troops, he wrote, was excellent, the roads were fair and supplies were normal. In such dry terms, without embroidery, do operations reports celebrate the end of a war.

A few hours after the Armistice was signed, Colonel Stephen Fuqua addressed a note to Marshall which may serve as a conclusion to the story of the march on Sedan. He wrote:

> G-3 First Army attention Colonel Marshall map reference 2000. No troops of First Division entered Sedan. Extreme advance 500 meters north of Hill 252, 1 kilometer south of Wadelincourt, Hill 307, 1 kilometer north-east of Chevenges, through La Garenne de St Aignan, 1 kilometer north of St Aignan. FUQUA.

During the forty-seven days of the Meuse-Argonne campaign, Marshall occupied a position of authority. Repeatedly he asked for a command in the field, and he was repeatedly refused; but he had the instincts of a regimental commander. He made plans as "Stonewall" Jackson would have conceived them, and only regretted that, unlike Jackson, he was unable to carry them out in the field. He spoke of Jackson to nearly all the war correspondents who came to the operations room of the Souilly *mairie*. One of them was Damon Runyon, at that time attached as a war correspondent to the First Army, who wrote on November 7:

> There is a mild-looking, retiring man at American headquarters called Col. George C. Marshall, Jr. . . . This man Marshall is Chief of Operations of Liggett's forces. It was Marshall who had much to do with planning of operations against Sedan, and he turned to the Great Master of Infantrymen for the general scheme. "Drive the infantry" was the word. They picked all of Liggett's crack divisions for the driving.

Damon Runyon was writing in the same mood of optimism as Roy W. Howard of the United Press who telegraphed the same day from Brest: "sedan taken smorning by americans." But there was no doubt that it was Marshall who had been one of the main inspirations of those last days, while "Drive the infantry" was to remain his watchword to the end.

The fates, which had removed him from an undeserved obscurity to place him in operational command of battles, now played him false. In the midst of the confusion resulting from Pershing's order to the First Division to capture Sedan, on November 8 he was appointed Chief of Staff of the VIII Army Corps and promoted to brigadier general. The promotion, though recommended by Pershing, was refused by the Senate, which preferred to take no action on nominations made after October 1. But Marshall retained the position without the rank, and for nearly a year he served as a temporary colonel under Major General Henry T. Allen, at first in France and then in the occupation of Germany. He had to wait eighteen years before he became a brigadier general.

CHAPTER SEVEN

Towards Obscurity

The hard tasks of the war were now over. Marshall had shown he had a talent for operations, a complex mind capable of sorting out the complexities of war, an intense loyalty and a way of dominating the battle even when he remained invisible in the Souilly *mairie,* where Pershing's car with the four stars on the pennant was always screaming to a standstill, where the bustle was continual, and only Marshall seemed calm. Damon Runyon spoke of him as "mild-mannered, retiring." It was not quite true. Others spoke of his nervous excitement, the sudden leaping energy of the man, the way he would flog himself to stay awake for four or five nights, while the reports came in by telephone and the maps were inked in and the obscure colonel helped to settle the fate of nations. He was one of the five or six men most responsible for the success of American arms in France, and the legend of the calm "wizard" was known throughout the Army. But the calm was mostly illusory: he had lived on his nerves, and when the war ended he was tired.

With tiredness went some bitterness. Pershing was to become General of the Armies, like Grant before him; the honors heaped upon him were deservedly earned. Fox Conner was to command a sector of the Panama Canal defense, Summerall became Army Chief of Staff, Drum and the rest were to hold important positions. Only Marshall seemed to have been forgotten, "the forgotten man," the one whose brilliance was such that he could not be trusted with high command, but must go through the weary lists of seniorities until at last he retired on a small pension. He had not led men in battle, and that was what he had wanted most of all. When someone offered him twenty thousand dollars a year to enter business, he said: "I must stay on the job. I must see that the Army is ready for the next war."

Partly, this determination came out of his long conversations with Fox Conner, who continually celebrated the young tactician, buttonholing anyone who would listen and saying: "Marshall is the nearest thing I know to a genius. We should have given him a high command, and we must be certain he has a high command in the next war." There were lengthy discussions on unity of command between them which were to bear fruit later. It was largely at Fox Conner's suggestion that Marshall was brought back to G.H.Q. in 1919 to work on the planning of American troop movements into Germany. Mostly, it was wasted labor, for nothing approximating a real occupation ever took place, and Marshall was glad to go off on a lecture tour with General Hugh A. Drum in March. The subject of the lecture was: "The Organization and Development of the A.E.F. and the Operations of its Armies." They showed films and slides to the First, Second and Third Armies: it was Marshall's first introduction to propaganda by means of moving pictures, and he was to remember these preliminary skirmishes when he became Chief of Staff and employed films on a scale which the Army had never envisaged before. He also showed the films at the staff college at Langres, where Henry Stimson first set eyes on him and marked him out as a man to be watched. By this time Pershing had also marked him out, and in May he became aide-de-camp to the General of the Armies.

On July 4, 1919, he attended the gala performance at the *Opéra* for Marshall Foch and General Pershing; there John Erskine met him briefly between the acts, remarking only that Marshall walked among the highest as though born to it. To celebrate the approaching withdrawal of American forces, Gounod's *Faust* was played—a strange enough choice, for though there is the resounding "Soldier's Chorus," the most soldierly character in the play runs his sword, not through the devil, but through the devil's guitar, while the devil calmly enquires whether he has an ear for music. There were two more months in France, then in September he sailed on the *Leviathan* with Pershing to New York. He was close to the seat of power, but he was still in a sense the "forgotten man," without any real power, a decorative addition to Pershing in those long parades through half the states of the Union which lasted through the autumn and winter, and, with a brief excursion to Panama, went on into the spring. In the summer of 1920 Pershing appeared at West Point, and then at Marshall's suggestion he appeared in June at the Virginia Military Institute, looking tired after his long journeys, but still upright, resembling the ideal portrait of the ideal soldier.

The two days spent by the General of the Armies in Lexington delighted Marshall. Pershing unbent. He was exceedingly gracious. He said he had heard that V.M.I, was referred to as "the West Point of the South," but having seen their parades he wondered why West Point was not called "the V.M.I, of the North." It was a gala occasion, with cannons booming and airplanes diving low, only just clearing the parade ground and the barracks parapets. There was a presentation of diplomas to the class of 1920 and the inevitable excursion to New Market, and Pershing was impressed by the sight of the alumni reviewing the corps of cadets and by the appearance of the cadets in their brilliant uniforms. But the parades and the fireworks came to an end, and in Washington Marshall, whose temporary wartime rank had lapsed (so that he was reduced first to being a captain and then promoted to major) was put to work sifting the records of the A.E.F. He had little taste for the work and little gift for writing, and he seemed to have lost the happy knack of describing a situation in a few words, for Pershing complained of his verbosity and sent back his reports for revision. His accounts of battles, like the *Summary of Operations of the First Division* for which he was at least partly responsible, read like dehydrated algebraic equations; he wrote better when he contemplated the huge wastefulness of the American effort in the war, the green men thrown into combat with insufficient training, the havoc caused by the influenza epidemic which resulted in such heavy losses that it was claimed that twice as many men died from sickness as from bullets, gas and shell fire.

Bravery, élan, readiness to die—the Americans had these; but they lacked training. There were needless losses. Gas casualties among untrained troops were twice as great as among trained troops. Tanks would rumble ahead and lose themselves deep in enemy lines, because the tankmen were not trained to maintain communications. When the First Division was attached to a French corps under General

Dubonnet, the French general remarked that American losses were twice his own—why?

The reason could only lie in insufficient training and insufficient preparation. When Secretary Bryan had spoken of a million men springing to arms overnight, he had forgotten to mention that they had no arms to spring to—a large quantity of the heavy guns, tanks, mortars, howitzers and machine guns employed by the Americans during the war were bought from the British and the French, and American troops were even transported in foreign ships. By the time of the Armistice the American First and Second Armies could have continued the war single-handed, but it had taken seventeen months to bring them to this point. Again and again American commanders were faced with the knowledge that it was more than a year after the declaration of war before they were able to take offensive action.

Here were lessons to be learned, and Marshall wrote concerning them at some length in an article which appeared in the January number of the *Infantry Journal*. He spoke, too, of the dangers of divided command, the danger of textbook tactics, the danger of believing that the war as it was fought by the Americans provided a useful basis for envisaging the tactics to be employed in any subsequent war—a whole catalogue of Cassandra-like warnings which few listened to. He said:

> The Americans who fought only at St. Mihiel and in the Meuse-Argonne probably will never realize the vast difference between their enemy then and the German of April or May. Even those who fought in the summer of 1918 will have some difficulty in visualizing the state of mind of troops who are opposed by an enemy far superior in numbers and confident of his ability to defeat them. For this reason it is possible that officers who participated only in the last phase of the war may draw somewhat erroneous conclusions from their battle experiences.
>
> Many mistakes were made in the Argonne which the Germans at that time were unable to charge to our account. The same mistakes, repeated four months earlier in the war, would have brought an immediate and unfortunate reaction. It is possible that methods successfully employed in the Meuse-Argonne would have invited a successful enemy counter-attack in the spring of 1918.

It is not intended by this discussion to belittle our efforts in the latter part of the war, for what we actually accomplished was a military miracle, but we must not forget that its conception was based on a knowledge of the approaching deterioration of the German Army, and its lesson must be studied accordingly. *We remain without modern experience in the first phases of a war and must draw our conclusions from history.*

Marshall had no desire to coat the bitter bill, but he was afraid that others would sweeten it, make it more palatable; and it could only be made palatable by deliberately avoiding the main issue of America's perpetual unpreparedness for war. Twice again in his lifetime he was to see that the lesson had not been learned.

There were other lessons. He had spent most of his military activity during the war in preparing operations. He had given orders and he was concerned whether they had been effectively carried out, and for a long time he had realized that they were rarely carried out exactly as intended. Somewhere at the heart of all battles there was a center of confusion, an almost unavoidable flare of purposelessness and obscurity. An order could be completely misinterpreted, and simply by being misinterpreted it could lead to victory. There was the classic example, which he referred to in his book *Infantry in Battle,* published nearly twenty years later, of the battles of Magdhaba and Rafa in which the British defeated the Turks. In both cases the British commander had made the decision to break off the fight, but before the order reached the front line the victory was won. The chronic obscurities of war demanded attention, and in the same article for the *Infantry Journal* he wrote:

In studying examples of the orders issued to our troops in France several important points deserve consideration in determining the relative excellence of the orders issued. It is frequently the case that what appears to be a model order was actually the reverse, and a poorly and apparently hastily prepared order will often be erroneously condemned. Many orders, models in their form, failed to reach the troops in time to affect their actions, and many apparently crude and fragmentary instructions did reach frontline commanders in time to enable the purpose of the higher command to be carried out on the battlefield.

In this exotic landscape where good orders are bad and bad orders are good he was hardly at home. His precise mind was baffled by the disorder which lay at the heart of war: he would have everything clear-cut, impersonal, clearly enunciated. He had no sympathy with Marshal Kutuzov who, according to Tolstoy, gave orders rarely and spent his time dozing at the war councils, quietly leaving events to take their course, because he knew that his orders would be mislaid or wrongly interpreted and the Unconscious of the soldiers would lead them wherever victory was possible. Indeed, throughout Marshall's writings there is an absence of psychological insight; he makes no effort to grapple with the depths of things; and his conceptions of tactics are logical, even mechanical, unconcerned with what T. E. Lawrence described as the "irrational tenth" which is "the test of generals" and "like the kingfisher flashing across a pool." Yet he had raised the problem of irrationality and was aware of its importance. To his notes on the giving and receiving of military orders he added the remark: "Our troops suffered much from the delays involved in preparing long and complicated orders." For the most part his own orders had been remarkably terse.

The essay in the *Infantry Journal* was not a consistently brilliant performance, though brilliance flares up at moments. A slight fatigue, a lack even of characteristic quality shows in its long paragraphs; we can even recognize the author of *Notes on Cordage and Tackle*. The explanation is probably not hard to seek. He had spent the war years sharpening his mind against problems of organization and tactics until his mind had grown razor-sharp; now the once powerful mind was dulled by lectures, by long and rather aimless tours, by the pleasantly easy tasks allotted to him. He wrote Pershing's speeches, and assisted Pershing in preparing those memoirs which remain, in spite of Marshall's assistance, among the dullest and most self-centered ever written, with no leaping quality of life.

Meanwhile the Army itself was growing impotent. There were 4,000,000 men in the Army in November, 1918. By 1933 there were to be no more than 117,000. Marshall could only watch the decline with bitterness in his heart, knowing that the issue of unpreparedness would be raised again. Preparedness became his watchword—he even called his horse *Prepare*—but no one listened to his warnings. Many years later he spoke of that haunting sense of insufficiency when he addressed a Senate Committee on Military Affairs:

> The great tragedy in France during the World War was, as I saw it—and it happened to be my opportunity to see twenty-seven divisions on the battlefield engaged in different kinds of fighting—the great tragedy was the wastage of the tremendous potential advantage we had in quality of our personnel, because of the very limited opportunity the men had for preparing themselves for what they were trying to do. No one has ever fully really told the full truth of what might have been, and what actually was; and the fault was that of a nation in not giving these men a fair chance to prepare themselves.

The clear warning went unheeded. He had said, as carefully as one can, that the American armies in France had avoided disaster by a hair-breadth. Would they avoid disaster again? He did not know. For nearly twenty years he was to be transferred from one minor command to another, rising gradually and steadily but always at a tortoise pace. He would retire in time and be forgotten, and perhaps someone reading through the operational orders of the First World War would chance upon the initials "G. C. M." and wonder who had written those oddly brilliant reports with their occasional notes of hidden malice or irony, and their occasional swift portraits of the war. He seemed, in fact, doomed for a decent obscurity.

CHAPTER EIGHT

The Dangerous Years

On April 28, 1924, there appeared in War Department Special Orders No. 100 the following announcement:

> Lieutenant Colonel George C. Marshall, Jr., Infantry, aide-de-camp, is relieved from his present assignment and duties, Washington, D.C. and is assigned to the 15th Infantry, effective July 1, 1924.

The Fifteenth Infantry at that time was stationed in Tientsin, the Chinese Treaty Port where America possessed extra-territorial rights. The choice of the appointment had been largely in Marshall's hands, and the journey to China represented the fulfillment of one of Marshall's ambitions: more than ten years before he had hoped for an assignment to China, only to be sent to the Philippines. For a long time he had been an occasional student of Chinese art; he had toyed with the idea of learning Chinese, and he was fascinated by Chinese history, with its perpetual crises and its anarchic stability. There had been Chinese merchants in the Philippines, and he had sometimes gone into their shops and bargained for curios. He had admired the grace and beauty of the Chinese, and he remembered that a distant relative of his, Commissioner Humphrey Marshall, had once exerted an extraordinary influence on Chinese history. He was coming to China at a time of upheaval not unlike the time of the Taiping rebels.

Tientsin, where Marshall arrived in September, 1924, is a coastal city with miles of monotonous stone streets and foreign houses, stagnant and foul-smelling canals and innumerable factories, a city which has very little of the real character of a Chinese city. Like

Shanghai, it has bowed down to foreign influence, and though there is an excellent Chinese University called Nankai and a number of temples, it was not by any means the best introduction to China. Yet there were some very real advantages in going there for anyone interested in the development of Chinese politics. China was then being ruled by warlords who had carved for themselves huge principalities covering whole provinces, and these warlords were gradually eliminating one another. Marshall arrived in time to see the remnants of General Wu P'ei-fu's army streaming towards Tientsin after the "Christian" General Feng Yu-hsiang treacherously attacked him, and though the warlords remained it was evident that they were doomed. The Kuomintang Party under the leadership of Dr. Sun Yat-sen was in possession of the southern province of Kwangtung, while the dictator Chang Tso-lin ruled over the north in uneasy alliance with Feng Yu-hsiang. The Kuomintang Party had embarked on its famous "march to the north," only to discover that its rear was threatened, and it had precipitantly returned to its base in Canton. During the next two years it was to prepare for the more successful march to the north which occurred in 1926-1927.

Marshall, then, had arrived in China at a time of flux. He was to watch the Chinese Communist Party growing from a small left-wing rump exerting hardly any political pressure into some semblance of power in 1927, and he was to see the decline of the warlords and the increasing power of the Kuomintang. He reached China for the first time during the critical years when the Kuomintang began to weld the whole of China together, and when he came to China twenty years later he presided over the abrupt decline of the same party. His experience of China therefore embraced the span of the active domination of the Kuomintang.

Marshall's interests in those days were hardly political, and problems concerning the garrison took most of his time. As Executive Officer, Fifteenth Infantry, he was interested in the morale of the troops stationed in a garrison where temptations were frequent and desires were easily satisfied: cheap liquor was available, and Tientsin after Shanghai was the chief center of the White Russians, and therefore of the traffic in White Russian women. Marshall was determined to safeguard his regiment from the temptations which China sedulously placed in front of foreigners in those days when there were three or four governments, and everything, including political power, could be bought with dollars. As usual, he drew up plans for keeping the regiment busy and in full training. He ordered the building of an ice rink, encouraged athletics, developed amateur theatricals, and saw to it that his men were rarely unoccupied. For himself, he decided to learn Chinese, and though he never mastered the language, he was able in three months to pick up sufficient colloquial Chinese to take the testimony of a Chinese witness at a summary court-martial without the benefit of an interpreter. He organized a language course for the officers of the regiment, and later he made the course available to enlisted men, producing a series of simplified Chinese textbooks. And all the time he was constantly frequenting the company of Chinese scholars and business men, determined to absorb as much as possible of the peculiar qualities of Chinese civilization, speaking in Chinese to anyone who would listen to him, absorbing into his system something of Chinese courtesy and not a little of Chinese fatalism, and at night when the work of the day was over he could be seen patiently inscribing on absorbent paper the shapes of Chinese characters. He was a man with three dominating passions: first, to produce a smart and disciplined regiment; second, to get to grips with Chinese culture; third, to go riding. In the pure air of dawn, when the Chinese were already beginning to crowd the roads, he would go riding among the maize fields.

Meanwhile he kept up his interest in the desperate strategems which were being employed by some of his friends who wanted to maintain a reasonably large Regular Army. He corresponded with John McAuley Palmer and a host of others, including General Pershing, whose fears Marshall shared. In December, 1924, Pershing wrote Marshall a letter which showed something of the despair of the aging General of the Armies. "I find on my return here," Pershing wrote, "that the War Department seems to be up against the real thing. The Budget Officer insists on reducing our estimates so that we shall not be able to have over 110,000 men. Just what this means I cannot understand. I do not know what is going to be done about it, but to my mind it is very discouraging." Marshall filed the letter away, and sixteen years later when he addressed an Encampment of the Veterans of Foreign Wars, he introduced the letter as evidence of a situation which was still virtually unchanged.

Marshall in China was something of a martinet. He was himself like a highly strung race horse, nervous, often irritable, capable of sweeping and grotesquely unfair judgments on men. The story has been told of a young lieutenant who was placed in charge of the training of the Mongolian ponies which Marshall had imported for the benefit of the garrison. When he saw the lieutenant slapping a pony across the face with a piece of harness, he was infuriated. The lieutenant's behavior was justified; it was a peculiarly recalcitrant pony, and there was no other way of getting it between the shafts. There was some kind of enquiry, the proper explanation was offered, but Marshall refused to change his opinion, and the lieutenant was relieved from the duty of training the ponies. The calm Olympian Marshall came later; at this time he was noted for his excitability and a curious facial spasm which sometimes occurred when he was speaking to his men and which would occur quite suddenly and inexplicably during the most ordinary conversation.

A man who lives in China for any length of time develops a sixth sense, and he inevitably changes his character. The subtle dusts of the Gobi fill the air in summer, the winters are freezing cold, only spring and autumn are tolerable. The northern Chinese winters tend to make the most gregarious men into recluses; the violent summers increase the sensitivity of dullards. Marshall changed, and it was observed of him that he would fall into long Chinese silences, and he would sit for hours contemplating a Chinese painting on silk. He was in his element in that exotic country, and there was nothing so pleasant as those early morning rides on his Mongolian ponies.

The war clouds were descending over China, and he began to pay more and more attention to the developing political pattern of the country. He was friendly with British and American journalists in Peking, and he spent long hours in argument with them. When General Pershing wrote to him, saying he was envious of Marshall's experience in China, Marshall wrote back giving his impressions, and there were phrases in his letter which may have haunted him twenty years later when he held power of life and death over the nation. He said:

> How the Powers should deal with China is a question almost impossible to answer.

There has been so much of wrongdoing on both sides, so much of shady transaction between a single power and a single party; there is so much of bitter hatred in the hearts of these people and so much of important business interests involved, that a normal solution can never be found. It will be some form of evolution, and we can only hope that sufficient tact and wisdom will be displayed by foreigners to avoid violent phases during the trying period that is approaching.

At the time his sympathies were with the Peking Government dominated by Feng Yu-hsiang, an enormously tall and boisterous warlord who inherited for a brief while the mantle of the Chinese Emperors, for it was Feng Yu-hsiang who held during those years the decisive role and manipulated the emergent forces according to his will, and it was the same man who invited Dr. Sun Yat-sen to Peking to inaugurate a national assembly. The death of Dr. Sun Yat-sen in the spring following Marshall's arrival put an end to people's hopes of a national assembly; no real assembly ever came into being. Marshall's prophecies in his letter to General Pershing were unhappily unfulfilled. China did not progress by evolution, but by a series of savage, hard-won revolutions.

When in the spring of 1927 Marshall completed his foreign duty in China, he could claim that the two and a half years had not been spent in vain. He had learned a great deal of Chinese, he had given some study to the complex problems of China, he was almost an authority on Chinese porcelain, and he had learned a great deal concerning contemplative Taoist mysticism, and he could see that there was something in common between the contemplations of the ancient Chinese philosophers and those of the great military commanders like Napoleon and "Stonewall" Jackson who trained themselves by prodigious efforts of the will to think problems out to their final conclusions.

The year 1927, which saw his departure from China in the spring and the victorious march of the Kuomintang forces to Peking in the summer, was a tragic one for Marshall. In the autumn his wife died. She had fought a long-delaying battle against heart disease, and now at last, while she was writing a letter to her mother in a hospital in Washington, her heart failed her. She had accompanied her husband to China and experienced the rigors of Chinese weather, she had continually comforted him and brought him the wealth of her sensitivity and her talent for friendship, and without her he was lost. He had been appointed an instructor at the War College in Washington, and now that she was dead he had no desire to live in the place. He asked for, and obtained, a transfer to Fort Benning in Georgia.

Lieutenant Colonel Marshall, Assistant Commandant of the Infantry School, with his deepset blue eyes and his sandy hair which was not yet beginning to grow grey at the temples, was the successor of the young lieutenant who taught at the School of the Line at Fort Leavenworth. Pedagogy suited him, and he had the air of a vigorous young don, never casual, always keeping the students up to the mark, absorbed in military theory and contemptuous of easy solutions. The battle exercises based on the experience of the War between the States were abandoned; he was concerned to discover the fundamental methods of future wars. He was blessed with an astonishing galaxy of instructors and pupils. There was Major Omar N. Bradley, who came first to the Tactical Section and was later assigned to be head of the Weapons Section. There was the fiery Major Joseph W. Stilwell, whom Marshall had admired at Tientsin when "Vinegar Joe" was in command of a battalion. There was Lieutenant Joseph L. Collins, who might have been a musician if his many-faceted mind had not been intrigued by the problems of military command. These three, Bradley, Stilwell and Collins were to become the most brilliant exponents of military leadership in the Second World War—such, at any rate, was Marshall's view and there is no reason to doubt his authority. Marshall would summon the three to his quarters at Fort Benning, and together they would debate endlessly about the high art of leading men into battle. Marshall usually led the discussion, and there was something about these meetings which resembled the private tutorial offered by a professor to his star pupils. There was at least one other student for whom Marshall showed a marked affection. This was Lieutenant Charles T. Lanham, who possessed a curious resemblance to Huckleberry Finn. Marshall admired his impetuosity and observed the sharp-pointed intelligence which "Buck" Lanham was often at pains to hide. To Lanham went the task of putting into shape the scattered notes on war which Marshall had begun when he was G-3 of the First Division, and the book *Infantry in Battle* was largely the fruit of their collaboration, though like nearly all the books which Marshall has been responsible for, a host of advisers, editors and draft-writers were called in.

The book was not written by Marshall, but it bears the imprint of his mind and thought, and here and there are to be found phrases which reflect the rhythms of his speech. Sometimes it gives the impression of simply elaborating upon arguments put forward in Marshall's article written for the *Infantry Journal* under the title "Profiting by War Experiences," as when in the chapter called "Obscurity" he speaks of the chaotic muddles of modern war:

> The leader must not permit himself to be paralyzed by this chronic obscurity. He must be prepared to take prompt and decisive action in spite of the scarcity or total absence of reliable information. He must learn that in war, the abnormal is normal and that uncertainty is certain. In brief, his training in peace must be such as to render him psychologically fit to take the tremendous mental hurdles of war without losing his stride.

To the layman, the chapter on Obscurity is by far the most interesting and it is written with considerably more art than the rest. The category of chaos is carefully examined; there are phrases which seem to echo the preoccupations of Chinese Taoist philosophers, and even a phrase like "He must learn that in war the abnormal is normal and that uncertainty is certain" seems to spring from Chinese origins. In this chapter there is a withering account of battles which were lost because the ordinary rules of war were blindly obeyed. The chapter headings: Obscurity, Simplicity, Terrain, Time and Space, Mobility, Surprise, Command and Communication, Battle Reconnaissance, Counter-Orders, Night Attacks, Miracles, Optimism and Tenacity suggest the quality of the book, which begins with the excellent statement: "The art of war has no traffic with rules, for the infinitely varied circumstances and conditions of combat never produce exactly the same situation twice." The statement is repeated with slight changes at intervals through the book. Practice in real war problems, not theoretical erudition and abstractions, is seen to provide mastery. "It is more valuable," he says, "to be able to analyze one battle situation correctly, recognize its decisive elements and devise a simple workable solution for it, than to memorize all the erudition ever written of war." Elsewhere he quotes approvingly from the writings of a French corps commander, General Cordelier, who wrote: "He who remains in abstraction falls into formula; he concretes his brain; he is beaten in advance."

Infantry in Battle, with its careful examination of actual battle problems, reflected the qualities of Marshall's mind. He had found textbooks almost useless during the First World War, and he was quite deliberately training himself for the uncertainties of the next. The dazzling group at Fort Benning, which also included Walter Bedell Smith and John R. Hodges, came under Marshall's influence, and each one of them showed the imprint of his mind. When Marshall became Chief of Staff, he was responsible for appointing to high position these soldiers he had trained and whose reactions, as they fought thousands of miles away from the Pentagon, he knew because they were likely to be his own.

Marshall took no delight in the monastic loneliness of garrison life. He was a man who flowered in the presence of children, and who was in need of a wife; and when at a dinner party in Columbus, Ohio, he met Mrs. Katherine Tupper Brown, the widow of a Baltimore lawyer, his mind was instantly made up: he would marry her and take her to Fort Benning. The marriage was delayed for nearly two years, but on October 16, 1930, they were married at Baltimore, and General Pershing acted as Marshall's best man. To his immense satisfaction Marshall found himself the head of a family which included the three delightful children of his wife. They will form no part of this chronicle, but it should be said here that in the long and arduous process which brought about the humanization of an erratic genius, the new family played an exemplary rôle.

With the coming of the world-wide depression, the Army suffered the inconveniences of poverty. In 1933, shortly after Marshall was transferred from Fort Benning to become Commander of the Eighth Infantry at Fort Screven, Georgia, all salaries in the Army were reduced by fifteen per cent. The reduction in salary did not seriously hurt Marshall, but he was aware how closely it touched the lives of the soldiers under his command and their families, and shortly afterwards he instituted a lunch-pail system by which on payment of fifteen cents each member of the family was fed: the price was the same, however many members there were in the family.

It was the time of the New Deal and the Civilian Conservation Corps. Marshall approved of the CCC, and when the veterans who composed the first CCC contingent in that region assembled at Fort Screven, he went out of his way to welcome them informally, and led them to their barracks. Mostly, the boys who entered the CCC camps were the poverty-stricken sons of bankrupt farmers, and Marshall had a great deal of sympathy for them. Looking them over, he was convinced they would make good soldiers once they were fattened a little. In time it fell to Marshall to organize, altogether, seventeen CCC camps in Georgia, Florida and South Carolina. They were model camps, and he would have been prepared to spend a few more years in active contact with these youngsters, but in the autumn of 1933 he was ordered by the Chief of Staff, General Douglas MacArthur, to proceed to Chicago as senior instructor with the Illinois National Guard. The order sounded suspiciously like a punishment. Twenty-three years before, as a young lieutenant, he had been appointed an instructor to the Massachusetts National Guard. He appealed against the decision, and MacArthur's reply appears to have been the inevitable brutal official letter stating bluntly that the appeal has been taken under consideration and has been refused. Marshall replied on October 9, saying that in view of the Chief of Staff's letter he would accept the new appointment. Until Christmas the wound bled. Like Washington, Marshall was naturally choleric and violent; he gave the appearance of calm only with the greatest difficulty and with the use of considerable artistry; and he showed quite openly how the wound had hurt him. Mrs. Marshall, remembering those early months in Chicago, spoke later of his "grey, drawn look which I had never seen before, and have seldom seen since."

By the end of the year his enthusiasm had returned. The friendliness of the people of Chicago worked a spell on him. If the National Guard rarely achieved a high standard in peace, at least he would do his best to prepare it for war. Hitler was now in command of the fate of Germany. Marshall, who had become a full colonel in September, 1933, devoted himself to the training of the National Guard. It was a slow, relentless, and grinding occupation, but the quality of the Guards perceptibly changed under his influence. He still maintained a close contact with General Pershing. Once Pershing came to his headquarters and was introduced to Marshall's aides. Such introductions involved cunning, for Pershing would send out orders in advance explaining that he had not the least interest in being treated as a visiting fireman and did not want to be "shown off." Marshall found pretexts for bringing his staff one by one into the room, and once they had entered Pershing was at their mercy, and the old gnarled General of the Armies, still upright in spite of great age, shook hands with the stenographers as though he had come deliberately for that purpose. Pershing was still impressed by Marshall's qualities. At some time during the year 1934 he wrote to the President and requested Marshall's promotion, for one of Roosevelt's memoranda reads:

> To the Secretary of War:
> General Pershing asks very strongly Col. George C. Marshall (Infantry) be promoted to Brigadier. Can we put in list of next appointments? 54 years old.

Marshall's name did not appear in the next list of appointments. Nor did it appear the following year when General Johnson Hagood added his own testimony to Marshall's right to be promoted. The Secretary of War at that time was Mr. George Dern. The Secretary had a fondness for visiting Army headquarters, and he arrived at General Hagood's office at San Antonio, Texas. Among other things he asked whether there were any good colonels who could be recommended for promotion.

"Mr. Secretary," General Hagood replied, "I have a great many good colonels whom I could recommend, but the best colonel in the Army is not under my command. His name is George Marshall, and he is on some duty over in Chicago."

"Yes," replied the Secretary, "I have heard that George Marshall is a very good man. But he is too young."

At that time Marshall was fifty-five.

Meanwhile Marshall remained in Chicago. He continued to train the Guards. In August, 1936, he commanded the Red forces in the Second Army maneuvers, and did this so well that his promotion could not be delayed any longer. He was promoted to brigadier general and assigned to command the Fifth Infantry Brigade at Vancouver Barracks, Washington. At last, at the age of fifty-six, he wore a star on his shoulders. The long years of waiting were over.

The two years spent in Washington were among the happiest of his life. He was a man who thirsted with the ambition to be a general in command of troops. During General Douglas MacArthur's tenure of office as Chief of Staff, Marshall felt slighted. Now, under the new Chief of Staff, General Malin Craig, the way was open to advancement. Vancouver barracks pleased him. He could look down through giant firs at the swift-flowing Columbia River or at the bright silver summit of Mount Hood, snow-capped summer and winter. He could hunt steelhead salmon, or go hunting after pheasants which were sometimes so tame that they roosted in his yard. The barracks stood on a place where the Hudson's Bay Company had once built a station, and where General Grant had spent some years in a log cabin which now formed a part of the post library. Marshall's duties included the command of thirty-five CCC companies scattered through Oregon and Washington, and this pleased him; there were good excuses for traveling across the land on tours of inspection. By an odd fate, people who had never heard of Marshall before heard his name when three Soviet airmen who were on their way across the North Pole from Moscow to San Francisco landed at the Vancouver airfield. Marshall immediately took charge, found an interpreter, put the weary men to bed in his house and set guards over them, and when the reporters gathered at the house there were complaints that Marshall, who refused to produce the airmen, was behaving highhandedly. It was an unfair accusation, for Marshall had simply insisted that they should have an uninterrupted sleep. While they were sleeping he arranged for a tailor in Portland to bring them twenty suits and twenty pairs of shoes to choose from, and so provided for their comforts that the Soviet Ambassador, Troyanovsky, was moved to come to Vancouver barracks and present his warm thanks to the General.

This was in June, 1938. There followed more tours of inspection—Marshall was now particularly pleased with the development of the CCC camps. In the autumn he underwent a thyroid operation in San Francisco. The operation, which was successful, had the effect of putting an end to the furious excitability which had so often made him miserable. From this period there begins the emergence of the calm Olympian mask which he was later to present to the world. Shortly after he had completely recovered from the dangerous operation—the operation is still dangerous, though methods have been devised since then to lessen its ill effects—he was called to Washington by a telegram from General Malin Craig. The order stated only that he was to report for special duty, but Marshall knew exactly why the order had been made—Pershing was ill and thought to be dying, and as Governor Charles Martin of Oregon, a close friend of Marshall, explained to the press, Marshall was the person in the Army closest to Pershing. When Pershing recovered, Marshall returned to Vancouver barracks.

He was not to remain there long. In the summer of 1938 he was ordered to Washington as Assistant Chief of Staff, War Plans Division, General Staff. It was the year of despair, of endless frustrations and agonized indecisions. Marshall was appointed to the War Plans Division in July, the month when the Republican forces in Spain made a daring attack across the Ebro and routed the Germans, Italians and Moors who were entrenched on the other side; but this was the last of the Spanish Republican victories, and by the end of the year the disintegration of Republican Spain was already taking place. In March, Hitler had entered Vienna in triumph. Immediately afterwards he had set the Sudeten Germans against the government of President Benes in Prague. September saw the diplomatic defeat of the British and French at Munich. The Americans, who took no part in the Munich agreements were nevertheless defeated *in absentia,* and without knowing that they were defeated, in those preliminary diplomatic battles which the Germans fought before they resorted to arms; and everyone knew that the resort to arms could not be much longer delayed. In the early winter President Roosevelt announced that the United States would build ten thousand military airplanes.

Roosevelt's announcement was a gauntlet thrown at the feet of the fascist conquerors. Marshall argued against it. The statement was made without warning to the Chief of Staff, and the two Generals, Malin Craig and Marshall, bearded the President at the White House and emphatically protested against the President's decision. It was one of those comparatively rare occasions when Marshall nearly lost his temper; he was coldly angry, for it seemed to him that the President was acting irresponsibly. The matter had not been discussed: it looked as though the President had surrendered to a momentary whim when he made the announcement, and as he left, Marshall exclaimed: "You are the Commander in Chief, Mr. President, and we will obey your orders, which are contrary to the considered judgment of the General Staff. You will, of course, never question the integrity of the Chief of Staff in these matters." The barbed conclusion, spoken in some heat, did not rankle with the President. He was pleased when men spoke openly, but he made no effort to alter the original announcement, which was calculated to demonstrate to the potential enemy the fabulous resources of American industry. Later the number of airplanes was reduced to fifty-five hundred, and on January, 1939, the new program was recommended by the President in his budget message to the Congress. At this time Marshall was already Deputy Chief of Staff, having been appointed to this position in October.

The first thing Marshall did after his new appointment was to study the full texts of all the military hearings and debates which the Congress had held during the previous five years. He knew there would be innumerable hearings before the Army could be put on a war footing. He also made a study of the Relief Program as it affected the Army, discovering that WPA and PWA between them had spent about $250,000,000 in War Department projects, and had in fact been the mainstay of the Army during the lean years. Unknown to the Army, Harry Hopkins had been its chief benefactor. Marshall had guessed at this truth before, and now it came to him with quite extraordinary force, and he began to pay particular attention to Army officers who possessed WPA experience. Among the Army officers whom he marked for advancement at this time was Brehon B. Somervell, who was to become Commanding General of the Army Service Forces.

But though Marshall was now learned in the past history of congressional debates, he still possessed little of that feeling which the President possessed in superabundance for the shape of things to come. In October, 1938, when the Spanish Republic was reeling and the Germans were vaunting their strength before the whole world, he spoke at the opening of the Air Corps Tactical School at Maxwell Field, Alabama, and said:

> With us, geographical location and the international situation make it literally impossible to find definite answers to such questions as: who will be our enemy in the next war, in what theater of operations will that war be fought, and what will be our national objective at the time? These uncertainties lead inevitably to the conclusion that the only sensible policy for us to follow is to maintain a conservatively balanced force for the protection of our own territory against any probable threat during the period the vast but latent resources of the United States, in men and matériel, are being mobilized.

He was counseling safety, where the President proposed daring. There were, however, many cogent reasons why a safe and conservative policy should be adopted. He was perfectly willing to recognize the importance of air power, but he was not yet in a position where he could arrive at simple solutions to the problem: what kind of air force should America have? He would ask such questions as: "Is it more desirable to have a large number of small planes or a small number of large planes?" He was not sure. New methods of air attack were still being worked out; and Roosevelt, demanding ten thousand planes, had forgotten, as Marshall pointed out, the crews and the trained reserves which would have to man them. More and more he feared that America might embark on a war unprepared. On November 6, when he made a speech at Brunswick, Maryland, his mind went back to the long conversations he had enjoyed with Pershing about the risks which had been taken by an improvised American force during the Mexican War. The same risks had been taken during the War between the States by both sides, but it was in the Spanish-American War that the Americans had shown themselves most unprepared. He said:

> Out in San Francisco an expedition was embarking to sail to the Philippines, to back up Admiral Dewey. They lacked all knowledge of the country, of the people, of the general necessities; they lacked training and organization; and yet they sailed off across the broad Pacific to fight, seven thousand miles from their base, with only one hundred and fifty rounds of ammunition available per man, just about one day of rifle fire on a battlefield. What was to happen the morning following the first encounter had to be completely ignored.

He went on, then, to speak of his own experiences during the First World War, and of how it had taken more than a year of preparation before the American Army was deployed in battle. The time element was critical, for war might come at any moment and there was no reason to believe that the enemy would offer the United States the privilege of waiting while the Army prepared. Bombs, even bullets, take time to be prepared:

> Remember that almost every weapon of war, certainly every gun—big or little—and every device for aiming and firing that gun, like the elaborate instruments necessary for antiaircraft artillery, require a year to a year and a half to manufacture. So, no matter how many billions of dollars Congress places at our disposal on the day war is declared, they will not buy ten cents' worth of war materiel for delivery under twelve months, and a great deal of it will require a year and a half to manufacture. In other words, whatever your son and my son is to use to defend himself and to defend us and the country, has to be manufactured in time of peace.

As the year came to an end, the threat of war could be felt like a cold breath coming out of Germany. As Deputy Chief of Staff to a Chief who would soon resign, he knew that the burden of carrying on the war if it broke out would fall to his hands; and though a few months before he had complained that the United States was never in a position to name the enemy, he knew now that Germany was the certain enemy. In a speech before the Rifle Training Association at Washington on February 3, 1939, he spoke of the overwhelming importance he attached to the infantrymen, for "no other group competed with them in hardships and casualties"; and something in the uncertainty of the times made him linger on the defenselessness of the infantryman, so that it was as though he was seeing the defenselessness of his own country in terms of the solitary infantryman on the battlefield. The infantryman unassisted by mechanical instruments, without even a horse, lacking the anchor of a field gun or tank, and with only a corporal to back him up—here was an object worth every man's attention. At considerable length, and with some passion, Marshall described the infantryman as he made his way towards the enemy, and he deliberately repeated the images of the man's loneliness:

He lacks a physical rallying point—no ship, no heavy gun, no fortification, nothing but a few scattered buddies. He is a young fellow, depressed by a heavy physical burden on his back, exhausted by long marches of concentration and deployment, and lack of food, and he is virtually alone under the terrific pounding of hostile fires of every kind. Of himself, by himself, he can apparently do very little, though collectively he can win the war.

He must be supported by artillery, which means in turn that his platoon commander must have a skilled knowledge of topography and be able to report exactly where his line is established—on ground never seen before and of which he probably has no map. This information . . . must be communicated through an elaborate but hastily established communications system, by runner, telephone, radio, through company, battalion, and regimental headquarters, to some distant battery of artillery, probably a mile to the rear, and which the platoon commander has never seen and possibly never will see. It may be necessary to coordinate his isolated activities with an infantry cannon or Stokes mortar, and certainly with distant machine guns. He may even have to initiate procedure to secure the support of tanks still miles to the rear. All this he does, lying on his stomach, under a hostile fusillade—with a diet of gas thrown in for good measure. And what he proposes must be coordinated with the scattered units along a regimental, a brigade, a divisional front, and through its depth of supports and reserves. Altogether it is *the* most complicated problem of troop leadership, and requires a higher degree of training and discipline, I believe, than for any other military preparation—except for the actual flying of an airplane. There are no convenient electrical buttons as on a battleship to launch a broadside; no hot meals, no rest, seemingly no end to a long-drawn-out battle of endurance.

The passage has been quoted at length because it represented Marshall's hymn of praise for the infantryman who would soon be engaged in war. He said much the same thing in *Infantry in Battle*, but never so passionately, never with such power of evocation nor with such a sense of overwhelming fear. One half of his mind seemed to believe that the war was near, while the other, the more conservative half, spoke of war from a distance and talked of the patient preparation of a balanced force. In May, 1939, he outlined the defense policy of the United States. "It is extremely simple," he said. "We have merely to maintain an immediate available force—the Regular Army and the National Guard—adequate to defend the continental United States, Panama and Hawaii, during the period our vast resources in personnel, matériel and industry are being mobilized for war." It was easy to say, as he did, that in natural resources the United States was supreme—the matter had yet to be proved. More to the point was his statement that though everyone was talking of the vast number of airplanes being produced in Germany, the Germans were producing something of even greater consequence than airplanes—for more than two years they had been producing more than a million rounds of ammunition a week.

In April, Roosevelt had made the decision to appoint Marshall Chief of Staff on the retirement of General Malin Craig. During the following month the Deputy Chief of Staff was sent on one of the strangest missions of his life. The German government had invited the Brazilian General Pedro Aurelio de Goes Monteiro, Chief of Staff of the Brazilian Army, to Berlin. He had been promised the high honor of leading a division of German troops on parade. American diplomats heard of the maneuver and hurriedly consulted Washington, and the President decided that the best way to offset the unfortunate situation would be to send Marshall to Brazil on a goodwill mission. Accordingly Marshall sailed on the U.S.S. *Nashville* and spent seven strenuous weeks in Brazil—it was the first time he had visited South America. He was accompanied during the journey by Colonel Matthew B. Ridgway, who spoke Spanish and who had served on the commission of inquiry and conciliation to settle the Bolivia-Paraguay border in 1929. Marshall had picked him from the ranks and was grooming him for high positions: later Ridgway was to become Deputy Chief of Staff and the inheritor of all MacArthur's commands in the Far East. There were receptions everywhere, school children paraded in his honor, he was perpetually surrounded with a motorcycle escort and he succeeded in visiting most of the large towns of Brazil. He discussed at considerable length the whole question of the defense of South America, which juts out into the Atlantic Ocean and provides either a bastion for American defense or a convenient foothold for an invader. During the early

George Catlett Marshall Jr. at the age of two.
Photograph taken at Uniontown, Pennsylvania, in 1882.

Second Lieutenant Marshall in dress blues shortly before graduation from the Staff College, Fort Leavenworth, in 1908.

months of the war Marshall was to be almost obsessed by the thought of a German landing in Brazil. Tired after the long journey, he returned to Washington to discover that General Malin Craig, his strength nearly broken by dissensions in the War Department, had applied for terminal leave, and Marshall was now Acting Chief of Staff. Two months later, on September 1, 1939, the very day on which Germany invaded Poland, he was sworn in as Chief of Staff. He had received the news of the German attack on Poland at three o'clock in the morning, when the telephone rang at his bedside. Later the same morning, wearing a white Palm Beach suit, he was sworn in in Secretary Woodring's office.

A week later the President declared a limited National Emergency and authorized the expansion of the Regular Army and the National Guard.

The war which was not to involve the United States for more than two years was now being fought in earnest. The need for a large mechanized Army had never been greater, and Marshall found himself towards the end of November testifying before a House Appropriations Committee for an additional $271,000,000 for purposes which were never clearly divulged (for part of the testimony was held in secret), though there could be no doubt that the money was to be spent on the immediate expansion of a perilously small army. When he became Acting Chief of Staff, the Regular Army consisted of 13,808 officers and 174,079 enlisted men, and this pathetically small Army was all he had to work with. It should be remembered that at that time Spain, Austria and Czechoslovakia had all fallen to the fascist powers. Addressing the American Historical Association at the end of December, he acknowledged the inefficiency of the Army, saying that "the Army machine is less than 25 per cent ready for immediate action."

While continually fighting for a larger army, better equipped and better trained than ever before, Marshall continued, at intervals, the long tour of American military defenses which had begun with his visit to Brazil. In February, 1940, he inspected the defenses at Puerto Rico, and remarked with satisfaction that Punta Borinquen, the Army's easternmost air base, had been nothing more than a canefield a year before. He still believed that America would be able to fight with a small army, but when he addressed the House

Appropriations Committee during the same month, he spoke of the time when it would be necessary to add to the number of seasoned troops in the Regular Army, and he added: "If Europe blazes in the late spring or summer, we must put our house in order before the sparks reach the Western Hemisphere. The Army was growing, but too slowly for his taste. He went on to inspect the military defenses of the West Coast, spending the night at the sanatorium in Tucson, Arizona, where Pershing was resting, before flying on to Hamilton Field. On June 12 he found himself addressing the Commencement Exercises at V.M.I. He had no time to prepare his speech, and spoke extempore, his mind racing back to the time when he was himself a student at the Institute. The past week had been overshadowed by the tragic unfolding of the war in Europe, and he spoke now with deep emotion. He said:

> It is your graduation day, but it may also be one of the most fearful in the history of the world. No man can predict the outcome of the tragic struggle in Europe. No American can foresee the eventual effect on the Americas. The world we have known may be revolutionized; the peaceful liberty we have accepted so casually may be a hazard in this ghastly game abroad.

The words were appropriate to the times, for on that day the German Army entered Paris. A week later, addressing the Veterans of Foreign Wars at Akron, Ohio, he declared: "The time for endless debate and other differences of opinion is past. We must get down to hard pan and carry out our preparations without vacillations or confusions."

From the grey-paneled room in the War Department on Constitution Avenue, the plans were sent out over the whole country. Sitting at the ornately carved desk which Phil Sheridan had brought to Washington after the War between the States, Marshall was mapping out the future. He was still hesitant, determined not to risk an expansion beyond the strength of the Army. He planned to have sixteen divisions fully organized by January 1, 1941. They were to consist of nine Regular Army infantry, four National Guard infantry, one cavalry and two armored divisions. He was faced with insoluble problems, impossible hurdles. He said in August:

> We cannot at present expand beyond a force of 1,200,000 without destroying our present organizations. While a larger force would be essential to prevent hostile infiltration in this hemisphere, we cannot create a larger force at the present moment.
>
> We cannot tell what final strength will be required. If danger threatens this hemisphere, we may require 3,000,000 men, even 4,000,000 or more, because our obligations are scattered in so many directions. We must consider the possibility of action over a wide expanse. The force required depends entirely on the extent and determination of the hostile forces. If we do not have the equipment we are lost.

Other difficulties confronted him. In the same month, during a recess of the Senate Appropriations Committee, he told Byrnes that he was faced with an extraordinary situation in the Army: it was simply impossible for him legally to promote young officers of unusual ability. He suggested an amendment to the existing law. The amendment read: "In time of war or national emergency determined by the President, any officer of the Regular Army may be appointed to higher temporary grade without vacating his permanent appointment." Byrnes promised to place the amendment before the Senate, and by September 9 it had become law. Byrnes noted with satisfaction that by the end of the year 4,088 new promotions of young officers were made. The law gave Marshall the weapon which would allow him to advance men at breakneck speed: a certain Colonel Eisenhower was advanced over 366 senior officers.

With a new law giving him power to create a capable officer corps and an expanding Army, Marshall began to face the future with a new confidence. There were desperate issues at stake. In December, when Secretary Stimson, Secretary Knox and Admiral Stark were in conference with him, there was not one of them who believed the United States could avoid being drawn into the war. His original aim had been the creation of a small, thoroughly equipped fighting force; after the breakthrough at Sedan he began to think in terms of armies of millions, and gradually, but far too slowly, this army was coming into existence. The creation of this army was, as he said in the first of his Biennial Reports published a year later, "a great experiment in democracy, a test of the ability of a Government such as ours to prepare itself in time of peace against the ruthless and arbitrary action of the Governments whose leaders take such measures as they see fit, and strike when and where they will with sudden and terrific violence." He was often to use the word "terrific"—it is almost the sign-manual by which one can recognize his hand in the anonymous papers published by the War Department. Within a year "the sudden and terrific violence" was to fall upon America.

CHAPTER NINE

The Volcano

The war was stealthily coming nearer to America, but where would the blow fall?

As Marshall looked at the battle reports which came into his office every day, he saw danger everywhere. There was danger inside America, where the people were still woefully unprepared—the theme of unpreparedness returns again and again in his speeches—and there was danger at all the perimeters of American power abroad, and the most frightening danger of all was that Great Britain might fall. Sometimes his mind would turn to dangers in the Pacific.

All through 1941 there were sporadic conferences concerned with the danger to American outposts in the Pacific. One such conference was held in Marshall's office on February 6; the subject was the defense of Pearl Harbor, and on the following day Marshall wrote to General Short his considered opinion of the risks involved. He wrote:

> If no serious harm is done us during the first six hours of known hostilities, thereafter the existing defenses would discourage an enemy against the hazard of an attack. The risk of sabotage and the risk involved in a surprise raid by air and by submarine constitute the real perils of the situation.

Shortly afterwards, on February 19, he said at another conference: "Out in Hawaii the Fleet is anchored, but we have to be prepared against any surprise attacks. I don't say any probable attack, but they have to be prepared against a surprise attack from a trick ship or torpedo planes." On February 25, at a conference held in his office attended by a galaxy of generals and colonels, he repeated what he had said earlier and at the same time he gave it as his opinion that he considered the risk slightly less: "It is necessary for the Fleet to be at anchorage part of the time and they are particularly vulnerable at that time. I do not feel that it is a possibility or even a probability, but they must guard against everything." These statements said no more than they were intended to say. Marshall regarded Pearl Harbor as one of many critical points on the American perimeter, and he was not prepared to give it special emphasis. The phrase "I do not feel it is a possibility or even a probability" indicated that he perhaps regarded Hawaii as less important than other American stations, such as the Philippines and the Panama Canal. A few days later he was to read the joint estimate made by General Martin and Admiral Bellinger, the commanders of the Army and Naval Air Forces of the Fourteenth Naval District. The report, dated March 31, 1941, written in Hawaii and immediately despatched to Washington, where it was read by Marshall, contained a brilliant analysis of the situation insofar as it affected Hawaii. The report read:

> (a) Relations between the United States and Orange (Japan) are strained, uncertain and varying.
> (b) In the past Orange has never preceded hostile actions by a declaration of war.
> (c) A successful, sudden raid against our ships and naval installations on Oahu might prevent effective offensive action by our forces in the Western Pacific for a long time.
> (d) A strong part of our Fleet is now constantly at sea in the operating areas organized to take prompt offensive action against any surface or submarine force which initiates hostile action.
> (e) It appears possible that Orange submarines and/or an Orange fast raiding force might arrive in Hawaiian waters with no prior warning from our Intelligence Service. . . .
>
> Possible enemy action:
> A declaration of war might be preceded by:
> > 1. A surprise submarine attack on ships in the operating area.
> > 2. A surprise attack on Oahu including ships and installations in Pearl Harbor.
> > 3. A combination of these two.
>
> It appears that the most likely and dangerous form of

attack on Oahu would be an air attack. It is believed that at present such an attack would most likely be launched from one or more carriers which would probably approach inside of 300 miles.

One of the major tragedies of the war was that insufficient importance was attached to this report, but every kind of fantastic and menacing possibility presented itself: destruction at Pearl Harbor was one of many. There was the possibility that Japan and Russia would form a team operating to hold American ships in the Pacific. Marshall had discussed this in the summer of the previous year as something to be considered even then with care: and with the signing of the neutrality pact between Japan and the Soviet Union on April 13, 1941, the danger only increased.

What if Great Britain fell as suddenly as France had fallen? As he looked at the map and discussed the possibilities with Stimson, Marshall saw that there were only a few remaining outposts in the East, and there was danger of being prematurely dragged into two major operations in the Atlantic, one in the neighborhood of Iceland and Great Britain, the other near Brazil, and there would not be enough naval strength to hold politics steady in South America. The whole of South America might erupt. These were real and pressing worries. It was a time when men clutched at straws. The Azores, those miniscule islands lying almost exactly halfway between Iceland and Brazil, suddenly acquired enormous importance, but could one hold off German power with a thing which looked on the map about the size of a pin? Nevertheless plans were made for the occupation of the Azores, while Cordell Hull, kept in ignorance of the plans, assured the Portuguese Minister on April 18 that he knew nothing about an intended occupation of the islands, and Dean Acheson, then Assistant Secretary of State for Economic Affairs, found himself called upon to pursue a mysterious policy towards Portugal, not knowing until later that secret negotiations were going on. Early in February, Marshall had written to General Short that it might be necessary to keep the Azores from falling into German hands. "To keep them from falling into German hands" was almost a euphemism. It had suddenly become quite conceivable that the Azores would become the springboard from which attacks might be launched against a totally occupied Europe.

Attacks might also be launched against Pearl Harbor, and at the President's request Marshall prepared an aide-memoire on the defense of Hawaii on May 3. "The island of Oahu," he said, "due to its fortification, its garrison and its physical characteristics is believed to be the strongest fortress in the world." It was a strange statement followed by an even stranger conclusion. Marshall still thought of the island chiefly in terms of sabotage. He said: "In point of sequence, sabotage is first to be expected, and may within a very limited time cause great damage. On this account, and in order to ensure strong control, it would be highly desirable to set up a military control of the islands prior to the likelihood of our involvement in the Far East." No military control of the islands was set up until the Japanese had attacked, and the dangers of the Pacific were largely forgotten in the War Department, where all eyes were set on the growing power of Germany. Like Singapore, Pearl Harbor suffered from its reputation for strength; and both were much weaker than Marshall imagined.

As the terrible spring moved into a still more terrible summer, part of the American Pacific Fleet had entered the Atlantic, German airplanes had been seen over Iceland, Lend Lease had been passed, Roosevelt had announced his Hemisphere Defense Plan No. 1, only to scrap it after the neutrality pact between Russia and Japan was signed, and the German submarines took their daily toll of ships. The *Bismarck* had emerged from Bergen, sunk H.M.S. *Hood* with a single lucky shell which blew up its magazine, and when last seen was heading for the coast of America. On Pan-American Day, May 2 7, Roosevelt had announced to an audience of ambassadors seated on gilded chairs in the East Room of the White House that a state of "unlimited emergency" existed, and on the same day the *Bismarck* was sunk by the Royal Navy. Then, on June 2, Hitler and Mussolini staged their meeting on the Brenner Pass, and, as though in answer to the pageantry of their meeting, President Roosevelt on June 14 quietly ordered the freezing of all German and Italian assets in the United States, and ordered the closing of all German and Italian Consulates. It was an act of incredible boldness, and a very dangerous one, and when Marshall went off the next day to Hartford, Connecticut, to speak to the students of Trinity College, so fulfilling a long-standing engagement, something of the brooding horror of the times came out in that grave speech, so unlike any speech he had made before, so urgent and so passionate and demanding that it seemed to be spoken by someone else inside him, someone who had broken through the austere mask he presented to the world.

He had been a lifelong Episcopalian, and this was an Episcopalian College: the Church had provided the buildings and presented them to the Nation. He had known Trinity men, and liked them, and in these surroundings he felt free to talk about the subjects which rarely, if ever, arose during congressional enquiries. He spoke without notes, and often haltingly, as if struggling with his ideas. The theme was a simple one: the spirit and the human body, and the war between them. But what had this to do with the coming war against the Axis powers? He talked briefly of the nature of that war, "long-drawn-out and intricately planned," a war which would not be a succession of mere episodes, but would continue perhaps for years, and the longer it continued the heavier would be the demands on the men engaged in it, until they were battered and had only the spirit to sustain them. A new discipline must come about. It was enough that soldiers should obey commands mechanically, with instinctive reactions, in the old days of small professional armies; it was not enough now. "We have sought for something more than enthusiasm," he said, "something finer and higher than optimism or self-confidence, not merely of the intellect or the emotions but rather something in the spirit of man, something encompassed only by the soul." There was the ancient discipline which relied on physical habits; there must be new disciplines relying on spiritual habits. "From a moral standpoint there is no question as to which of these two disciplines is the finer if you admit that respect is to be preferred to fear; the white flame of enthusiasm to the dull edge of routine; the spiritual to the instinctive." He spoke of the new American Army as a Christian Army, which was not asked to live on rations alone. He spoke of the chaplains and the five hundred new chapels built by the Army, and how they were building the Army on beliefs that made men invincible. He concluded: "This army of ours already possesses a morale based on what we allude to as the noblest aspirations of mankind—on the spiritual forces which rule the world and will continue to do so. Let me call it the morale of omnipotence."

The morale of omnipotence! It was a strange phrase coming from an American Chief of Staff, for very similar phrases were employed by the Japanese in their dreams of world empire. The words would have pleased Emerson and frightened Jefferson, who cultivated no omnipotent ambitions. The words echoed across the years a sentence which General Drum had once inserted in a memorandum: "Boundaries will not be considered as binding." But though the words have the look of danger, as though quite suddenly a window had opened to reveal a blinding glimpse of ambitions which went beyond all reason, they sprang almost naturally from the strains of the time. He called upon omnipotence out of a sickening realization of the country's desperate weakness. He need not have worried so greatly. A week later Hitler, who planned to conquer the world and believed devoutly in his own omnipotence, invaded Russia.

The War Department had known for some time that there was a possibility that the Nazis would attack Russia, but for some reason never sufficiently explained they had not taken the possibility seriously. For half a year Cordell Hull had received confidential reports from the American commercial attaché in Berlin saying there was excellent reason to believe that Hitler would attack, and the British were reasonably certain of an attack from the beginning of April: to Stimson and Marshall the news came as a bolt from the blue. Their first reaction was a sigh of relief. With the weight of Germany moving towards Russia, the tension on the American outposts must inevitably decrease, there would be no German effort to attack Iceland, no invasion of Great Britain, no pressure on Brazil. As for the outcome of the new invasion, they believed the war would last "a minimum of one month and a possible maximum of three months." Neither had the remotest conception that there would be a protracted campaign in Russia.

After the momentary relief came a period of deep gloom. The German armies rolled into Russia, driving deep with their first massive onslaughts, and the War Department came to believe that it was within the bounds of possibility that after a quick victory the combined weight of Germany and Russia would be thrown into the battle for the conquest of the world. On July 2, Stimson's pessimism, which Marshall for a while had shared, reached the lowest depths it was to reach during the war. "I feel more up against it than ever before," he wrote. "It is a problem whether this country has it in itself to meet an emergency." He knew, as Marshall knew, that everything depended upon a race against time. Before them both lay the appalling prospect of America being drawn into a war which was not of her choosing with an inadequately prepared Army, an America able to offer only a token resistance to the aggressor.

It was as simple as that; and the key to the whole problem lay in Selective Service. If an army could be trained quickly, on a prodigiously large scale, there might still be some hope. Now more than ever it was necessary to make the Americans realize their plight. While out riding one day, it had occurred to Marshall that he had declined to prepare the usual annual report of the Chief of Staff the previous summer; he would therefore prepare a Biennial Report covering the period July 1, 1939 to June 30, 1941. He would show it to no one; not even the President would see it before it was published, and Stimson would see it at the same time it was released to the press. He felt that affairs had reached a critical stage several months before, nothing was being done and it was therefore necessary, by some kind of dramatic act, to show the people and the Congress how dangerous the military position was. With the help of his staff working at top speed, the Report, which was begun immediately after the German attack on Russia and completed in five days, was released to the Press on July 1.

The first Biennial Report is conveniently short. Marshall's hand can be detected in it throughout, but it possesses none of the magisterial lucidity of the third Report, perhaps because it is not dealing with the excitements of far-flung battle lines but with the intricate and complex details which concern the assembling of an army. He begins with a recital of the state of the Armed Forces on July 1, 1939, when the United States had no field army, when there were no corps troops, almost no Army troops or G.H.Q. special troop units, and there was only the framework of three and a half divisions. The Air Corps consisted of only sixty-two tactical squadrons. Since then, of course, there had been a vast improvement, and the expansion of the Army from 172,000 men to approximately 1,500,000 men had imposed great, but necessary strains on the War Department. He examined some of these strains, and went into considerable detail in describing the reorganization of the staff and the command; there followed his "Recommendations for the Elimination of Certain Legal Limitations and Restrictions." All that had gone before was no more than an introduction to these closely written pages designed to force new legislation upon the country immediately.

> What has happened [he wrote] is history. Of grave concern today are the contingencies of the present and future. There are legal restrictions on the use of the armed forces which should be removed without delay. Events of the past two months are convincing proof of the terrible striking power possessed by a nation administered purely on a military basis. Events of the past few days are even more forcible indications of the suddenness with which armed conflict can spread to areas hitherto considered free from attack.
>
> It is therefore urgently recommended that the War Department be given authority to extend the period of service of the Selective Service men, the officers of the Reserve Corps and the Units of the National Guard.... In the light of the situation it is believed that our interests are imperiled and that a grave national emergency exists. Whatever we do for the national defense should be done in the most efficient manner. Differences of views regarding national policy should not, it seems to me, be permitted to obscure the facts relating to the preparation of the armed forces for service, which has been the purpose of our vast program of the past twelve months. When and where these forces are to serve are questions to be determined by their Commander-in-Chief and Congress, and should not be confused with the problem of their readiness for service. All, it is believed, will admit that the time factor has been of dominant importance in the march of events since September, 1939, in the availability of matériel, in the effect of the complete readiness of huge, highly trained units for employment in chosen theaters. The matériel phase of our task is generally understood. The personnel phase is not, and it is here that legal limitations, acceptable at the time of their passage, now hamstring the development of the Army

into a force immediately available for whatever defensive measures may be necessary.

Within an hour of the publication of the Report, there was a furor. It was believed by some that he was attempting to introduce in peacetime an American Expeditionary Force, and Senator Burton K. Wheeler, who had described the Lend-Lease Act as a measure designed to plow under every fourth American boy, plunged into the attack, with half or more than half of Congress applauding him. There was a violent storm of discussion, and some of it may have arisen as a result of the unfortunate title Marshall gave to the paragraphs where he discussed his recommendations. Stimson was furious and bitter, his bitterness leading him to an unfair and inaccurate attack against Senator Wheeler. Marshall had expected the furor, and came to the conclusion that no one had really read the recommendations—nearly everyone had been content with the headlines. He ordered an examination of the letters received, and noted without surprise that there was evidence of collusion in the writing of them, for there could be no other explanation of the fact that so many came from the neighborhood of Passaic, New Jersey, and were couched in similar terms. He noted the fact that 23 per cent of the letters examined contained extreme personal abuse or threats of violence against the President or himself. These were small matters. What was far more important was that the recommendations should be met. He did not particularly mind being called a militarist, but he objected intensely to the assumption that his basic principles were wrong. Alarmed, Roosevelt called a White House Conference with Congressional leaders, and it was decided to introduce three bills to cover a declaration of national emergency, the extension of enlistments, appointments, and commissions and other matters which had arisen out of the Report. Marshall took the witness stand before the Senate Committee on Military Affairs. He spoke with some bitterness. It seemed to him that the national crisis of unpreparedness was there for all to see; it was inescapable; then why the furor? Why was it necessary that he should be continually resented, when he demanded only that America should survive? He was not always a good witness. He spoke tartly sometimes, his cold eyes blazing with sudden fury, his mind racing beyond the thought, stern and lean, looking a little like a prophet of doom, repeating with a hundred variations the phrases he had already employed in the Report, as though he thought he could hammer through the Congressional defences by the simple process of repetition. They were, for the most part, lawyers: he was a soldier. "Lawyers and legal complications," he said, "are inappropriate on a battlefield." The barb pierced, and did little to increase his popularity with the Congress. Often he employed his "statistical talk" and sent them half to sleep; but a new note appears in his prose. He declared: "We have seen nation after nation go down, one after the other, in front of a concentrated effort, each one lulled, presumably into negative action, until all the guns were turned on them and it was too late." He was still thinking of the possible defeat of Russia. There were no words fit to express his horror of what could so easily happen: in these Congressional meetings the word "tragic" was often on his lips. Again and again, with only the slightest variations, he repeated: "I do emphatically believe that the safety of this country is imperiled."

In command of 1,400,000 men scattered from the Philippines to Alaska, Newfoundland and Trinidad, he was perfectly aware he held no command over the Congress. He spoke patiently enough. He explained that he had wanted to build an army as one builds a fire: "If too much wood were piled on suddenly the fire would be put out. I did not want to put out the fire. I wanted to build it gradually to where it could accommodate large quantities of wood." People had hinted that he belonged to the war party, and it amused him to remember that the former Secretary of War, Newton D. Baker, the thin spindly little man who had come as near as any Secretary of War had ever been to the front lines, during the St. Mihiel battle, once wrote a letter to General MacArthur. That letter, written in 1935, declared that he knew no case in history where an Army officer had fomented war in the United States. He offered this as evidence of the clean bill of health of the War Department, yet he was aware of a deep-seated, unchangeable hostility towards himself, because he represented symbolically the war which everyone feared, and in fact the clean bill of health offered by Newton D. Baker was not an altogether valid document, and not all the doubts expressed in Congress were unreasonable. But on one ground there could be no debate. He said on

July 22: "An emergency exists whether or not the Congress declares it. I am asking you to recognize the fact—the fact that the national interest is imperiled and that an emergency exists. I am not asking you to manufacture a fact."

So the great debate went on, while irrascible Congressmen attempted to trick him into an admission that the American Expeditionary Force was being planned, that he wanted war, that he was incapable of seeing possibilities of peace. Then he replied that in the early summer there had been a time when the Chief of Staff did not know whether the British Empire would be in existence at the end of the next six weeks or two months, and whether America would find herself with the Atlantic completely open to enemy naval forces. There had been desperate fear in the War Department: it seemed impossible to convince Congress that a Chief of Staff had a right to his fear.

Occasionally, to relieve the tension, Marshall wandered off into brief anecdotes, memories of former wars, solemn little disquisitions on the nature of modern war. He had long ago come to the conclusion that the American people possessed a profound knowledge of matériel—machines. They could see readily enough that a vast quantity of machines were necessary; they could not convince themselves so easily that a vast number of men were also needed. He tried to drive the lesson home by comparing war at sea and war in the field:

> Only a team can fight a ship, and it requires much technical preparation to develop that team, both as to the individual's knowledge of his job, and as to coordination among members of the team. The team has to be so developed that despite the shock of battle, explosions, and so forth, it will continue to function according to a prescribed procedure. However, nobody runs from a ship, because there is no place to run, and hiding in the hull is of no advantage. The ship is full of buttons and fixed gadgets that the electric companies have built into them. And you will agree with me that you never saw a button on a battlefield. There communications are not welded or built into the structure. They are scattered over the face of the earth. Your first glimpse of a modern battlefield would be when you first plunge forward on it. You do not see the

artillery unit that is supporting you. You may never see it in your lifetime, yet it is the unit that has to pour down the artillery fire at the time and place you need it.

It was not an altogether clear exposition: buttons are in fact found on battlefields in the shape of electrically-operated mine detectors and in a number of other forms, but the main contention is clear; more than most people realized, the Army needed a long technical training, and with the present dangers it was necessary that the largest Army, with the greatest amount of technical training, should be formed, and it was nearly too late.

The debate continued throughout July, 1941. Suddenly, at the beginning of August, Marshall received word that he was to accompany the President on the U.S.S. *Augusta* to a secret meeting off the coast of Newfoundland with Winston Churchill. He packed his winter clothes and set off from Fort Myer in a mood of guarded despondency, for the final conclusions of the debate had not been reached. With him, representing the American war potential, went Admiral Stark, Admiral King and General Arnold. The last two were later to form, with him, the Joint Chiefs of Staff.

After the meeting of the warships in Placentia Bay on August 9, a debate of an entirely different kind occurred. All of the Americans present felt that America would be drawn into the war, willingly or unwillingly, that time was short, that there was no longer any reason to dissemble, and that the danger of German occupation on the outposts of American defense was now as critical as it had been before the German attack against Russia. The threat from the Far East was as great as the threat from Germany, for Japan had already occupied southern Indo-China, and Roosevelt, just before sailing, had issued an Executive Order freezing Japanese assets. There was however no specifically military agenda to be discussed at the meeting, which took place for political reasons and brought about a singularly potent political victory in the shape of the Atlantic Charter. There were some military matters connected with the battle of the Atlantic to be discussed, but it was not yet, of course, the time to make war plans. Nor was Marshall in any position to make promises, or even hint at promises. The American overseas garrisons were pathetically small: the total number of men in the garrisons extending from Newfoundland to the Philippines was only 120,000 men. Equipment, field training, nearly everything else was lacking; and Marshall was facing the grim fact that he was Chief of Staff of an army which might dissolve in his hands. The Selective Service men had been drafted for a year only; and they could not, except in the event of war, be sent anywhere outside the Western Hemisphere, and no one was quite crtain what the words Western Hemisphere could be interpreted to mean—was the east coast of Iceland in the Western Hemisphere? There were other reasons why no military agenda had been prepared. By law, no soldiers could be sent to Great Britain, but matériel could be sent, and the President, with Marshall's advice and assistance, had sent to Great Britain all the matériel America could afford to send without endangering her own security. But if there was nothing of immediate military consequence to discuss, Marshall's first meeting with Sir John Dill, the Chief of the Imperial General Staff, was important. Sir John Dill resembled an eagle. He was tall, precise, a little pedantic, given to long silences and ironic understatements, with a passion for mountaineering and riding. He was also an expert on the subject of the War between the States. Almost exactly Marshall's age, their careers had followed almost identical paths. While Marshall was in the Philippines, Dill had fought in the South African war against the Boers. Since then he had risen slowly, becoming Commandant of the Staff College at Camberley when Marshall was Assistant Commandant at Fort Benning. Afterwards Dill became director of military operations and intelligence at the War Office, and in the early stages of the war he had commanded the First Army Corps in France. Their instincts were the same, they were both experts in operations, they spoke the same language and even resembled one another, not so much in obvious physical characteristics, but in the way they held themselves, their lack of mannerisms, the play of expression on their features, in the posture, partly physical, partly spiritual, they assumed towards life. They had one other thing in common: they were both profoundly pessimistic about the immediate prospects of the war, Marshall because he did not know whether the extension to the Selective Service Act would be passed, and Dill because he feared an armored landing on the coast of Britain while Britain (in his view) was squandering her forces in Africa. Churchill blithely ordered a continual flow of reinforcements to the Middle East, and castigated Dill for his pessimism: his pessimism, however, remained.

Harry Hopkins, the perennial marriage-broker, had insisted on their meeting—Roosevelt had originally contemplated a meeting with Churchill without the participation of his military advisers—and the result went beyond his expectations. As often as possible they were together, and since neither has published an account of their conversations we can only surmise what they talked about.

Some of the things they discussed can be inferred by later events, others have been recorded briefly by other participants. The political discussions dominated the rest, but there was time for a prolonged examination of Western hemispheric defense, a projected landing on the Canary Islands by the British, the occupation of Icelandic ports by American marines, Lend-Lease priorities, the change in production schedules brought about by the opening of the Russian front. There were round-table talks with the President and Churchill in attendance, while they discussed the production of tanks and big bombers, and for the first time there were hints of an American occupation of northwest Africa. How should it be done? Someone spoke of Liberia and the establishment of air bases there, and from there they went on to discuss airfields at Dakar—Liberia was eventually forgotten, but the importance of Dakar remained. There were many informal talks at small gatherings, some on the *Tuscaloosa,* in Arnold's cabin, some on the *Augusta,* others on the *Prince of Wales.* It rained, and the fog hung over Placentia Bay. There were minor excursions. Marshall flew off, with Roosevelt's permission, to Gander Bay and St. John, simply to look at these places from the air: very soon they were to become an important stage in the ferry service from Scotland. Churchill spoke endlessly of armor: how this war had become more than any other war in the past a war of machines: it would become more mechanical before it was over. He called for more tanks and more airplanes than America was producing, and he outlined a strategy of cutting the German tentacles, hammering at their extended lines of communication, till the octopus in the end collapsed from exhaustion. The strategy did not commend itself to Marshall; he would have preferred a single lethal blow at the heart of the octopus; but he had not yet made up his mind on how Germany should be attacked—there were to be endless discussions on this subject later. On the last day of the conference, just as the British and American ships were about to start away, some good news came in: the extension to the Selective Service Act had been passed. Marshall's joy was tempered by the knowledge that it had been passed by the slenderest possible margin in the House of Representatives—203 votes against 202. When the conference ended, he climbed up on the bridge with the President and Admiral Stark, and watched the *Prince of Wales* steaming away in the fog, her band playing "The Star-Spangled Banner," as she disappeared in the direction of Iceland. Four months later she was to sink off the coast of Malaya.

The Atlantic Charter had been signed, but few military decisions came out of the conference. Dill had hoped to discuss major strategical problems, only to be confronted with Marshall's bland statement that he was empowered only to discuss the defense of the Western Hemisphere. Because Roosevelt was impatient with geography, the Western Hemisphere had come to include considerable portions of the Eastern Hemisphere: it included perhaps—no one was quite sure—the Cape Verde Islands, Dakar, Liberia, French and Spanish Morocco. Within these restricted areas Marshall could advance opinions on strategy; outside them he could advance no opinions whatsoever. They had talked briefly of the extension of Japanese influence in Asia, but there was no serious consideration of Japan as an enemy: Germany was to remain the main enemy. Dill proposed American-British-Dutch-Australian staff talks in Singapore. Again there was no decision. Marshall could receive the British reports, but he could not yet promise anything. He was wary, and he suspected the motives of Churchill, and he was never to be entirely at ease in Churchill's company.

Returning to Washington, Marshall's task was now clear. By the mercy of one vote he could produce an efficient army. Meanwhile he was faced with deficiencies in matériel as well as of men, shortages of tanks and airplanes—the production for July was seriously behind schedule. There was a desperate shortage of small arms .30 caliber bullets. These were the most severe shortages, but there were other shortages in guns and ships which would last until the late summer.

There were gasoline shortages, strikes in the defense industry, no immediate prospect of the mobilization of industry on the scale he desired. The studies which would lead later to the atomic bomb were already in progress; study of the proximity fuse had advanced so far that it would be test-fired a little later. The huge expansion of the armed services did not concern him particularly now, for the groundwork of the expansion had already been laid long before the extension of the Selective Service Act. His job now was to pore over maps, design plans against invasion or sudden attack, see that the Army machine was working smoothly. There were two enemies to be considered and two immense fronts; and it was probably inevitable that he should have been more concerned with the defense of America against Germany than against Japan. He did not know Japan, he could only guess at the motivations of the Japanese mind, and he was aware, from a constant stream of military reports sent by advisers in China, of deficiencies in Japanese military techniques.

At the end of July the situation in the Far East had taken a turn for the worse. On July 24 the Japanese had occupied southern Indo-China in flagrant defiance of the warnings of Roosevelt and the Secretary of State. Roosevelt had acted at once by freezing Japanese assets, an act which the Japanese regarded as only a little short of an act of war. On the following day Marshall and Stark sent a warning to the Pearl Harbor commanders saying that the embargo order was about to be issued, and concluding:

> Chief of Naval Operations and Army Chief of Staff do not anticipate immediate hostile action by the Japanese through the use of military means, but you are furnished this information in order that you may take appropriate precautionary measures against any possible eventualities.

Stark alerted his command under the pretence of sending it on maneuvers, and a few days later, for the first time, the threat of an attack on Hawaii began to appear very real, for Naval Intelligence advised Admiral Kimmel that "Japan has marshalled its full naval strength and is on a full wartime footing." They were woefully undermanned and underplaned. It was more than a month after the embargo order that the first B-17 Flying Fortresses made their difficult journey to the Philippines, having to go by way of Midway and Wake Islands and then south through Rabaul, Port Moresby or Port Darwin.

As for Hawaii the situation was clearly desperate. In the middle of August, General Martin, the air commander of the islands, sent in his report on the probable Japanese method of attack. He envisaged a strike by planes from six carriers, launched at dawn from a position two hundred and thirty-three miles out, and he said it would probably come from the north, west or south rather than from the east. He asked for a force of 180 B-17 Flying Fortresses as the minimum number required to provide complete aerial reconnaissance and protection from attack. At that time there were exactly 109 Flying Fortresses in the United States.

There were other factors besides the appearance of the Japanese Navy in full strength which suggested that the Japanese already considered their main enemy to be America. On July 7 the War Department sent a strangely complacent note to General Short in Hawaii, stressing the probability that the Japanese movements indicated only the possible seizure of development bases in Indo-China, "although an advance against the British and Dutch cannot be ruled out." There was at that time no mention of any possible advance against America, but there was an ominous footnote, which read: "They have ordered all Jap vessels in U.S. Atlantic ports to be west of Panama Canal by 1st of August."

This mysterious accumulation of ships in the neighborhood of the Panama Canal puzzled Marshall. He declared later:

> In August, I think it was, it was discovered that Japanese shipping on the East Coast of the United States had been directed to proceed immediately to the Caribbean, through the Panama Canal, certain boats on certain days, and finally sizeable numbers of boats in a very short period of time. Just what that meant we didn't know, of course. Since the Canal had been developed, we had always thought of sabotage there as being our greatest menace.

The discovery had come about as a result of the successful breaking of the Japanese naval code: the movements themselves did not necessarily mean that preparations were on foot for possible hostile action against the United States, but they could be interpreted in this way; and President Roosevelt wisely ordered the closing of the Canal to Japanese shipping "for technical reasons."

The danger was now beginning to creep closer. During this

period Marshall's mind was concentrated on the danger to the Canal, the Philippines and Hawaii in that order, and as far as American installations were concerned they were to remain in that order until the attack on Pearl Harbor.

There were good theoretical reasons for this choice. Anticipating Japanese movements in the Gulf of Siam, against the Malay Peninsula and the Dutch East Indies, he guessed that the Japanese would attack the British and the Dutch first, and only after the defeat of the British and Dutch empires in East Asia would they attack the American outposts; or if they attacked the Philippines, where General MacArthur, field marshal of the Philippine Commonwealth, had been recalled to active duty as a lieutenant general of the United States Army, they would do so as part of a concerted drive against Southeast Asia, a drive which would temporarily exhaust their energies. An isolated adventure against Hawaii was regarded as far too hazardous. It would have to take the form of a surprise raid, and surprise, as Marshall said later, "is either a triumph or a catastrophe." He expected the Japanese would "proceed somewhat conservatively rather than dash into great distances." In all this he showed, together with his G-2, General Sherman Miles, who had never had any duties in the Far East, a complete misapprehension of Japanese military psychology. Only two people, General Martin, the commander of the Army Air Force, and Admiral Bellinger, the commander of the Naval Air Force, appear to have foreseen what would happen; and though Marshall read their joint estimate of March 31, 1941, it did nothing to change his conception of the relative importance of Hawaii in comparison with the other outposts in the Pacific.

It was perhaps understandable. From every corner there came to his office urgent requests for matériel and men. To have sent adequate reinforcements to Hawaii and the Philippines would have left the United States in peril if there was a break in the defenses of Great Britain. He was not convinced that Great Britain would hold out. There was Alaska to be considered; there were the Maritime Provinces of the Soviet Union, which might be expected to fall to a Japanese attack; and there were the Dutch East Indies and Malaya loudly clamoring for arms. In the developing war, as it was fought by the Japanese, there were no certainties; the Japanese were assumed to be incalculable, and might therefore be expected to attack in any direction. It was impossible under these circumstances to make lists of countries which were in various degrees of danger: all were in danger.

How, then, did he decide which countries would receive American supplies?

Partly, as he admitted in the second Biennial Report, he was swayed by emotional impulses. Towards the end of August, 1941, representatives of the Dutch Government called at his office, and made a moving appeal for an initial allotment of twenty-five million rounds of small arms ammunition, to be sent immediately to the Dutch East Indies. As Marshall related the incident:

> They stated that they feared the disintegration of their ground forces unless at least a small amount of ammunition was promptly issued. We had an extremely critical situation here in the United States but the dilemma of these fine people was so tragic in the face of the Japanese threat that it was finally decided to accept the hazard of reducing the ammunition reserve for the troops in movement to Iceland to an extreme which would permit seven million rounds being turned over to the Dutch. Four million of these rounds were to be made quickly available by shipment from Manila, replacement shipments being started from San Francisco immediately.

Marshall also noted that the seven million rounds, which were then so urgently debated, were no more than the expected *daily* delivery of a plant due to go into production early in October.

Through July and August the attitude of the American government towards Japan had changed. Previously there had been hope of a working agreement for a Pacific peace. Now hope gradually disappeared, and at the same time the greatest confusion existed in the highest quarters about how America would meet the crisis; for even if Japan attacked only the British and Dutch empires, America was threatened. Desperately it was hoped that Japan could be contained by China, or exhausted by China, or in some mysterious way her power would be dissipated. Marshall and Admiral Stark, writing a memorandum for the President in the early days of September, assumed that Japan would attack northward towards

Russia, westward toward China, southward towards Malaya and the Dutch East Indies, and afterwards the Philippines.

This memorandum, called the "Joint Board Estimate of United States Over-all Production Requirements," was dated September 11. It had been called into existence by the President, who desired a professional summary of the military position on which to base production requirements. The document, in spite of its title, therefore says nothing about production, but goes into great detail on the military possibilities of the time, and there is internal evidence to show that Marshall was responsible for about two thirds of the report.

In this extremely lucid report, where the areas of danger are analyzed under twenty-six headings and a number of sub-headings, a posture is assumed, an attitude of mind is formulated. This attitude was strangely at variance with what might have been expected. Comparatively little importance was attached to the possibility of a Japanese onslaught on American Pacific bases other than the Philippines, it was hopeful about the progress of the war in Russia and extremely pessimistic about the possibilities of survival of the British Commonwealth. "Unless the losses of British merchant ships are greatly reduced," wrote the authors of this report, "or unless there is an internal collapse of Germany, it is the opinion of the Joint Board that the United Kingdom cannot continue indefinitely, no matter what industrial effort is put forth by the United States." Such sweeping verdicts occur throughout the report. The complexities of the situation are reduced to simple formulas; the dynamic of the fascist power was almost entirely overlooked. It was assumed, for example, that once Germany had conquered all Europe, she would wish to establish peace with the United States for several years; the same assumption was made of Japan, which was expected to establish an "East Asia Co-Prosperity Sphere" after conquering China, Russia, Siam, Malaya and the Dutch East Indies, and would thereupon welcome a period of established peace in which to gorge on her gains. Why either Germany or Japan were expected to grant the world the blessings of peace is never explained. References to the establishment of a comparatively long period of peace by Germany after the conquest of Europe occur twice, although in one paragraph it is admitted that "this concept cannot be accepted as certain, because it is conceivable that Germany might at once seek to gain footholds in the Western Hemisphere." One may well ask the underlying purpose of a memorandum which offers two diametrically opposed possibilities, and does nothing to assist in any judgment of probabilities.

As a military document the memorandum was not very valuable. As an indication of the minds of the men who were to become America's war leaders on the eve of the war, it possesses quite extraordinary importance. The pessimism concerning the fate of Great Britain probably derives from Sir John Dill, with his dark apprehensions of a German landing on the southwestern coast of Britain with twenty-four hundred tanks, which would fan out and envelop the country. As for Japan, the predominant attitude throughout the report is that she must be contained. "The principal strategic method employed by the United States in the immediate future," says the report, in italics, "should be the material support of present military operations against Germany, and their reinforcement by active participation in the war by the United States while holding Japan in check pending future developments." The optimism concerning the function of Japan in any future war seems to derive from Cordell Hull, who refused until the last moment to believe that war with Japan was inevitable. If Japan entered the war the Joint Board suggested that the proper strategic methods to be employed were "a strong defense of Siberia and Malaysia; an economic offensive through blockade; a reduction of Japanese military power through raids; and Chinese offensives against the Japanese forces of occupation."

The rather vague discussion of the ways a Japanese drive in the Pacific could be met becomes clearer when the Joint Board comes to discuss the security of the Western Hemisphere. Except for one sentence the whole of this paragraph bears the mark of Marshall's writing:

> The security of the Western Hemisphere against the extension into it of European or Asiatic political or military power is an essential of United States strategy. To provide this security under all eventualities, the United States must have naval, land and air forces in such positions that they can be made promptly available in both the Atlantic and

Pacific Oceans in strengths adequate for preventing invasion should the British Isles and Russia collapse. In this connection, an important question is whether or not Northwestern Africa and the Atlantic Islands are in German or in friendly hands. Similarly, Alaska, Hawaii and the Islands of the South Pacific Ocean have an important relation to the security of the Eastern Pacific. United States naval strength, built up in accordance with the approved program, should be adequate for defensive needs until 1944. However, if Germany is successful in Europe, and Japan is successful in the Far East, naval strength for defensive purposes must be increased even in excess of the present approved program. United States land and air forces may be required for the defense of the Western Hemisphere within the next few years, and it is necessary for Latin American countries to be provided with munitions and manufactured articles.

In these statements, delivered so categorically, can be discovered the seeds of the strategies which were to be developed later. Not all of them were to be accepted. There are moments as we read this document when the Chiefs of Staff appear like children playing with empires, their minds reeling at the wonders they behold, so that at times they speak almost incoherently. In this respect Stark's contributions are the more naïve, the more magnificently vague. A sentence like "If Germany and Japan are successful, naval strength must be increased . . ." suggests that the leader-writers could do this kind of thing better; and there is little satisfaction to be derived from the author's style, which is thick with clichés. Neither Stark nor Marshall were gifted with great imagination: nor was the report adequate to their responsibilities.

But if the report failed to give a likely picture of America in a world of arms, it showed clearly how Marshall had pinned his hopes on the Russian Army. An infantryman, believing like Napoleon that the infantry was "the queen of battles," he could see no hope of a German defeat without crushing blows by the Russian Army. He wrote:

The maintainence of an active front in Russia offers by far the best opportunity for a successful land offensive against Germany, because only Russia possesses adequate manpower, situated in favorable proximity to the center of German military power. For Russia, ground and aviation forces are most important. Predictions as to the result of the present conflict in Russia are premature. However, were the Soviet forces to be driven even beyond the Ural Mountains, and were they there to continue an organized resistance, there would always remain the hope of a final and complete defeat of Germany by land operations. The effective arming of Russian forces, both by the supply of munitions from the outside and by providing industrial capacity in the Volga Basin, or to the east of the Ural Mountains, would be one of the most important moves that could be made by the Associated Powers.

This belief in the near-invincibility of Russian land forces was to remain with Marshall throughout the war, and it was responsible for the bitter struggle which ensued between Marshall and Churchill, who was not prepared to open a second front at the risk of the annihilation of his own forces. It was characteristic of Marshall that in this passage, the most cogent of all, he should have succeeded in introducing one sentence ("For Russia, ground and aviation forces are most important") which might have been written by a child.

The report can be attacked for its insufficiencies, but it demonstrated certain fixed objectives which were of vast importance when the war broke out. The most important of these was the statement: "National policies can be effectuated in their entirety only through military victories outside this hemisphere." This meant that an imaginary wall could be constructed thousands of miles from the American coast, and on this wall the battle would be decided. The second most important statement concerned the nature of the war itself: it was seen clearly that Germany could not be defeated by the European powers then at war with her. If America's European enemies were to be defeated, it would be necessary for America to enter the war. The report foresaw the possibility that Russia might be militarily impotent by July 1, 1942, and that America would probably have to take part in an attack on Germany no later than July 1, 1943. At that date the American armed force would have to be increased to 10,045,658 men, made up of 1,100,000 men in the Navy (including the Naval Air Corps), 150,000 men in the Marine Corps, 2,050,000 men in the Army Air Force, and 6,745,658 in the Army Ground Forces. It was no wonder, when the Chicago *Tribune* succeeded in releasing a copy of the secret memorandum three days before Pearl

Harbor, that people gasped. So vast an army had never been envisaged in America before; nor had so vast an act of treachery occurred, for when the full details of the Joint Army-Navy Board were taken from the secret files, the Germans and the Japanese were in a position to read, in all its strength and weakness, the American military mind.

Meanwhile Marshall was hard at work on the reorganization of the Army, selecting new officers, regardless of age and the seniority lists, and preparing plans for the sharp increase in enlisted men which would begin at the end of the year. September was the month when the wheels began to turn. The destroyer deal transferring fifty American destroyers to Great Britain had been announced on September 3; two days later, unknown to the American Government, Prince Konoye had presented to Emperor Hirohito his "Plans for the Prosecution of the Policy of the Imperial Government," which gave the first resounding threats of war, for the plans stated that if Japanese terms were not met by the beginning of October, "then we shall immediately get ready for war against America, England and Holland." There were signs and portents. Unknown to the War Department in Washington, though known in Hawaii, was the ominous request from Tokyo to the Japanese consul in Honolulu dated September 24, asking for information concerning types and classes of ships at Pearl Harbor, all this to be mapped out according to five sub-areas. There were to be more requests for information about the ships in the harbor; mysteriously, they were thought to be unimportant. There were dangers closer at hand. The Governor of Dutch Guiana, an important source of bauxite, was threatened, and American troops on Trinidad, now leased from the British, were alerted. As Marshall pored over his maps in the War Department, and then spread them out after dinner at Fort Myer at night, it began to seem a reasonable possibility that the war would begin with an attack on one of the innumerable islands. Which one was waiting for the blow?

He did not know, and he could only guess, hoping the pieces of the jigsaw puzzle would fit together before it was too late. Until December 7, they refused to fit together. He was in charge of preparing the country for an inevitable war, but his mind was preoccupied by a hundred details which should have been dealt with by others. There were Congressional hearings, more than he could bear, for they were more time-consuming than any other chore. He complained bitterly and ineffectively about them to an American Legion Convention held at Milwaukee on September 15:

> I submit to you men of the Legion the impossibility of developing an efficient army if decisions which are purely military in nature are continually subjected to investigation, cross-examination, debate, ridicule and public discussion by pressure groups, and by individuals with only a superficial knowledge of military matters, or of the actual facts in the particular case. I submit that there is a clear line of demarcation between the democratic freedom of discussion which we are determined to preserve and a destructive procedure which promotes discontent and destroys confidence in the army.

Unhappily, there was no clear line of demarcation, and public discussion by pressure groups was to haunt him long after the war had been finally won.

There were other fears. He saw a strange similarity between the plight of America in the autumn of 1940 and the plight of France the previous spring. Then there was the matter of the divided command, which he discussed at length in the same speech to the American Legion. He pointed out that in Belgium, France, Norway, Greece, Crete and the Middle East the lack of unity of command between air and ground forces had led to reverses; the air arm had been independent during the Battle of Britain, but this, he explained, was an exceptional case with little application to the problems of hemispheric defense. He spoke of the Italian air force, "which nurtures the theory of total war from the air," though it had failed to be effective. He pointed out that the Germans were in better case, a whole campaign involving all three arms being organized by a single Chief of Staff responsible only to Hitler. He saw, too, that the characteristics which make Americans potentially the best soldiers in the world could be a source of weakness. "Racially, we are not a homogeneous people like the British, who can glorify a defeat by their stubborn tenacity and dogged discipline," he said. "We have no common racial group, and we have deliberately cultivated individual initiative and independence of thought and action. Our men are intelligent and resourceful to an unusual degree. These characteristics may be explosive or positively destructive in a military organization, especially under adverse conditions, unless the leadership is wise and determined, and unless the leader commands the complete respect of his men."

It was strange that he should subscribe to the heresy of a racial myth; nor is it true that the British are a homogeneous people. At those moments he was a little like Sun Yat-sen who complained to the end of his life that the Chinese were like shifting sand, and like Sun Yat-sen he knew that if one could find the appropriate mold they could be made to assume hard shapes. It was partly weariness. There were more long appearances at the House of Representatives, this time before the Subcommittee on Appropriations, where he defended at length a defense-aid estimate of $2,255,575,667, and was confronted with a lead article in the Washington *Post* which spoke of military decisions involving stopping the draft and sending all arms output to Great Britain and Russia. Against such articles he could only plead that they did a tragic disservice to the American cause and offered hostages to Germany. To the committee he explained in detail the bases upon which Lend-Lease were made under six sub-headings, and pointed out that the needs of Great Britain continually outran the supplies available. It was the same in other parts of the globe. The Chinese appealed for matériel and men. The decision was in Marshall's hands, and he decided against sending armed forces to China except for a strengthening of the American Volunteer Corps, which came to be known as the "Flying Tigers." He also ordered the sending of matériel, and at the same time he begged Roosevelt to deliver no ultimatum to Japan. There were insoluble problems connected with the sending of Lend-Lease to Great Britain and China: he was obsessed with the thought that when matériel was removed from the United States, it would become increasingly difficult to train the soldiers. The most urgent requests were being made by MacArthur in the Philippines. By October half a million tons of supplies and twenty thousand fully equipped and fairly well-trained troops were available as reinforcements for the Philippine Islands. The desperate race, which would affect the fortunes of the Pacific, was on. There were few troopships available. Marshall arranged for passenger ships to be converted hastily to troop carriers. Eleven of these troopships were scheduled to sail between

November 21 and December 9; none of these troopships arrived at their destination.

In early November the signs of war came crowding one on top of the other. On November 3 Ambassador Grew reported to Secretary Hull: "Japan may resort with dangerous and dramatic suddenness to measures which might make war inevitable with the United States." On November 5 General Hideki Togo became curiously expansive on the subject of the date on which the war would break out. "It is absolutely necessary," he wrote to Nomura, "that all the arrangements for signing of the agreement with the United States be completed by the 25th of this month." A few days later the British Ambassador in Tokyo reported that he believed a Japanese attack on the Dutch East Indies was imminent; a little later the official British view was that the attack would come on Thailand. As far back as January there were rumors, reported by Grew, that an attack employing all the Japanese military facilities would fall upon Pearl Harbor; Grew added the note that "the plan seems fantastic."

About this time in November a photograph of Marshall was taken by Wilfred Morgan in the Chief of Staff's office in the War Department Munitions Building. The Chief of Staff sits with his elbows leaning on the desk. The face is hardly recognizable, gaunt and hollow-cheeked, with heavy bruised shadows under the eyes which stare straight ahead, the lips are pursed in a tight line and he has the expression of a man quivering under intolerable strains. Understandably, the photograph has not been published.

By November 25 it had become reasonably certain that the Japanese would launch their campaign, and that it was not directed towards small islands only but to the conquest of the world. On that afternoon a Japanese task force sailed from the Kuriles for Pearl Harbor.

That morning there was a meeting of the War Council in the White House. There Secretary Hull gave it as his view that "the last stage had been reached and the safeguarding of our national security was in the hands of the Army and Navy." Marshall remembered later that the Secretary said: "These fellows mean to fight; you will have to be prepared." In the afternoon the War Department received news of five Japanese divisions which had embarked at Shanghai and were now sighted south of Formosa. In this atmosphere Churchill's message to the President, received at dawn the next day, saying that "we feel that the Japanese are most unsure of themselves," was strangely discordant. In fact, the Japanese were very sure of themselves, and the task force was one day nearer to Pearl Harbor. Later in the morning the Army-Navy Joint Board met to prepare a memorandum for the President on the military steps to be taken if negotiations with the Japanese failed. The memorandum, written by Stark and Marshall, read:

> If the current negotiations end without agreement Japan may attack the Burma Road; Thailand; Malaya; the Netherlands East Indies; the Philippines; the Russian Maritime Province.
>
> There is little probability of an immediate Japanese attack on the Maritime Provinces, because of the strength of Russian forces. Recent Japanese troop movements all seem to have been southward.... The most essential thing now, from the United States viewpoint, is to gain time.... The process of reinforcement is being continued. Of great immediate concern is the safety of the Army convoy now near Guam, and the Marine Corps convoy just leaving Shanghai. Ground forces to the total of 21,000 are due to sail from the United States by December 8, 1941, and it is important that the troop reinforcements reach the Philippines before hostilities commence.

On the afternoon of November 26 Marshall left Washington to attend the First Army's maneuvers, then reaching their climax along the Peedee river in North Carolina. For the next thirty-six hours the military head of the Army was unavailable. He had asked desperately for a breathing space, he had compiled a list of possible Japanese objectives, which omitted Hawaii, and he had no means of knowing that while he was away a communication would be sent from the War Department which would be the subject of long enquiries afterwards. This communication, partly written by Secretary Stimson, partly by Admiral Stark and partly by Brigadier General Gerow, the chief of War Plans, was sent to the Pacific commands in slightly different forms according to the needs of the commands. The message to General Short read:

> #472 Negotiations with Japan appear to be terminated to all practical purposes with only barest possibilities that Japanese Government might come back and offer to

Lieutenant Colonel Marshall as a member of Pershing's staff in Washington, about 1920.

General Marshall as Chief of Staff, in 1939.

General Marshall after landing in France, June 1944.

General Marshall at the Pentagon, January 1945.

continue. Japanese future action unpredictable but hostile action possible at any moment. If hostilities cannot, repeat cannot, be avoided the United States desires that Japan commit the first overt act. This policy should not, repeat not, be construed as restricting you to a course of action that might jeopardize your defense. Prior to hostile Japanese action you are directed to undertake such reconnaissance and other measures as you deem necessary but these measures should be carried out so as not, repeat not, to alarm civil population or disclose intent. Report measures taken. Should hostilities occur you will carry out the tasks assigned in Rainbow 5 so far as they pertain to Japan. Limit dissemination of this highly secret information to minimum essential officers.

Though the cable went out under Marshall's name, it was not written by Marshall. According to Stimson, the message was sent primarily to guide MacArthur in the Philippines, and Stimson was responsible for the first sentence, which originally read: "Negotiations with Japan have been terminated." This was later softened after a telephone conversation with Hull. The second sentence was inserted either by General Gerow or by Colonel Charles W. Bundy, who was to be killed in an airplane accident shortly afterwards when on his way to Hawaii to make an examination of the situation for Marshall. The third sentence—"If hostilities cannot, repeat cannot, be avoided, the United States desires that Japan commit the first overt act"—was inserted, according to Marshall's later testimony, on the specific instructions of the President. The following sentence was inserted by Gerow or Bundy, who seems also to be responsible for the wording of the rest. The final message, the work of many hands, was confusing, as such messages generally are, and no lessons appear to have been learned from the failure of this message to accomplish its purpose.

When Marshall returned to Washington on the next day, the 28th, the damage had not yet been done, for there was still time to clear up the confusion of the long message with its cautious restrictions. The message, which could be divided into two parts, one dealing with what General Short should do in the event of war, the other with what he should do before the war, gave the appearance of being deliberately designed to minimize in General Short's mind the seriousness of the situation; or so at least General Henry D. Russell believed, commenting on the peculiarly repetitive message at the board of enquiry which was set up later. He added that he was not sure this was a fair question; it might be pure opinion; and to this Marshall agreed.

The trap was sprung by General Gerow in the words: "Report measures taken." The reply came shortly afterwards. It read:

> Reurad (*Re* your radio) #472 twenty-seventh report Department alerted to prevent sabotage. Liaison with Navy.

This extraordinary reply, which meant that General Short had alerted his command to prevent sabotage and nothing else, was received by General Gerow, and together with another reply from General MacArthur, was passed into Marshall's office. The two replies were clipped together, the one from MacArthur on top. Marshall signed the top one, left the other unsigned and confessed afterwards that he had no recollection of having seen it. The presumption is that he did not see it. Whatever the cause, the message from Short seems to have passed unobserved, and its implications were not weighed until later; and though the primary responsibility inevitably falls on General Gerow, the secondary responsibility falls heavily on Marshall for not following-up the November 27 order to the Pacific commands. He had not mentioned Hawaii in his memorandum to the President, and was clearly not thinking in terms of an attack on the Island. He had written in a letter to Short on February 7: "The risk of sabotage and the risk involved in a surprise raid by air and submarine constitute the real perils of the situation." Short had taken precautions against the first risk and none against the second.

The alarm bells were ringing in Washington, but the War Department heard them as though they came from a long way away. The roar of the bells was deafening by the time Marshall went on another inspection trip in the first week of December. Everyone knew that Japan would begin with a surprise attack, but everyone hoped it would be directed against Thailand, Malaya, the Dutch East Indies or the Russian Maritime Provinces. Perhaps it would fall on the Philippines as the Japanese cut a huge swath southward. It was conceivable that there would be a shattering attack on the United States' west coast. "I would not have been a bit surprised if Japanese submarines had appeared off San Francisco," said Admiral Stark. "I was not expecting an air attack on Hawaii." "We did not, as far as I recall, anticipate an attack upon Hawaii," Marshall admitted three years later. It was as though the place marked Hawaii in their minds had been anesthetized in their minds, as though the warnings of Grew and Knox in January, Marshall's instructions to Short, Martin's brilliant report of March and Admiral Kimmel's Confidential Letter to the Fleet on October 14, speaking of the possibility of a surprise attack on ships in Pearl Harbor, had all passed by default. For the most part they had hoped there would be no attack, but if it fell they believed it would fall on the Philippines.

On the night of December 5, the Japanese naval radio sent a coded message which was picked up by the radio in Washington. The message read: "Climb Mount Niitaka." In the strange pattern of clues which, like criminals, the Japanese had provided, here was perhaps the most obvious clue of all. Mount Niitaka is a volcanic mountain, and on December 7 the volcano exploded.

CHAPTER TEN

The Morning of Pearl

We may never know exactly what happened in the War Department on the morning when Pearl Harbor was bombed. The testimony is conflicting, the memories of officers were clouded by the quick pace of events which occurred immediately afterwards, a confusion of loyalties was aroused, and conscious or unconscious efforts were made to shield some of the participants; but even now, so various were the testimonies, we do not know who was shielding or who was being shielded.

The story, as it was unfolded later in four separate enquiries, was never completely elucidated, but the main outlines are clear and can be told simply.

At noon on Saturday, December 6, there began to emerge from the Army's code machine in Washington the opening statements of a long message from Foreign Minister Togo to Nomura, the Japanese Ambassador, in reply to the American proposal of November 26. The third paragraph of the statement explained that the time for presenting the memorandum to Cordell Hull would be divulged later, while the second paragraph stated that the whole message would comprise fourteen parts and emphasized the extreme delicacy of the occasion. During the next seven and a half hours the message continued to come through the code machine, until thirteen of the expected fourteen paragraphs were received. By 9:30 p.m. the message had been taken to the Oval Study of the White House, where Roosevelt was in conference with Hopkins. The thirteen clauses were repetitious, frenzied and evidently written by Togo himself in a mood of capricious anger: there is something exceedingly artificial in their constant repudiation and rejection of the President's proposals. There were the often-repeated claims that America had failed to understand the realities of East Asia, was attempting to encircle Japan and had disregarded her honor and prestige. In the thirteenth paragraph Togo rejected the American proposal outright. There remained the missing fourteenth paragraph, which would presumably contain the Japanese counter-proposals or a declaration of war. Roosevelt was perfectly aware of the seriousness of the message and discussed it briefly with Hopkins, saying how much he regretted that America could not strike the first blow and prevent any form of surprise, but though he regarded the message as serious, he did not regard it as urgent. He was awaiting the answer to a direct message to the Emperor Hirohito, which was sent to the Tokyo embassy only half an hour before. "I address myself to Your Majesty at this moment," he wrote, "in the fervent hope that Your Majesty may, as I am doing, give thought to the definite emergency to ways of dispelling the dark clouds." There was at least a reasonable chance that a message addressed by one head of a state to another would delay the approach of the war, even though war had become almost inevitable. He asked for a call to be put through to Admiral Stark, but Stark was at the National Theater. The President decided not to have the Admiral paged, because this might cause public alarm. He called the Admiral later, and discussed the situation briefly. He did not ask for a call to be put through to Marshall.

About the time the President received the thirteen paragraphs Marshall was returning after an inspection tour to his house at Fort Myer. At some time during the afternoon he had received the "pilot message," but he had failed to see its significance and took no steps to arrange that subsequent paragraphs should be telephoned to him at Fort Myer; yet he was, or should have been, aware of the extreme danger of the time because two weeks previously the President had discussed with him, Knox, Stimson and Stark the possibility of an attack without warning "perhaps as soon as next Monday." He evidently forgot he had seen the "pilot message," for he afterwards denied having seen it, though General Sherman Miles and Colonel Bratton both remembered they had delivered the message to him. It is possible that he failed to realize the importance of the message, or the message may have been mislaid—nothing is known with certainty.

At one point during the Congressional enquiry Marshall said: "I don't know where I actually was" (on the Saturday night), and at another time he stated categorically: "I was not aware on the late evening or night of December 6 that a long intercepted message was coming in and was in process of being deciphered, translated and submitted to the Secretary of State."

By midnight on the Saturday the thirteen paragraphs had been seen by the President, Harry Hopkins, Secretary Knox, Admiral Wilkinson (the head of naval intelligence), Captain John Beardall (the President's naval aide), General "Pa" Watson (the President's military aide) and Commander Kramer, who was in charge of the translation and distribution of intercepts—altogether eight people. They were not seen by four people who should have seen them. These were Cordell Hull, who found them waiting on his desk the next morning, General Gerow (in charge of military war plans) who was never able to remember where he spent the evening, Admiral Richmond Kelly Turner (in charge of naval war plans) and General Marshall. It has never been explained why General Miles did not telephone Marshall as soon as he heard the news.

Marshall's habits were fixed. He would reach his office at the War Department on weekdays around seven-thirty, and around nine on Sundays. During the winter on Sundays he usually breakfasted at eight o'clock, and within half an hour he would be on his way to the office. But it was a fine clear day, and he decided to take a long canter through the Virginia woods on horseback. He liked, during these rides to think out his problems, and that Sunday there were a number of very pressing problems indeed. The most important of them were the possibility of war with Japan and the fact that the Chicago *Tribune,* with an incredible lack of regard for the safety of the country, had just published the secret documents forming the report of the Joint Army-Navy Board; and to Marshall the very publication of these documents brought the war nearer. No one knew how the documents had been obtained. These documents contained plans for a total military establishment of over ten million men and an expeditionary force against Germany by the summer of 1943. Their publication would inevitably harm the Army; and with these somber thoughts Marshall started out on his morning canter, apparently oblivious of the possibility that decisive actions were about to take place, were in fact taking place while he was out riding.

At about the moment when Marshall set out on a fifty-minute canter, Colonel Bratton, the chief of the Far Eastern section of Military Intelligence, tried to reach him by telephone. The orderly at Fort Myer answered that the General was on horseback. Bratton then told the orderly to find Marshall: "Get assistance, if necessary, and find Marshall. Ask him to—tell him who I am and tell him to go to the nearest telephone, that it is vitally important that I communicate with him at the earliest possible moment." Colonel Bratton continued to phone at intervals. The orderly apparently made no serious effort to find Marshall, who received news of Bratton's attempts to reach him only after he had returned to his house and taken his shower. On the telephone Marshall learned that some documents had come in—the messages which had been received in code could not be discussed over the telephone—and realizing the seriousness of these messages, he decided to drive straight to the War Department. It was then a few minutes before 10:30 a.m. For roughly two hours the fourteenth paragraph had been lying on his desk, and for more than five hours it was known in the War Department, for the paragraph had come through at about 5 a.m. Colonel Bratton who had reached his office at about eight o'clock saw the message shortly after he arrived. For a brief while the destiny of America had been in Colonel Bratton's hands. If he had come to the office a little earlier, if he had read the message a little more quickly, if he had telephoned to Marshall even a few seconds before he actually telephoned, if it had occurred to him to order an airplane up to find Marshall as he went riding alone on that sunlit morning, if any of these things had happened, the message which should have been sent to Hawaii might have been received in time. Meanwhile, in a kind of divine remoteness from the world and its activities, Marshall was riding the horse which was called *Prepare*.

In the Austrian Army a special medal was awarded to those who deliberately disobeyed the orders of their superiors, and so brought victory about. One of the tragedies of that tragic morning lay in the fact that orders were implicitly obeyed when they had become meaningless. There was no real reason why the contents of the message should not have been delivered to Marshall by telephone, for the chance that a Japanese was tapping the telephone line was excessively remote. Sitting in his house at Fort Myer, Marshall could still have saved Hawaii; and the time he spent in his car driving to the War Department was time wasted when every moment was precious.

In the various enquiries which followed, the time of arrival of the fourteenth paragraph acquired enormous importance. In fact, it was no more important than the rest. The new paragraph said very little that was not already included in the previous thirteen, but it spoke with greater finality. It stated that the Japanese Government no longer regarded an agreement as possible, and the hope of peaceful cooperation was finally abandoned. The mysterious message still made very little sense. Togo was evidently repeating his weary accusations against America to keep his courage up. But why? Something was still missing. Sinister clues were being unraveled by the code machine, but the time and place of the murder were still uncertain. Admiral Wilkinson had come to the conclusion that there were "fighting words" in the fourteenth paragraph, but Admiral Stark was not certain and advised against sending a further warning to the Philippines.

At almost the same time that Marshall finally contacted Bratton, Commander Kramer came upon the one clue he had been searching for ever since he arrived at the office earlier in the morning. The message had been monitored at 4:37 a.m. on the Pacific Coast. It had then been teletyped, then decoded and translated in Washington by 10:30 a.m. The message read:

> Re my #902
> Will the ambassador please submit to the United States Government (if possible to the Secretary of State) our reply to the United States at 1:00 p.m. on the 7th, your time.

Commander Kramer decided rightly that the Japanese had decided to present their ultimatum and launch their first attack instantaneously; by 1 p.m. Washington time the first bombs would have fallen. This message was sent off at once to the eleven people who were entitled to receive the intercepts.

Marshall arrived at his office at the War Department shortly after 11:00 a.m.* to find the fourteen paragraphs laid on his desk. He read them carefully, weighing the implications of each phrase, and at 11:25 Colonel Bratton and General Miles entered the room with the last brief final message which knit all the other paragraphs together. Marshall was absorbed in the reading of the paragraphs, and it was five minutes before they were able to attract his attention. When he saw the "1 o'clock" message he called General Gerow to his office by telephone and held a conference with the three men who were now in his office.

The conference was brief. He said he felt that the Japanese Government's instructions to deliver the note at an exact hour and time might have considerable significance; he did not quite know what the significance was, but the warning was clear—as he said afterwards, there passed through his mind the thought that "something, somewhere, was very definitely related to that hour." An alert message must be sent out at once. He picked up the telephone and reached Admiral Stark. Did Admiral Stark agree that the Pacific commanders should be alerted? Stark did not think so. There had after all been a large number of warnings; why add to them? Marshall put down the telephone and began to write in longhand the penciled draft of an alert message to be sent to the four commands principally affected. These were MacArthur's command, the Caribbean Defense Command, the Hawaiian Department and the Fourth Army with its headquarters in San Francisco. Marshall's message read:

> #529 7th Japanese are presenting at 1 p.m. eastern standard time today what amounts to an ultimatum also they are under orders to destroy their code machine immediately. Just what significance the hour set may have we do not know but be on alert accordingly.

He had reached thus far when he decided that the message was unsatisfactory without a similar message from Stark to the naval

---

*The exact time of Marshall's arrival at his office is of some crucial importance, and either Marshall himself or the stenographers at the various hearings have unwittingly confused the scholar who attempts to be precise. Marshall is reported in the monumental pages of the Congressional Enquiry as having said: "I arrived about ten o'clock" (Vol. 37, p. 826), "I arrived about 11 o'clock" (Vol. 29, p. 2308), and "Incidentally I am quite certain that I arrived at the office before 11:30 a.m. on that morning" (Vol. 29, p. 2409). The evidence would seem to show that the second of these statements is correct.

commanders. He again telephoned to Stark, who was at the White House, and discussed the sending of a similar message by the Chief of Naval Operations. Once again Stark pointed out that a plethora of warnings had been issued, but he agreed to Marshall's suggestion that the words "Inform naval authorities of this communication" should be added. Marshall read out the message. His three advisers agreed that this was the proper message to send. Colonel Bratton was told to take the penciled draft to the Message Center. There was some discussion about whether the message should be typed, but time was against them—it was typed later in the day and entered in the records. A few moments later Colonel Bratton returned to Marshall's office. Asked how soon the message would arrive in Manila and Oahu, Colonel Bratton said it would arrive in both places in half an hour. The messages, filed at the Message Center at exactly twelve noon, would if they were delivered according to plan provide each of the four commands with exactly half an hour warning. In order to be entirely clear in his own mind how long the message would take to reach its various destinations, Marshall then sent Colonel Bundy, an officer of the War Plans Division in immediate charge of all matters pertaining to the Pacific, together with Bratton, to the Message Center. They returned with the same information as before. As Marshall remembered the events afterwards, he sent them out once again, saying he could not understand their explanations of how long it would take to decode the message. When Bratton had been to the Message Center three times, and Bundy twice, he felt reasonably satisfied that the messages would be delivered on time. On one of the occasions when Bratton was leaving the room, General Gerow said: "Tell them to give first priority to the Philippines." According to the information now in their hands, the message would be encoded in three minutes, on the air in eight, and in the hands of the commands in twenty minutes or half an hour.

  The surprising thing is that the matter was not pursued. It was assumed that the Message Center would operate with normal efficiency. Marshall made no effort to use the scrambler telephone, which could have brought him into direct contact with Short in Hawaii, claiming that a number of factors influenced him against using the telephone. He was afraid the Japanese would detect the message and put the blame for the war on the War Department. He said later: "The Japanese would have grasped at most any straw to bring to such portions of our public that doubted our integrity of action that we were committing an act which forced action on their part." Above all, he felt there was a need for extreme secrecy in the whole matter, for it was necessary to prevent the Japanese from knowing that their code had been broken. The message therefore had to be sent by code, though a coded message often and nearly always takes hours to decode, while the scrambler telephone could have brought the message to Hawaii instantaneously. The scrambler telephone was not as safe as code, but it was reasonably safe, and in a time of crisis the reasonable safety of the scrambler telephone was preferable to the hazards of a coded message which had to be decoded and delivered within half an hour to be of any use.

The fate of the message was now in the hands of the Message Center. They discovered there were static difficulties which prevented them from raising Pearl Harbor over the Army radio, and they decided to send the message to Western Union for commercial transmission. The message was accordingly sent through the Western Union connection in San Francisco to Hawaii. The Honolulu office of Western Union was some distance from Fort Shafter, where Short had his headquarters. The telegram was given to a messenger boy a few minutes before the first bombs fell. The boy spent the next two hours hiding in a ditch, and the telegram was not decoded and delivered to Short's adjutant general until 2:58 p.m. (Honolulu time), a little over seven hours after the raid began. Marshall could reflect, with an eerie sense that the fates were working towards a climax, that he had been unwittingly used by them to make the biggest blunder of his life. A single word delivered on the scrambler telephone or even in clear would have alerted Short in time. He had not delivered the message, though a number of other messages had been sent previously to Short urging him to meet preparations for an attack; but it was only during the space of an hour that morning that the full scope of the attack had been envisaged in the War Department. When the real test came, the Chief of Staff acted with an overwhelming fear that the country was divided and that the Japanese must be placated to the very last minute. The failure was in psychology as well as in communications.

If the blame rests squarely on Marshall, who later admitted that he had made "a tragic mistake" in not replying to General Short's report of November 27 and accepted the responsibility for not giving a full war alert to General Short, the blame lay also on the pattern of American command with its water-tight compartments, the Navy existing in isolation from the Army; and there was pathos in those wasted moments spent by Marshall in telephoning Admiral Stark, asking whether the Navy should be informed. One error lay in the divided command, the lack of liaison between them. Another error lay in the inefficiency of General Short and Admiral Kimmel, who had received many alerts and should have realized that the danger of attack was growing progressively nearer, for they had only to read the Honolulu newspapers to know that the Japanese were approaching the point of no return. These were serious errors, not to be minimized, but there were also other errors which lay within the military mind and were remarkably evident in Marshall's mind. Stimson had written in his diary on November 25: "The question was how we should maneuver them into the position of firing the first shot without allowing too much danger to ourselves." Commenting on these words at a Congressional hearing, Marshall replied: "I took a decision of this kind—at least I take it now—was a discussion of the diplomatic procedure involved, having in mind that it was the accepted thought in all our minds at that time that if we were forced to take offensive action, immediate offensive action, that it would be a most serious matter as to its interpretation by the American people, *whether we should have a united nation, or whether we would have a divided nation in getting into a world conflict.*" His fear of a divided country sprang from many causes, as much from his knowledge of the War between the States as from the extraordinary power of the isolationists, but it was essentially a fear which, as the chief responsible military officer, he had no right to show or even to admit to himself. The halting sentence betrays him, and perhaps explains the delay.

The mind of the military officer, accustomed to give sharp commands and receive implicit obedience, is usually at a loss when dealing with the complexities of international and social affairs, where there are no strict demarcations of rank, where orders are not necessarily obeyed, where there are no fixed traditions, and loyalties are often abandoned at the first sight of danger. Small countries can exert pressures out of any relationship to their size; small social groups can bring huge forces into play without anyone outside the group suspecting that the forces have come into existence. The subtleties of the play of social forces are normally incomprehensible to the military mind; and Marshall, with no training in sociology and little enough in international affairs, was in no position to compute how the Japanese would employ the social forces of Asia to their own ends, or how inevitable it was that they should attempt to conquer Asia. Every kind of warning had been given to him; when the time came he was unprepared. He had thought, inevitably, in terms of a surprise attack. He had not considered the possibility of a surprise attack *in all directions.* Because he was cautious, he assumed the Japanese would be cautious. To his extreme surprise they threw caution to the winds. "As it was," he said later, "they went without regard to any fears, and went out on the end of the plank through all of Malaysia, Indonesia and the New Guinea district." They also went to Pearl Harbor.

  The news of the attack reached the War Department shortly after it was received in the Navy radio station at Washington. The message, very brief, said: "Air raid on Pearl Harbor. This is not drill." This was at 1:50 p.m. It was not until 2:28 p.m., more than half an hour later, that Stark was able to confirm to the President that the attack had caused severe damage and some loss of life, though no one suspected that the single raid had produced more than three thousand casualties. Two minutes later the President was in his study on the second floor of the White House, writing a news release to be given to the press at 3 p.m., and still the telephone from the Navy Department kept ringing: it continued to ring all afternoon and part of the night, giving more details of the raid. It rang at intervals during the first war conference which began at 3:05 p.m., attended by Secretary Stimson, Secretary Knox, Harry Hopkins and Captain John Beardall. A little later Secretary Hull and Marshall appeared, both grey with shock, Hull shaking his head nervously as he recounted how the Japanese envoys had delayed seeing him until long after the bombs had fallen, and then he had turned to them and spoken of their "infamous falsehoods and distortions on a scale so huge that I never imagined until today that any Government on this planet was capable of uttering them," a strange enough statement to make, for Hitler had then been in power for more than six years. The President turned to Marshall. What was being done? Where were the troops? What dispositions had been made? Was there news from MacArthur? Marshall replied quickly and impatiently, explaining the dispositions of the troops and the Air Force. He had ordered General MacArthur to execute the war plan especially designed to come into operation in the event of a Japanese attack. Haunted by the possibilities of vast outbreaks of sabotage and assassination, he explained that he had given orders for the War Department to be guarded by the military and suggested a military guard to the White House. The President refused the last request, and summoned a conference for 8:30 p.m.; by then perhaps there would be some certainties to report. Marshall worked through the afternoon. At 8:30 the Cabinet meeting took place, with Stimson, Knox, Hull, Stark, Marshall and a few others, but the ground had already been gone over, there was little to add, and they retired in less than an hour to make way for the Congressional leaders, who debated whether the President would issue a declaration of war, while the President kept his own counsels.

The war was now on. Speaking the next day to a conference of Negro newspaper editors, Marshall said: "It is now only a few hours since this nation was attacked by one of the great armed forces of the world. . . . I know that this news has brought to all our people a new realization of our common destiny as free men." He spoke for a while of the one or two Negro divisions which would be activated shortly, about the training of Negro officers and how he hoped there would be increasing understanding between the War Department and the Negroes; then he hurried away to the maps which showed the American Pacific outposts looking like pebbles flung up by the advancing Japanese wave.

CHAPTER ELEVEN

The First Gropings

That Christmas, Washington was in turmoil. The news of continual defeats crackled over the radio, lights burned in the Pentagon and the White House late at night, there was frost on the ground, a brooding storm in the air, an atmosphere of desperate urgency. This was the beginning of a long war, a time of shadowy confusion and insoluble problems, before the broad strategic lines could be painted on the maps, and the springs were uncoiled. The Western Allies were separated by three thousand miles of ocean. It was necessary that Churchill and Roosevelt should meet and hammer out a technique for thwarting the Axis powers; and in those early days of the war both knew that there could only be an improvised technique. The enemy had gained surprise. The Allies could only stiffen and resist and plan a long-term strategy. Later there would come the sharpening of the claws, the huge deliberate blows which would rip the enemy apart. Some ironist called the first of the great conferences held during the war by the name of Arcadia.

When Churchill arrived in Washington on December 22 for the Arcadia Conference he brought with him a document written on the *Duke of York* during the Atlantic crossing. This brilliant document, about the same length as the memorandum composed in September by Stark and Marshall and covering the same ground, contained conclusions which were sometimes diametrically opposed to the conclusions arrived at by the Chiefs of Staff. Briefly, Churchill envisaged a war in the West which would comprise the occupation and control by Great Britain and the United States of the whole of the North- and West-African possessions of France, and Britain would control the North African shore from Tunis to Egypt—Africa was the springboard. Churchill expected the Germans to swallow all of France. He felt reasonably certain that the Germans would not penetrate into Persia, Iraq or Syria. He believed that the Spanish would refuse the Germans free passage to Gibraltar. He was sure the British Isles would remain intact. He thought the war could be ended only by the defeat of the German armies in Europe, and he hoped that by the spring of 1943 forty armored divisions with a million men of all arms would be poised ready for an attack on the European mainland. As for the Japanese enemy, he saw that the battle would have to be waged largely by the use of aircraft carriers and convoys, and this meant the creation of a superior battle fleet in the Pacific. They must be fought from island to island, "at every point where we have a fair chance, so as to keep them burning and extended." Japan was to be worn down by a process of slow bloodletting, as each small tentacle in the Pacific was cut off, while Germany was to be crushed by huge, accumulated forces based on North Africa and Great Britain.

A week before Churchill arrived, Marshall had come to roughly the same conclusions, though he was never to attach to the North African campaign the importance which Churchill attached to it. He agreed with Churchill's verdict on the Pacific. There were high military officers prepared to write off the Philippines. Stark, shocked by the slaughter of his ships at Pearl Harbor, could see no way by which the Navy could keep the line open. Marshall insisted that it had to be held open whatever the cost, and there began in the middle of December the long, hazardous and (as it happened) nearly valueless despatch of blockade-runners which tried to make their way into Cebu. In the ten days between December 7 and December 17 a reasonable degree of protection against air and sea attack had been provided for the critical areas on the Atlantic and Pacific coasts, and reinforcements had been sent to Panama, Hawaii and Alaska, with anti-aircraft units on their way. Australia and New Zealand were threatened. Marshall began to occupy himself with the creation of strong bases on Midway, Port Darwin and New Caledonia to keep open the lines of communication to Australia, which suddenly assumed immense importance. Australia was virtually undefended. So was India. No one knew where the main blow would strike next, and as Marshall saw it in those early days it might be possible to hold the Dutch East Indies even if the Philippines and Malaya fell. Information about losses in the Philippines was still unknown. A convoy sailing for the Philippines was diverted to Australia. There were jobs to be done nearer home: air bases to defend the Panama Canal were hastily set up in Brazil. And for the moment this was all that could be done. America was still on the defensive, weakly parrying blows from a superior enemy. With Churchill's arrival the grand strategies could be prepared.

On the afternoon of Tuesday, December 23, the Combined Chiefs of Staff held their first official meeting at the White House, the President presiding. As often happened, others besides the Chiefs of Staff were present, and these included Lord Beaverbrook, Captain Beardall, General "Pa" Watson, Secretary Knox and Secretary Stimson. The meeting was addressed by the President and by Churchill. The general outlines of Churchill's memorandum were approved, though by this time the President was thinking of an invasion of Europe in 1944. There followed on the afternoon of Christmas Day the first real meeting of the Chiefs of Staff where matters were discussed without the dominating presence of the President or the Prime Minister. This meeting was dominated by Marshall.

Again and again Marshall had grappled with the problem of divided command. He had spoken of the necessity of unity of command in his speech to the American Legion on September 15, and he had seen less than three months later how lack of unity had affected Pearl Harbor. During World War I a final and satisfactory unified command was never completely worked out, and he was concerned that there should be established at the very beginning of this war some principles which would allow a unified Allied high command to operate at the highest potential. At the Christmas afternoon meeting he declared:

> I am convinced that there must be one man in command of the entire theater—air, ground, and ships. We cannot manage by cooperation. Human frailties are such that there would be emphatic unwillingness to place portions of troops under another service. If we make a plan for unified command now, it will solve nine-tenths of our troubles.

There are difficulties in arriving at a single command,

but they are much less than the hazards that must be faced if we do not achieve this. We never think alike—there are the opinions of those on this side of the table and of the people on the other side; but as for myself, I am willing to go the limit to accomplish this. We must decide on a line of action here, and not expect it to be done out there. I favor one man being in control, but operating under a controlled directive from here. We had to come to this in the first World War, but it was not until 1918 that it was accomplished and much valuable time, blood and treasure had been needlessly sacrificed. If we could decide upon a unified command now, it would be a great advance over what was accomplished during the World War.

To the British the statement came as a bombshell, for they could see that inevitably under these conditions supreme command would pass into American hands. Their shock was not lessened when, at Marshall's suggestion, it was proposed that the first supreme commander to be appointed should be General Sir Archibald Wavell, who should take over under his single command a vast area extending from the Bay of Bengal to Australasia including all the islands of the East Indies. All land, sea and air forces would be assigned to him, and he would have an American officer as his deputy. The suggestion was greeted with something approaching horror by Churchill, who saw that this was precisely the area which the Japanese were in the act of plundering, and it might be overrun at any moment. Wavell would bear the load of defeat. By the 29th, Wavell, who was then in Chungking, had received his command. It was of little use to him, for by this time the area was already overrun, and there was never again to be a supreme commander covering this immense territory. At the end of the war Lord Louis Mountbatten, General MacArthur and the commander of the American Pacific Fleet each possessed separate commands over the area which for a few days constituted Wavell's Pacific empire.

Though Marshall's first effort to produce a unified command failed, the second and third were more successful. On December 29, the same day that Churchill sent instructions to Wavell, Marshall drafted a memorandum proposing a unified command over China, northeast Burma, Thailand and Indo-China. At Churchill's insistence

Burma was removed from the list. Generalissimo Chiang Kai-shek was offered the supreme command of Allied land and air forces in the Chinese Theater. Under him there would be an American Chief of Staff.

The situation in China was so complex, so fluid and unpredictable that it was necessary to send a military representative who would carry great weight with the Chinese. Marshall at first thought of sending General Hugh A. Drum, who had been Chief of Staff of the First Army in World War I. Drum was stubborn, pompous, occasionally ignorant, but he possessed an overriding ability for hard work. He had been Marshall's senior officer in the first war, and did not think the post offered to him in China was big enough. There was a row. Stimson called Drum into his office and was shown a paper in which Drum outlined his understanding of the situation, whereupon Drum was bowed out politely from the office of the Secretary of War. Marshall knew General Joseph W. Stilwell well. They had both commanded battalions at Tientsin, and they had worked together at Fort Benning. He believed Stilwell to be the only American officer who had any chance whatever of correcting the military situation in China. Stillwell was blunt, tactless, uncomfortable among officials, but he had a mind like "Stonewall" Jackson's, which worked by sudden fiery leaps from prejudice to prejudice. He had a mordant humor and some savage hates, but he was also a tactical genius with a flair for improvisation. Marshall sent him to meet Stimson, who professed a grudging admiration for the officer's record and a dislike for his manner. According to Stillwell's diary, Stimson refused to consider him because "he had his head down." Marshall reported to the Secretary of War that the only reason why Stilwell had his head down was probably because he was "getting ready to butt something." Under pressure from Marshall, Stilwell's appointment was confirmed on January 16. Three weeks later Stilwell left for China with the promise from Dr. T. V. Soong that the new Chief of Staff would have virtual command over all China's land and air forces.

Stilwell's mission to China was close to Marshall's heart. At a time when southeast Asia was falling, it seemed in those early days eminently desirable that the Chinese should launch a great offensive against the Japanese. It was assumed that the main Japanese strength had been removed from the mainland, and there was encouraging news from General Hsueh Yueh's armies which were about to throw the enemy back across the Milo River. No one then knew that this was the last successful battle to be fought by the Generalissimo's troops.

There were problems of organization and strategy; there was the interminable problem of choosing adequate commanders. "It's hard as hell to find anybody in our high command who's worth a damn," Marshall told Stilwell. "There are plenty of good young ones, but you have to reach too far down." It was an odd remark from someone who had suffered intensely because no one had reached down for many years to give him the high position he desired. The choice of Stilwell, later to be bitterly criticized, was welcomed by the Chinese High Command; and if in the process of galvanizing the demoralized Chinese Army, he gave it a shock from which it never recovered, this was hardly his fault, for nothing can be galvanized without the passing of an electric current. Marshall came to think of Stilwell's later Hukawng Valley campaign as the most brilliant of the entire war. It is not difficult to understand why. Of all the battles fought in the war, this was the one which most resembled the Shenandoah Valley campaign during the War between the States.

Meanwhile there were daily conferences with the Combined Chiefs of Staff, to be known later (on February 8) as the Joint Chiefs of Staff. Usually the British and American Chiefs would spend their mornings in separate conferences, then meet together in the afternoon. It was arranged that Sir John Dill, who was no longer Chief of the Imperial General Staff, a position he had surrendered to Sir Alan Brooke, should be the chief British representative with a permanent office in Washington. The Joint Chiefs of Staff assumed vast powers. They were the fountainhead. They largely controlled basic strategic directives, priorities, intelligence and supplies, and though Churchill and Roosevelt between them ran the war and made the final decisions, they very rarely opposed the recommendations of the Joint Chiefs. Some such organization might have come about during the course of the war, but Marshall was responsible for its creation in its earliest stages and remained long afterwards in a privileged and dominant position within it.

The organization of the Joint Chiefs of Staff meant a radical change in the conduct of the war. Other radical changes followed. At the end of January, General Joseph T. McNarney produced a memorandum recommending a drastic change in the organization of the Army itself. McNarney, the son of a Pennsylvania attorney, a poker-playing lieutenant colonel at twenty-six, a tall man with a high forehead and a ruthless intelligence, simply cut the complex organization of the Army into its minimum components: the Army Ground Forces, the Army Air Forces and the Services of Supply, later called the Army Service Forces. Marshall approved the plan at once and fought for it against the objections of the Secretary of War and the further objections of the President: they were not very strong objections. It was necessary to streamline the Army, and if it had to be done while the war was in progress, this was one of the inevitable results of Army traditions which had long ago lost their usefulness. The Chief of Infantry and the other Chiefs of the Arms were abolished. In their place were the Commanding General of the Army Ground Forces, General Lesley J. McNair, the Commanding General of the Army Air Forces, General Henry H. Arnold and the Commanding General of the Service of Supply, General Brehon B. Somervell. They were men of ordinary middle class origins. McNair was the son of a dry goods storekeeper in Minnesota, Arnold was the son of a Pennsylvania doctor, Somervell was the son of a lawyer, a West Pointer, an authority on Turkey and a former WPA administrator in New York City. The most brilliant of the three was McNair, who became a brigadier general in France at the age of thirty-five, the youngest general in the A.E.F. With his hooked nose, his fierce blue eyes and his passion for riding, he looked as though he had stepped out of the War between the States. When Marshall placed him in command of all the ground forces, so instituting the first drastic reorganization of the War Department since Elihu Root created the General Staff in 1903, he said: "Now that I have put this in your hands I can forget all about it." By March 9, when the reorganization was made effective by Presidential order, the teams which were to win the war were already in existence.

While these reorganizations were going on, plans for the invasion of Europe were advancing. There were long and involved discussions. Two areas had to be heavily defended: Great Britain and Australia. They were at the ends of long lines of communication, and convoys sent in both directions were threatened by submarines. Was it possible to prepare an invasion without crippling Britain or Australia? Risks had to be taken, including the major risk of sending out the *Aquitania* with a full American division comprising more than fifteen thousand men without a protecting escort. Some of the complexities which faced them can be seen from the minutes of the meeting of the Joint Chiefs of Staff on January 12. Marshall is explaining the plan of expeditions to Northern Ireland and Australia:

> 21,800 American troops were to sail from the East Coast on January 20 to arrive in the ABDA [American-British-Dutch-Australian] Area approximately February 14. This convoy to consist of 10,000 ground troops for New Caledonia, which with the artillery brigade now in Australia, would furnish approximately a division for New Caledonia. The remainder of the expedition would consist of engineers and other ground service troops for the bombers then arriving in the ABDA Area. Also moving out were 20 cargo ships, carrying 250 pursuit, 86 medium bombers, 57 light bombers, 220 ship tons of cargo, and four and one-half million gallons of gasoline. The airplanes involved were to replace those lost by attrition.
>
> General Marshall further stated that in order to permit this expedition to depart, the following changes would have to be made in existing plans:
>
> In the first convoy for MAGNET [the expedition to North Ireland] the 8,000 troops scheduled for Iceland on January 15 would be reduced to 2,500; the 16,000 scheduled for Ireland would be reduced to 4,000. The *Queen Mary* could carry 7,000 troops to Ireland February 1; then transport the British troops desired to the Middle East. 9,000 troops would be carried to Ireland on the *Andes, Oronzay,* and *Orion,* to sail February 15-20.
>
> Three Navy transports—the *West Point,* the *Wakefield,* and the *Mount Vernon*—then being used to transport troops from the Middle East to the Far East by Suez, would be available

for another round trip to move British troops over the same route. In addition, 4,400 more troops could be moved to Ireland on the *George Washington,* February 24. Under the plan approximately 24,000 troops would be in or en route to Ireland by February 25.

Marshall's duties included those of traffic officer, and they were not very dissimilar to the duties he had assumed in 1918. These bare statements concealed important decisions and paralyzing risks. The risk of submarine attack had to be accepted. As he listened to Marshall's calm recital of traffic on infested seas, Arnold was openly frightened; and Stilwell, when he heard about them, objected strongly. "Why, there were Jap troops all round the Philippine Islands," he wrote. "Our submarines could not get at them, the air and surface defense was so good." How does one penetrate into enemy waters? Marshall shrugged and spoke of small convoys so closely guarded that the enemy would be unable to penetrate. It was a risk that had to be taken. Buoyed up by the thought of the inevitability of victory, Marshall accepted the risks with fatalism.

The general pattern of his life as Chief of Staff was already established. There were few changes during the war. He would rise around 5:30 a.m., ride for an hour, take a shower, breakfast, and motor to the Pentagon, slipping through the door around 7:00 or 7:30, though officially the War Department did not open until 8:30. Rested by the long ride along the Potomac, he would then go through his mail. He liked to have his letters untouched; he would open them himself, unlike General MacArthur, who ordered that the corners of his letters should be ripped off for easier opening. His replies were brief to curtness, and invariably signed, no matter to whom they were addressed, with "Faithfully yours." On some letters he would write in pencil: "Take action," "No," "Yes." After disposing of about fifty letters, he would study reports, call in his assistants, ponder the wall maps where there were no flags on colored pins—he knew precisely where the armies were. It was a simple room, barely furnished, with a clean desk and only a memo pad, a pair of steel-rimmed spectacles and a mahogany paper tray. After consultations with his assistants there were conferences with the President, with the Secretary of War or with the Joint Chiefs of Staff. These meetings began at nine and lasted until noon. There were more appointments in the afternoon, but by 4:30 he was usually on his way back to his rambling red-brick house at Fort Myer. He smoked not at all, reduced his drinking to an occasional highball, and ate like a monk: his lunch was usually a small slice of pie and a cup of milk, enough to keep the engine ticking. Outwardly, it was a quiet and calculated life. Underneath the storms were continually boiling up. Incompetence, as usual, was punished silently and mercilessly: such storms were over quickly. Other storms arose as the result of the violence of his conflicts with Roosevelt, who lacked his orderly mind. He threatened to resign at least three times during the war. At one time he threatened to resign if the Munitions Assignment Board was not placed under the authority of the Joint Chiefs of Staff; there was a dramatic meeting with Roosevelt and Hopkins; he attacked their opinions heatedly, and was only mollified when he learned that Hopkins had supported his view all along. He was wary of Roosevelt, and often suspicious of Hopkins, who also possessed a distressingly disorganized mind. He was closest perhaps to Stimson, who had met him first at the staff college at Langres in 1918 and ten years later had invited him to accompany him as his aide to the Philippines. Their minds worked in the same way, but there was one cardinal difference: Marshall's mind worked ten times faster than Stimson's. Now, as the war progressed, there was need of a mind which could race with phenomenal speed. Sudden decisive military decisions had to be made, often on insufficient evidence. And brilliance was often dangerous. Among these decisions was one to call for the resignation of General Short, in command of the Hawaiian Department. The resignation was probably inevitable: the country demanded a scapegoat for the defeat at Pearl Harbor, and General Short became the first of a number of scapegoats whose guilt was never decisively proved. His application for retirement was announced on February 26, 1942, "without condonation of any offense or prejudice to any future disciplinary action." Marshall was clearly determined that General Short should be removed, but he appears to have been hesitating in his own mind about the degree of guilt of the unfortunate general, for his own memorandum which was later introduced among the exhibits of the Pearl Harbor enquiry lacked his usual concision. The hurried and unfinished note read:

> *General Short's retirement is accepted, we to be*
> *to future action in*
> *effective—, without prejudice to the interests of the government.*

The memorandum was abandoned, for a more streamlined version was later presented to the public. General Short had been recommended to Marshall by General Hugh A. Drum to take command of a division or a corps, and Marshall was evidently hesitating not only about the degree of the general's guilt but whether he was guilty at all, and what effect the retirement would have on General Drum, and on a hundred other matters. The scrap of paper was illuminating, because it showed how much faster his mind was running than his pencil and because it showed him in the actual process of thinking on paper.

Such decisions were the order of the day during February which saw the fall of Singapore, the invasion of the East Indies and a desperate appeal from President Quezon of the Philippines for the neutralization of the Philippines. Quezon asked for complete and unconditional independence, the withdrawal of troops and the disbandment of the Philippine Army in the belief that the Japanese would thereupon look favorably upon his Government. No troops had arrived, almost the whole of the air force had been destroyed on the ground, and they were in desperate straits. Even MacArthur, who sent a covering note to President Quezon's message, appeared to agree that no other solution except a quiet surrender was possible. The messages shocked Marshall as much as they shocked Stimson, that New England conscience on legs, who possessed puritanical objections to the mere thought of defeat. It was decided to refuse Quezon's request. There could be no independence, no disbandment of the armies—the war must be fought to a finish. The President, Stimson, Welles and Marshall, with the help of some secretaries drew up on February 9 an appeal to be signed by the President, urging them to stand firm whatever the cost. It is a long appeal covering four pages of closely printed type. As one might expect when so many different minds have been at work on it, it shows a variety of styles. There are sentences which are clearly by Roosevelt: "By a malign conspiracy of a few depraved but powerful governments this hope [for political and economic independence] is now being frustrated and delayed." And again: "The service that you and the American members of your command can render to your country in the titanic struggle now developing are beyond all possibility of appraisement," where it is as though Roosevelt was borrowing the forms of language employed by MacArthur to instill courage into him. But here and there, dropped like rocks on velvet, are phrases which have the icy impersonality and definition of Marshall: "I particularly request that you proceed rapidly to the organization of your forces and your defenses so as to make your resistance as effective as circumstances will permit and as prolonged as humanly possible."

This message was despatched on the night of February 9. On the afternoon of February 22, less than two weeks later, MacArthur's defenses were crumbling and MacArthur himself was ordered to leave Corregidor. The decision came about at a meeting in the White House between the President, Marshall, Hopkins and King. The responsibility for the decision was very largely Marshall's. It was a decision clearly dictated by military necessity, and it was totally misunderstood by MacArthur, who brought his whole staff to Australia and left General Wainwright only in command of Bataan. MacArthur hoped to direct the Pacific campaigns by remote control from Brisbane. Marshall, with his usual belief that the man on the spot knew more than others what was happening, immediately asked Roosevelt for permission to promote Wainwright to lieutenant general with full powers to command all forces in the Philippines, while MacArthur was ordered to relinquish his former command: his duties now were to safeguard the approaches to Australia. On April 18, which happened to be the day of the Doolittle raid on Tokyo, Marshall sent a radio to Wainwright on Corregidor:

> The continued demonstration that you and all members of your command are giving to the world of hardihood, courage and devotion to duty is worthy of the finest traditions of American and Filipino soldiery. We are immeasurably proud of every individual serving in the fortifications of Manila Bay. I request that you convey the special commendation and gratitude of the War Department to the nurses on Corregidor whose service is a source of inspiration to all of us.

It was characteristic of Marshall that he should have employed a succession of dry military clichés; it was also characteristic of Marshall that we should be able to see through his clichés to the real emotions hiding beneath, while the inflated language of MacArthur's messages during this same period is suspect and sterile.

When the Philippines were lost, the need for a victory in the West became urgent, and throughout January and February and far into the spring there were discussions on how this should be brought about. The innumerable theaters which Marshall had at one time contemplated were reduced to three on March 8: on this day it was decided that America should take responsibility for the Far East, Great Britain for the Middle East and both together should assume responsibility for the recovery of Europe; and it was against Europe, where their combined forces could be directed, that plans were now being prepared. Marshall did not waver in the belief that forces could be landed in Europe in 1942. He relied on Napoleon's maxim that the strength of an army, like power in mechanics, is a product of mass multiplied by velocity, and he thought that holes could be punched wherever desired in Hitler's fortress of Europe, providing that a large mass could be assembled with speed and sent off with determination and velocity. In this he was probably wrong. Statistically, such an army could have been produced, but questions of morale entered the grand design. The British Army in Britain had not yet recovered from its mauling in France, and through the first six months of the year the American Army was still not a first-class force. As General McNair described it in February: "It was capable of fighting creditably, but with excessive losses." Though both would have attacked magnificently, it is doubtful whether they would have possessed the resolution for victory which comes with the knowledge of one's own superiority over the enemy.

On March 25 the President, Hopkins and the American Chiefs of Staff lunched together at the White House. It was a meeting of some significance for the future of the war. The President was discussing the possible direction of attack against Germany. He mentioned the Middle East and the Mediterranean basin, and the last charmed him. Marshall, with some help from Stimson, turned the conversation to the Atlantic, and held it there, giving an outline of his own views. The President finally agreed with Marshall and suggested that the whole matter be laid before the Joint Chiefs of Staff. Thereupon Hopkins made the plea that it should not go to the Joint Chiefs at all, but should be presented by someone—he meant, according to Stimson, Marshall—to Churchill and the British Chiefs of Staff in London, Admiral Sir Dudley Pound, Air Chief Marshal Sir Charles Portal and Field Marshal Sir Alan Brooke. The reason was simple: Hopkins hoped a confrontation in the conference room at 10 Downing Street would be more decisive than memoranda passed through the hands of Sir John Dill from Washington to London and back again. Hopkins had always talked about "the marriage of minds" and always worked on the assumption that documents interfered with agreements. The plan, as Marshall envisaged it, involved a vast preparation in Great Britain (this phase was called BOLERO), to be followed by a preliminary operation which looked forward to a beachhead on the Contentin Peninsula at some time before September 15, 1942 (this phase was called SLEDGEHAMMER), and a massive onslaught during the following spring (this phase was called ROUNDUP, and later OVERLORD). President Roosevelt gave his final approval to the plan, which would involve thirty American and eighteen British divisions, on April 1. Immediately afterwards Marshall and Hopkins, accompanied by a small staff, prepared to leave for London, having given themselves the code word MODICUM, prophetic of their own lack of success in their mission.

Leaving Baltimore on April 4, they were forced down over Bermuda by engine trouble. They were in Bermuda for two days, one of those days being Easter Sunday. Lord Knollys, the Governor, requested Marshall to read the lesson in the Cathedral; the lesson happened to be Revelations 1:4-18, which includes an impressive recital of messages from the angels of the seven churches: Ephesus, Smyrna, Pergamos, Thyatira, Sardis, Philadelphia and Laodicea. Marshall boggled over Thyatira and Laodicea, but he pronounced Philadelphia with considerable enthusiasm. Bermuda was one of the many British islands in the Atlantic with American military establishments: Marshall inspected the defenses, and then continued his flight in a Pan-American Clipper to Scotland. He arrived in London on April 9, a day which has some historic significance, for Bataan fell and there occurred the first flight of the Air Ferry Command over the "Hump" to China on the same day.

By the time the Americans reached London, Hopkins was ill: he had been under the care of a doctor throughout the journey. Marshall met with the British Chiefs of Staff alone. With him he brought a document prepared by the American Joint Chiefs of Staff, approved by the President and largely written by Marshall. "The decision," said this extraordinary document, "to launch this offensive must be made *at once.*" There could be no delays, no changes in the plan, which must be accepted in its entirety or not at all. The document hints at an autocratic temper, outlines its objectives boldly and simply, and covers a vast territory; and while it dealt with pressing problems of the moment, there hovered over it the shadow of Marshall's memories of another war:

> Speed [said Marshall] is the essence of the problem. The principal limiting factors are shortages of landing-craft for the assault and of shipping to transport the necessary forces from America to the United Kingdom. Without affecting essential commitments in other theatres, these forces can be brought over by April 1, 1943, but only if 60 per cent of the lift is carried by non-U.S. ships. If the movement is dependent only on U.S. shipping, the date of assault must be postponed to the late summer of 1943.
>
> About seven thousand landing-craft will be needed, and current construction programs must be greatly accelerated to achieve this figure. Concurrently, preparatory work to receive and operate the large U.S. land and air contingents must be speeded up.
>
> The assault should take place on selected beaches between Havre and Boulogne, and be carried out by a first wave of at least six divisions, supplemented by airborne troops. It would have to be nourished at the rate of at least one hundred thousand men a week. As soon as the beachheads are secure armored forces would move rapidly to seize the line of the Oise-St. Quentin. Thereafter the next objective would be Antwerp.

Churchill's first reaction was favorable. He delighted, as Marshall did, in vast plans expressed in the simplest possible terms, but he saw objections. Marshall no longer believed that an attack by September 15 was absolutely necessary, though the plan also provided for the operation SLEDGEHAMMER in the event of a disaster to the Russians or if the German forces in western Europe became critically weakened. The first might very well happen; there was no reason to believe that the second would happen except under attack. But though Churchill wrote approvingly to Roosevelt, his mind was elsewhere— he was appalled by the possibility of a Japanese invasion of India and a consequent meeting of German and Japanese forces in central Asia. He had other plans. He thought of a quick raid on northern Norway; he still looked forward to operation GYMNAST on the coast of Africa. Churchill played for time. Marshall found himself mostly in the company of Field Marshal Sir Alan Brooke, who raised objections to SLEDGEHAMMER—there were not enough landing craft available. Roosevelt had spoken to Lord Mountbatten some time previously of a "sacrifice" landing in France; it was assumed that Marshall and Roosevelt were in agreement; SLEDGEHAMMER was to be largely a British operation, and Churchill could not bring himself to look pleasantly at the inevitable losses. Marshall came to the conclusion that Sir Alan Brooke did not possess the brains of Sir John Dill, and that Churchill was being evasive. Churchill spoke of the "momentous proposal" which Marshall and Hopkins had brought from the President. He went on to paint a gloomy picture of India, where the Cripps mission was then attempting to solve an insoluble problem. He was obsessed with the dangers of a German and Japanese junction of forces, just as a little later Marshall was obsessed by the thought of a Japanese invasion of the Russian Maritime Provinces. Marshall stuck to his guns when he replied to Churchill, emphasizing that American troops would take a large share of SLEDGEHAMMER if a Russian disaster occurred. He emphasized, too, the importance of commando raids on the French coast and he was not particularly worried by the shipping crisis, though a few days previously Hopkins had cabled Roosevelt to the effect that in the four months from January 12 to April 11 the shipping losses in the western part of the Atlantic Ocean totalled considerably more than a million gross tons, and half of these were tankers. "Our need for ships during the next few months is going to be desperate," said Hopkins. Later Marshall spoke about the Alaska-

Hawaii-Australia line. He believed this could be held and he was reasonably certain the Indian Ocean could be safeguarded. By the end of the discussion it was clear that SLEDGEHAMMER was about to be abandoned by the British and only the most determined efforts by the Americans would keep the British to the plan. Marshall left the meeting in the belief that the plan was agreed upon "in principle," and after a short visit to the American troops in Northern Ireland he flew back to America, encouraged by the hope that the war might be over in a year and elated by the news of the Doolittle raid, which had demonstrated for the first time that the Japanese were not themselves invulnerable to surprise attacks.

The major problem in London had been to convince the British that the Americans could put a vast, well-trained army in the field. The British seemed dubious, remembering the long period of training which had elapsed during World War I before the great body of American troops were able to take the field. Marshall decided there was a perfectly simple way of showing the British that large and powerful American forces were already in being. He would show them the new troops at their training.

On May 1, accompanied by Sir John Dill and Lord Louis Mountbatten, he flew off to Fort Benning in Georgia. There, General Mark Clark took them to a hilltop which gave them a good view of an infantry assault. Live ammunition was used; tanks and fighter bombers supported the attack. They watched the running of a bayonet course, the throwing of grenades and the firing of the latest mortars and 37mm. guns. In the afternoon they flew to Camp Gordon, also in Georgia, where they saw the Fourth Division in review, and then they flew on to Fort Bragg where they saw a parachute drop by the Ninth Division and inspected sixty thousand troops, including the Negro engineer units. For two days, without interruption, they were constantly inspecting and apprizing the new American Army; and Marshall was as impressed as his visitors. He was also impressed by the incisive mind of General Mark Clark. A few days later he appointed Clark to the Army War College at Washington.

May was a month of hope, for the battle of the Coral Sea halted the Japanese advance in the southwest Pacific, and Washington was still hoping for the opening of a second front in Europe that year.

Marshall sent Mark Clark and Eisenhower to England for a ten-day visit for staff conferences and a tour of inspection; and though he had known Eisenhower only casually in the past—the first meeting had come about through Mark Clark—he was coming more and more to the opinion that Eisenhower was the right choice for commander of SLEDGEHAMMER. Eisenhower was human, had a wry sense of humor, and worked well with his subordinates and superiors; there was no sign in him of those terrible god-like qualities which military commanders too often saw in themselves. Eisenhower had shown that he could make brilliant war plans, and he wrote out his plans with a trenchant sense of the importance of simple, hard-hitting phrases. Marshall came in time to have complete trust in him, and the relationship was not unlike that between General Lee and "Stonewall" Jackson. "I had such implicit confidence in Jackson's skill and energy," wrote Robert E. Lee, "that I never troubled myself to give him detailed instructions. The most general suggestions were all that he needed." There were to be occasional passages of arms between them, for Marshall remained the aristocrat and Eisenhower was determined to remain the plebeian—it would occur sometimes to Marshall that Eisenhower was behaving in a manner calculated to demean himself—but there were never to be serious differences between them on the field.

The results of Eisenhower's visit to England were so gratifying that at the end of the month Marshall spoke to the graduating class at West Point as though victory was already in the air. He said:

> Current events remind me of questions which were put to me by members of Congress prior to December 7, as to where American soldiers might be called upon to fight, and just what was the urgent necessity for the Army that we were endeavoring to organize and train. In reply I usually commented on the fact that we had previously fought in France, Italy and Germany; in Africa and the Far East; in Siberia and Northern Russia. No one could tell what the future might hold for us. But one thing was clear to me: we must be prepared to fight anywhere, and with a minimum of delay. The possibilities were not overdrawn, for today we find American soldiers throughout the Pacific, in Burma, China and India. Recently they struck at Tokyo. They have

General Marshall and Mrs. Marshall at Hickam Field, Honolulu, on his return from China. January 1947.

Secretary Marshall at the Pentagon, September 1950.

wintered in Greenland and Iceland. They are landing in Northern Ireland and England, and they will land in France. We are determined that before the sun sets on this terrible struggle our flag will be recognized throughout the world as a symbol of freedom on the one hand and of overwhelming power on the other.

The speech was important, for it introduced a new note. If the Chief of Staff was more confident of victory than he had a right to be on the available evidence, it showed that he had emerged from the troubled perplexity of mind which companioned him through the winter. As usual he had written the speech himself in longhand, without benefit of ghost writers, a brood he thoroughly despised, though he employed them of necessity in writing his Biennial Reports: then, so evident is his own style, it is easy to recognize the passages written by Marshall and those interpolated by his assistants. The speech showed that he was in command of a forceful rhetoric for the first time; and never before had he spoken quite so humanly as when he concluded the speech with his appeal to youth—"It is on the young and vigorous that we must depend for the energy and daring and leadership in staging a great offensive"—and a prayer: "May the good Lord be with you."

If May was a month of calms, June which began with the successful battle of Midway in the dead center of the Pacific was a month of renewed turmoil and spectacular defeats, of mounting forces in the Pacific and in Great Britain, of disasters in the Middle East. Marshall was still hopeful. When Molotov visited Washington and asked whether the Americans were preparing a second front, Marshall replied "Yes," and the President authorized Molotov to tell Stalin that the second front would be opened that year. Marshall explained that the troops were already trained; the only difficulty lay in transport; the problem was to land on the continent of Europe sufficient troops to make the Germans engage in an all-out air effort; then, with their air force largely destroyed, victory would inevitably follow. It was not, of course, quite as simple as that, and he hastened to explain that while Stalin demanded an American and British force which would divert forty German divisions from the Russian front, the British and Americans were concerned with the number of men they could ship to France: the problem, as always, was indissolubly connected with shipping. The danger, however, to Russia was very real, with Sevastopol under seige and a major drive towards the Caucasus under way; and Roosevelt and Hopkins, then at Hyde Park, wrote a melancholy letter to Marshall and King asking where American ground forces could compel the withdrawal of Germans from the Russian front, assuming Leningrad and Moscow were threatened and there was a breakthrough towards the Caucasus. At the end of the letter there was the curt statement: Marshall to come to W.H. 11 a.m. Sunday, Brooke ditto 12. The day before Churchill had arrived accompanied by his Chiefs of Staff, and it was clear that the strategic plans were once more in the melting pot.

Marshall had a premonition of what was coming. He guessed that Churchill was hoping to revive GYMNAST, the assault on North Africa, and he had prepared a paper against it. Churchill had also prepared a paper, in which he asked rhetorically: "In case no plan can be made in which any responsible authority has good confidence, and consequently no engagement on a substantial scale in France is possible in September 1942, what else are we going to do?" The answer was provided dramatically in a cable received from Admiral Harwood at Alexandria. "Tobruk has fallen," he wrote, "and situation deteriorated so much that there is a possibility of heavy air attack on Alexandria in near future." From that moment all eyes were turned on Africa and the Middle East, for the situation in the Valley of the Nile and the southern end of the Russian front threatened, in Marshall's words, "a complete collapse in the Middle East, the loss of the Suez Canal and the vital oil supply in the vicinity of Abadan. It was a very black hour."

With Tobruk fallen, Britain's need became greater than the rest. The President asked what could be done. Churchill asked for Sherman tanks. Marshall was summoned and told of Churchill's request. His words, as Churchill remembered them when he came to write *The Hinge of Fate,* were brief and generous: "Mr. President, the Shermans are only just coming into production. The first few hundred have been issued to our own armored divisions, who have hitherto had to be content with obsolete equipment. It is a terrible thing to take the weapons out of a soldier's hands. Nevertheless, if the British need is so great, they must have them; and we could let them have a hundred

105mm. self-propelled guns in addition." Marshall was as good as his word. Three hundred Sherman tanks and a hundred self-propelled guns were sent round Africa to the Red Sea, and when one ship carrying these weapons was sunk off Bermuda by a submarine, Marshall ordered a further seventy tanks to be put on a fast ship to overtake the convoy. Later the tanks were used with decisive effect at El Alamein.

But if all eyes were turned on Africa, there was still the problem of the major strategic move to be settled. There was still no certainty about SLEDGEHAMMER and BOLERO. GYMNAST had been carefully worked out, largely by Eisenhower, and Marshall had told him that "you are the man who is going to carry it out." But Marshall found it difficult to think of GYMNAST as anything more than a large-scale raid. He was still uncertain whether Churchill realized the potentialities of the new American Army. He had shown Dill and Mountbatten the tremendous unleashed forces in the training camps, and now he prevailed upon Churchill to see them. On June 23 they left Washington by train for South Carolina and the next day they attended maneuvers at Fort Jackson. They watched a parade of American armor and infantry, a parachute drop, and field exercises with live ammunition. Churchill was impressed, but not as impressed as Marshall hoped he would be. Churchill grumbled a little about "mass produced divisions" and he was skeptical of their quality, saying it would take two or three years to hammer them into shape. In his skepticism he proved himself wrong, as he admitted gracefully before a meeting of military men at the Pentagon three years later. But the harm was done; and seeing Churchill so intractable, Marshall began to think of withdrawing American forces from the European and Middle East theaters, and concentrating on Japan. He hoped to commit the British to BOLERO by threats or by a ruse.

As he well knew, he was in no position to carry the threats through. Military decisions rested with Marshall in part, but the larger part was Roosevelt's, and Roosevelt was more concerned with the problems of the Middle East than with the fate of Japan. Roosevelt asked for a complete report on the military situation in the Middle East on June 30. Marshall replied dismally, explaining that though the Suez Canal could be effectively blocked by the British, this was the only happy prospect on a menacing landscape. Army Intelligence was estimating that Rommel would reach Cairo within a week, or perhaps two weeks. With a week's rest Rommel would be able to proceed with the annihilation of the remaining British forces in the Middle East, and then go on to occupy Cyprus, Syria and the great oil areas of Mosul and Basra. There was also the very real danger that Rommel's occupation of the Middle East would result in the breakdown of the American Air Ferry route across Africa to the Far East and to the Soviet Union. The crisis in the Middle East was desperate.

Marshall, the old cobbler sticking to his last, saw only one solution: a massive attack on Europe. He raged against Churchill, who by now was assuming something of the characteristics of the devil in the piece. Stimson recorded in his diary under the date July 10 that Marshall spoke of "a new and rather staggering crisis that is coming up in our war strategy." The crisis however was no more than the old crisis under a slightly different form: BOLERO *versus* GYMNAST. Marshall complained of the constant shifting of plans, and spoke openly of his desire to abandon the British and concentrate on Japan. It was an unpleasant and dramatic interview with Stimson, and there were to be more unpleasant passages before the decision to invade North Africa was taken.

July began with a curious balance of forces. While on July 1 Sevastopol fell to the Germans, the British were barely holding the El Alamein line. It was a reasonable assumption that the Germans would make the most of their Russian victory, and perhaps with a gigantic pincer movement envelop the whole Mediterranean basin. In this crisis, Roosevelt cabled to Churchill: "Marshall, King and Hopkins leaving for London at once." How desperate the crisis was in the eyes of the President and the American Chiefs of Staff can be seen from the memorandum written by Roosevelt, which calmly contemplated the loss of Egypt, Syria, the Suez Canal, the Mosul oil fields, Tunis, Algiers, Morocco, Dakar, Liberia and Brazil, and suggested that plans should be made to offset the loss of any or all of these. He also announced his decision, which Marshall entirely agreed with, that United States ground forces should fight the German army some time that year.

Hopkins, Marshall and King flew by Stratoliner to Prestwick on July 16, and then took train for London, where they set up their headquarters at Claridge's Hotel. Churchill had invited them to meet with him as soon as they arrived; Marshall had counseled a first meeting of the American staffs before seeing Churchill. Churchill, who had made arrangements for his visitors to see him immediately, was not unnaturally in a bad humor. Marshall went to work on the technical details of SLEDGEHAMMER, convinced that Churchill would finally agree to the adventure. He knew he had the backing of Sir John Dill. He was convinced that the Allies possessed sufficient forces for a cross-Channel operation, and he worked quietly and calmly on this assumption; and within four days the assumption was ripped to pieces. There were many reasons, including the British naval view that an operation of this kind in September or October involved perils of weather. On July 24 Stimson made his final appeal to the President in favor of SLEDGEHAMMER, and on the same day the President accepted the verdict of the British Chiefs of Staff. GYMNAST, renamed TORCH, became the order of the day; and Marshall, once convinced, became its most ardent defender. He wrote in his Biennial Report: "The psychological effect of the conquest of North Africa would be tremendous." By July 27, after a brief inspection of American forces in Iceland, Marshall was once more back in Washington.

The problem of TORCH now possessed overriding importance, but there were a host of other problems. In particular there was the problem of China, now splitting at the seams. Chiang Kai-shek sent one of his periodic messages saying that Chinese resistance might collapse at any moment. Marshall received the Generalissimo's request for 500 planes, 5 divisions and 500 tons to be sent monthly. Marshall, perplexed by the dominance of the number 5 and the urgency of the message (for Stilwell's reports were guardedly optimistic) did his best to increase the flow of munitions and airplanes over the Hump but refused the request for 5 divisions. There was also the problem of morale. Characteristically, Roosevelt had decided to send his most powerful political enemy on a world tour in the hope of stimulating the morale of the Allies and he wrote to Marshall:

> I think that for many reasons Willkie should take this trip—especially to put some pep into the officials of Egypt, Palestine, Syria, Irak, Iran and China. I do not know what capacity he should go in—perhaps as a special representative of the President. What do you think?

Marshall replied, offering his blessing to the project and assuring the President that military facilities would be given to Willkie. At least the journey would do no harm. Marshall was in a profoundly depressed mood, still not convinced that there was a real drive behind the British plans, and he was largely indifferent to the interminable discussions concerning the supreme commander of the Allied forces—would it be Marshall, Eisenhower, or someone else? Admiral King had suggested Eisenhower; Sir John Dill thought Marshall should assume the command and would probably accept it. The President had not yet approached Marshall. In the end, with some misgivings which arose from Eisenhower's lack of political experience, Marshall proposed that Eisenhower should be placed in charge of TORCH.

July had seen a change in the general arrangement of the American Chiefs of Staff. For some time there had been felt the need for a closer liaison between the Chiefs and the President, and with the resignation of Admiral William D. Leahy from his embassy at Pétain's strange court in Vichy, a liaison officer with the proper qualities was now available. Tall, blunt, ponderous and nervous, Leahy's admirable impassivity and desire to serve could now be set to work. Close to Stimson, he possessed some of Stimson's pontifical sense of his own importance, but he also possessed a sense of fair play. He was able to prevent the President from making the wild decisions which were his inveterate delight; and if he adored the President, he admired Marshall and set himself, as well as an admiral could, to understand the workings of the military mind.

Marshall's depression over TORCH continued in August, and in the middle of the month he cabled to Eisenhower in London:

> There is unanimity of opinion of Army officers here that the proposed operation appears hazardous to the extent of less than a fifty percent chance of success. To what extent are you prepared to meet possible German air assaults

launched from Spain or from Spanish Morocco? Give me your completely frank view and similarly frank expression from Patton.

By the 25th Marshall was disposed to believe that the operation might continue on a more limited scale. "The hazard is too great," he wrote, "especially considering the extreme seriousness of the effect on the peoples of occupied Europe, India and China if the United States should fail in its first major operation." He suggested that the operation should be contracted to eliminate the Algiers-Bône area.

Marshall's fears were not groundless, but they were exaggerated by the knowledge that the day of decision was soon coming, that China was in a disastrous position, there was still no solution of the Indian problem and messages were coming from occupied Europe suggesting there was a limit to the endurance of suffering under the Germans. Fourteen poorly equipped French divisions occupied North Africa. What if they should offer sharp resistance to the invaders? Marshall had no high opinion of De Gaulle; he had indeed treated him with undeserved contempt in London at a frosty meeting in which Admiral King and Eisenhower were participants; but he possessed a healthy respect for fourteen divisions, however ill-equipped. Throughout September he was still apprehensive. The preparations for GYMNAST were being made at the expense of BOLERO. Even if GYMNAST was successful, there would be inevitable delays in launching the invasion of Europe. Roosevelt had originally set the date of GYMNAST at October 30; it was finally set for November 8. And when at one o'clock in the morning of November 8, the first assault landings began in Algiers, the ships having steamed safely through the Straits of Gibraltar, he knew that the vast logistical preparations had not been in vain. A few days before there had come the welcome news of the victory of the British Eighth Army over Rommel's Afrika Korps, and four days later there was to begin the victorious battle of Guadalcanal, which avenged a multitude of American defeats at the hands of the Japanese. He admired Eisenhower's skill in operating the landings, and spoke shortly afterwards of the "perfection of the performance of our forces up to this time." The casualties were surprisingly light; he asked Eisenhower's consent to publish them. He wrote in his next Biennial

Report: "The landings were carried out in accordance with plans and with a boldness and efficiency which secured the initial objectives, the major airfields and ports of North Africa, within a period of 48 hours."

There followed the long-drawn-out consultations with the French military leaders, which began with Giraud's belief that he had been smuggled out of France to assume supreme command of the invading forces and ended with Darlan's assassination. Darlan had been discovered visiting his sick son in North Africa; his presence there had been entirely unforeseen. Eisenhower had made use of him. There were popular protests against the use of generals who had sworn allegiance to Vichy. On the second Sunday after the landings Marshall decided to hold an off-record conference, and summoned about thirty newspaper- and radio-men to the Pentagon. He spoke with complete frankness. He admitted that Eisenhower had acted like a political innocent, and then for an hour he read Eisenhower's voluminous despatches on Darlan. In these despatches Eisenhower had expressed his astonishment, his fears, even his bewilderment at the swift turn of events, but he had also expressed an unalterable determination to bypass Darlan wherever possible. When he had finished reading, Marshall said:

"Well, gentlemen, there it is, fair and square. If you want to go on beating hell out of Eisenhower for something he didn't do, I can't help it."

Surprised by the success of the off-record conference, Marshall began to use this method increasingly. He would use it to give newsmen background material, to provide warnings, to correct mistaken conceptions on the course and conduct of the war. He spoke against strikes, he explained how they not only hindered the production of war matériel but made changes in strategical plans inevitable; and once he described how a strike had altered the whole military picture as it affected the Balkan states. He was often brutally frank; and sometimes, in a mood approximating braggadocio, he would reveal far more than he should have revealed, as when he disclosed the battle order of the British, the Americans and the Russians to the surprised correspondents. Someone raised the question whether such disclosures would alarm the Russians. Marshall answered casually that if the Russians knew their dispositions had been disclosed they might do anything short of quitting the war. These conferences were informal, but few correspondents dared to argue with Marshall, who held himself conspicuously upright, always reserved, always polite and always mysterious. He neither asked for nor succeeded in gaining the intimacy of the newsmen, who complained of subtleties where none perhaps existed and were tormented by the thought that every statement made by Marshall concealed a hidden purpose. In this they were wrong. He was incapable of Admiral King's informality or of Roosevelt's generous delight in listening to his own voice; but in his curt way he was being as informal and garrulous as he could be, and it was not his fault that they saw mysteries where none existed.

Meanwhile the African campaign was moving towards a conclusion. On November 25 he was sufficiently optimistic to tell Roosevelt that the occupation of Tunisia would probably be accomplished in two or three weeks, provided that two divisions were sufficient to accomplish the task. The Axis powers would soon find themselves in an intolerable situation in Tunisia. He was still afraid of a German occupation of Spain, he did not believe they would halt their drive through the Caucasus and he still feared an attack on the British Isles, but they were fears that he had lived with for a very long time and they were beginning to lose their sharp luster. American forces were now involved in the war against Germany; he had pleaded for the early contest, and this had been given to him, and by the end of the year he knew that the first stage was over. On his sixty-second birthday Stimson, without telling him, issued a statement to the press, which read:

> The Army moves into the New Year confident and sure of its mission, backed by a country that today is the best equipped for war the world has ever seen. The men of our Army, now over five million strong, one million overseas, are being trained with more solicitous care for their health and welfare than any Army in history. As the citizen who is the head of the department to which the Army belongs, I am proud of the magnificent work which has been done by the Chief of Staff, General George C. Marshall.

Mrs. Marshall, with a greater knowledge of her husband's

desires, made no speeches: she gave him a present of some gardening tools instead.

For some time before the end of the year Marshall had been thinking of a gift to the President and the Prime Minister which would somehow symbolize the incredible changes which had occurred during the year. Finally he settled upon the gift of a globe as a most appropriate introduction to the New Year and a presage of victories to come. The President was delighted, and wrote back shortly afterwards:

> I am made very happy by your letter and by the special globe which I have set up in my office directly behind my chair. I can swing around and figure distances to my great satisfaction.

For Marshall there was less satisfaction in figuring distances. As he gazed at the large vertical relief map in the Pentagon, he knew that everything depended upon the bridging of those distances between obscure islands in the Pacific and the mainland of Japan, between England and the mainland of Europe. The war had only just begun.

CHAPTER TWELVE

The Rage for Victory

"The hand of the Lord was over us," Marshall said in December, when he spoke of the North African landings, and sometimes, when he looked back at the venture he shuddered at the thought of how close they had come to the razor's edge. The date had been set months before. On the night of the landing there were reports of two storms approaching the coast. By a miracle the storms neutralized each other; an old Frenchman in Casablanca said the sea was calmer that night than he had seen it in sixty-eight years. Marshall had not hoped for calm. He knew that Atlantic rollers had a habit of driving huge swells on the exposed beaches, and that only on seven days out of thirty were landings possible: nevertheless the fleet had passed unmolested through the narrow Straits of Gibraltar, taking the same risk which the Japanese had taken in the Coral Sea, at Midway and again in the Solomons, but with a different outcome, and the army was safely landed against his most sanguine hopes. He had visions of the convoys being subjected to mass air and naval attacks, of transports sunk and thousands of soldiers drowned, the entire expedition forced to turn back mutilated and defeated. It had not happened; the Germans watching the Straits had come to the conclusion that the convoys were taking reinforcements to the Far East or to the starving garrison at Malta, or perhaps they were intended to land in the rear of Rommel in the Middle East—they had thought of all the possible objectives except the one deliberate objective.

"The hand of the Lord was over us." It was almost credible, as December turned towards January, with the Allies in North Africa driving against Rommel and the Russians opening their final drive against the surrounded German Sixth Army in Stalingrad. There was so much hope in the air that even the British, who were usually prepared to believe the worst, began to think that the Germans would surrender by January 1, 1944. The time had come to call another conference, for there was no doubt that the Germans would soon be thrown out of North Africa and the main strategy for the defeat of the Germans in Europe had not yet been settled. Roosevelt had been concerned for some time with the choice of a meeting place. Khartoum, Bhagdad, the Bermudas had all occurred to him, and all had been given up for various reasons. Then he settled on "a satisfactory and safe place just north of Casablanca," choosing it perhaps because the name meant "the white house." Churchill suggested the code name SYMBOL, which was not one of his more brilliant suggestions, and then Roosevelt made the final arrangements, reaching Casablanca by way of a sea voyage to Dakar and a swift flight across the fertile fields of North Africa and the snow-white Atlas mountains.

Early in the morning of January 9 Marshall, Arnold and Sir John Dill flew off from Gravelly Point in one C-54, to be followed by Admiral King and General Wedemeyer in another. They flew through a heavy overcast until they reached Borinquen Field in Puerto Rico, and were off again in the early evening, with Arnold at the controls. There was some discussion between Arnold and Marshall about filling C-54's with fifty to seventy-five men and using them as troop transports, but no decisions were reached. They flew to Belem and Natal in Brazil, and then across the Atlantic to Bathurst in West Africa: a short and dangerous stretch of water, for it was a German trick at the time to send submarines out in these lonely wastes: they would fire rockets, American planes would dive low thinking there was somewhere a ship in distress and then the submarines' guns would be trained on the planes. Some Liberators had been lost in this way. While Arnold was piloting the plane, the rockets flared up about thirty miles away; he made no attempt to investigate, but hurried on towards Bathurst, alarmed by the news they had received in Brazil that their movements were already known along the coast of Africa. They flew to Marrakech without incident, and set off the next morning for Casablanca, arriving there only half an hour before the British delegation: Churchill had seen no flares over the Atlantic but he complained that they had to fly so high up that he was nearly frozen to death.

There were to be many conferences, but no others were held in such pleasing surroundings. The days were high and windy, with indigo blue skies, and fifteen-foot waves roaring against the rocks; the hotel at Anfa was lost among palms and Arab mosaics. It was a place which threatened no storms, though the storms came.

The first storm came in the shape of a memorandum which Churchill, as usual, had prepared for the occasion. Written originally after the conclusion of the battle of El Alamein, it read:

> The paramount task before us is, first, to conquer the African shores of the Mediterranean and set up there the naval and air installations which are necessary to open an effective passage through it for military traffic; and, secondly, using the bases on the African shore to strike at the underbelly of the Axis in effective strength and in the shortest time.

This was not the kind of argument which commended itself to Marshall though he was outnumbered among the American Chiefs of Staff: Arnold approved the prospect of obtaining air bases in Italy and King saw the advantages of occupying the Mediterranean. Marshall preferred the direct attack on the German heart from bases in England. He wanted this more than he wanted anything else; and he saw the slow drain of resources flung against Italy as something to be avoided: for clearly, when Churchill spoke of the soft underbelly of the Axis he meant Italy. There was still no indication when the invasion of Normandy would take place. TORCH would become a sponge. There was the danger that the Allies would regard the soft underbelly as the enemy regarded Tunisia, which became, as Marshall said in his third Biennial Report, "a lure into which the German command continued to pour great quantities of men and matériel, commitments that were certain to be disastrous for the enemy." He had prayed and hoped for ROUNDUP, spoken to Sir John Dill of a "modified ROUNDUP" in the summer of 1943, and wherever he turned, he was faced with the accusing stare of the Prime Minister, who seemed to be determined to thwart him. "You have certainly fixed my clock," he told Churchill when the conference was over. The remark puzzled one of the members of Churchill's staff, who enquired later: "Did the Prime Minister really repair one of your clocks so it would run?"

Though Marshall's favorite project was thwarted, hope ran wild at Casablanca. The Allies for the first time were taking the offensive. General Montgomery's Eighth Army had driven Rommel back to Tunisia. Though German supplies were coming over the Sicilian Strait, they would cease when the winter rains ended, and the overwhelming Allied superiority in the air would pound them out of the sea. There were, after all, advantages in attacking the soft underbelly; the very softness of the belly was tempting. Churchill was in his element. He showed how Italy could be knocked out of the war by hardly more than a cuff from a lion's paw: in this he proved to be a bad prophet, for the lion's paws were bloodied and mangled before they were done with the affair. He hinted at a drive through the Ljubljana Gap into Hungary. He showed how operations in Burma, the Middle East and the Pacific would become possible with the release of so many troops from the North African campaign. There were advantages in having large bomber bases in Italy. He listed the possibilities happily; and Marshall, still outnumbered by his Chiefs of Staff, was finally swung round, basing his decision on the fact that America was still in the process of a vast mobilization and "because we will have in North Africa a large number of troops available and because it will effect an economy in tonnage which is the major consideration." On January 23, Eisenhower received the directive to attack Sicily:

> The Combined Chiefs of Staff have resolved that an attack against Sicily will be launched in 1943 with the target date as the period of the favorable July moon.

This operation, which came to be known as HUSKY, was not the only operation decided upon at Casablanca. Plans were made to reduce Rabaul on the island of New Britain in the Pacific, and to open the Burma Road in an operation curiously named ANAKIM, which means "the race of giants." Rabaul remained an obstinate fortress until the end of the war, and ANAKIM was to be delayed for many months. A more surprising, and far more dangerous decision was reached: Roosevelt and Churchill both demanded the unconditional surrender of the enemy, with the result that German resistance was stiffened and one more hostage was given to fortune. But the giants were beginning to be conscious of their might.

When the conference was over, the delegates went their separate ways. Marshall went to Algiers, where Eisenhower had set up his headquarters. At Casablanca they had met briefly; now he stayed at Eisenhower's villa, and even occupied the immense double bed with the maroon silk covers where Eisenhower had slept. Marshall was gay and talkative; he told anecdotes; he was like a man from whose shoulders a great weight has been lifted. He still called Eisenhower by his full name, and he went out of his way to praise Eisenhower for his accomplishments. He liked the younger general's clear simple reports—Eisenhower was aware of Marshall's desire for brevity and kept reminding himself, sometimes in little notes addressed to himself, to obey the Chief of Staff's injunctions about brevity. Above all, Marshall liked and admired the man, and behaved like a father towards him, ordering him to take three days rest from his duties, urging him to play tennis and ride horseback, though Eisenhower was an indifferent performer at both, and commanding Eisenhower's naval aide to be sure that there was a capable masseur on the premises. Eisenhower was notoriously indifferent to his own health and generally disliked exercise; he had no alternative but to obey. "You must keep him refreshed," Marshall explained to the naval aide, "but knowing him as we do, it will take ingenuity. It is your job in the war to make him take care of his health and keep that alert brain from overworking." In this he was a little like a fussy aunt deploring the late hours of her most brilliant nephew.

For once, Marshall was full of enthusiasm. He praised Admiral Cunningham, who had thrown his fleet across the Mediterranean with the skill of the Elizabethan raiders. He was delighted with General Mark Clark's plans for a training center for the Fifth Army. He was pleased with the eleven-page document containing proposals for the year 1943 which had been presented at the final full-dress meeting between Roosevelt, Hopkins, Churchill and the Combined Chiefs of Staff. Finally, his distrust of the British was temporarily in abeyance: they had not suggested any transfer of the command to a British commander, though they had an enormous superiority of divisions in Tunisia.

With Eisenhower appointed a full general, Marshall flew back to Washington to fight for the Manpower Bill. He had 5,000,000 soldiers, and wanted 8,200,000 to launch the offensive which might put an end to the war by January, 1944. There were more interminable conferences with the House Military Affairs Committee; the misery of the conferences was not brightened by news of the Kasserine Pass disaster in Tunisia. The picture was rapidly changing. Stalingrad had been relieved by the Russians. There had been a sharp increase in the production of airplanes. MacArthur had won a resounding victory over the Japanese in the battle of the Bismarck Sea, his bombers under the command of Lieutenant General Kenney having attacked a Japanese convoy passing through the Vitiaz Strait in exactly the same circumstances as the Allied convoys passed through the Straits of Gibraltar. MacArthur claimed that his airmen in this battle had sunk twenty-three major Japanese ships, including all the transports carrying troops for an invasion of New Guinea at the cost of four Allied aircraft. "We have achieved a victory of such completeness as to assume the proportions of a major disaster to the enemy," wrote MacArthur. "His campaign for the time being at least is completely dislocated."

Marshall, who possessed a high opinion of MacArthur's tactical abilities, appears to have been wary of the good news. Exactly what passed between him and MacArthur has never been revealed. The victory was apparently not reported to MacArthur's satisfaction in one of the official accounts of the war published at the time, and MacArthur immediately took umbrage, saying that the report questioned his honor, integrity and reliability, and he demanded to be called before a jury of his peers—a demand which was astonishing only because, in a very real sense, MacArthur possessed no peers in the Army who could serve on a court-martial. Marshall replied that he was not responsible for the report, that no one questioned MacArthur's integrity, and when he came to write the second Biennial Report he gave MacArthur full credit for the victory.

There were many quarrels among the generals during the war, some of them, like the quarrel with General Hugh A. Drum as reported by Secretary Stimson, of quite extraordinary violence, even though the violence was well-mannered. When Patton was told by Marshall he would have only a limited number of transports to carry his troops to

North Africa, Patton demurred. He said he must have many more. Marshall immmediately ordered him back to the West Coast. From there, having cooled his heels, he telephoned plaintively to say he had thought the matter over and was prepared to take the transports, would in fact be delighted to take them. Marshall ordered him back to Washington, saying: "This is the way to deal with Patton." There was even a quarrel between Marshall and Eisenhower, when Eisenhower used publicly the phrase "lost his pants" and found himself vigorously corrected for unseemly language. But these were small matters in a war which tried every man's temper, and Marshall, who always gave the impression of holding himself in reserve, held his temper in check with surprising self-command. Inevitably, the most violent of his explosions occurred when he was among civilians, but that will be told in its proper place.

The battle for Tunisia drew to an end. The Afrika Korps abandoned a succession of defensive positions and withdrew into Tripolitania, then established itself on the Mareth Line in southeast Tunisia, later to join forces with von Arnim's command. It was this junction of forces which brought about the defeat at Kasserine Pass, but the defeat was quickly avenged; and by March 11 Eisenhower was telegraphing a message to Marshall saying he contemplated a rising scale of offensive operations. Early in May the German and Italian forces in North Africa were defeated. In these campaigns altogether a quarter of a million enemy troops surrendered.

Marshall was delighted. The victory had been brought about, he said later, by three decisive factors. They were:

(1) The perfect example of coordinated leadership for Allied action.
(2) The assemblage of overwhelming military power, air, land and sea.
(3) The explosive effect of the skillful application of that power.

A great deal of the credit went to Eisenhower, and Marshall sent his congratulations immediately. He was pleased, too, with the terse manner of an order written by the headstrong Major General Terry Allen at one phase of the campaign—so pleased that he sent a copy to the President. On a tour of inspection he had seen General Mark Clark's training centers in Tunisia, and these too pleased him. He said they were among the most remarkable training schools he had ever seen; they took in everything; they trained men in amphibious operations, mountain operations, village fighting and everything else in the most practical fashion. They were magnificent, but they contained an unavoidable error. He said it should never have been necessary to have training quarters in Africa at all, for all the training should have been done in America. He seemed to be remembering the long year wasted in France during the First World War.

With all of North Africa in Allied hands, HUSKY could now be put into operation, but the problem of OVERLORD remained, and to solve this problem (among many others) the President called another conference. This conference, which came to be known as TRIDENT, the first of the "numerical" conferences, was distinguished from the previous ones by the presence of Chennault and Stilwell from China, and of Wavell from India. There were the usual disagreements and the usual tempests. In the end, the conference, so elaborately planned, reached agreements already arrived at in Casablanca and added some necessary footnotes. The Cross-Channel Operation, which Marshall had hoped to see in December, 1942, was fixed for May, 1944, the initial assault consisting of nine divisions (two airborne) to be followed by twenty more when a bridgehead had been opened. ANAKIM was to be pursued vigorously. Ploesti in Rumania was to be bombed; the Japanese lines of communication were to be cut; the Azores were to be seized. Except for the decision to intensify on a hitherto unprecedented scale the bombing of Germany, no decision was so important as the decision to postpone the Cross-Channel operation until 1944, with its inevitable repercussions in Moscow. From Washington or London the plan looked reasonable: the conquest of Sicily in the autumn to be followed by the landings in Normandy in the spring. It was not so certain that the plan looked reasonable in Moscow, where there was considerable belief that Churchill was deliberately prolonging the opening of the second front. On the last night the President and Churchill sat together over the draft of a memorandum to Stalin. Inevitably the memorandum would be unpleasant. It was written and rewritten until it was a mess of scribbles, and at two o'clock in the morning Churchill suggested it was time for him to go, he would take the draft and work on it in the plane to Gander, and from Gander he would send it back to the President with whatever amendments he had thought of during the journey. The President agreed. As Churchill was rising, Marshall entered the room. Both Churchill and Marshall were leaving fairly soon for North Africa, but they had not intended to travel together. Then the President suggested that Marshall should accompany Churchill and they could work over the memorandum to Stalin in the airplane. Marshall waved his hand, said: "I will be there," and made his departure.

With six hours notice, on the morning of May 26, Marshall flew off with Churchill. In the flying boat Churchill worked on the memorandum and then gave it up in despair. It was sent to Marshall, who carefully revised the memorandum and presented the Prime Minister with a clean draft some two hours later. Churchill was astonished and delighted. The crisp new version said everything he had intended to say with a clarity which had escaped him. The new draft was sent to the President from Botwood, New Brunswick. Shortly afterwards they began a direct flight across the Atlantic to Gibraltar, a distance of twenty-seven hundred miles. This particular journey had never been flown before.

At Gibraltar, Marshall was coaxed into a tour of inspection. He was shown the distillery, the guns, the monkeys, the hospitals. He reviewed the troops, dined with the Governor and was sent on a tour of the rock galleries from which quick-firing guns commanded the Straits. He was not altogether impressed with the galleries. He said: "I admired your gallery, but we had one like it in Corregidor. The Japanese fired their artillery at the rock several hundred feet above it, and in two or three days blocked it off with an immense bank of rubble." Marshall, as so often, was thinking of the worst. When Eisenhower went down into the galleries of the rock he was overjoyed. "I have operational command of Gibraltar, the symbol of the solidarity of the British Empire," he wrote. "An American is in charge, and I am he. Hundreds of feet within the bowels of the Rock itself I have my command post. I simply *must* have a grandchild or I'll never have the fun of telling this when I'm fishing, grey-bearded, on the banks of a quiet bayou in the deep south."

The main reason for Churchill's flight to North Africa was to discuss with Eisenhower the next stage of the offensive against Germany. In a spirit of fairness, Churchill hoped to convince Eisenhower that OVERLORD could not take place before the spring, and he wanted to do this in the presence of the arch-defender of an immediate OVERLORD. There were a number of important details to be settled, and there was the question of bombing the Italian marshaling yards. When the conferences were over Marshall was asked to meet the correspondents. There were sixty of them. He began by asking each one of them to phrase a question, and then he reviewed the whole course of the war, organizing his statement in such a way that all the questions were answered, and whenever he came to the point where the precise answer of a question was answered, he nodded gently in the direction of the correspondent who had asked it. It was an uncanny performance. He had done much the same kind of thing during the previous war when correspondents interviewed him in the operations room at the Souilly *mairie,* but never on so prodigious a scale, nor with such *elan.* Though he said little that was new, he gave a precise history of the development of the war, with all the relevant facts in order: it was as though he was testing his own knowledge of these developments by marshaling them together and placing them before the correspondents.

He returned to Washington with the knowledge that the minor operation HOBGOBLIN—the capture of Mussolini's prison island of Pantelleria—was well under way and the plans for the invasion of Sicily were in a high state of preparation. He also had the mission of obtaining from the American Government approval for the bombing of the marshaling yards in Rome. This might be difficult, for Cardinal Spellman had raised some objections previously. He had spent some pleasant days with Eisenhower—he noted that Eisenhower had paid some attention to advice concerning his health, and had even taken to horseback riding—and he had inspected the troops. He was pleased with their bearing. If there was little news of importance from the South Pacific, there was excellent news from Alaska, where the battle of Attu had been fought and won. In heavy fog and deep snow, on a roadless island, supported by Navy and Air forces, part of the Seventh Infantry Division had fought its way across the hills to encircle the Japanese troops defending Chichagof Harbor. Twenty days after their landing, at the cost of 512 Americans, they had annihilated 2,350 Japanese. This was a small victory, but an important one, for Kiska had been bypassed, and there had arisen the possibility that innumerable islands in the Pacific could be similarly bypassed. Island-hopping had begun.

Marshall was in an elated mood when he addressed the Conference of State Governors at Columbus, Ohio, on June 21. It had become his practice to make these addresses as an alternative to meeting the press. He knew that he was considered to be the only American in a position to see the war situation as a whole, and he therefore phrased his speeches carefully, writing them himself, his style becoming more robust as the war progressed. He told how the American troops had passed through the period of military adolescence, and the initiative had passed to the Allies. He cast a passing horrified glance at the arguments and conferences of the past, and the terrible days when they had planned their strategies piecemeal. All that was over. He declared: "The pattern for victory is clear. If we had set the stage we could not have provided a more sharply defined picture than that offered by the battle of Tunisia." He explained how the Germans had been humbled by an improvement of the same technique which brought about the defeat of France. "The Superman has had his day. The democracies have called his bluff."

But to speak of Tunisia, a model campaign, was one thing; there remained the Pacific; and when he went on to speak about the conquest of Attu, he was describing the same kind of conditions which existed in the Pacific where the soldiers fought as much against the weather as against their enemies. In such areas the tasks would be increasingly difficult, with over-extended lines and a heavy battle to be maintained beyond the beaches. Yet the end was certain, though great battles lay ahead.

When he described the battle of Attu he wrote with a heavy keen-edged style which is rare in his writings. He said:

> The recent battle in Attu has special significance. There we encountered probably the most difficult of fighting conditions. An amphibious operation in uncharted waters over a stormy sea, deep snow and high mountains, with a complete absence of roads and trails; an enemy dug in with complete cover and communication and our own troops transferred through necessity from the pleasant climate of California to a battle with the elements over an extremely

> difficult terrain, against a desperate enemy. It was a severe test of the American soldier, but today we hold Attu, with more than one thousand nine hundred Japanese graves as a memento of their previous occupation.

He turned to the civilian front: there he was not so sure that the battle was being fought as it should be fought. "Sometimes," he said, "I am discouraged by the democratic processes in a great and critical emergency like that of today." What had aroused his anger was the report in some newspapers that a secret agreement had been reached between the War Department and the Women's Army Auxiliary Corps that contraceptives would be furnished to the WAAC's. He regarded these rumors with more bitterness and horror than they probably deserved. They were evidence, he thought, of an element of self-destruction among the people. "Some seem to be intent on the suicide of our own war effort," he declared. "If we cannot be decent in such matters we at least should not be naïve enough to destroy ourselves." It was strange that he should pay so much importance to a matter which reflected only upon the inevitable moral disturbances of wartime, but he was on safer ground when he warned against optimism. "The great battles lie ahead. We have yet to be proven in the agony of enduring heavy casualties, as well as the reverses which are inevitable in war. What we need is a stoic determination to do everything in our power to overwhelm the enemy, cost what it may."

When General Giraud arrived by plane in Washington on the afternoon of July 7, Marshall greeted him as one who possessed these stoic virtues to an almost unparalleled degree. General de Gaulle, perpetually listening to the mysterious and divergent voices of the past, speaking with the authentic voice of the Middle Ages, so tall that he felt at ease only among the gods, had incurred the large wrath of Roosevelt and the lesser wrath of the Chief of Staff. Giraud was humble, brave, generous and predictable. There had been one incident: a furious argument in the caverns of Gibraltar when he insisted upon being the commander in chief of the Allied forces in North Africa, but after this display of emotion he behaved with an understanding tolerance of American ways. Marshall took him in tow, presided at a dinner for him at the Mayflower Hotel, and then, because the heat in Washington was unbearable, removed him to Dodona Manor in Leesburg, Virginia, a colonial mansion which Marshall had bought shortly after becoming Chief of Staff.

Marshall had fallen in love with Dodona Manor. There were five acres of ground, fruit trees, spreading oaks, a vegetable garden of tomatos, beans, eggplant, turnips and squash. There was also a compost heap which Marshall regarded with a great deal of affection. It was his custom to prune the trees and keep the compost heap "boiling." He enjoyed pottering in the garden, pruning the oaks and ashes, or hunting pheasants nearby. Part of the house was built in 1784, and once a ball for Lafayette had been held there. Indeed, the manor reeked of history at remove, for Leesburg was at the heart of the Virginia from which he derived his strength. Here Washington had his headquarters when he served the King in the French and Indian wars under General Braddock. Leesburg had grown respectable, but it was still possible to guess, among those shaded southern houses, at the tumult of the past. General Giraud, solid, distinguished and adventurous, found himself sitting under an oak tree with an iced drink, and the war seemed a million miles away. But on July 10 the assault on Sicily began, and the invasion of the German fortress of Europe had begun.

As usual, Marshall prepared his summary of the course of the war during the two years which ended July 1, 1943. The second Biennial Report has none of the brilliance of the third: a quiet, cautious, slightly repetitive document which seems to have been written passionlessly and in a great hurry. The situation as he saw it was simple: the Allies had already witnessed the turning point of the war and everywhere they were on the offensive, with a mounting power and a freshness which the enemy could never imitate or surpass. He wrote:

> The British Isles are stronger than ever before and a new France is arising from the ashes of 1940. Strategically the enemy in Europe has been reduced to the defensive and the blockade is complete. In the Pacific the Japanese are being steadily ejected or rather eliminated from their conquered territory. The Aleutians are about to be cleared of all tracks and traces of the enemy. In the South and Southwest Pacific two facts are plainly evident to the Japanese command as

well as to the world at large: our progress may seem slow but it is steady and determined, and it has been accompanied by a terrific destruction of enemy planes and surface vessels. This attrition must present an appalling problem for the enemy High Command. Whatever satisfaction they may draw from the fanatical sacrifice of their soldiers with whom our forces come in contact, the destruction of their air power and shipping continues on an increasing and truly remarkable scale.

The Report, which was published in September, was supplemented with thirty-one appendices, which offered short notes on various phases of the organization for war. One of the longest concerned the problem of unity of command. It discussed the operation of the Joint Chiefs of Staff and Combined Chiefs of Staff, and explained how these organizations led inevitably to "the unity of command principle which places the responsibility and authority for a contemplated operation under one commander." But who was the commander? The answer was given in a secret decision reached at the conference called by Churchill and the President in Quebec in August.

For the first time Marshall was now able to attend a conference where he could report that his army was in process of conquering part of Europe—the news of the fall of Messina,, the last remaining outpost in northeastern Sicily under Fascist domination, came while the conference was sitting. The campaign had lasted thirty-nine days, and though the scale of American losses was incomparably lower than the scale of enemy losses, they were far higher than expected and gave a foretaste of the future: there were 170,000 German and Italian losses, while Allied casualties numbered 31,158 dead, wounded and missing.

Once again the conference was concerned with plotting a course. The course hardly commended itself to Marshall. He had left Washington in an Army plane in the rain; the plane had been forced down at Montreal, and the weather was bleak and cold. For Marshall the atmosphere of the conference was as bleak and cold as the weather. Churchill insisted on widening prospective operations to include an assault on southern France; Marshall was against a Mediterranean commitment. In Marshall's eyes this was one more sign of Churchill's desire to postpone indefinitely the main attack through Normandy. The British were insisting on expanding the Italian operations: again Marshall disagreed. However, the target date for OVERLORD was reaffirmed, even though Churchill was still not reconciled to the Normandy landing. It was decided to step up the bombing of enemy communications—the code names for these bombing offensives were POINTBLANK and STRANGLE, which suggest the change in the weather of their minds. The problem of Russia was discussed, and Harry Hopkins was in possession of an important document headed *Russia's Position* which quoted from "a very high level United States military strategic estimate," otherwise unnamed. The quoted passage, which is printed in Robert E. Sherwood's admirable *Roosevelt and Hopkins,* appears on internal evidence to be written by Marshall. It read:

> Russia's post-war position in Europe will be a dominant one. With Germany crushed, there is no power in Europe to oppose her tremendous military forces. It is true that Great Britain is building up a position in the Mediterranean vis-à-vis Russia that she may find useful in balancing power in Europe. However, even here she may not be able to oppose Russia unless she is otherwise supported.
>
> The conclusions from the foregoing are obvious. Since Russia is the decisive factor in the war, she must be given every assistance and every effort must be made to obtain her friendship. Likewise, since without question she will dominate Europe on the defeat of the Axis, it is even more essential to develop and maintain the most friendly relations with Russia.
>
> Finally, the most important factor the United States has to consider in relation to Russia is the prosecution of the war in the Pacific. With Russia as an ally in the war against Japan, the war can be terminated in less time and less expense in life and resources than if the reverse were the case. Should the war in the Pacific have to be carried on with an unfriendly or negative attitude on the part of Russia, the difficulties will be immeasurably increased and operations might become abortive.

This estimate, which clearly continues the argument outlined by the Joint Board of September, 1941, was, like so many of the Army estimates, accurate in delineating an existing political force and inaccurate in its deductions; and it was to have great and tragic importance in guiding the policy which brought about the decisions reached in Teheran and Yalta.

At this conference in Quebec it was agreed by a secret decision that Marshall should be Supreme Commander of OVERLORD, and Eisenhower should be recalled to act as Chief of Staff. This decision was brought about largely at the prompting of Secretary Stimson who had visited London that summer and discussed the appointment with Churchill, a little hesitantly, not knowing that Churchill had already promised the position to Field Marshal Sir Alan Brooke, whom the Americans found strangely forbidding. On one of the last days of the conference, to Stimson's extreme pleasure, he was summoned by the President and told that Churchill had voluntarily come to him and spoken of his acceptance of Marshall as the Supreme Commander.

The decision, though apparently final, was kept secret, for any announcement would have given the Germans a clue as to what kind of attack to expect. Marshall had now been Chief of Staff for four years and would normally have retired from the post on September 1. He was told to carry on. He imagined he would be Supreme Commander, and even began to remove his furniture to Dodona Manor from the house at Fort Myer in the expectation that he would not be attending his office at the Pentagon but would have his headquarters in London, and when the war was over he would retire quietly to Leesburg. He had not counted with his friends. Among these were Major General Stanley D. Embick, who was concerned with the dangers which might arise if Marshall left his dominating position among the Combined Chiefs of Staff. Embick had taken part in the first real American-British staff talks held in Washington at the end of January, 1941. He was close to Harry Hopkins. He had been Deputy Chief of Staff and after his retirement he was recalled to duty as chairman of the United States-Canada Permanent Joint Defense Board, a post where his tremendous energy had few outlets. He now began to fight a one-man battle for the retention of Marshall in Washington. He approached Hopkins, who allowed the matter to rest with the President: Hopkins would do nothing to change the appointment. Embick thereupon called up General Malin Craig, who had succeeded MacArthur as Chief of Staff and preceded Marshall. Malin Craig had bushwhacked through the Philippine jungles with Major General J. Franklin Bell, he had served in China against the Boxers and fought at Santiago. He was a West Pointer who had enjoyed a brilliant military career, and it was not his fault if he was a more or less undistinguished Chief of Staff: he had only the stump of an Army to rule over. In 1941 he was recalled to duty as head of the Personnel Board of the War Department, and he still retained this office. Close to Pershing during World War I, he now used his friendship with Pershing for the purpose of keeping Marshall in Washington. He also arranged that the *Army-Navy Journal,* which usually expressed the views of the Army, would print an editorial lamenting Marshall's transfer to London, saying that "Marshall has come into conflict with powerful interests which would like to eliminate him from the Washington picture." The statement was not happy, nor was it particularly true, but Pershing seized upon it, and other similar reports, and wrote with the help of General Embick a letter to the President emphasizing that Marshall had already played the part of master-coordinator in the global war, and "to transfer him to a tactical command in a limited area, no matter how seemingly important, is to deprive ourselves of the benefit of his outstanding strategical ability and experience."

The President replied four days later:

> You are absolutely right about George Marshall—and yet, I think, you are wrong too! He is, as you say, far and away the most valuable man as Chief of Staff. But, as you know, the operations for which we are considering him are the biggest that we will conduct in this war. And, when the time comes, it will not be a mere limited area proposition, but I think the command will include the whole European theater—and, in addition to that, the British want him to sit with their own Joint Staff in all matters that do not pertain to purely British island affairs.
>
> More than that, I think it is only a fair thing to give George a chance in the field—and because of the nature of the job we shall still have the benefit of his strategical ability.
>
> The best way I can express it is to tell you that I want George to be the Pershing of the second World War—and he cannot be that if we keep him here. I know you will understand.

The President, who may have suspected that Pershing did not write the whole of the letter submitted under his name, had written a clever response. He seized upon the phrase "a tactical command in a limited area" and showed that it was largely meaningless. He still hoped Marshall would be the Supreme Commander, and when he left for the Teheran conference in November he intended to inform Stalin and Marshall formally of the appointment, but as often happened he temporized, made no clear announcement, waited for time to solve his own problems, and he did this deliberately and purposefully, for there were advantages in temporizing. These advantages, however, were unknown to the popular press. When a few days later the *Army and Navy Register,* which usually reflected authoritative opinion, announced that "the European command would not be a promotion from his place as Chief of Staff of our Army, but only removal from Washington, where it is said that some concerned with strategy do not want him," the fat was in the fire. The Washington *Times-Herald* came out with banner headlines: "GLOBAL W.P.A. SEEN AIM IN MARSHALL 'PLOT.'" There were denunciations of the "dismissal" of Marshall in newspapers all over the country. It was assumed wrongly that Hopkins was in the Churchill camp and Marshall in the opposing camp, that this was only one more piece of evidence to demonstrate the evil hand of Hopkins, and that Marshall was being attacked by a group of enemies who included Hopkins, Justice Felix Frankfurter and Henry Morgenthau. None of these statements were true, and General Embick was hardly responsible for the *furore* he had aroused. Stimson appears to have played some part in General Embick's unhappy crusade, but about this and many other things he remained discreetly silent when he wrote his memoirs. One of the minor results of the affair was Marshall's appointment as President of the United States. This occurred after a Nazi broadcast from Paris saying that Marshall had been relieved of his duties and President Roosevelt had taken over his command. Marshall attached this announcement to a note to Hopkins: "Dear Harry: Are you responsible for pulling this fast one on me? G.C.M." The note came back with another note scribbled at the bottom: "Dear George. Only true in part. I am now Chief of Staff but you are President. F.D.R."

Of all the people concerned in the public quarrel Marshall was the least affected. He had stated repeatedly his desire to serve in whatever place the President thought best, and he had no desire to depart from his rule. But if he was determined to remain silent Stimson was equally determined to take every opportunity for pressing

Marshall's case. He wrote to the President on August 10, reminding him that he was far luckier than Lincoln or Wilson, for he possessed a Chief of Staff who had "a towering eminence of reputation as a tried soldier and as a broadminded and skillful administrator." In this letter he asked for Marshall's appointment as Supreme Commander, and now he returned to the charge. He wrote:

> I do not think we can safely postpone the date of his taking command beyond November 1st. The fatal delays and diversions which may sabotage OVERLORD will begin in the U.K. this autumn and nothing but his direct presence and influence will save us from them. No one dreads more than I do the loss of his influence in theaters other than the European theaters, but I hope that the rank and title which I have suggested [he proposed that Marshall should hold the rank of General of the Armies] will help to preserve that influence indirectly in those faraway theatres even if not directly. I have talked this over with Harry and I think on most of these points he is in full sympathy with me.

It was a typically Stimsonian approach, indirect but at the same time challenging, but Roosevelt had no desire to be stampeded into making a formal decision. The newspaper hullabaloo lasted for two weeks, then quietly died, becoming, as Roosevelt remarked a little later, "pretty much of a dead cat." It was not, however, a dead cat in the eyes of Churchill who was alarmed by the wild rumors and who was not certain of the precise connotation of the words "Supreme Commander." Did this mean that Marshall would have complete powers over the R.A.F.? Would he be allowed to make decisions outside the sphere of OVERLORD?

While the newspapers were debating the question of the future Supreme Commander, Marshall was preoccupied with his appearance before the Senate Committee on Military Affairs, which was then debating whether the pre-Pearl Harbor fathers should be exempted from the Army. Marshall was still in search of a large and overwhelming Army; he regarded the processes of exemption with considerable distrust. He explained, as General McNarney had done before him, that there had to be seventy-five thousand replenishments each month, and in the light of the Salerno casualties these were probably insufficient. The War Department was being pressed daily by the field commanders for more men, and it was impossible to plan operations without a sufficient reserve. All this was a familiar argument, which he had stated in a slightly different form before the war and was to repeat again later long after the war was over. The usual objections were raised, and Marshall employed his usual tactics to remove them. By giving the Senators secret information he hoped to make them more malleable. He said:

> I am possibly getting into the dangerous ground of publicizing information, but maybe the end justifies the means. At the present time we are shipping to England, this month, some fifty thousand special troops, engineers, mechanics, signal troops, and so on, to keep that place operating. We are sending over some six hundred bomber crews, not to increase the bombers we have in England, but to maintain the bombers we have in England, and we are being pressed very heavily to send them as rapidly as possible, to keep that great operation going. There is a constant drain, and we must have the people in time, trained and ready to sail when they are required.

The drain was uppermost in his thoughts. It seemed impossible sometimes that the Senators would understand that the drain was perpetual, and that there were often as many losses from fatigue as there were from battle. Disease and discharges made nearly as much havoc of the army as casualties. Italy had surrendered, but the fighting went on in Italy almost as though no surrender had taken place. He noted that after the loss of the Italian divisions the total of Axis forces in Italy was still within fourteen of the grand total in 1942. The assumption that Germany had been bled white at Stalingrad had to be combatted. So did the assumption that the Pentagon was brimming with young officers who could be spared from their desks. Senator Wheeler spoke of those young men who sat in their comfortable chairs at the Pentagon and had no better view of the war than that which can be provided from a glimpse of Arlington Cemetery. Were there such young men in the War Department? Senator Wheeler asked. Marshall answered that such men did indeed exist: there was one, for example, who had his hand shot off at Hawaii. The Senator went on to complain that innumerable soldiers were writing to him on this matter, but they dared not allow their names to be known. Marshall was puzzled. He said the War Department was not running a Gestapo, and if there was any foundation for what they had to report they would probably be promoted.

The meeting with the Senate Committee occurred on September 20. On the next day Marshall addressed the American Legion at Omaha, Nebraska. He repeated much that he had told the Senate Committee, and he repeated ironically the statement made by some Senators that the Army was already too large, saying: "I do know that I am profoundly grateful that for once in the history of the United States there is suggested the possibility that we have too much of something or other." He talked of "the flood of power" which was being massed against the enemy, and he concluded his speech with a statement which was to haunt him in later years, for it described a dream which seemed incapable of being made a reality: "We must proceed in the most businesslike manner possible to make this war so terrible to the enemy, so overwhelming in character, that never again can a small group of dictators find a sufficient following to destroy the peaceful security of a civilized world."

Perhaps the dream itself was insufficient; perhaps the word "businesslike" concealed elementary errors; perhaps the vision of "the peaceful security of a civilized world" dominated by American power lacked definition; but it is more likely that the logic was at fault, for there is no reason to believe that dictators ever learn lessons from their defeats. Until the end of the war, and long afterwards, Marshall's mind was to play with the same phrase, repeating it under slightly different forms, restlessly attempting to define the undefinable: will the dictators ever be crushed? in what way does America play her part in the world? on what premises reposes the *pax americana?* He was to find the answers—some of them—when the time came to underwrite the Marshall Plan.

The problems of OVERLORD and the unified command were still uppermost in Marshall's mind, and by November they were to flare up again during the two great conferences held at Cairo and Teheran. These conferences were by far the most decisive held up to this time. Previously neither Chiang Kai-shek nor Stalin had attended the conferences held by the Western Allies; by now their attendance could no longer be delayed; and when Marshall set out with the Chiefs of Staff on a cold, rainy day from Washington on Admiral King's flagship, the *Dauntless,* to meet the new battleship, U.S.S. *Iowa* sailing up from Hampton Roads, he was perfectly aware that decisions were about to be made by heads of states which might wreck his carefully laid plans. He was not feeling well; he had a bad cold which he shook off with difficulty. Unknown to him, Stimson had once again urged Marshall's claims, saying that Marshall's command of OVERLORD was imperative and he must be sent immediately to London, even though Marshall himself had written with Admiral Leahy a memorandum pointing out that there were advantages in appointing a deputy—it was more important at this point to appoint a deputy than to appoint a Supreme Commander. Roosevelt was still undecided, and the Joint Chiefs were prepared to accept a British commander "provided the man named is Sir John Dill." Leahy, King and Arnold were all working for the retention of Marshall in Washington. The secret agreement made in Quebec was now a thing of the past. Once more final decisions were in the melting pot, with no obvious solutions in sight; and once again among the American Joint Chiefs there was the general suspicion that Churchill was at his Fabian tactics, delaying OVERLORD with countless arguments in favor of Mediterranean adventures.

To Marshall as he sat in conference, the progress towards these final decisions was a little like the progress of his ship which zigzagged across the Atlantic and was once very nearly torpedoed by a torpedo launched accidently from one of the escorting destroyers. This strange event happened one afternoon during firing practice. The air was full of screaming antiaircraft shells firing at balloons when someone observed the wake of a torpedo advancing towards the *Iowa*. Somebody shouted the dread warning: "This is not a practice." The *Iowa* veered in time, missing the torpedo by a scant twenty yards and proceeded on its way. The lesson of the accidental torpedo attack was not lost on the Chiefs of Staff.

On the second day out there was a long conference. Plans were prepared for placing the R.A.F. and A.A.F. under a single commander, and for placing the whole Mediterranean area under a single commander. The question of the commander of OVERLORD came up. Sir John Dill, Sir Harold Alexander, Montgomery and Eisenhower were all passed under review, and once again no decisions were reached. On the morning of the 20th the *Iowa* nosed into the harbor of Oran, having passed through the Straits of Gibraltar without being observed by enemy airplanes, though rumors of their coming were already rife—on the 17th the censor had released a report in Cairo saying that the conference was about to begin there. There was some astonishment at the news, and there were discussions about changing the locale of the conference to Khartoum. In the end it was decided to proceed as though security regulations had not been infringed. They flew from Oran to Carthage, where Eisenhower had his headquarters, and the next morning they were on their way to Cairo, to discover that Churchill had already spent two days there and Chiang Kai-shek's party had already arrived.

At Carthage, Roosevelt had gone through one of those disarming changes of mind which were so characteristic of him. He told Eisenhower that he had come to the conclusion that Marshall must be Supreme Commander of OVERLORD. He spoke of how chiefs of staff were always forgotten—who, for example, could remember the names of the chiefs of staff under Lincoln? He was concerned that Marshall's name should be remembered. He explained that Eisenhower would be recalled to take Marshall's place in Washington. Eisenhower was confused. From King and Arnold he heard a contrary story, while Harry Hopkins was reasonably certain that Marshall would be leaving Washington shortly for London. There was no agreement on this subject, and in Cairo disagreement between the British and American Chiefs of Staff only increased. "It is going to be a hot meeting," Hopkins announced before it began, and in this he was as accurate as he usually was.

All they had suspected happened to be true. Churchill produced a series of brilliant arguments in favor of operations in the Aegean and against the island of Rhodes. The American Chiefs of Staff had long ago rejected the idea, but Churchill returned to the attack, convincing while he was talking, unconvincing the moment he was silent. There was agreement to expand ANAKIM, though even there Churchill was wary. Admiral King and Admiral Nimitz discussed their well-known plan of defeating the Japanese largely by sea power: they would cut the Japanese tentacles and blockade the coast. This conception of the war in the Pacific was sufficiently like Churchill's conception of war in the Mediterranean to meet objections from

Marshall; and with the discovery that the American Chiefs of Staff were themselves not united, Roosevelt was once more in the position of being the prime mover—the decisions as far as they affected America were made by him alone, though he followed Marshall's advice in rejecting Churchill's plan to "turn to the right" after reaching the Pisa-Rimini Line. Churchill was in favor of a breakthrough through the Ljubljana Gap, and he pressed his case vigorously. Marshall regarded this as only one more example of Churchill's desire for strategic diversions, and in this Marshall was probably fatally wrong. With the conclusion of the Cairo conference no final agreements had been made except to assist Chiang Kai-shek with all the power at their command; and everyone knew that these vague promises would be kept only if a miracle occurred.

In all these conferences Marshall had played his role quietly and relentlessly. He was not concerned with brilliant solutions. He wanted a landing on Normandy; nothing less would satisfy him. As the conferences succeeded one another his stature increased. He would analyze a situation trenchantly and with a lucidity which was often lacking in Arnold and King and which was wholly lacking in the Commander in Chief. There was something awe-inspiring in the mere processes of his orderly, logical mind, a mind which behaved like a hammer and continually repeated: "There is OVERLORD. This must be settled. There must be the blow to the heart, and then it will be all over."

In Carthage Roosevelt had informed Eisenhower he would be the next Chief of Staff. In Cairo he told Arnold that Marshall could not be spared from Washington, and a few days later at Teheran he was still undecided, deliberately postponing the date of decision.

At the Teheran Conference, which began on November 28, Marshall missed the most exciting, though it was the least dramatic, of the meetings between the three heads of the states; he had taken a staff car and driven away on a sight-seeing tour in the direction of the Elbruz Mountains, and with a vague idea of testing how far Russian territorial power extended north of Teheran. When he drove off with Arnold, exactly one half of the American Joint Chiefs of Staff were absent from the preliminary conference. Marshall heard later that Stalin had quietly embarked on a discussion of the next phase of the campaign against the Axis, and everything he said reinforced Marshall's position. Stalin was dubious about Turkey's desire to enter the war; he threw scorn on extensive operations in Italy; he was in no way impressed by the thought of a drive through the Ljubljana Gap; and he wanted OVERLORD to be synchronized with a vast westward movement of the Russian Army. He promised that once the war against Germany was ended, Russia would throw in her eastern armies against Japan. He was against all diversionary activities in the Mediterranean, but he agreed with the necessity of an attack against southern France— the sooner the better. Marshall found himself treated with the greatest respect by the Russians; and when Stalin pressed for the immediate appointment of the Supreme Commander, it was clear that his choice lay with Marshall. By this time Churchill was insisting on Marshall's appointment, and Roosevelt found himself facing the heads of two powerful states both clamoring for the same thing, and he was still unable to make a decision.

On November 29 there was held the first meeting of the military chiefs. It was a small meeting, attended only by Sir Alan Brooke, Voroshilov, Portal, Marshall and Leahy. Voroshilov urged an immediate decision concerning the flank attack through southern France—it was characteristic of both Voroshilov and Stalin that they were always asking for immediate decisions and did not comprehend that the Western Allies were often completely unable to make decisions on the spur of the moment. Sir Alan Brooke talked happily about an invasion of the Dodecanese, and Voroshilov, who possessed no knowledge of naval matters, wondered why the Americans and British were obsessed with problems of landing craft and transports. The Russians, after all, had experience of crossing rivers, and they were usually able to get their men across. Marshall then explained that he wished to offer a comment. He said: "The difference between a river crossing, however wide, and a landing from the ocean is that the failure of a river crossing is a reverse while the failure of a landing operation is a catastrophe. . . . My military education and experience in the First World War has all been based on roads, rivers and railroads. During the last two years, however, I've been acquiring an education based on oceans and I've had to learn all over again. Prior to the present war I never heard of any landing craft except a rubber boat. Now I think about little else."

Voroshilov seems to have been convinced, for though it is unlikely that he ever understood the problems of supporting supplies across three thousand miles of ocean, he beamed at Marshall and said: "If you think about it, you will do it."

But if there was an atmosphere of generous understanding between the Americans and the Russians, it was largely on the surface. The Russians were pleased with OVERLORD. They spoke of synchronizing it with their attacks from the east, but they were not prepared to name a date. They agreed with Arnold's suggestion of "shuttle bombing" across Germany with the great bombers landing in western Russia, but when the time came for the operation to be carried out, they lost interest rapidly—Arnold believed they objected to fraternization and particularly objected to the American magazines, The *Saturday Evening Post, Collier's* and others, which reached the American squad rooms in Russia. They told the Americans to go ahead with the planning of bases in Siberia, to be used when Russia declared war on Japan, and then forgot about it. There were limitless difficulties of interpretation, which were not lessened by the fact that Stalin knew some English and Churchill knew some Russian and both were attempting to conceal their knowledge. It was a time when the air shivered with beginnings—on a scrap of paper Roosevelt outlined the shape of the United Nations. He discussed the dismemberment of Germany, as one might tear a wild animal to pieces, scattering its legs to the four corners. But inevitably—it happened shortly after Churchill's ceremonial presentation of the "Sword of Stalingrad"—they returned to the question of the Supreme Commander of OVERLORD. It was Stalin who asked, refusing to believe that the operation would ever come about until its commander was named. Once again Roosevelt was silent, not perhaps because he was unsure of himself but because he had not yet assessed all the complex decisions of the conference and it was still not certain whether the commander of OVERLORD would command all operations in western and southern Europe. Was OVERLORD to be delayed again? Even this was not certain. Meanwhile he wanted a few more days to consider the matter. Perhaps he would ask for one commander over the Normandy operations, another over southern France, another over the Mediterranean. Someone seems to have told Stalin that Marshall would certainly be appointed. He is supposed to have answered: "Excellent—now we can get on with the job." It may be true. Certainly he regarded Marshall more than Roosevelt as the American engineer of victory.

The three-power conference came to an end, and was followed by a two-power conference in Cairo between the Americans and the British—conferences had become endemic and there seemed no hope that they would ever cease. Though the date of OVERLORD had been finally decided, there were more discussions concerning Rhodes, the Dodecanese, the Andaman islands: Churchill, an islander, saw victory in terms of islands. There were discussions with General Smuts and President Inönü of Turkey; there were wagers about the date the war would end—Marshall and Sir John Dill were the most hopeful, believing it would end in February, 1945, while Admiral King and General Ismay were the most pessimistic, believing it would not end until the fall. There were discussions on landing craft, but in all the multitude of discussions the question of the Supreme Commander of OVERLORD was not mentioned. Tacitly, the decision had been left to the President. He made the decision on December 4—Marshall would remain Chief of Staff, and Eisenhower would be Supreme Commander. It was three days later, while he was flying from Cairo to Tunis on December 7, before he told Admiral Leahy. The next day they reached Sicily. There he asked Arnold where Marshall was, and learned to his surprise that Marshall was already a thousand miles away on his way to Australia and the islands of the Pacific.

The journey to the Pacific had long been contemplated. As Chief of Staff he was responsible for the operations in the Pacific insofar as they were military operations, and for some time he had been perturbed by MacArthur's maneuvers, and by the tragic failure of the Joint Chiefs of Staff to institute any real unity of command in the Pacific. The Fourth Marine Division was at that time poised to attack the northern tip of the Marshall Islands; Tarawa and Makin had fallen; and the long chain of islands from the Gilberts to the Marianas and Iwo Jima was gradually coming under American command. The islands themselves were reduced to a bloody rubble and the usefulness of the operations was often debatable. Marshall never showed the interest in the Pacific operations which he showed in the operations for the conquest of Europe. Admiral King and MacArthur had carved up the Pacific between them, regarding it as their own preserve, but at odds with one another; and though Marshall served as a cushion between them it was not a rôle in which he was particularly adept. He returned to Washington on Christmas Eve, to discover that the President was ill with flu and the Army was about to take over the railroads. On the day of Marshall's return the news of Eisenhower's selection as Supreme Commander was released.

On the last day of the year Marshall called together a group of correspondents for an off-record discussion of the coal strike and a threatened steel strike. General Strong, head of Army Intelligence, had shown him monitored Axis broadcasts which were jubilant about the strikes. Marshall was furious. At the press conference he denounced the labor leaders roundly, savagely; they were demoralizing the country; they were gambling away the lives of the soldiers; they were irresponsible allies of the Axis. He spoke with a cold fury against William Green, the president of the AF of L. "I feel," he said a little later, "that here at home we are not yet facing the realities of war, the savage desperate conditions of the battle fronts." He felt, as he had felt before, that Americans behind the battle lines were not sufficiently dedicated to ending the war in the shortest possible time; there were malingerers everywhere and no stern resolution on the part of the people, no fire. It was not a temperate speech, nor was it intended to be, but it was an unfortunate one. From the cold eminence of his office in the Pentagon, weary after his long journeys, baffled by his own terrible responsibilities, possessed of no instinctive understanding or sympathy for the problems of labor and a harassed people, he took the part of an accusing Jeremiah, and he seemed astonished when the newspapers turned on him and asked for reports of the monitored broadcasts, only to discover that they consisted of only a few brief announcements concerning American industry, no better and no worse than those which had appeared through the course of the war, and the broadcasts were neither as dangerous nor as disturbing as Marshall had thought. Ill-advisedly William Green asked for a presidential enquiry of the incident, and then the tide turned. But there was no doubt that

Marshall had committed an error, and if he could commit comparatively small errors of judgment, there were many who wondered why this man, who had assumed such vast powers to himself, was regarded as though a blessed destiny prevented him from committing errors at all. The giant had been asleep before Pearl Harbor. He had shown in the September report that he had no real knowledge of the immense political, social and psychological implications of the coming war. He had thought in purely military terms, as though the complexities of political and social activity had no meaning. Then, as the war unfolded, he had demonstrated that his mind could expand and embrace the subtle complexions of human behavior. At times the ice-cold military mind asserted itself, and this was dangerous when it came to dealing with people who wore no uniform and were not obedient to military commands. There was a streak of the dictator in him, something forbidding and proud: he could not hide it. But those who said he had set his heart on being Supreme Commander of OVERLORD and had given way to this outburst of military temper because he was replaced by Eisenhower were wrong: there were too many of these outbursts to make one believe there was any cause and effect at work. The outbursts were the signs of his irresponsibility; he belonged to the military caste and he could not escape the military's disdain for labor. Also, the carelessness which dogged him at important moments, was once more in evidence. He had seen the monitored reports: he failed to understand their import: and he had flared into hot temper.

Though Marshall's fury was well-known, he usually kept it in reserve when dealing with the press. He had a healthy respect for the press and a genuine respect for industrial managers, but he has never completely overcome an instinctive distrust of labor. Of the press he said shortly after Pearl Harbor:

> We of the War Department General Staff sit here at the moment with the destiny of our nation resting on our judgment and our ability. We think we are competent. We think we can fulfill the responsibility. But how can we be sure? As far as I am concerned, the press is one of my best inspectors general.

There were times when his rage was exercised in favor of the press. When the President, through Hopkins, sent him a peremptory note demanding that a news magazine which had published an article he thought scurrilous should be banned in the Army, Marshall answered dramatically and furiously: "I won't obey that order unless I get it in writing, and if I do, it will come back with my resignation as Chief of Staff."

Human rage is rarely beautiful, but the rage of the gods and of nations can be profoundly beautiful. So it was now. All the accumulated resources of the Allies were to be turned in hot rage against the enemy in 1944. In the previous year the enemy had made mistake after mistake; now they were to receive the full force of punishment.

CHAPTER THIRTEEN

The Winning of the War

By the end of 1943 the foundations of victory were laid, and with the appointment of Eisenhower as Supreme Commander of all Allied forces in the European Theater in January, 1944, and with the climax of the air war over Germany in the following month, Marshall could feel reasonably satisfied. He expected desperate resistance from the Germans, but he knew that no army had ever been better equipped than the Allied armies which were now gathering in England. "I have no fears," he said in February, "regarding the ability of the American soldier to meet the situation." He saw the well-trained and well-disciplined Allies opposed by the disintegrating forces of Germany, whose homeland was being bombed by American daylight bombers and R.A.F. night bombers: they were expected to fight vigorously but their strength was already weakened. There was good news from other quarters. The American assault on the Marshalls was the first operation against a stronghold which the Japanese were able to fortify over a long period of years—the Marshalls had in fact been in Japanese occupation for more than twenty-five years. The Americans captured the islands with small losses in an extraordinarily brief time. This might be—probably was—a foretaste of future victories, and beginning with the winter of 1943-44 there can be seen in Marshall's writings and speeches a note of profound optimism, and there are no more of those long involved sentences heavy with dread which were so frequent during the early years of the war.

Now, as spring came, he spoke more and more often of the coming triumph over Germany as though it was something to be expected, something as natural as the air one breathed, as inevitable as air. There had been giant conflicts between the Americans and the British on matters of policy, but they were over now; or he thought they were over. Halfway through February he spoke at Yale when the Howland Memorial Prize was offered to Sir John Dill, and then for a brief while he talked about the possibilities of confusion which would arise if there was any discord between the Anglo-Saxon Allies. "The harmful possibilities of discord have been serious in the past and will continue to be so in the future because of the necessity in the European Theater for combined operations. That we have been able to master these very human difficulties, that in fact we have triumphed over them to the disaster of the enemy is, in my opinion, the greatest single Allied achievement of this war." And if the suggestion suffered from Marshall's characteristic desire to make sweeping statements (for in a war of this nature there could be no "greatest" single achievement) there was considerable justification: without the unity of the Allies there could be no victory. Above all, he derived his satisfaction from the knowledge that the long-promised attack on Germany could not be delayed beyond the summer.

Spring was a time of promise, of continual tours of inspection which took him to Texas and the West Coast, of telegrams to Eisenhower in London and news of victories in Russia. The Allies were blocked at Cassino on the march to Rome, and the useless bombing of the monastery at Cassino was only one of the tragedies which marked the slow progress up the soft belly of Italy. But triumph was close at hand, and when at the Thanksgiving Service at Arlington Memorial Amphitheater on April 9, Marshall delivered the Easter morning prayer, something of his own determination and humility came clearly through the closing words: "Give us strength, Lord, that we may be pure in heart and in purpose to the end that there may be peace on earth and goodwill among men. May we be mindful this Easter morning 'still stands Thine ancient sacrifice, an humble and a contrite heart.'"

Rome fell on June 4. It was like the first dawn which heralds an exploding sunrise; the fall of Rome, like the fall of Stalingrad, announced far more than a military victory. When Eisenhower set the hour for the invasion of June 6, he knew that the Russians were preparing for an attack against the Germans in the Leningrad area, that half of Italy was conquered and all North Africa was in the hands of the Allies, while good news came speeding from the Pacific. The huge, carefully planned and terrible attack on the Normandy beaches owed a great deal to Marshall's advocacy, and as soon as the landings were reported, he hastened to go to the scene of operations. On Thursday, June 8, he flew with General Arnold and Admiral King to England by way of Nova Scotia, the journey sunny and eventless, though sometimes they came upon enormous icebergs so large that they had their own lakes within their surfaces, and there was a heavy overcast by the time the great C-54 came over north Wales. For an hour and thirty minutes the Chiefs of Staff circled above Prestwick, the airdrome hidden by low-hanging clouds, while three other planes attempted to come down. The plane with the three Chiefs of Staff was hovering over north Wales while the Allies were securing their beachheads, but the sun came out the next day, clear and strong, and Eisenhower at headquarters was talking happily about the way the French were hindering the Germans and still more happily about the drive into Normandy. Carentan was captured on the following Monday, and on Tuesday Marshall, King and Arnold embarked on the destroyer *Thompson* and headed for France, with Eisenhower accompanying them. It was like a journey of sovereigns to a captured land.

When they were recognized the sovereigns were cheered, but mostly the soldiers were too busy with their own affairs. The three-quarter-ton reconnaissance car which took them along the Normandy roads was white with dust and surrounded by dust: it was a dust-splattered crew which arrived at General Bradley's headquarters and fed on rations. Marshall, according to his custom, gave a curt briefing on the whole global situation at the First Army Command post, while Bradley, Hodges, Gerow, Collins and a host of other high brass listened gravely. There were no ceremonies, though the meeting was not unlike one between Napoleon and his marshals. From the moment when the Chiefs of Staff left Portsmouth Harbor the day was remarkable for its quietness: hundreds of ships were scurrying calmly across the Channel unopposed by enemy bombers or the enemy navy. They saw a few German dead, spoke with the wounded in a C-53, examined the effects of the naval guns and the aerial bombardment and pored over Bradley's maps, but there was little for them to do: the war was proceding on its own momentum. When the newspaper correspondents found them, Marshall announced that Guam was being attacked that day: he had no news to offer them of Normandy. In the evening, as quietly as they had come, the sovereigns departed.

Marshall had enjoyed a glimpse of France and now decided to see the Americans in Italy. He reached Naples on June 18, and flew over the Salerno beaches the next day; and having inspected the beaches where every square yard showed the marks of enemy shells, the holes so thickly clustered that it seemed impossible for anyone to have survived, he went to the Anzio Cemetery and stood alone beside the grave of his stepson who had been killed during the landing operations. Once more the experience near the front was one of extraordinary quietness, for German airplanes rarely bombed American positions, and indeed there were no more than two hundred German planes left in Italy. Then he flew back to America by way of Casablanca, Algiers and the Azores, facing a storm all the way to New York.

Marshall had enjoyed no real rest during the war. Exhausted, he decided to take a short holiday in the High Sierras with Arnold. They flew to Bishop, California, and then by car and horseback made their way to the mountains. Airplanes came and dropped locked pouches by parachute over their camp, they listened to the Army radio, sent out orders and fished contentedly. They slept in sleeping bags. For long hours they did nothing at all except relax in the sun. Marshall's temper had been short during the Italian journey. At a meeting at the headquarters of Field Marshal Sir Henry Maitland Wilson, the British Supreme Commander in the Mediterranean, he had tried to sound the various commanders on Churchill's project of an attack through the Ljubljana Gap. General Ira C. Eaker, who was mainly responsible for directing the daylight bombing raids on Germany, was asked what he thought of Churchill's project. He is said to have replied that he preferred it to the invasion of southern France, which had been set for August 15. He explained that in his view a trans-Adriatic operation could be more easily supported from existing bases in Italy. Marshall disagreed, and after the meeting was over he is supposed to have said: "You have been too damned long with the British." There were other signs of high temper. Now, in the High Sierras, with the colored smoke-flare flying like a pennon over the camp to show the Army plane with the pouches where they were, the frayed tempers healed and Marshall was able to take a longer view of the war. July brought bad news, for in that month General Lesley J. McNair was killed by bombs dropped accidently by American planes. General McNair, known as "Whitey" because of his ash-blond hair, had been very close to Marshall, and he more than anyone else was responsible for the hard battle-conditioning training which brought the American soldiers to the pitch of efficiency. He had made the men crawl on their bellies under barbed wire while live ammunition exploded around them; and men who cursed his name while they were training were grateful to him when they entered battle.

Victory was already in the air when Marshall on September 1 was sworn in as Chief of Staff, the normal five-year period of tenure having come to an end. He believed the war would end before December. He had good reasons for his beliefs: MacArthur was attacking Biak, Nimitz had captured Saipan, the Russians were racing beyond the Warsaw-Budapest Line and Eisenhower's Army was moving towards the German border, where there was no heavily defended Siegfried Line, as in the last war, to keep the invaders at bay. On the day he was sworn in before Secretary Woodring, Marshall told the post-war planners that he did not believe in a large peacetime Army. He advocated a small professional Army backed by trained citizen reserves. Of the large standing Army he said that it had no place among the institutions of a modern democratic state, but at the same time he hoped the Congress would approve universal military training so that "every able-bodied young American shall be trained to defend his country." It was a day of quiet contentment, for the news of the capture of Antwerp and Brussels had come in shortly before. There were trials of strength ahead. The second Quebec Conference, known as OCTAGON, was coming up, and he knew there would be more disagreements with the British.

OCTAGON was the first conference where post-war problems were discussed at length. The uprising in Warsaw, which the Russians watched from a distance, gave a foretaste of things to come. There were talks on British participation in the Pacific, and the collapse of Italy, and long discussions on the various plans for the dismemberment of Germany, but the statesmen and generals at the conference table deliberated at length and came to no conclusions concerning the fate of Germany. The problem of Germany, like many of the problems discussed at these conferences, was solved by history without the assistance of the Combined Chiefs of Staff.

But the results of the conference were reasonably hopeful. To his astonishment, Marshall found himself in agreement with British plans, there was little wrangling, it was decided that Lend-Lease should continue after the war and agreement was reached on British munitions requirements. The Russians were proving strangely cooperative; in October they even asked that Allied forces should go through Austria and assist the Red Army then making its way through Hungary. But for Marshall the best news was that the report of the Combined Chiefs of Staff was accepted with almost no alteration by the aging President and an unusually calm Prime Minister.

There occurred at Quebec an incident which Marshall recounted with great relish in his third Biennial Report. The Joint Chiefs of Staff had received a copy of a message from Admiral Halsey to Admiral Nimitz, suggesting that three islands on the chain of advance to the Philippines should be bypassed, and that an immediate attack on Leyte in the central Philippines had become feasible. Such a maneuver was audacious, but it was exactly what Marshall had come to expect from Halsey, whom he described a few weeks later as a man possessing "the fighting heart of a Farragut, a Nelson or a John Paul Jones." Nimitz had thereupon offered MacArthur the use of the Third Amphibian Force, and the Joint Chiefs asked for MacArthur's views. MacArthur was then engaged in a landing at Biak, but two days later he sent a radiogram to Quebec saying that in view of Nimitz's offer he was prepared to advance his plans for the landing on Leyte by two months; the American forces would land on October 20 instead of December 20.

> The message from MacArthur [said Marshall] arrived at Quebec at night, and Admiral Leahy, Admiral King, General Arnold and I were being entertained at a formal dinner by Canadian officers. It was read by the appropriate staff officers who suggested an immediate affirmative answer. The message, with their recommendations, was

rushed to us and we left the table for a conference. Having the utmost confidence in General MacArthur, Admiral Nimitz and Admiral Halsey, it was not a difficult decision to make. Within 90 minutes after the signal had been received in Quebec, General MacArthur and Admiral Nimitz had received their instructions to execute the Leyte operation on the target date 20 October, abandoning the three previously approved intermediary landings. General MacArthur's acknowledgment of his new instructions reached me while en route from the dinner to my quarters in Quebec.

It was characteristic of Marshall that in his formal report to the nation he should speak of a message being received "while en route from the dinner to my quarters," as though he was tracing the plan of his own military progress across the map of Quebec. The message was received, according to Mrs. Marshall who also described the incident in her book *Together,* when Marshall was entering the elevator on his return to the Hotel Frontenac. Even General Arnold, accustomed to think in terms of supersonic airplanes and the fabulous scientific wonders which his brood of scientists were already planning, was stunned by the incredible speed of these messages, for only a few minutes had separated the instructions to MacArthur, then in the middle of a landing operation, and the reply.

The Joint Chiefs of Staff spent their last day in Quebec attending the final conferences, then sauntered out to examine the Heights of Abraham, which General Wolfe had scaled. Wolfe's campaign had something in common with the landings in the Pacific and the landings on the coasts of France and Italy. All the advantages lay with the defenders on the heights, and only by the greatest cunning could Wolfe claim advantages for himself. Marshall and Arnold had studied the campaign at length, and both knew exactly how Wolfe had landed his small force of British troops and Colonists from the river: they knew considerably more than the bumbling lecturer who addressed them. Afterwards they began to trace the course of the battle by the markers and fell in with a Catholic priest who had studied the Battle of Quebec, and who was prepared to speak about it at great length in French. Soon the Combined Chiefs of Staff were all listening intently to a long sermon on the battle delivered expertly by a man who had no idea that he was addressing the military heads of Great Britain and America.

On September 18, following his custom, Marshall addressed the American Legion at Chicago. He spoke of the rapid advances in the Pacific, "until today the enemy admits to his people the precarious nature of the situation." As though to reemphasize the need for a small, compact and highly trained Regular Army, he spoke of the "small, but extremely potent" force of United States troops in the Pacific. He praised General Stilwell's leadership in the North Burma campaign; a month later Stilwell was to be recalled. He noted that the breakthrough in the West had been carried out by three Army Corps which had never before been engaged in battle, proof that the maneuvers in Louisiana and California had borne fruit. Sixty divisions had reached the Western Front, and eight more were on their way. It was an intoxicating prospect, but he did not minimize the difficulties ahead and he mentioned in passing some of the difficulties he had faced as Chief of Staff: "In a global war of the present stupendous proportions the logistical requirements have ramifications so diverse and so numerous that one has the feeling of picking his way through a veritable maze of obstacles and uncertainties." But these "obstacles and uncertainties"—these were favorite words in the early stages of the war—were now passing, and he found himself immediately afterwards speaking of the one hundred and fifty thousand Japanese troops "cut off from their supplies and withering on the vine, with the same fate now in store for even larger garrisons."

These magnificent prospects were the result of training. Again and again he spoke of the lengths to which training had been continued. There were no easy roads to success. Training was the heart, core and kernel of success. He said:

> A conspicuous factor in the sustained successes of the past six weeks has been the steady flow of well-trained men to replace combat losses. Our divisions have been kept at full strength from day to day. The losses suffered by battle casualties are usually made good within twenty-four hours and the missing matériel in trucks, tanks and guns is being replaced at the same rate. On the German side of the line, divisions dwindling in strength and gradually losing the bulk of their heavy equipment, always find themselves beset by full American teams whose strength never seems to vary and whose numbers are constantly increasing. These German

deficiencies will bring about their downfall if we on this side of the Atlantic see to it that our forces are maintained day in and day out at full strength, and supplied with every possible need. We have a stern duty here at home if our attacks are to surge forward during what we hope are the last hours of this great European conflict.

But the last hours were many months away, there were to be major setbacks on all fronts and the course of the war, which seemed so smooth at last, was in the very nature of things to produce a few more catastrophes to add to the large number of catastrophes which had already occurred. One of these catastrophes was concerned with General Stilwell, an excellent soldier and a poor diplomat, who was finally recalled from China at the end of October. Marshall, who had known and liked Stilwell at Fort Benning, was grieved. Stilwell's brilliant campaign in Upper Burma, culminating in the capture of Myitkyina, had seemed to him one of the classics of the war. He was in no mood to view the recall dispassionately, and when Chiang Kai-chek had roared against Stilwell in the presence of General Brehon Somervell exactly a year before, Marshall who received reports of the interview, dismissed the matter as one which had very little importance in the course of the war: Stilwell in his eyes was still the best general for China. Early in October Secretary Stimson produced a long, detailed report on the situation in China. On the same day Marshall told him that if Stilwell were removed, he would not allow another American general to be placed in the position of Chief of Staff and Commander of the Chinese Armies, a judgment which he subsequently reversed. Stilwell was recalled on October 28 by order of the President, who had never possessed Marshall's complete faith in the general whose sobriquet of "Vinegar Joe" concealed, as it also revealed, the man's acid contempt for all those whose opinions he refused to share. Marshall praised his "extraordinary vigor"; he would have been less likely to offer such high praise if he had read Stilwell's diaries.

On the day before Stilwell's recall Marshall made a speech at the Navy Day Banquet in Washington. He had made a brief visit to France earlier in the month, flying with Byrnes direct from Newfoundland to Orly in *The Sacred Cow,* and he now gave a brief resumé of his findings. He had visited most of the command posts, spoken with Field Marshal Montgomery in Holland and General de Lattre de Tassigny near Belfort, and most of the American commanders, and now once again he was concerned to praise the infantryman fighting through mud and cold. They knew little of what was happening outside their own battlegrounds. He hoped they would never hear how the people at home were already speaking of the war as something of the past, for victory was so close at hand, while the soldiers were still dying, and then he made one of those oblique references to politics which illuminated the whole of his political thinking during the war. He said: "Let's have no nonsense, no superficial thinking or selfish purposes until we have won this great struggle in which Allied forces on the Western Front and in Italy are attacking along almost one thousand one hundred miles of a raging battle-line." What he was saying was simple: the war comes first, politics comes afterwards. It was a reasonable enough statement, if it had been spoken by anyone else, but it suggested a continuing blindness to political considerations. The British had hoped to place themselves in such a way that their armies could provide in central Europe a bastion against the advancing Russians. To Marshall such a desire seemed almost treacherous. He was not concerned with the future of Europe, had little feeling for the subtleties of the European mind and put little value on the desperate desire for safety of the western European powers. The war had to be won; nothing else mattered. It was as simple as that, and politics must be abandoned in the winning of it. So overriding was the desire to win the war that he never came wholly to believe that politics and the managing of the war could proceed simultaneously, and a huge distrust for politicians haunted him until he became Secretary of State, and even then he behaved more like a general in command of armies than a Secretary in command of policies. Perhaps it was inevitable: the complexities of the war absorbed him to the exclusion of everything else.

Thinking in military terms, Marshall was at a disadvantage in dealing with politicians. When, towards the end of October, he heard that Dewey had made a speech at Tulsa, Oklahoma, which showed that Dewey knew the War Department had broken the Japanese code, he sent a colonel from the Military Intelligence Division directly to Dewey with a sealed message. Dewey was invited to open the letter and read the first two sentences, but he was told that he must not read further unless he swore to keep the rest of the letter secret, never divulging what he had read. Dewey refused, suspecting that the information in the letter might include facts already known to him from other sources. He therefore returned the letter unread. Two days later, at Albany, the same colonel returned with a second letter from Marshall; and this time Dewey read the letter through. Dewey had attacked the administration in his speech at Tulsa: the presidential campaign was in full swing: and he was alarmed by what he called the interference of the military in presidential politics. He agreed, however, not to divulge in his speeches the information he had received in such strange fashion from the Army, and there the matter ended. He had not suspected that the information he possessed involved a knowledge of the breaking of the Japanese code. Marshall's urgent messages had been delivered in a peremptory manner, without informing the President who should have been consulted, with no knowledge of Dewey's peculiarly sensitive psychology, and with an instinct for drama which may have seemed spurious to Dewey, who possessed his own instinct for drama. Soon the incident was forgotten. It was not, after all, an important incident, and if it showed that Marshall had little flair for dealing with Republican candidates for the Presidency (he came from the South, and may therefore be presumed to be a Democrat), it also showed his sense of the desperate urgency of keeping secret the fact that the Americans had broken the code.

In November Sir John Dill died in the Walter Reed Hospital. Marshall felt the loss keenly. They had worked together continually since the Arcadia Conference, and in all his life there was hardly anyone else whose mind he understood as well as he understood the mind of that calm, brilliant and methodical soldier. He said in a prepared statement to the press: "The fact that the Allied Forces stand poised at the gates of Germany is due in no small measure to the breadth of vision and selfless devotion of Field Marshal Sir John Dill to our common cause. I know of no man who has made a greater contribution to complete military co-operation between British and American forces." Sir John Dill had asked to be buried in Arlington Cemetery. This was accordingly arranged, and Marshall read the lesson at the burial, arranged that the Senate should pass a resolution in honor and praise of the Field Marshal and in due time arranged that an equestrian statue of him should be placed at Arlington. When six years later the statue was unveiled, Marshall spoke once again of the man "whose high character shone so clearly in the honest directness of every action," and it pleased him that the statue should stand in Arlington Cemetery at the intersection of Roosevelt and Grant avenues, and that anyone making the journey to the Tomb of the Unknown Soldier would have to pass within a few feet of it. Marshall has been accused of coldness; all this was a sign of natural warmth.

Marshall had few intimates, but those he possessed he bound to him with ropes of steel. Among his close friends was Colonel Charles T. Lanham, who possessed the bravado of a poet and who was in nearly every way different from Marshall. They had met first when Lanham was a first lieutenant at Fort Benning, and Marshall had come upon him playing blackjack when he should have been studying tactical problems. In the same month that Dill died, Lanham had escaped from death by a miracle. In command of the Twenty-Second Regiment, Lanham had fought through eighteen days of battle in the Huertgen Forest. Of the 3,200 men of the regiment who entered the battle, 2,600 were casualties.

While the hard winter battles were being fought, Congress began to deliberate on the titles of the four-star Army and Navy commanders. Marshall regarded their discussions as supremely unimportant. The matter had been raised before, and he had always attempted to defer the question of titles. But now, as the war came to an end, the Congress was determined to show signal honor to the military leaders. On December 8 a bill was passed to create eight five-star commanders, and a week later Marshall, together with MacArthur, Eisenhower and Arnold, became Generals of the Army. The title "General of the Armies" was not revived, because it was thought that Pershing was entitled to his lone eminence. But Pershing had commanded only two armies during the First World War. Marshall commanded nine U.S. armies, and for long periods he was in direct or indirect command of British, Dutch, French and Chinese armies scattered over the whole globe.

The time for the military conferences was now over; the political conferences were beginning. The conference at Yalta was the inevitable sequel to the conference at Teheran. The political problems concerning a defeated Germany and a defeated Japan were still unsolved: there had not even been a beginning to their solution, and in fact no real solutions were ever arrived at during the course of the war. The conferences were gestures, attempts towards an understanding of the unity and determination among the Allies, occasions for the display of fantastic skills by the heads of states. So it had been during the previous conferences, but the conference at Yalta in the Crimea, which opened on Sunday, February 4, 1945, on a rising tide of Allied victories, possessed darker implications: for the first time one of the Allies was to employ threats of force and to exert his diplomatic skill in order to obtain immense post-war advantages.

Marshall left Washington for Yalta on January 24 and breakfasted the next morning in the Azores. There he found Secretary Stettinius, and together they walked across a terrace, deep in conversation over the dangers of the coming peace, that new age which was dawning in an atmosphere of distrust and terror. Stettinius had been informed about the progress of the Manhattan Project. It was a reasonable assumption that the Russians might have heard some rumors of the project, and Stettinius remembered afterwards that he asked Marshall what should be said if the Russians raised the question. Marshall hoped they would not raise the question, and in any event it was too early to plan ahead. He flew on to Marseilles for a secret rendezvous with Eisenhower, which was held at the Château Valmante. There had been arguments between Eisenhower and Sir Alan Brooke concerning the conduct of the war against Germany. The British had proposed that Eisenhower be directed by the Combined Chiefs of Staff to concentrate the American strength behind Montgomery's force; they were afraid he would concentrate his forces on the southern crossing of the Rhine, and do nothing to help the British offensive. Marshall discussed the matter at length with Eisenhower and came to the conclusion that the second crossing in the south was dictated by the over-all strategy. He reasoned that the British were in a dangerous situation in the north, for they were approaching the German jet aircraft bases, and a secondary crossing by the Americans offered the advantages of a broader front. He also objected to the idea that the Combined Chiefs of Staff should give tactical orders to a field commander; from the very beginning of the war Marshall had in practice given the field commanders the largest possible degree of autonomy. At Marshall's suggestion General Walter Bedell Smith was detailed to explain the situation to the British Chiefs of Staff who were waiting in Malta for a preliminary discussion with the American Chiefs.

With Bedell Smith Marshall flew on to Malta, staying at Montgomery House at Valetta, overlooking the ancient harbor which had seen the rise and fall of so many nations and empires. King and Arnold were already in Malta; they had vehemently opposed the British plan; and Marshall, suffering from a cold and in no mood for procrastination, added his own categorical denunciations. They were phrased politely, but acidly. He said he refused to accept the thesis that Eisenhower should be obedient to the Combined Chiefs, because this would in effect prevent him from taking advantage of situations as they arose, and he refused to order Eisenhower to place his forces behind Montgomery's. To the British plan that there should be an officer under Eisenhower in command of ground forces—the officer they had selected was General Sir Harold Alexander—Marshall suggested an alternative; they should simply wait upon developments before complicating the heirarchy of command. On all three questions Marshall was able to convince Roosevelt and Churchill, who shortly afterwards arrived in Malta. Soon they were all flying towards the Saki airfield on the west coast of the Crimean Peninsula, and there they arrived, with an escort of P-38 fighters, on the afternoon of February 3. Marshall occupied the imperial bedroom of the Tsarina on the second floor of the Livadia Palace during the conference, while Admiral King occupied the Empress's boudoir next door. On the journey from Saki to Yalta they saw the evidence of the German occupation; they also saw the grim and thickset Russian sentries who lined the whole ninety-mile route between the airfield and the Emperor's summer palace overlooking the sea.

On February 4 the first plenary session of the conference was held in the ballroom of the Livadia Palace. Churchill suggested that Marshall should give a brief outline of the situation on the Western Front. As so often before, Marshall gave one of his extemporaneous and carefully prepared summaries of operations. He explained how the Ardennes bulge had been eliminated and the Anglo-American forces had advanced beyond the lines held by the Germans before their counter-offensive. The damage brought about by von Runstedt's attack had now been set right, and Marshall believed that the Rhine would be crossed shortly after March 1—in fact it was not crossed in force until March 22. Meanwhile the German transportation system was under heavy aerial bombardment, there had been concentrated attacks on German oil refineries and German oil production was now one fifth of its former capacity. Tank factories and submarine assembly yards had been bombed. As Marshall concluded his recital of the Anglo-American gains, ending with a reference to a recrudescence of German submarine warfare and the statement that German submarine bases were under heavy attack, Churchill took the occasion to point out that Danzig was a great submarine center, and the Russians were now advancing on that city. It was as though Churchill were attempting to raise the ghost of the city which a little more than four years before had been the battleground between the Germans and the Poles, and the indirect cause of the war.

Marshall's faculty for making precise and brilliant descriptions of battle operations was well-known, but he had never enjoyed a more exalted audience. Victory was in the air, and he was describing the mounting tide of the Allied offensives at a time when the German counter-offensive had been stopped in the bloody snows of the Ardennes and the drive across the Rhine was already being prepared. Stalin asked whether the Allied reserves were sufficient. Marshall answered that by March 1 Eisenhower would have 89 divisions stretching from the Mediterranean to Holland, and one out of every three would be a tank division. There were nearly 10,000 Allied tanks and 4,000 heavy bombers in the European Theater. It was an impressive display of figures, but Stalin was able to counter with a still more impressive figure: he stated that he had 180 Soviet divisions in Poland facing 80 German divisions. Against such overwhelming odds German power could resist only for a little while; inevitably it must crumble and be broken on the field. For the first time the Western Allies realized the prodigious forces which Stalin was commanding.

Whether Stalin's statement was strictly true has never been settled, but it explains much which happened afterwards. Most of the conference was held in secret—the agreements were not published to the world until the following October—and inevitably Stalin was in a position to manipulate the conference. The President was ailing, and Churchill, nettled by the decisions made in Malta, found himself playing a lone hand; and when Stalin demanded as the price of his entry into the war against Japan a commanding position in Manchuria, the richest province in China, no one was in a position to gainsay him. He promised to enter the war against Japan within three months of the termination of the war against Germany, and he faithfully kept his promise, but the price was higher than the Allies could reasonably be expected to pay. Stalin demanded the restoration to Russia of the right formerly possessed by the Imperial Russian Government to dominate Manchuria through control of the Chinese Eastern and South Manchurian railway; he demanded the internationalization of Dairen and the return of South Sakhalin and the Kurile islands, and these concessions were to be made partly by a defeated Japan and partly by a victorious China. In addition, north Korea was designated a Soviet area of military occupation, and south Korea was to become an American area—the decision to divide Korea at the 38th parallel was not reached until the Potsdam Conference in July. The conference demonstrated the extent of Soviet imperialism. Unhappily no American or British historians were present at the conference, and the emerging pattern passed unnoticed. It is only fair to add that the tragic decisions of Yalta were for the most part arrived at directly by Roosevelt in conference with Stalin, and neither Churchill nor Marshall took any great part in the agreements as they referred to the Far East. But Marshall, who had little knowledge of Japanese psychology, grossly overestimated the cost in lives of an assault on the Japanese mainland, and just as at the beginning of the war he had desperately appealed for a political settlement with Japan which would delay the outbreak of the war, so now he appealed for political settlement with the Soviet Union which would have the effect of bringing the Russians into the Far Eastern war. Towards the end of the conference, on February 9, Marshall received from the Russians the promise that bases in the Russian Maritime Provinces would be placed at the disposal of the American Air Force—it was a promise as empty as the rest.

Though Hopkins and Roosevelt were elated by what they regarded as the victory of Yalta, Marshall seems to have left the conference in a mood of profound disquiet. There had been unsettling incidents at the conference, and not the least of them was the knowledge that Roosevelt and Stalin were making secret commitments concerning the Far East which would throw their shadow over the future. Then there was the mysterious incident which occurred on the evening of February 8, when Marshall and Admiral King found themselves excluded from the formal dinner given by Stalin at the Villa Koreis. No explanations were offered, and no one knows whether the two Chiefs of Staff regarded their exclusion as an insult, or a blessing in disguise.

Hopkins referred to the Yalta Conference as the dawn of a new day. It was hardly that. It resembled one of those false dawns common in India: for a moment the sky is illuminated in red flames, for a brief while you hear the rumbling of the sun and then the flames sink below the horizon. There was more hope in the forthcoming World Security Conference than in this congress of emperors who sought to carve out the world, and compiled secret agreements for their own purposes. On February 8 Secretary Stettinius found himself discussing the site of the forthcoming Security Conference with Marshall. Remembering Eden's desire to see California, Stettinius suggested San Francisco. He asked Marshall's opinion. Was San Francisco too congested with military traffic? Marshall answered that all the great cities of America were congested; one might as well hold the conference at San Francisco as elsewhere. Shortly afterwards, strengthened by Marshall's guarded commendation of San Francisco, Stettinius approached the President and enquired whether he was ready to choose San Francisco. The question, so carefully and lovingly loaded—Stettinius had a great affection for San Francisco—received an approving answer from the President. Far from the Crimea, half a world away, there was to be held the opening session of the United Nations in congress.

Long before he left Yalta, Marshall had determined to pay another visit to the Mediterranean Theater. Accordingly, he sent a telegram to General Mark Clark, giving warning of his visit and ordering as usual that there should be no honor guards. Arriving at the Fifteenth Army Group headquarters, Marshall discovered to his astonishment that General Mark Clark had disobeyed the orders of his Chief. Marshall was received by an honor guard composed of

Brazilians, Poles, Canadians, New Zealanders, Italian Army and Partisan troops, together with British and American troops, and there were American Negroes on parade. Angry at first, Marshall softened when he saw the glint in General Clark's eyes, for the General had gone to great pains to assemble a concourse of the United Nations, and no Chief of Staff in history had ever been presented with an honor guard comprising so many different nations before.

The rest of the journey to Italy was less happy. In the Apennines Marshall detected a note of weariness among the American troops, who had been fighting from one mountain ridge to another in an unrewarding campaign, with little glory attached to it. Marshall visited the command posts, and spent five days touring the Apennines, speaking to the soldiers, commending them for their gallantry in the past and warning against failure in the present. He made about twenty-five speeches in the field, and then returned sadly to America, more than ever convinced that the Italian campaign, which he had agreed to reluctantly, was basically a mistake.

The war in the West was nearly over; within three months the Russians would be throwing their blinding searchlights on the last defenders of Berlin, and fighting in the Berlin sewers. The war which had begun on the borders of Poland was to end on the banks of the Elbe, with the Western Allies holding a precarious frontier against the Russians. Again and again in those last months Marshall had made tragic mistakes. Thinking as always in military terms, he had failed to see Europe politically, and indeed he was very ignorant of European political history. Churchill had called for the invasion of Hungary through the Ljubljana Gap and a massive onslaught on Berlin, and Marshall had set his face against both these stratagems, not knowing the way the world was going, and perhaps at that time not worrying overmuch, for victories on the field seemed ends in themselves. He shared the opinion of Bradley, whom he regarded as the best field commander without exception that the war had seen. "I could see no political advantage accruing from the capture of Berlin that would offset the need for quick destruction on our front," wrote Bradley afterwards. "As soldiers we looked naïvely on this British inclination to complicate the war with political foresight and non-military objectives." The naïveté remained through the first years of the peace, and was to assume its most extraordinary form in China.

Some hint of what was coming was provided shortly after Marshall's return to Washington. A message from Stalin was received in Washington which could only be interpreted as a direct accusation that the American Chief of Staff had been lying. Marshall and Leahy together wrote a memorandum to Stalin explaining carefully that the head of the Russian state was misinformed. It was a gracious letter deliberately designed to mollify the Russian leader's feelings, and five months later Stalin was still smarting from the gentle rebuke, for he went to considerable pains to explain to Eisenhower, then in Moscow, that he had acted regrettably, and he agreed that the information he had received from Marshall concerning the strength of German forces was sent in good faith. Stalin charged Eisenhower with the errand of conveying his regret to the Chief of Staff.

But the damage was done, and the following month which saw the death of the President and the inauguration of the United Nations at San Francisco marked the turning point. Early in the month, a week before Roosevelt's death, Marshall declared in a speech before the Military Order of the World Wars: "It is difficult to realize how vast and how successful our military forces are today. It is almost inconceivable that they should have reached such heights of efficiency and power, when we turn back to the military poverty of four years ago." The military victories had indeed been awe-inspiring, and there were more to come, but the war was still being fought as though politics existed in a vacuum.

With the death of Roosevelt and the accession of Truman a new age was ushered in. Marshall found himself largely in charge of the funeral arrangements of the dead President, for Mrs. Roosevelt had asked that there should be a military funeral. Standing beside Admiral King he attended the burial in the rose garden at Hyde Park. In a sense, he was chief mourner over the period which had passed and herald of the period about to come.

Less than a month after the death of Roosevelt, in a final paroxysm, the Third Reich, which Hitler had described as "the God-given force destined to rule the world," perished in the abject surrender of the state. At noon on that day Secretary Stimson, already ailing, his face white with emotion, summoned his Chief of Staff to his office, together with fourteen generals and high officers. The Secretary had stood staunchly by Marshall throughout the war, and now the time had come to pay tribute to the aging man who, from his office in the Pentagon, had commanded the American Armies all over the world. He said:

> I want to acknowledge my great personal debt to you, Sir, in common with the whole country. No one who is thinking of himself can rise to true heights. You have never thought of yourself. Seldom can a man put aside such a thing as being the Commanding General of the greatest field army in our history. This decision was made by you for wholly unselfish reasons. But you have made your position as Chief of Staff a greater one. I have never seen a task of such magnitude performed by man.
>
> It is rare in late life to make new friends; at my age it is a slow process but there is no one for whom I have such deep respect and I think greater affection. I have seen a great many soldiers in my lifetime and you, Sir, are the finest soldier I have ever known.

It was a simple speech and a very long one, for there was much more of it, and there were passages which were not strictly true. It was not true, for example, that Marshall had willingly set aside the prospect of becoming "the Commanding General of the greatest field army in our history"—the decision belonged properly to the Commander in Chief, and Marshall had simply obeyed orders. But the tribute was welcome and very largely deserved, and as Marshall gazed around, seeing the eyes of generals moistening as they listened to a sick man's valedictory, with a quarter circle of generals on each side of him and the Secretary at his desk intoning the speech like a sermon, it may have occurred to him that the end was in sight and he could now retire on his laurels to become a gardener at Leesburg. In ancient days there would have been a triumph: the commanding general would have been allowed to enter the capital with the senators and lictors marching in front of the prisoners and the spoils, while the *triumphator* rode in a gilded carriage drawn by four snow-white horses. But those times were over; now there were to be more speeches, more valedictories, more medals pinned on his breast which was already overloaded with them, and perhaps later, after he was dead, an equestrian statue in a public park. Marshall hardly cared. Like Aristotle's "high-souled man" he possessed a supreme contempt for honors, but he was concerned that the lesser generals should receive the acclamations of the people; and it was Marshall who prepared the ground for Eisenhower's tumultuous reception in New York, the ovations of Spaatz and Bradley in Philadelphia, of Hodges in Atlanta and Devers in Louisville. There were more important matters than triumphs to keep him awake at night. Above all there was the thought that the triumph in the West would be hollow unless peace were preserved, and he began to think that when he retired he would dedicate the rest of his life to ensuring American strength. Speaking before the Select Committee on Postwar Military Policy of the House of Representatives on June 16, he declared roundly: "Whatever the terms of peace, the fundamental basis of our defense must be universal military training." He had no desire to see a large standing army: the cost was prohibitive, the men needed to fill its ranks could not be hired in peacetime and it was repugnant to the whole American tradition. But how else could American strength be respected? Universal military training provided the only answer to the problem, and he went on to declare that all the evidence went to prove that the Army could become one of the pillars of democracy. He said:

> I assert that we have produced a democratic Army, one composed of self-respecting soldiers whose spirit has not been crushed and who have shown splendid evidences of high morale. I submit that the Army has demonstrated that it can efficiently and expeditiously instruct men and that it does this without detriment to the mind and character of the individual, rather the contrary. I firmly believe that universal military education would be a stimulant to education rather than a deterrent. It would be a perfect demonstration of democracy, with rich and poor alike, side by side, rendering a common service.

The war against Japan had still to be won, and there were signs that the going would be hard. General Hodge had telegraphed from Okinawa that the Japanese were using their artillery more intelligently than ever before; the *kamikaze* attacks were mounting in ferocity and the Japanese were beginning to use their deadly Baka planes, which resembled small rocket-accelerated V-bombs slung underneath their medium bombers. The losses were considerable, and amounted to nearly 40,000 casualties in the Okinawa campaign by the end of June. In this extremity the Chiefs of Staff were perturbed by the thought that the Japanese who had behaved with suicidal disregard for their own losses on Okinawa would be even more suicidal on the Japanese mainland. In June, Marshall was of the opinion that the invasion of Kyushu, the southern island of Japan, would cost 63,000 casualties out of the 190,000 combatant troops necessary for the operation. The cost was high; it would be higher when the time came to invade Honshu. Asked how many casualties would follow a landing on the Tokyo plain, Marshall answered that a million men would be necessary for the landing, a million would be needed to hold, and there would be half a million casualties—the figures, however, were very nearly meaningless and could not be interpreted as having been arrived at by any process of logic. They represented his own emotional reaction to the problem, and meant only that the forces involved would be very large indeed. King and Marshall advocated the invasions; only Leahy refused to see any justification for the invasion of an already defeated enemy. But Leahy was overridden, and at the June 29 meeting of the Joint Chiefs of Staff, November 1 was set for the invasion date of Kyushu. The date for the invasion of Honshu was to be determined later. On July 16, in a deserted area of New Mexico the first atomic bomb was exploded; and the carefully constructed plans of the Joint Chiefs of Staff were once more abandoned.

In the construction of the atomic bomb Marshall had played a decisive role. In the fall of 1941, before Pearl Harbor, he was appointed to the committee which came to be called the General Policy Group, which included Vice-President Wallace, Secretary Stimson, Dr. Vannevar Bush and Dr. James B. Conant. The committee was set up to consider policy relating to nuclear fission, and on them had fallen the responsibility of deciding whether to develop the atomic weapon. In June, 1942, the major part of the program fell to the War Department, and therefore came directly under Marshall's supervision. When the time came to decide whether the bomb should be dropped, Secretary Stimson appointed still another committee, which included George L. Harrison (who acted as chairman of the committee in

Secretary Stimson's absence); Justice James F. Byrnes, the personal representative of the President; Ralph A. Bard, Under Secretary of the Navy; William L. Clayton, Secretary of State for Economic Affairs; Dr. Vannevar Bush and Dr. Karl T. Compton, the two last from the Office of Scientific Research and Development; and Dr. James B. Conant, who was then the Chairman of the National Defense Research Committee. Marshall was not invited to form part of this committee, though he exerted his influence when he was summoned to appear before the Presidential conference which occurred later, and it was at this conference that Marshall quoted his famous figures concerning the casualties which would follow a landing on the Tokyo plain. This conference was attended by the President, King, Leahy, Byrnes, Eisenhower, Marshall and Stimson. It was decided to drop the bomb. On Monday, August 13, in the midst of obscure surrender negotiations and seven days after the first bomb was dropped, President Truman directed Marshall to proceed with all planned offensive operations against Japan. But the war was over, and shortly afterwards General MacArthur's troops landed on the Japanese mainland without opposition: to the surprise of the invaders they were welcomed with open arms. With the ending of the greatest, the most terrible and the most fiercely contested war in history, Marshall asked to be retired.

By that late summer of 1945 he had achieved his greatest triumph. The threads of Allied command throughout the world had passed through his hands. He, often alone, had made the gravest decisions, assumed the most urgent responsibilities, performed the most terrible tasks, for the fate of nations had depended upon his judgment. If, for example, he had not sent the Sherman tanks to Egypt in 1942, the British Army of the Nile might have been defeated and the whole of the Middle East might have been opened up to the Germans. There had been many other similar decisions; and in the landscape where he moved there were dangers everywhere. The perils were surmounted; the war was won; that summer he stood at the highest pinnacle of his achievement. As winter came on the victory would gradually pass from him, as it passed from the nation of which he was in a very real sense the greatest living representative, and in the following year, entangled in a Chinese swamp, he was to suffer his gravest defeat: so quickly did victory and defeat follow one another in those critical days. But the summer of 1945, which saw the United States in the full possession of her greatest strength, saw him at his best.

From early spring into the summer he worked on the book which was the nearest thing he ever wrote to an autobiography. He had said often that he would never write a formal autobiography—the truth hurt, and he had made too many enemies to make an honest account of his life palatable—but inevitably, in his own way and in his own time, he would write about himself; and it was characteristic of the man that the book in which his own voice is heard most clearly and in which he describes himself at the greatest length, though always by implication, should have been called *The Winning of the War in Europe and the Pacific: Biennial Report of the Chief of Staff of the U.S. Army 1943-1945*.

This book, which amounts to no more than 123 pages, was begun in Washington in April and completed during the Potsdam Conference. Much of it was written during airplane journeys, scribbled hurriedly and tempestuously in that terrible backward-slanting handwriting of his, where the strains and the violent impulses of his character show themselves as though they were on parade. These penciled scribbles were given to a secretary who copied them on a typewriter. Afterwards there were many revisions, some pages being rewritten six times until he was finally satisfied with them. As the work progressed Marshall called upon various authorities for information; every statement was checked and double-checked. He sought advice avidly, employed all the resources of the Chief of Staff's office and submitted passages concerning the actors in the drama to the actors themselves. There are places where he has merely made a précis of existing operations reports, or someone else has done it for him. But the mark of the man is on the whole book, even in its confused arrangement, and his style, no longer sluggish but swift and clear as a salmon stream, is on every passage. Though perhaps a hundred people contributed to it in various ways, it is his book bearing his sign manual, and it is among his greatest achievements.

From the beginning everything was against him. He was attempting to put down on paper, within a limited compass, his impressions of the whole course of the war; and since the war was so vast in its scope and he was in daily contact with all its remotest details, so short an account may have seemed impossible. He had rarely shown any real gift for writing. From *Notes on Cordage and Tackle* to the second Biennial Report, he had shown only an occasional gift for the happy phrase; his writing was like his speech, colorless and diffuse, with the slow passages oddly balanced by little quick runs which occurred when his thoughts overreached his words. His best writing had occurred in the brief notes he wrote in his operational reports during World War I, when he was in physical contact with war and shared tire immediate excitement of war. He had spent a large part of World War II in Washington, rarely coming into contact with the physical details of war and therefore unable to draw sustenance from violent experience. The men in the field wrote best: so Stilwell in those brief letters written with the cutting edge of high temper, and Patton writing as one imagines a bulldog would write if it could. The writings of the "high brass" were generally pompous: they were men who had a high regard for themselves and were not afraid to strike attitudes: Leahy in particular is almost insufferable with his air of condescension and immutable virtue. And most of the American war-leaders, including Roosevelt, were bad writers who employed ghosts to write their speeches and memoirs, and it never seems to have occurred to them that to employ a ghost is uncommonly like an act of prostitution. Their writings lacked quality; Marshall's *Winning of the War* is brimming with it. All his life he had trained himself to make lucid and accurate reports, but mostly they were colorless, without any sense of life, as accurate as an algebraic formula. Now at last, with a quiet appreciation of his own accomplishment, forging a new style to suit a new purpose, he wrote with energy and precision and a sense of life, a history of the war which could only be written at a time of triumph by the man most responsible for the triumph, and through it all there shines the peculiar quality of the man at his best: complex and unyielding, stripped like a runner for the race.

The book is not in any real sense a simple report on the war, for issues far larger than the war are involved. He recounts the story of a victory, but within the victory there is implicit the possibility of defeat. The note of warning is heard continually. Indeed, the form of the book resembles the ancient musical arrangement called a *passacaglia* where one theme is repeated throughout and secondary themes evolve to provide elaborate complications, but the major theme remains constant, always present, never to be forgotten. For Marshall the major theme was the duty to salvage and safeguard the civilization we live in.

The book begins on a note of triumph. Addressing himself to Secretary Stimson, Marshall announces complete victory in words which at one place echo the Biblical rhythms of Miriam's exalted song after the defeat of the Egyptian hosts:

> Our forces in Europe, air and ground, have contributed mightily to the complete destruction of the Axis enemy. In the Pacific Japan has been compelled to sue for an end to the war which she treacherously started. For two years the victorious advance of the United States sea, air and land forces, together with those of our allies was virtually unchecked. They controlled the skies and the seas and no army could successfully oppose them. Behind these forces was the output of the American farms and factories, exceeding any similar effort of man, so that the peoples everywhere with whom we were joined in the fight for decency and justice were able to reinforce their efforts through the aid of American ships, munitions and supplies.

Almost immediately the note of warning is sounded. The Nation had only just emerged from one of its gravest crises; Germany and Japan had come so close to complete domination of the world that even now people did not realize "how thin the thread of Allied survival had been stretched." Nor was America mainly responsible for the survival of the Allies. "In good conscience," wrote Marshall, "this Nation can take little credit for its part in staving off disaster in those critical days. It is certain that the refusal of the British and Russian peoples to accept what appeared to be inevitable defeat was the great factor in the salvage of our civilization." He listed the Axis mistakes, and showed how, with a little more perspicacity, the Germans and the Japanese might have retrieved their errors or not committed them at all. Chance played its part. A terrific snowstorm on the Russian front, the bitter cold during Christmas week of 1941 which precipitated the defeat of the German Army—what if the weather had been a little less cold? He showed how accurately the Germans had sometimes gauged their enemies: they were reasonably sure that General Patton would be placed in charge of one of the American armies in France, and they guessed both the general direction and the strength of the initial assault on Normandy with surprising accuracy. He says bluntly that the decisive battles of the war were not fought by the Americans: these battles were fought at Stalingrad and El Alamein. "Had the U.S.S.R. and the British Army of the Nile been defeated in 1942, as they well might if the Germans, Japanese and Italians had better coordinated their plans and resources and successive operations, we should have stood today in the western hemisphere confronted by enemies who controlled a greater part of the world."

Then he went on to speak of the future. The immensely destructive weapons, invented or brought to perfection during the course of the war, offered alarming prospects. The bombers which originally flew at 200 miles an hour with a bomb load capacity of 6,000 pounds could fly at the end of the war at 350 miles an hour with a bomb load capacity of 20,000 pounds; and there was no end in sight to the speed and range and carrying power of airplanes. New bombs, one weighing 45,000 pounds, were being developed, and ordnance engineers were quietly blueprinting a bomb weighing 100,000 pounds. There were in existence new rockets controlled by electronic devices which sought out their own objective. "Drawn by their own fuses such new rockets will streak unerringly to the heart of big factories, attracted by the heat of the furnaces. They are so sensitive that in the space of a large room they aim themselves toward a man who enters, in reaction to the heat of his body."

A strange and savage drama rides through the opening pages of the book. The style, so clean and swift, was part of the man; so were the dire prophecies. Having examined the nature of the weapons which could tear the world apart, Marshall wrote gravely of the consequences. He had never written so well before, nor so honestly. He spoke of the danger which lies before us: the terrible weapons, the desperate measures which would inevitably be invoked, but the most dangerous thing of all would be to rely implicitly on the new weapons. He said:

> This doctrine [of relying upon machine power] will be closely akin to the doctrine of negative defense which

destroyed France. The folly of the Maginot line was proved early in the war but too late to save France. The folly of the new doctrine which has already begun to take shape in the thinking of many Americans would also be proved early—but probably too late to save America.

The only effective defense a nation can now maintain is the power of attack. And that power cannot be in machinery alone. There must be men to man the machines. And there must be men to come to close grips with the enemy and tear his operating bases and his productive establishment away from him before the war can end.

The classic proof of this came in the battle of Britain. Even with the magnificent fighter defense of the Royal Air Force, even with the incredible efficiency of the fire of thousands of anti-aircraft guns, controlled and aimed by unerring electronic instruments, the British Islands remained under the fire of the German enemy until the final stages of the war.

Not until the American and British armies crossed the channel and seized control of the enemy's territory was the hail of rockets lifted from England. Not until we had physical possession of the launching sites and the factories that produced the V weapons did these attacks cease.

Such was the pattern of war in the 20th Century. If this nation is ever again at war, suffering, as Britain did in this war, the disastrous attacks of rocket-propelled weapons with explosive power like our own atomic bomb, it will bleed and suffer perhaps to the point of annihilation, unless we can move armies of men into the enemy's bases of operations and seize the sites from which he launches his attacks.

As he wrote these words he was half-hopeful that war could be outlawed through the United Nations, but it was a desperate hope. The thought of America bleeding and suffering to the point of annihilation was not offered for the purpose of alarming Americans: such a blood-letting under modern conditions was eminently possible and might, under slightly different circumstances, have occurred in the war against the Axis. He was stating what might very well happen; and he could see that there were forces in the world which regarded another war as unavoidable. Then what should be done? Once before he had appealed to historians to write more honestly and more accurately. He said that all the trouble in the world comes from misunderstandings of history; but to put the blame on the historians was to avoid the issue: the soldiers are as much responsible for war as the politicians, who never listen to historians. He hoped that the atomic explosion would "spur men of judgment as they have never before been pressed to seek a method whereby the peoples of the earth can live in peace and justice." But in whose keeping was the roll of honor in which the men of judgment are listed? He did not know. He could only tear savagely at a problem which had gone beyond him, and for the rest he would see to it, with all the power he could, that America would look to her defenses. He said:

> We have tried since the birth of our nation to promote our love of peace by a display of weakness. This course has failed us utterly, cost us millions of lives and billions of treasure. The reasons are quite understandable. The world does not seriously regard the desires of the weak. Weakness presents too great a temptation to the strong, particularly to the bully who schemes for wealth and power.
>
> We must, if we are to realize the hopes we may now dare have for lasting peace, enforce our will for peace with strength. We must make it clear to the potential gangsters of the world that if they dare break our peace they will do so at their great peril.

These words served as prelude to the drama which Marshall thereupon describes in five chapters written deliberately with an emphasis approaching that which history was likely to give to the story. These chapters give the progress of the war in clear outline. It is as though the war was seen from another planet, in miniscule, by someone completely detached from its overwhelming problems and simply because they are succinct and well-written and given the sharp edge of Marshall's style, these chapters are quite unusually instructive. Caesar wrote his account of the wars with a detailed brilliance, basing his writing upon endless staff reports; Marshall eschews detail; everything is seen in terms of the tremendous sweeping forces of American character and industry. Eisenhower's letters are quoted, but he becomes no more than an American symbol: a curious anonymity surrounds the actors in the drama. Only Stilwell is praised at length and in words which suggested real emotion. Marshall described how

Stilwell was sent out to take command over one of the most difficult campaigns of the war:

> He was out at the end of the thinnest supply line of all; the demands of the war in the Europe and Pacific campaigns, which were clearly the most vital to final victory, exceeded our resources in many items of matériel and equipment and all but absorbed everything else we had. General Stilwell could have only what was left and that was extremely thin. He had a most difficult physical problem of great distances, almost impassable terrain, widespread disease and unfavorable climate; he faced an extremely difficult political problem and his purely military problem of opposing large numbers of enemy with few resources was unmatched in any theater.
>
> Nevertheless General Stilwell sought with amazing vigor to carry out his mission exactly as it had been stated. His great efforts brought a natural conflict of personalities. He stood, as it were, the middle-man between two great governments other than his own, with slender resources and problems somewhat overwhelming in their complexity. As a consequence it was deemed necessary in the fall of 1944 to relieve General Stilwell of the burden of his heavy responsibilities in Asia and give him a respite from attempting the impossible.

The final sentence provides a clue to the simplifications with which the Report abounds. They were, of course, necessary simplifications, but they occasionally conceal the truth as much as they reveal it; no one reading the Report would be made aware of the thunder which accompanied Stilwell's recall, or the extraordinary tensions involved. There are times when Marshall's mind moves like a flooded river over a broken landscape, and in the bright silvery surface of the river the landscape lies concealed.

There are faults in the Report, as there are faults in the man; places where the involved grammar shows spiritual knots; the words "terrific" and "tremendous" begin to lose their force after too many repetitions; there are times when his mind appears to find consolation in the recital of vast and not very helpful figures, as when he mentions that "rations for our troops in the United Kingdom were supplemented by 436,000,000 pounds of foodstuffs, principally fresh fruit and vegetables, grown in Britain," while Australia provided 1,835,000,000 pounds of foodstuffs, and India 524,000,000.

Here and there his own private obsessions come through. His belief in the American soldier could not be greater, but he distrusted the excitability of Americans, and said so in one of the few barbed passages in the Report:

> The American soldier has a very active imagination and usually, at least for the time being, covets anything new and is inclined to endow the death-dealing weapons of the enemy with extraordinary qualities since any weapon seems much more formidable to the man receiving its fire than to the man delivering it. If given slight encouragement the reaction can be fatal to the success of our forces. Commanders must always make every effort to show their men how to make better, more effective use of what they have. The technique of handling a weapon can often be made more devastating than the power of the weapon itself. This was best illustrated by the correct, the intended, tactical employment of the United States medium tank.

Marshall did not explain how a technique could be more devastating than a weapon or what he meant by "usually, at least for the time being"; but this hardly matters, for the sense comes through. What is strange is that the words were written by a man who demanded clear-cut thinking and accuracy from his subordinates, but did not always think clearly and accurately himself. He confused names easily, refusing promotion to Van Fleet because he confused the officer with another, who was a heavy drinker. But there are few confusions in the Report, and the passage just quoted does not give the quality of the whole.

Some of the best passages in the Report occur in the concluding chapter called "For the Common Defense," where he restates more firmly and against the background of American history the conclusions which were reached in the beginning of the Report. He dismisses the isolationists with the statement: "We are now concerned with the peace of the entire world. And the peace can be maintained only by the strong." Again and again he makes his plea for strength. The great democracies, he says, were sick nations when Hitler began the war. As sick as any was the United States, a third-rate power when the President proclaimed in September, 1939, a state of limited emergency. The consequences of weakness were nearly disastrous:

> The German armies swept over Europe at the very moment we sought to avoid war by assuring ourselves that there could be no war. The security of the United States of America was saved by sea distances, by Allies, and by the errors of a prepared enemy. For probably the last time in the history of warfare those ocean distances were a vital factor in our defense. We may elect again to depend on others and the whim and error of potential enemies, but if we do we will be carrying the treasure and freedom of this great Nation in a paper bag.

It was on these matters that he wrote best, for he had lived long with them. The style is sharp and clean; and even when he goes into lengthy details concerning universal military training, repeating the substance of many speeches, saying over and over again things he had said a hundred times before, the passion comes through. Significantly the Report ends with one last appeal for universal military training:

> We can be certain that the next war, if there is one, will be even more total than this one. The nature of war is such that once it now begins it can end only as this one is ending, in the destruction of the vanquished, and it should be assumed that another reconversion from peace to war production will take place initially under enemy distant bombardment. . . .
>
> If this Nation is to remain great it must bear in mind now and in the future that war is not the choice of those who wish passionately for peace. It is the choice of those who are willing to resort to violence for political advantage. We can fortify ourselves against disaster, I am convinced, by the measures I have here outlined. In these protections we can face the future with a reasonable hope for the best and with quiet assurance that even though the worst may come, we are prepared for it.

The final words of the Report are Washington's: "There is a rank due to the United States among nations, which will be withheld, if not absolutely lost, by the reputation of weakness—if we desire to avoid insult we must be ready to repel it; if we desire to secure peace, one of the most powerful institutions of our rising prosperity, it must be known that we are at all times ready for war."

The third Biennial Report was published to the world in October during the beginning of the massive demobilization which followed the end of the war; and there was some irony in the fact that Marshall, who had clamored loudest for a strong citizen-army, should have presided over its decline. It would be some years later before the new citizen-army he envisaged became a reality: in June, 1951, for the first time, the kind of army which Washington had wanted and Marshall had fought for became law.

In October, 1945, Marshall was finally allowed to retire from the post he had occupied since September, 1939. Judge Robert P. Patterson had assumed the place occupied by Secretary Stimson, and in the private ceremony at the Pentagon which marked Marshall's retirement there was still another of those long memorial speeches which attend the resignation of high military figures, the judge pronouncing the words of praise as though they were a kind of doom, while the generals listened and fidgeted like schoolboys. By this time Marshall was weary of speeches. Only the previous month Stimson had resigned, and once again he had pointed to Marshall as the greatest general of his generation. The speeches seemed endless. Marshall's own valedictory message as retiring Chief of Staff was shorter than most and more to the point. Echoing Washington, he said: "Are we already shirking the responsibility of victory? . . . Are we inviting the same international disrespect that prevailed before this war?" This was in November, when already the tensions in Europe and the Far East announced the beginning of another and even more dangerous war.

Marshall was now ready for a long rest. He knew he would remain on the active list until the end of his life, but he believed that a grateful country would allow him to pass his days quietly. There were still a few more ceremonies to attend. On November 26, six days after he was succeeded as Chief of Staff by Eisenhower, there was a ceremony at the White House where the President presented him with the Oak Leaf Cluster to the D.S.M. he had earned in France during another war, and there were more speeches, and then, as he thought, he would be allowed to retire to Leesburg. The next day, shortly after reaching Dodona Manor, the telephone rang. It was the President saying that General Patrick Hurley, the United States Ambassador to

China had resigned, and would Marshall leave at once for Chungking?

He did not leave at once. The Navy Court of Enquiry on Pearl Harbor was sitting, and once more it was necessary to give his testimony and recite the protracted events which led up to the catastrophe of another December four years ago. His testimony added little to what had been said at other enquiries; an airplane was kept ready for him; there were further delays as the President, the State Department and Marshall's staff hammered out the policy statement which was given to Marshall on December 15. Then, on December 19, he flew off towards China, a land he hardly knew, so much had it changed in the twenty years since he was stationed at Tientsin.

CHAPTER FOURTEEN

Debacle in China

When in the early fifties of the last century Commissioner Humphrey Marshall reached China, he saw the country in the throes of a revolution. An impotent, ignorant and conceited dynasty—the words are his own—ruled by mandate from Peking; in the south the revolutionary Taipings were masters of the Yangtse Valley. These revolutionaries were Christians, though their Christianity differed from Christianity as it is practiced anywhere else in the world; they put forward vast programs of agrarian reform; they deified their leaders; they ruled by naked force. Commissioner Marshall was at first attracted by the Taipings. They represented, he thought, the aroused revolutionary feeling of the people confronted with the decay of the imperial régime. He wrote home in April, 1853: "Any day may bring forth the fruits of successful revolution, in the utter confusion of the existing dynasty."

The mandarinate was reeling, but its overthrow, which Commissioner Marshall predicted within a few months, was delayed for another sixty years. As the years passed with no great victories on either side, he saw that the protagonists were about evenly matched: a small hard-hitting force applied to one or other of the sides might resolve the issue. But which side should receive American aid? He heard in July, 1855, rumors that the Chinese Government was calling upon Russia for aid. He wrote to Secretary of State Marcy: "Her [Russia's] assistance would probably end in passing China under a Russian protectorate, and in extension of Russian limits to the Hoangho, or the mouth of the Yangtse. . . . I think that almost any sacrifice should be made by the United States to keep Russia from spreading her Pacific boundary, and to avoid her coming directly to interference in Chinese domestic affairs."

The situation was grave, but Humphrey Marshall's belief that the Russians were about to intervene was founded on nothing more than rumor. The Russian Government was not yet in a position where it could employ force; and Marshall, observing that the Russians were then impotent and that the Taipings had exhausted themselves with feuds among their own princes, decided that American aid should be offered to the imperial dynasty. Frederick Townsend Ward and General Gordon placed their military knowledge at the service of the Manchus, and the Taiping armies were chased across the whole length of China. Marshall's reasons for assisting the Manchus were clear. He wrote:

> Whenever the avarice or ambitions of Russia or Great Britain shall tempt them to take the prizes, the fate of Asia will be sealed, and the future Chinese relations of the United States may be closed for ages, unless *now* the United States shall foil the untoward result by adopting a sound policy. It is my opinion that the highest interests of the United States are involved in sustaining China—maintaining order here and engrafting on this worn out stock the healthy principles which give life and health to governments, rather than to see China become the theater of widespread anarchy, and ultimately the prey of European ambitions.

Though the doctrine of the Open Door was to come later, Commissioner Marshall's statement remained for nearly a hundred years the policy of the American Government towards China. Beneath Humphrey Marshall's drab prose a desperate purpose can be discerned: at whatever the cost China must be saved from Russia, Great Britain and anarchy. For a few years Humphrey Marshall possessed the power to decide the fate of China; and though he left China before the Manchus won their victory over the Taipings, he more than anyone else was responsible for bringing them foreign military advisers and foreign weapons. By a strange stroke of fortune his collateral descendant, George Marshall, stood in an almost exactly similar position in 1945.

When Marshall flew to China the official policy of the United States Government was based upon conceptions of collective security.

It was believed that "a strong, united and democratic China" would play her part in the family of nations. There was imminent danger of civil war, of a gigantic flare-up which might be expected to reach far beyond the borders of China. If the civil war broke out, the consequences to the rest of the world might be disastrous. "A breach of the peace anywhere in the world," said President Truman in a prepared statement which became a part of Marshall's directive, "threatens the peace of the entire world." If China could eliminate conflict in her own territory, the United States would provide China with huge credits. If China could not maintain peace—but President Truman saw no reason to contemplate the grim alternative. He had sent Marshall out, and he was prepared in due time to receive news that Marshall had discovered a formula which would reconcile the Communists with the Kuomintang, a "strong, united and democratic China" would come into being and the American credits would flow into a peaceful China.

    The phrase "a strong, united and democratic China" owed its origin to the fertile brain of Chiang Kai-shek.* It was an unhappy phrase, for it contained within it the seeds of many corruptions and many contraries. China could become strong only under a ruthless dictatorship; she could become united only when one of the warring protagonists had decisively beaten the other; she could become democratic only by jettisoning her whole culture. Yet the phrase, however meaningless and impossible of attainment, did represent the very real desire of many Chinese of all classes and all political complexions; and insofar as he could, Marshall was determined to bring it about.

    A foretaste of Marshall's attitude was supplied when his airplane reached the Kiangwan Airport in Shanghai. He hurriedly inspected the American honor guard and then drove immediately to Cathay House for his first conference. There were no frills; he moved directly to the target. He no longer regarded himself as a military figure, though he wore military uniform. As a special emissary with the rank of Ambassador he was charged with the almost impossible task of bringing peace to China, and this could be done, as he knew,

    * The phrase was first used officially by Secretary Byrnes at a hearing of the Senate Committee on Foreign Relations on December 7, 1944. It had however appeared in a number of memoranda and in the Generalissimo's speeches.

only on political levels; and it was as a man wielding immense and sometimes hypothetical political powers that he flew off to Nanking, where the Generalissimo was then staying.

Marshall had acquired a Chinese name. There were three or four variants, but the generally accepted Chinese version of his name was Ma Hsieh-erh, which meant "Resting Horse" or "Peaceful Horse." The "horse" part of his name represented "power" or "force"; the remaining part represented "passivity." It was agreed that the name was remarkably consistent with the man who would possess vast powers but would be constrained to use them only passively, by threats or by suggestion or by the promise of aid from America which could be withheld, never by the direct employment of American arms. The name, so subtly devised, described his own dilemma, for though he represented a huge power he was never able to use power except in argument; and in argument, from the moment he arrived in China, he showed himself a master. He was faced by men with subtle powers of argument equal to his own. They, too, were masters, and to the very end there was to be something heroic in that terrible debate between champions which was to decide the future of China.

There were many people involved in the debate. Some like Mao Tse-tung remained hidden in the mountain fastness of Yenan, and though they exerted enormous powers and made tremendous decisions, their exact contribution to the debate is still unknown. There was Chen Li-fu, the former Minister of Education, the man who had welded the Kuomintang party into a tough bureaucratic machine instantly obedient to his orders, at the mercy of his mystical adoration of force, hot-tempered and willful under a calm, frozen exterior. He, too, remained in obscurity, taking no part in the argument while controlling the course of the argument from a distance, since he was closest to the Generalissimo, possessed large powers over the secret police and was in constant contact with the Kuomintang generals. There was Chou En-lai, the son of a mandarin, hot-tempered and volatile with a brilliant analytic brain and a devotion to Stalin as great as his devotion to Mao Tse-tung, whose representative he was. There was Lo Lung-chi, a former professor of political science who had been debarred from teaching by the direct order of the Generalissimo for his criticisms of the régime, a man who lived on his nervous energy. He represented the liberal groups which had come together under the name of the Democratic League, and he was the most tragic of the disputants, for he possessed no army. Finally, there was the Generalissimo himself, a man who believed himself to be the descendant of ancient Chinese kings just as his Minister of Finance believed himself to be the descendant of Confucius, a man who showed in his stern gestures the effects of his early military training in Japan, where he attained the rank of a second-class corporal. He was unyielding, proud, brave, dedicated and ignorant; and when he entered a room some almost magical process of theatricality occurred, for one was made immediately aware of a Presence. Marshall immediately liked him as a man, while distrusting his judgments. Stimson was to characterize him as "an ignorant, suspicious, feudal autocrat with a profound but misconceived devotion to the integrity of China and to himself as her savior." This picture of the Generalissimo was based on the reports of General Stilwell. Marshall, who read and approved of Stilwell's reports, at no time shared Stilwell's belief in the idiocy of the Generalissimo. Years later when he was asked what he thought of the Generalissimo, Marshall replied: "A very fine character and I was really fond of him. The question of his handling of the situation was another matter." The Generalissimo's handling of the situation was to precipitate one disaster after another.

Reaching Chungking, Marshall immediately went to work. He had received definite directives from the State Department, but his overriding objective could be stated simply: a China "disunited and torn by civil strife" was not a proper place for American economic assistance, and his major task quite simply was to prevent civil war. Some mystery attached to the original directive. It was said, and widely believed, that the Far Eastern Division of the State Department rewrote his directive under the guise of removing unnecessary verbiage. This directive was favorable to the Communists, and Marshall's staff is supposed to have intervened at the last moment, tearing up the draft composed by the Far Eastern Division and substituting another closer to Marshall's wishes. The draft composed by the State Department is said to have been written by John Carter Vincent with Dean Acheson's approval. The story may be true; it is certainly irrelevant. Marshall's mission arose as the result of forces which had little enough to do with the writing of directives. The Moscow conference of the three foreign ministers held during the same month had urged "the participation by all democratic elements in all branches of the National Government," while America, Russia and Britain had affirmed their adherence to "the policy of non-interference in the internal affairs of China." Neither the Americans, the Russians nor the British seriously regarded the second as binding; they did however regard the first as overwhelmingly dictated by the logic of events. All of the three great powers were war-weary, and all were agreed that the situation in China was fraught with danger. Here, if anywhere, a third world war might break out. In the end, of course, it did break out on the confines of China, but by then the great powers had maneuvered themselves into a position where the war was inevitable.

Marshall came to China with qualities which were rare in Americans and rarer still in American generals. He was deeply sympathetic towards Chinese culture. He had some knowledge of spoken Chinese. His friendship with General Stilwell had given him an understanding of the forces opposing Chiang Kai-shek. He was under no illusions about the desperate stratagems which would be necessary to prevent war from spreading in China. If the Yalta agreement of February 11, 1945, made his task immensely difficult insofar as it affected his relations with Chiang Kai-shek, he was faced with other difficulties from the uncompromising nature of the Chinese Communists' demands, though they were no more uncompromising than the demands of the faction headed by Chen Li-fu. The miracle was that he accomplished so much during his preliminary talks. Nineteen days after his arrival in China the Government and the Communists signed a truce. Six weeks later they signed a formal agreement to reduce and merge their armies from three hundred divisions to sixty within eighteen months.

The astonishing progress in those early days was due as much to Marshall's determined advocacy as to the legends which surrounded him. In those days he was more than man. He had captivated the Chinese imagination. He was the master-organizer of victory against the Axis. Neither the Kuomintang nor the Chinese Communists could dare to treat him with indifference. But it is one of the qualities of legends that their brightness fades unless they are continually fed, and

The Marshall Story

Marshall was in no mood to feed his own legend. He rarely appeared publicly. There were no heroic gestures. His most important work was done in the seclusion of a living room, round a charcoal fire, with the Kuomintang and Communist delegates beside him, while cups of hot tea were brought in silently by servants. The turning-point had come on January 1, when Chiang Kai-shek agreed that Marshall should have full powers to arbitrate the dispute. Such a solution had been canvassed before, for Vice-President Wallace had once suggested to the Generalissimo that the warring factions in China should combine to fight against Japan, if necessary by using the President as arbitrator. How such an arbitration could be accomplished was never explained; nor was any explanation offered about how Marshall could be both arbitrator and special emissary from President Truman to Chiang Kai-shek. That he succeeded for a while, in spite of the ambiguity of his position, was a testimony to the extraordinary hold he possessed over the Chinese imagination, to his patience and to his understanding of the forces at work.

As Marshall saw it, the war was basically a simple one and had much in common with the subterranean war which broke out after the American revolution. Privilege fought against the disinherited; the powers of high finance fought against the masses. What was necessary was that each should show signs of compromise. When on January 9, the Kuomintang insisted on its right to take over the Communist-occupied border provinces of Jehol and Chahar, Marshall appealed directly to the Generalissimo for a compromise: the Communists should open the railroads into Manchuria, and the Kuomintang should halt their armies at the border. The Kuomintang delegate at that time was General Chang Chun, a former Minister of Foreign Affairs and Mayor of Shanghai. When he heard that the Generalissimo had agreed with Marshall's suggestion, he appealed to the Generalissimo, saying he had lost face. "You do the negotiating, and I will do the fighting," the Generalissimo said. By this time the outlines of the confused war which lay ahead could already be seen. There was to come a time when Marshall was to be manipulated and employed as a smokescreen by both sides. On the surface both sides were negotiating; at the same time they were maneuvering for position, acquiring advantages, threatening, waiting for the moment when Marshall's legend would be dissipated in the eyes of the Chinese, only too anxious that by some slip of the tongue Marshall would compromise himself. It is the kind of game which is sometimes fought in Chinese families, where the relatives are endlessly engaged in the pursuit of favors from the head of the family—a bitter game fought with endless cunning. Marshall was aware that the game might be fought in this way; he did not always take sufficient precautions to prevent the adversaries from claiming favors which he had never granted. The Kuomintang through its press releases claimed that Marshall was in favor of their cause. Was he not President Truman's special emissary to Chiang Kai-shek as President of China? The Chinese Communists, who originally welcomed Marshall with open arms, perceived that the scales were weighted against them and gradually increased their demands, even though outwardly they gave the impression of being determined upon compromise.

Compromise! This was the word, according to the delegates, which was perpetually on Marshall's lips. "He says 'compromise' as though he really believed in it," Lo Lung-chi told me. "He does not know that the word has never been used before in Chinese political discussions." Marshall did not care if the word had never been used before; it was enough that it should be used now, unsparingly, passionately, as though the word itself possessed the magical property of bringing about solutions. Once, when he was talking about compromise, he showed Chou En-lai the address the eighty-year-old Benjamin Franklin delivered to the Convention which produced the Constitution of the United States:

> When you assemble a number of men, to have the advantage of their joint wisdom, you inevitably assemble with those men all their prejudices, their passions, their errors of opinion, their local interests, and their selfish views. From such an assembly can a *perfect* production be expected? It therefore astonishes me, Sir, to find the system approaching to perfection so near as it does; and I think it will astonish our enemies, who are waiting with confidence to hear, that our councils are confounded like those of the builders of Babel, and that our States are on the point of separation, only to meet thereafter for the purpose of cutting one another's throats. Thus I consent, Sir, to this

Constitution, because I expect no better, and because I am not sure that it is not the best.

Unfortunately, the contenders were much closer to cutting one another's throats than he realized; and there was about all the agreements a curiously provisional character, as though everyone realized their necessity and no one believed they would ever be carried out.

The major agreement aimed at preventing civil war was one entitled "Basis for Military Reorganization and for the Integration of the Communist Forces into the National Army." This agreement, signed on February 25, provided for the reduction of the Chinese Armies from three hundred to sixty divisions. This was to be a gradual process. The Nationalist Armies were to be reduced to ninety divisions at the end of twelve months, and the Chinese Communist forces were to be reduced to eighteen divisions during the same period. In the following six months there were to be further reductions: the Nationalist Armies would be reduced to fifty divisions, and the Chinese Communist armies to ten divisions. On paper the plan had everything to commend it; in practice nothing could be more difficult. There had to be a comparative rate of demobilization, but how could one demobilize armies which possessed no divisional organizations and whose numbers were unknown even to the high command? No one knew accurately what was contained in these armies; there were no basic units; it was impossible to say how many Communist units were equivalent to how many Kuomintang units. It was agreed that after seven months the armies should be integrated in the proportion of two Nationalist divisions to one Communist division; but even if tables of procedure had been drawn up, the integration would have been impossible simply because there was no method for bringing integration about. Probably Marshall knew that the scheme was impracticable, but even if it was impracticable it provided a necessary breathing space. Somehow, by means only dimly seen, he thought that an integration of armies could be brought about after a period of comparative peace; the army so formed would be a non-political force which could be used as a democratic army on the model of the Western armies and not as an authoritarian weapon. The agreement necessitated a list of armies with their strengths, their positions and weapons from both sides. The Kuomintang submitted such a list on March 26. When examined, it was seen to be largely inaccurate. The Communists never supplied such a list and there was therefore no need to enquire into the accuracy of their dispositions; nor could the Communists have supplied such a list, for their armies consisted of scattered units continually on the move, small in numbers but able at any moment to accumulate large resources from the countless villages of north China. The fact that accurate lists were not provided was the first real warning of trouble ahead. There was Marshall's clear-cut mathematical plan, to which everyone had given his assent; and there were the ghostly uncounted armies already wheeling across China and taking up their positions.

Two days after the February 25 agreement, a directive was issued to the Executive Headquarters which went a long way towards establishing peace in China. If peace could have been established, the method Marshall evolved was probably the best for the purpose. Three-men committees were to set out to the troubled areas with power to enforce the pledges of peace made by both sides. An organization called Executive Headquarters was set up, composed of American, Kuomintang and Communist members; the headquarters of the new organization were in the palatial building of the Peiping Union Medical College. From there field teams were to be sent out to all areas where fighting was taking place.

Marshall's preliminary moves occurred in an atmosphere of extraordinary good will. At the People's Consultative Conference in January the Generalissimo had announced a program of reform so far-reaching that the Chinese, who had listened so often to his anathemas against reform, could be forgiven if they thought the millenium was at hand. Chiang Kai-shek announced that the Government had decided to invoke freedom of person, belief, speech, publication, assemblage and association. All political parties were to be equal before the law; all political prisoners were to be released; popular elections were to be held throughout China. It is doubtful whether he intended at any time to carry these reforms through, but they were significant of the popular demand for reform; and the People's Consultative Assembly went on to introduce agrarian, educational and industrial reforms and to revise the 1936 Kuomintang Draft Constitution. Though few realized it at the time, the Constitution was to supply the brake to the reforms, and this became inevitable once it was decided that a three-fourths vote of the National Assembly would be required to ratify the Constitution. The seats in the National Assembly were so manipulated that the Kuomintang always arranged that it had a large majority; the party was therefore able to ensure its own survival and the survival of its most reactionary policies.

But all this belonged to the future. As Marshall accompanied by Chou En-lai and the Kuomintang General Chang Chih-chung flew over north China during the first week of March, covering nearly 4,000 miles, visiting a dozen cities, the three men always together until they seemed to be one man with all the hope of China gathered in their arms, a wave of extraordinary joy swept the country. On both sides of the fighting lines (for there was sporadic fighting even during that miraculous week) there was a wild enthusiasm for the man whom the banner-bearers called: "The Saviour of China," "The God of Peace" and "First Lord of all Warlords." From Hopei, Shansi and Shantung there came news of the successes of the three-men teams. At Yenan Marshall met Mao Tse-tung and Chu Teh for the first time, and he was a little surprised to find the chairman of the Chinese Communist Party at the landing field dressed as a peasant with a woolen scarf wrapped round his neck, while the Commander in Chief of the Red Armies wore a ragged soldier's uniform and a purple cape with a fox-fur collar. The Chinese Communists welcomed him with open arms, offered him a banquet, commented privately that he behaved with perfect propriety, unlike General Patrick Hurley who had jumped down from the airplane on the Yenan landing field and uttered a series of piercing Indian war-cries for no reason they were ever able to discover. Marshall was taken to the large brick building which served as the assembly hall of the Chinese Communist Party, and there he noticed the immense portraits of Stalin and Lenin which stood on the wall near the proscenium arch. He had never doubted that the Chinese Communists were in fact Communists; but now, quite suddenly, looking on those portraits, he realized that their loyalty to the Soviet Union was absolute, that nothing except defeat would change them and that they were in full possession of the mysterious power whose origin lay in Moscow. Afterwards, when Marshall had left Yenan, and every gesture and word he spoke there was submitted to analysis, the only fault they found in him was his momentary annoyance, as he stepped off the plane, concerning the absence of protocol. As he inspected the honor guard, Chu Teh and Mao Tse-tung had walked by his side; and it was remembered that he had made a gesture suggesting that he should walk with the Commander in Chief of the Chinese Communist Armies, and not with Mao Tse-tung. But these were not important matters. Chou En-lai had informed the Communists in Yenan that Marshall's integrity was unquestioned. Many Americans had visited Yenan. They already knew the kind of man he was; and they were not disappointed. If they were more critical than the students and the schoolboys who waved banners and crowded the streets in the expectation of seeing his automobile pass, it was because they were by nature critical and unable to think outside the Marxian categories. In these categories it was difficult to discover the place which was occupied by the tall American general who had brought the Western Allies to victory.

Nothing like this triumphal tour had ever occurred in China; nothing like it was to happen again. Everything Marshall did or said was carefully recorded, weighed, commented upon at length; and every editorial was a sigh of relief. Almost single-handed it seemed that Marshall had warded off the threatened war. Towards the end of his tour he spoke at Hankow. He said: "Last month and the next two months are the most critical months in the history of China." The historian may quibble over such a sweeping statement, for the history of China has been a continual repetition of crises, some of them of desperate gravity. Yet in the history of modern China those two months were dramatically decisive, and for reasons which he never made clear Marshall chose to leave China for five weeks out of those two months.

No one knows what course history would have pursued if Marshall had elected to stay in China during the whole of those fatal two months. One can only guess, but it is a reasonable guess that he would have been able to exert his authority and prevent the more intolerant of the disputants from exerting theirs.

As Marshall saw it, the reasons which led him to leave China were simple. The American White Paper on United States Relations with China prints the reasons in full in a paragraph which is evidently based on a memorandum written by him in his characteristic style. He said:

> He felt that he should report to the President on the situation in China and he was particularly anxious to take up the question of the transfer of surplus property and shipping and the problem of loans to China. He also wished to make a personal presentation of the situation in China regarding UNRAA and famine conditions. He was of the opinion that he should make a brief visit to obtain financial and economic facilities to aid China and return to China in time to assist in adjusting differences which were certain to arise over the major problems connected with the agreements reached. It was his opinion that steps had to be taken to assist China and its people in the increasingly serious economic situation and to facilitate the efforts being made toward peace and unity in China and toward the establishment of a unified defense force. General Marshall felt that Chinese political and military unity could only be consolidated and made lasting through the rehabilitation of the country and the permanent general improvement of economic conditions. President Truman approved the recommendation and formally recalled him to Washington for these purposes. He accordingly departed for Washington on March 11, 1946.

These reasons were of course real and serious enough to suggest that a visit to Washington would be rewarding, but there were compelling reasons, including the one he had himself stated when he spoke about the following two months as being the most critical in China's history, which demanded that he should stay in China. He belonged to legend and possessed the powers of a legend; his substitute, Lieutenant General Alvin C. Gillem, Jr., possessed none of these powers, nor did he have Marshall's understanding of the problem. During the five weeks of Marshall's absence the carefully constructed house of peace began to crack wide open. It was as though, as on the morning of Pearl Harbor, Marshall were illustrating his own fatal tendency to be absent at those critical times when he alone could decide the course of events.

In China Marshall had assumed the role of the envoy extraordinary of the American people. In Washington he spoke as though he was the envoy of the Chinese people, speaking of their hopes and fears, the terrible possibilities of famine and war, of ruin and decadence. He rarely mentioned his own role, though he had played a lone hand and was wholly responsible for the creation of the Executive Headquarters. He said:

> The Chinese people are engaged in an effort which should command the grateful cooperation of the entire world. It is an effort almost without precedent. Their leaders are making daily progress towards the settlement of deep-seated and bitter conflicts which have lasted for twenty years. . . . They are succeeding in ending hostilities, and are now engaged in the business of demobilizing vast military forces and integrating the remainder into a national army. They have agreed to basic principles for the achievement in China of political and economic advances which were centuries coming to Western democracies. . . .
>
> If we are to have peace—if the world wants peace—there are compelling reasons why China's present effort must succeed. This depends in a large measure on actions of other nations. If China is ignored, or if there is scheming to thwart her present ambitious aspirations, her effort will fail. . . .
>
> The next few months are of tremendous importance to the Chinese people and to the future peace of the world.

He had a proper right to speak in this way. He had understood the problem and realized its gravity; and he refused to believe that the problem was insoluble. Stalin told Secretary Byrnes in December, 1945, that if anyone could settle the situation in China, Marshall could. At the time the statement was almost certainly true. Now in Washington he hoped to convince the Senate Foreign Relations Committee that large credits and sympathetic aid of every kind should be sent to China. He emphasized that he could not continue to act without the acknowledged support of the legislators. It was necessary to demonstrate that America had a stake in the peaceful recovery of China. Before he left China he had succeeded in convincing both sides to extend the cease-fire order to Manchuria. It seemed then that the most potentially dangerous corner of China was under control. Unfortunately it was not under control. On March 11, the day Marshall left China, the Generalissimo finally agreed to the entry of Executive

Headquarters teams into Manchuria, but the agreement was so involved, so full of clauses invoking special stipulations and conditions that it was impracticable from the beginning. The directive for the field teams did not reach them until March 27, and even then the fighting continued. There was to be fighting in Manchuria during all the eleven months Marshall spent in China.

In Marshall's absence the civil war began in earnest. It was not war as we know it in the West. All over the country, from Canton in the south to the northern outposts of Manchuria there were continual skirmishes. It was largely a war of guerrillas, the same kind of war which was fought by Quantrill in Kansas, John Hunt Morgan in Tennessee and Moseley in the Carolinas. There were raids by men who wore no uniform, possessed no certain organization and had little discipline among themselves, but they tore up railroads and captured ammunition depots and deliberately traded for arms with the enemy. The Kuomintang troops as well as the Chinese Communists fought this kind of war, but the Chinese Communists were the acknowledged masters. More than their adversaries they had studied partisan theory; they could destroy supply lines; they haunted the railroads; they could eat up the railway tracks as a caterpillar eats up a leaf, and they were not alarmed by the thought that by destroying communications they were spreading famine. They were footloose and could operate wherever their information—always correct—led them to believe they could do the greatest damage. They were raiders and infiltrators, and Marshall knew their kind by his long study of the War between the States. What he apparently did not realize was that they were profoundly conscious that they had evolved a technique which would, if the conversations broke down, give them victory within a few years or even a few months. While Marshall was in America, it became increasingly clear that neither side really wanted peace: the Chinese Communists believed they would win alone, while the Kuomintang believed that they could win with the help of America. Quite suddenly the mask was lifted: the quiet debates by the fireside, the long discussions on the nature of compromise and democracy, the insistence on peace and the benefits to be derived from peace, all these were seen to be, at best, indications of America's disturbed and ambivalent attitude towards the Chinese. Why did the Americans want peace so desperately? Why did they promise so much? How could a man be both an ambassador to Chiang Kai-shek and a mediator between Chiang Kai-shek and his opponents? The Chinese, naturally suspicious, began to see themselves not as Marshall's willing prisoners but as his captors.

The weakness of Marshall's design for peace lay in the fact that the truce could be effective only as long as there was a real hope of a political settlement. Marshall had hardly left on his airplane when the Kuomintang put an end to any hope of such a settlement. The Central Executive Committee of the Kuomintang met to approve of the decisions of the People's Consultative Council. Despite their previous pledges, they tore the program of the PCC to pieces. Chen Li-fu and his brother, Chen Kuo-fu, emerged into the open, denounced the agreements already made and refused their assent to a new democratic government: the Generalissimo's dictatorial powers were reaffirmed. At the same time the Chinese Communists strengthened their position in Manchuria. On April 18, the day of Marshall's return to China, they attacked and occupied Changchun, the capital of Manchuria. Marshall returned to find the pot boiling over.

The task he had to accomplish was now greater than ever. The signs which pointed to possible failure were clearly visible. It was not only that the Kuomintang had jettisoned the PCC agreement and that the Communists were basing their claim for a continuation of the civil war precisely on the fact that the PCC agreement had been broken, but there was a subtle alteration in the Chinese themselves: they began to see that war was inevitable, that nothing Marshall did could alter the fact, that a civil war—if it was short and did not severely damage the country—would provide the only possible solution to the conflict between irreconcilable forces. Civil war, indeed, was to be welcomed, since the uncertainties of the present could only be ended by war. These beliefs were not spoken openly. They were not stated in editorials. They were spoken in whispers, with bated breath, by people who knew the cost and were afraid of it.

Though Marshall had returned to discover that everything he had fought for was in dispute, he gave no sign that he thought the situation was hopeless. Some of the factors which made it hopeless were unknown to him. He did not know that General Gillem had been making remarks about the Chinese Communists which should never have been made by anyone who was charged with the duty of mediation. General Gillem intensely disliked the Chinese Communists, and said so. Reports of his speeches came into the hands of Chou En-lai, and were transmitted to Yenan, and from that moment the Chinese Communists claimed to see a change in the American attitude towards their party. On February 26, the Military Advisory Group in China, known as MAGIC, had come into existence. In theory, its purpose was to train both sides; in practice it could train only the Kuomintang troops, because the Generalissimo refused to allow it to proceed into Chinese Communist territory. Large quantities of American equipment were now coming to China: tanks, antiaircraft guns, airplanes were being placed at the service of the Nationalist forces. The Chinese Communists saw only one purpose for these new weapons, and from this time onward they were to grow increasingly bitter towards the Americans. The capture of Changchun had alarmed the Generalissimo. He was determined to recapture the city. The Kuomintang newspapers were ordered to print exaggerated accounts of Communist troop movements: the Communists were about to enter Tsinan, they had sprung traps on Nationalist forces all over the Northeast territory, they were springing up in Kwangtung and Hopei. Nor were the Kuomintang alone to blame: the Yenan radio attacked the Nationalists with savage fury, and soon both sides were shouting curses and imprecations upon one another as though they were deliberately fanning the flames, as though nothing less than the fiercest threats were satisfying. Marshall himself was immune from attack for a little while longer. Marshall was so irritated by the irresponsibility shown by both sides that he issued on May 23 his first public statement in China. The statement was written in the third person. He said:

> General Marshall is daily engaged in discussions with representatives of Chinese political parties and others concerning the restoration of peace in Manchuria. He is deeply concerned over the critical situation in north China and is endeavoring by every means within his power to avoid the spread of the fighting in Manchuria to this region.

The present publicity or propaganda campaign conducted by both sides naturally enflames feelings and increases the possibility of some hot-head precipitating a general conflagration. This reckless propaganda of hate and suspicion seriously aggravates the present serious situation and can lead to results that would be disastrous for the people of China.

Operation of truce teams has been made especially difficult by the spreading of propaganda among the officers and soldiers of both sides, and it is on the success of these teams that China must largely depend for the effort at least to localize, if not suppress, conflict. The American members of the team are coping with conditions that involve, not only hardship, but the risking of their lives in a determined and impartial effort to better the situation.

May 23, the date of this statement, was important for other reasons: on that day the Nationalist forces recaptured Changchun and the Generalissimo, borrowing Marshall's plane, flew to Manchuria in order, he said, to control the situation. Marshall expressed the hope that the Generalissimo would not be long away. The Generalissimo said he would be away for a few days, perhaps five altogether. His departure, said Marshall later, was the first of a chain of events which were almost completely disastrous in their effect on the situation. The Generalissimo was away for eleven days, and during the whole time of his absence negotiations were impossible. Worse still, in his public statements and speeches the Generalissimo was vaunting the successes of Kuomintang arms and proceeding as though he was on a triumphal tour, although his armies had entered Changchun unopposed. There had, however, been desperate fighting at the railway town of Shihpingchieh. According to the Kuomintang newspapers published at the time the battle for Shihpingchieh involved one hundred thousand casualties. According to Chu Teh, the battle which had lasted nearly a month was the first example of positional warfare ever fought by the Chinese Communists. Though he denied the heavy casualties, and regarded the battle as a victory for the Chinese Communists, the truth seems to be that the battle was costly and that both sides disengaged themselves when they were exhausted. But now for the first time and on a truly immense scale the Kuomintang troops and the Chinese Communists were at desperate war with one another.

All over the world, forces were at work which made civil war more and more likely. It was still a "dark war," never openly declared, fought by harassed troops who hardly knew what they were fighting for, and it was still possible to mediate a temporary peace, but such periods of peace could be no more than breathing spaces, while the armies took up their positions and waited for the signals. It was the custom in the ancient Chinese armies to beat a copper drum before the assault, and now all over China the clamor of the drums could be heard. For years afterwards there were to be arguments about whether Marshall had unconsciously favored the Chinese Communists and whether he had put such pressure on the Kuomintang leaders that they were unable to fight against the Chinese Communists. The arguments were futile. He had shown no favors to the Chinese Communists, unless it is a favor to recognize what exists, and American airplanes were still transporting Kuomintang troops to Manchuria and supplying equipment to the Kuomintang—the Chinese Communists were beginning to talk of the strange kind of mediator who armed one side and refused to let the other fight.

During Marshall's absence the weather had changed, and there were to be more subtle changes later. The capital was transferred from Chungking to Nanking. Chungking with its crags and muddy slopes, resembling a defiant rock-fortress at the confluence of two rivers, was a place where arguments were drowned in the uproar of the city. Chungking was without pretensions, bone-hard and cruel and close to life. Nanking, with its lotus lake and soaring modern palaces, was full of pretensions. Marshall found Chungking oddly exhilarating, but Nanking was depressing, and most depressing of all was the former German Embassy where he lived, where the linen and silver were marked with the initials of the German Reich. In Chungking the Generalissimo was surrounded by evidence which went to prove that he was the chieftain of beleaguered garrisons; in Nanking, close to the Purple Mountains and the Ming tombs, he could give way to visions of imperial grandeur.

These visions remained, for they had always been part of the man, although, as Lo Lung-chi observed, "he would rein in his horse on the edge of a cliff." At the beginning of June the visions began to fade, and even the Chinese Communists saw advantages in a temporary truce. The truce which lasted for fifteen days, beginning at noon on

June 7, was Marshall's work. He had insisted on it, counseled both sides, served as errand boy and mediator and postman and organizer, and he had good reason to believe that the negotiations following the truce order would result in a period of comparative quiet. He had not calculated on the ultimatum which the Generalissimo issued on the 17th. The Generalissimo required the immediate evacuation of Jehol, Chahar and Shantung provinces by the Chinese Communists, who were also to abandon their strong points throughout Manchuria. The Chinese Communists could not accept such an ultimatum without seriously weakening their positions, and they were offered nothing in return. Once again, at Marshall's insistence, the truce was extended, and the Generalissimo took the opportunity to make further demands—the Chinese Communists were to withdraw from the Tsinan-Tsingtao railway, and the procedure by which the Executive Headquarters in Peking was compelled to reach an unanimous vote was to be abandoned. The first stipulation was designed to blunt the Chinese Communist spearhead in north China, while the second was designed to disrupt the working of Executive Headquarters. In answer Marshall produced a lengthy document designed to bring about the reorganization of the two armies at a quicker tempo. There were provisions for mapping out the places where Chinese Communists and Kuomintang armies were to be located, the Chinese Communists were to agree to a Kuomintang garrison in Harbin, there was to be no change in the 5:1 ratio of the two armies, and the areas which the Chinese Communists had relinquished were not to be immediately taken over by Kuomintang troops, but to be governed by the existing local governments and Peace Preservation Corps. This dry document, written towards the end of the truce, might have solved the problem if the Generalissimo had not riddled it with so many amendments that the whole force of Marshall's memorandum was vitiated. Marshall thereupon turned roundly on the Generalissimo. According to the American White Paper which once again quotes from Marshall's own notes in the third person, he accused the Generalissimo of desiring to perpetuate an army dictatorship not unlike that of Japan; and he reminded the Generalissimo that dictatorship had led to the destruction of the Japanese Empire. Marshall had no confidence in the partial truce; there must be a real truce, or nothing at all. He said he believed that "an extension of the existing form of partial truce would probably result in violent military ruptures due to the tense and explosive situation, the bitterness of the commanders in the field, and the strong desire of Government military leaders to settle matters by force, for which the National Government plans were complete and fairly well known to the Communist Party."

The Kuomintang, believing itself stronger than it was, its leaders filled with a wanton pride in their own strength and out of touch with the social forces which moved the country, was going to its doom; and nothing Marshall could do, however ably he presented his case, could change the determination of the Generalissimo to achieve a military conquest.

By the beginning of July the Chinese Communists, exasperated by the Generalissimo's inflexibility and believing that Marshall was actively taking his side, were also determined upon military conquest. By July 11, when the aged Dr. Leighton Stuart, the President of Yenching University, was appointed Ambassador, the battle was on. The first casualty was Marshall himself, who no longer found himself in a position where he could exert his influence. He had reached the point of no return. For the rest of his stay in China he became increasingly the spectator rather than the active participant in China's affairs. At this point he should have left the scene. Instead, he elected to stay, believing that American prestige would be affected if he left the Kuomintang and the Chinese Communists to tear at each other's throats. There was always the hope that he would be called upon for active mediation, but by the end of July it had become a slender hope, so slender indeed that for the first time he began to talk pessimistically of his mission, saying that he had been brought to China on a fool's errand and that both sides were determined to make him the scapegoat of their own failure.

Towards the end of July a group of United States Marines were ambushed and shot at Anping, near Peking. The circumstances of the attack were investigated, and the blame was placed on the Chinese Communists. Marshall, incapable of believing that the Marines could be at fault, accused Chou En-lai of deliberate misrepresentation when the Communist General insisted that the Marines were taking part in local "Red-hunting" expeditions. "The American investigators," said

Marshall, "have made no attempt, and do not intend to conceal facts or bend them to their advantage." The guilt was plain, and straightforward action was demanded. Unfortunately, the guilt was not so plain, and more than one Marine confessed privately that he joined expeditions against the Chinese Communists out of boredom, or for "the fun of it." For the first time the American and the Chinese Communist exchanged bitter words, and "the friendship and personal esteem" in which Marshall held Chou En-lai suffered a mortal blow. From this time onwards Marshall was to become more and more critical of the Chinese Communists.

By August 10 the situation was already out of hand. The Generalissimo was in Kuling, far away in the Chekiang mountains, and removed from the prevailing tensions. There Marshall had visited him, and together they had walked along the mountain pathways under the shadow of extinct volcanoes, among the sweet-smelling pines, but retirement to the country did nothing to make the Generalissimo less determined to conquer the whole of China and install a military dictatorship. From Nanking, Marshall and Stuart issued a document designed to prod both sides into new concessions. The statement said:

> General Marshall and Dr. Stuart have been exploring together every possibility of terminating the present growing conflict in China and for the initiation of preliminary steps in the development of a truly democratic form of government. The desire for a peaceful solution of political problems appears practically unanimous on the part of the people. The economic situation demands prompt solution if disastrous collapse is to be avoided. Fighting, daily growing more widespread, threatens to engulf the country beyond the control of those responsible.
>
> Government and Communist leaders are anxious to put an end to the fighting, but there are certain issues concerned in the immediate settlements involved regarding which agreement has not been found. It appears impossible for the two parties to reach a settlement of these issues which would permit a general order to be issued for the complete cessation of hostilities in all of China.

The style of the statement suggested that it was written by tired men, discouraged by the evidence that the Kuomintang and the

Chinese Communists were preparing for an all-out war. In one particular the statement was erroneous: the economic situation was no more dangerous than it had been during the war, and neither the Kuomintang nor the Communist leaders were very much exercised by the possibilities of economic collapse. China was an agricultural country, without any large-scale industries except in Manchuria and in the neighborhood of Shanghai, and both sides in various ways saw that economic collapse might be advantageous.

The statement by Marshall and Stuart did nothing to make the Generalissimo more pliant. Three days later, on August 13, the Generalissimo issued a public statement in which he blamed the Chinese Communists for their intransigence, and placed the entire blame for the breakdown in negotiations on their heads. The statement concluded with the ironical peaceful gesture which had become traditional. He declared that he would continue "to favor a peaceful settlement and abide by the agreements and formulas of which the government is a party." This broadside meant nothing at all, and the Five-Man Committee which was set up shortly afterwards inherited the task of bringing order out of chaos. Marshall was not a member of the Five-Man Committee. He had been gradually removing himself from the position he had occupied earlier in the year. It was at his suggestion that Dr. Leighton Stuart had been appointed Ambassador, and it was at his suggestion that the Five-Man Committee had come into existence. Behind these he would move mysteriously, following an established Chinese custom, his powers unknown and his decisions carefully guarded, a shadow representing the determined strength of America. Unfortunately, although America was still strong, there were signs that determination was sometimes lacking. The confused reports from China, the innumerable small battlefields, the knowledge that the Russians were on the Chinese frontiers, the strange stories of the removal by the Russians of the Manchurian heavy industries, the constant streams of propaganda in favor of the Kuomintang and the Chinese Communists, all these produced a peculiarly conflicting impression upon the American mind. No one knew what was happening, and because China was a long way away few cared to study the problem at length. Marshall saw it in terms of military forces, and he was largely uninterested in social forces. He surrounded himself with military advisers, sought the advice of his own officers and treated the problem in terms of military logistics, and seemed to be completely unaware of the huge convulsive revolutionary movement which was spreading over Asia and was not in the least Communist in its origins.

On August 30 China and the United States signed an agreement for the sale of United States surplus property in the Pacific. Huge floods of surplus war material were now to be handed over to the Kuomintang government, and the Chinese Communists objected. They pointed out that even though the material did not include guns, the Kuomintang would be able to use the trucks and communications equipment in the war against the Communists; and if they did not use them in the war they could sell them and use the profits for military purposes. The allegation was not unfounded, and Marshall found himself, in the words of the White Paper, "in the untenable position of mediating on the one hand between the two Chinese groups while on the other the United States Government was continuing to supply arms and ammunition to one of the two groups, namely, the National Government." This had indeed been the position for some considerable time, and Marshall was aware of the dangers involved, for the Chinese Communists could, and did, charge him with duplicity, and it was not easy to reply. At Marshall's request the agreement for the transfer of surplus property was suspended insofar as it referred to purely military property. The suspension, however, had little effect on Kuomintang military plans. By November the Kuomintang forces were at the highest peak of their military efficiency and they had gained large areas from the Communists.

The Five-Man Committee, with Dr. Leighton Stuart at the head, continued to meet in Nanking through September, but the pretence of mediation was wearing thin. There was no active mediation, and the time had passed when the two opposing sides could be made to see that the Chinese people demanded a reasonable peace. On October 1, weary of his long conversations with minor figures in the negotiations and with the intransigence of the chiefs, Marshall wrote to the Generalissimo suggesting that unless a basis for agreement could be reached without further delay, he would recommend that he be recalled and that the American Government take no further part in the mediation. He also stated his views on the two parties actively engaged in the struggle:

> I am not in agreement either with the present course of the Government in regard to this critical situation or with that of the Communist Party. I disagree with the evident Government policy of settling the fundamental differences involved by force, that is by utilizing a general offensive campaign to force compliance with the Government point of view or demands. I recognize the vital necessity of safeguarding the security of the Government, but I think the present procedure has gone well beyond that point.
>
> On the part of the Communist Party, I deplore actions and statements which provide a basis for the contention on the part of many in the Government that the Communists' proposals can not be accepted in good faith, that it is not the intention of that Party to cooperate in a genuine manner in a reorganization of the Government, but rather to disrupt the Government and seize power for their own purposes.

The Generalissimo, as though in contempt of Marshall's efforts, had often shown himself more demanding whenever Marshall sought to temper his demands, and he did not fail Marshall now. He ordered an attack on Kalgan, north of Peking, which the Chinese Communists had occupied since the previous August, in defiance of a June agreement which said that Kalgan should be left in Chinese Communist hands. Thereupon Marshall went to see the Generalissimo, explained his own ambiguous position and called once more for moderation, while the Generalissimo listened in silence and then explained that the forces of history were larger than himself, that nothing could be done to avert the show of force which would soon be over and that Marshall's insistence on mediation was praiseworthy and welcomed by the whole Chinese people. In fury Marshall returned to the American Embassy and penned out a provisional message of recall to be sent by the President to the Generalissimo, though in fact it was never sent:

> General Marshall recommends that his mission be terminated and that he be recalled. He has explained to you that he feels that a continuation of mediation under present

circumstances of extensive and aggressive military operations would place the United States Government in a position where the integrity of its actions as represented by him would be open to serious question. I deplore that his efforts to bring peace to China have been unsuccessful, but there must be no question regarding the integrity of his position and actions which represent the high intention and high purpose of the United States Government. I, therefore, with great regret have concluded that he should be immediately recalled.

The message was illuminating, for it introduced a phrase which Marshall had used before during a discussion with President Roosevelt at the White House, when Marshall had inveighed against the ten thousand bomber program. "There must be no question regarding the integrity of his position and actions." One wonders why the question ever occurred to Marshall: the integrity of his position and actions was not something to be settled by proclamation, while the ambiguity of his position and many of his actions remained.

The Generalissimo's decision to capture Kalgan was partly an act of revenge against the Americans, for having suspended the transfer of military supplies. He would show his strength, and with the fall of Kalgan on October 10 his appetite increased. October 10 is the anniversary of the outbreak of the 1911 revolution; the date of the capture had been carefully chosen, and the Generalissimo celebrated the occasion by ordering the resumption of nation-wide conscription of men between eighteen and forty-five. At the same time he introduced an administrative system which completely subordinated civilian officials to provincial military commanders. The war went on. Kuomintang forces moved north along the Peiping-Hankow railway and opened a drive against Antung in Manchuria. By this time the Chinese Communists were no longer participating in the field teams sent out by Executive Headquarters except at four places, and their broadcasts were becoming as virulent against the Americans as against the Kuomintang.

On October 28 Marshall had another interview with the Generalissimo. There he explained that "the Communists had no intention of surrendering and that, while they had lost cities, they had not lost armies, nor was it likely that they would lose their armies since they had no intention of making a stand or fighting to a finish at any place." This was a clear statement of the Chinese Communist position, and the Generalissimo agreed that the time had come to halt the fighting: the alternative might very well be the disruption of Marshall's mission and the complete cutting off of American aid. The Generalissimo had, as he thought, secured his position in Manchuria. The Third Party was clamoring for a continuation of the mediation. The war was proving unpopular among the people. The time had come for another breathing space. In this peculiar situation, with the Generalissimo speaking of a truce while at the same time preparing for an all-out war, a draft statement representing the Generalissimo's views was prepared by Marshall, acting, says the White Paper, "as a staff officer might on behalf of the Generalissimo in drawing up documents containing the latter's views." These words, which appear in parenthesis, evidently originated with Marshall and were designed to explain a quite unusual occurrence; in addition to the functions of mediator, envoy extraordinary and presiding genius of Executive Headquarters, Marshall had also become the speech-writer of the Generalissimo. This new task, though extraordinary, Marshall had assumed in an effort to modify the intransigence of the Generalissimo: the draft statement called for the convention of the National Assembly on November 12. In the final paragraph of the statement Marshall repeated, with some slight changes, the message he had delivered shortly before leaving China earlier in the year. He said:

> The next few weeks are of fateful importance to China. It is within our power to lay the foundations for a strong and prosperous democratic nation. We must overcome natural serious divergence of views as well as deep suspicion and bitterness. The time has come to rise above these difficulties and dedicate ourselves to the service of the people.

But the time for such praiseworthy calls for national benevolence were long since over, and the Generalissimo, having ordered his troops to cease fire, "except as necessary to defend present positions," went on to summon a National Assembly on November 15, which was packed with his own supporters who had been chosen more than a decade earlier. The Communists were absent, and there were no delegates from the Democratic League parties except the

Social Democrats, a small group which had been bought over by the Kuomintang. On the following day Chou En-lai, the principal Communist delegate to the negotiations, called upon Marshall and asked for transportation to Yenan, explaining that he had little hope in the continuance of the negotiations and he feared that the Kuomintang would attack Yenan. At this point Marshall asked Chou En-lai to discuss with the Communist leaders in Yenan the question of his continued mediation. Once more the White Paper gives Marshall's words in the third person:

> He said that it was useless for him to endeavor to mediate if he were not trusted as being sincere in an effort to be impartial and that under such circumstances it would be useless for him to remain in China. General Marshall stated that he wished General Chou to determine formally from the Communist leaders at Yenan whether specifically they wished him to continue in his mediation role and asked that the matter be viewed as a plain business proposition without regard to Chinese considerations of "face" since he was not interested in "face." He explained that his sole interest was the question of whether he could render some service to China by way of mediation.

Chou En-lai promised to place these questions before the Communist leaders in Yenan, and three days later he left Nanking in an American plane. The negotiations which had begun in the previous December now came to an end. Marshall received no answer to his request that he should be informed by the Chinese Communists whether they desired his services, and he guessed correctly—for it is the habit in China to render a negative answer by silence—that they rejected his efforts of mediation. The time had come, as Marshall saw it, to pull out. There were more desultory conversations with the Generalissimo, and once again Marshall noted the inconsistencies of that strange, relentless and untrustworthy genius who would say at one moment that he would do everything he could to bring the Chinese Communists into the Government by peaceful negotiation and the next moment he would explain how he would force the Chinese Communists to attend the National Assembly by defeating them in battle. He was a man with an obsession. He had said in June, 1946: "Given time, the ripe apple will fall into our laps." He had said the same thing in 1934 and in all the years afterwards, and the Chinese

Communists had grown stronger with every assault by the Generalissimo's forces. Marshall was forced to the conclusion, which he expressed to the Generalissimo, that "the Communists were too large a military and civil force to be ignored and even if one disregarded the brutality of the inevitable procedure necessary to destroy them, they probably could not be eliminated by military campaigning." To that view he held firmly, and indeed it was inescapable.

Why did Marshall remain in China when his usefulness was over? He hardly knew. He was a man with a mission, and he refused to believe in the failure of his mission until he saw the concrete evidence of failure. He had staked his reputation on success and he was stunned by failure, for he was not accustomed to fail. He explained in the White Paper his reasons for refusing to continue as mediator:

> General Marshall remained in China during this period in the hope that he might be able to use his influence toward the adoption of a genuinely democratic constitution. In the past he had often felt that the National Government had desired American mediation as a shield for its military campaigns and at this time the Communists had no desire for further American mediation but feared being placed in an unfavorable position if they were to reject formally such mediation. He was not willing to allow himself thus to be used by either party, nor did he intend to serve as an umpire on the battlefield. He felt that his continued usefulness as a negotiator had practically been wrecked by the recent Communist rejection of all Government overtures, actions which played directly into the hands of the reactionaries in the Government, from whom his chief opposition had always come.

It was not an entirely satisfactory answer. The situation described here was already in evidence in April. Both parties *had* used him for their own purposes and he *had* become inevitably, through his control of Executive Headquarters, an umpire on the battlefield. His chief opposition came, as he admitted, not from the Chinese Communists but from the Kuomintang reactionaries, who believed themselves entitled to receive American aid, while rejecting American advice.

In the last weeks Marshall made one last bid to ward off the threatened full-scale war. In private conversations with the more liberal Kuomintang officials he explained that it was necessary to remove the dominant military clique and to substitute "the organization of a patriotic liberal group under the indirect sponsorship of the Generalissimo." Except through revolution, he did not know how this would come about. The patriotic liberal groups formed the Third Party, which possessed no military power, no experience of government and no acceptable program. Their leaders were scholars and professors who belonged to innumerable splinter groups; and the best of them had been killed by the Kuomintang secret police or were under arrest. Why the Generalissimo should be expected to sponsor even indirectly a Third Party, which he had done his best to destroy, was never explained. Only the removal of the Generalissimo and the military clique by assassination would have saved the issue; and for different reasons neither Marshall nor the Chinese Communists saw advantages in assassinating the leaders of the military factions of the Kuomintang.

On January 6, 1947, the President announced that Marshall had been recalled to Washington. The end of the long mission, which lasted altogether eleven months, had come at last. Patiently, helplessly, he had watched himself being caught up in a Chinese web. He had attended more than three hundred formal conferences and informal meetings. Some mysterious quality of the Chinese mind eluded him: he had thought of himself as a mediator, and had not realized he was a pawn in the game, and so he never came to grips with the problem. The Chinese people also failed to come to grips with the problem, for they attempted to seek a solution in war, which solves some problems but leaves the most important unsolved. The victory of the Chinese Communists was now inevitable. Marshall had not delayed their victory or helped it onward. He had assisted the Kuomintang to the best of his ability, but the Kuomintang had sedulously resisted his advice. The embargo on the transfer of military supplies to the Kuomintang Government was due to his advocacy, but if there had been no embargo it would not appreciably have affected the course of the war between the Chinese Communists and the Kuomintang: the Chinese Communists came to victory by the massive employment of captured Kuomintang weapons. If there had been no embargo, they might have conquered China more quickly.

For Marshall the strain had been terrible. He demanded in his own conduct the utmost integrity, but there was no day in China when he was not conscious that his position was ambiguous, and that he was distrusted by the two most powerful factions in the country. His position was comparable with that of Chief Justice Marshall who, in the celebrated case of *Marbury v. Madison,* rendered a decision which not only dismissed the motion but also entered into a discussion of the merits of the case in which he, the Chief Justice, had been a participant. It was not his fault that he had been placed in a position of ambiguity; the fault lay in the wide discrepancy between American foreign policy and her conduct of international relations.

When Marshall left China finally, there was a balance of power between the two contending parties. There would have been exactly the same balance of power if there had been no effort of mediation. From the military point of view it was as though Marshall had never been in China, but from every other point of view American intervention was disastrous: for there had grown up in China, fanned by the extremists of the Kuomintang and Chinese Communists, such a hatred of America that a war between China and America became inevitable. The hatred was largely the product of propaganda, but its roots lay in the American failure to lead the social revolution in Asia.

During the weeks before he finally left China, Marshall prepared a long summary of operations which was issued the day after the President announced his recall. In this statement Marshall denounced both sides in the conflict, and he found it impossible to blame one more than the other: they were equally guilty, for they had equally desired war. He said:

> The greatest obstacle to peace has been the complete, almost overwhelming suspicion with which the Chinese Communist Party and the Kuomintang regard each other. On the one hand, the leaders of the Government are strongly opposed to a communistic form of government. On the other, the Communists frankly state that they are Marxists and intend to work towards establishing a communistic form of government in China, though first advancing through the medium of a democratic form of government of the American or British type. . . .

I think the most important factors involved in the recent breakdown of negotiations are these: On the side of the National Government, which is in effect the Kuomintang, there is a dominant group of reactionaries who have been opposed, in my opinion, to almost every effort I have made to influence the formation of a genuine coalition government. This has usually been under the cover of political or party action, but since the Party was the Government, this action, though subtle or indirect, has been devastating in its effect. They were quite frank in publicly stating that cooperation by the Chinese Communist Party in the government was inconceivable and that only a policy of force could definitely settle the issue. This group includes military as well as political leaders.

On the side of the Chinese Communist Party there are, I believe, liberals as well as radicals, though this view is rigorously opposed by many who believe that the Chinese Communist Party discipline is too rigidly enforced to admit of such differences of viewpoint. Nevertheless, it has appeared to me that there is a definite liberal group among the Communists, especially of young men who have turned to the Communists in disgust at the corruption evident in the local governments—men who would put the interest of the Chinese people above ruthless measures to establish a Communist ideology in the immediate future. The dyed-in-the-wool Communists do not hesitate at the most drastic measures to gain their end as, for instance, the destruction of communications in order to wreck the economy of China and produce a situation that would facilitate the overthrow or collapse of the Government, without any regard for the immediate suffering of the people involved. They completely distrust the leaders of the Kuomintang and appear convinced that every Government proposal is designed to crush the Chinese Communist Party. I must say that the quite evidently inspired mob actions of last February and March, some within a few blocks of where I was then engaged in completing negotiations, gave the Communists good excuse for such suspicions....

The salvation of the situation, as I see it, would be the assumption of leadership by the liberals in the Government and in the minority parties, a splendid group of men, but who as yet lack the political power to exercise a controlling influence. Successful action on their part under the leadership of Generalissimo Chiang Kai-shek would, I believe, lead to unity through good government. . . .

I have spoken very frankly because in no other way can I hope to bring the people of the United States to even a partial understanding of this complex problem. I have expressed all these views privately in the course of negotiations; they are well-known, I think, to most of the individuals concerned. I express them now publicly, as it is my duty, to present my estimate of the situation and its possibilities to the American people who have a deep interest in the development of conditions in the Far East promising an enduring peace in the Pacific.

Marshall's final statement on his mission to China has the lucidity and force of his third Biennial Report. It is among the best things he wrote, and among the most honest. "Though I speak as a soldier," he said, "I must here also deplore the dominating influence of the military." There were phrases like these which catch fire, perhaps because they reflected at a distance a universal complaint. He had seen the key to the plan of the integration of the Kuomintang and Communist armies in the separation of military from civil functions, but he had failed completely to reach the civilians. He reported all this with admirable fairness, giving credit where it was due and drawing up an assessment of guilt, and his very fairness had tragic consequences. When he dismissed the Chinese Communists as "irreconcilable" and the Nationalists as "reactionary," it was as though he was saying, "I cannot deal with you. You are both brigands, and therefore I wash my hands of you." But the whole history of the world depended upon a choice being made, and he was incapable of making a choice. The course of history is such that one must take sides.

Years afterwards, Admiral Leahy expressed his opinion of Marshall's mission to China. He said: "I was present when Marshall was going to China. He said he was going to tell Chiang that he had to get on with the Communists or without help from us. He said the same thing when he got back. I thought he was wrong then, both times." Marshall was fatally wrong, but not for the reasons which

Leahy suggested. He was wrong because he left China at a critical time in the negotiations, he was wrong because he continued his mission long after he had exhausted his own usefulness, and he was wrong because he was unable to make a choice. The question of assistance to the Kuomintang hardly arose; they were assisted throughout, and they employed American assistance to their own eventual destruction. The question of a coalition between the Kuomintang and the Chinese Communists, which was uppermost in China when Marshall first arrived, was not one to be decided from Washington: such a coalition was desired by the majority of the Chinese people as the only alternative to civil war.

As Marshall flew off to America, he knew he would soon be appointed Secretary of State and would have to deal with the problem of China for many years to come. Landing at Honolulu, he was asked whether he thought the Soviet Union was actively engaged in the Chinese civil war. He answered that he knew nothing of their engagement in the war, and there was no evidence that the Chinese Communists were using Russian weapons. He seems to have suspected that the Chinese Communists would win the war, but there was nothing he could do about it. The nightmare was over, but only for a time. Two years later, at the head of a vast concourse of captured American tanks, Mao Tse-tung entered Peking in triumph.

Footnote

* The phrase was first used officially by Secretary Byrnes at a hearing of the Senate Committee on Foreign Relations on December 7, 1944. It had however appeared in a number of memoranda and in the Generalissimo's speeches.

CHAPTER FIFTEEN

Mr. Secretary

All through Marshall's life a strange fatality accompanied him; there was about him the air of someone who was destined for great things, for responsibilities greater than mortal man may fairly assume, and by some peculiar accident of destiny the dates of his appointments to high office coincided often with vast upheavals. So on the day when he was appointed Chief of Staff the Germans invaded Poland and set the world aflame, and on the day when he was appointed Secretary of State the British resigned from their long preoccupation with Greece and announced that they could no longer assume the burden of stemming the tide of Communism in the eastern Mediterranean, and though this resignation did not appear to be a matter of great importance at the time, it was fraught with enormous consequences. Marshall had failed to stem Communism in China; could Communism be stemmed in Europe? For the next two years his major task was to shore the ruins of Europe.

He was appointed Secretary of State on February 21, 1947, and he had no illusions about the difficulties of his task. On the following day he made a speech at Princeton University in which he outlined the critical situation as he saw it. He offered no simple solutions, for there were none, and he expressed, as so often before, his belief that the Americans were neither sufficiently austere nor sufficiently united to cope with the desperate stratagems of the times. He said:

> We are living today in a most difficult period. The war years were critical, at times alarmingly so. But I think the present period is, in many respects, even more critical. The

problems are different but no less vital to the national security than those during the days of active fighting. But the more serious aspect is the fact that we no longer display that intensity, that unity of purpose, with which we concentrated on the war task and achieved the victory.

The same fears had occurred to him before the war. They were reasonable fears. He was haunted by what might have happened if the Germans and the Japanese had played their disastrous game a little more intelligently. If they had attacked the British Empire and left America alone, they could have conquered all of Asia, Europe and Africa, and then turned their accumulated might on the Western Hemisphere. Between them they could have eaten up the rest of the world, absorbing one country after another while America looked on, hamstrung by a policy of "non-intervention." What if there had been no attack on Pearl Harbor to galvanize the whole of America into action? The Russians were behaving with greater cleverness than the Axis powers. One by one they had absorbed the countries of eastern Europe, and their appetite was limitless.

When Marshall became Secretary of State he became Chief of Staff in a war which was being fought without visible weapons. In this war, information assumed critical importance. His first instructions therefore concerned the methods of gathering information on which foreign policy decisions were made; there was need to separate the fact-finders from the policy-makers. The Department of State was a jungle housed in more than thirty buildings in Washington. With his profound belief in unified command, he saw that he could not exercise his authority over so many scattered areas, and he ordered that steps should be taken to find a new building. He was in a mood to cut things to their essentials. "If you want to cut red tape," he said once, "you must be deadly accurate." Now he cut the tape to ribbons and hardly cared about the accuracy of the cutting: all that was necessary was that the Department of State should strip for action. In the process it came to resemble the Pentagon. His office staff was largely composed of men brought with him from the War Department who still addressed him as "General." It was noticed sometimes that when he was addressed as "Mr. Secretary," he would turn his head to one side as though trying to discover the invisible Secretary; it was some weeks before he became accustomed to the new title. Sometimes, too, he would make unconscious references to "the European Theater," as though the armies were still fighting one another.

On February 27, 1947, a week after he assumed office, President Truman called an important conference at the White House. The Greek problem was uppermost on his mind, and the President outlined "the whole Greek thing from hell to breakfast." The military and civil advisers were called in. Marshall was asked for his views, and these, as usual, he stated clearly and calmly—he believed that Greece could be safeguarded, and that America could fulfill the role in Greece which Great Britain was no longer in a position to fulfill. Senator Arthur Vandenberg of Michigan, the President of the Senate, was also called in. When the President had explained the nature of the problem, Vandenberg said simply: "If you will state a full case to the country and the world, I'll stand with you." The President was more successful in his approach to Vandenberg than Marshall, who was preparing himself for the Moscow Conference and began to seek out Congressional representation. When he invited Vandenberg and Tom Connally of Texas to come with him to Moscow, Connally agreed, but Vandenberg refused in the belief that his position would be compromised. Marshall emphasized how necessary it was that the Republicans should join him at the Conference. He attempted to break down their defenses, and sometimes he employed his famous strategy of diversion: he would talk about something else altogether, the China problem or Communism within the United States, talking on and on until his listeners were bored, worn down, their defenses breached. On the whole it was not a good strategy, and he made more enemies than friends by these impassioned speeches in which, by a process of exhaustion, he hoped to induce agreement. His mind still worked along military lines. All documents must be brief, clear, the statement reduced to its simplest logical form. Routine matters were dismissed under brief subheadings: Facts, Conclusions, Recommendations. The halting professors were dismissed, for he had never been able to tolerate their indecision; he preferred to have around him men with razor-sharp minds who spoke with the clipped voices of the parade ground or who were known for their incisiveness—men like Robert A. Lovett, a former banker and pilot; George Kennan, a student of Russian history who was later to outline a fatal theory concerning the containment of Communism; and Charles E. Bohlen, whose knowledge of the Russian language had enabled him to act as interpreter at Teheran, Yalta and Potsdam. Though now a civilian, Marshall's habits were unchanged. He arrived at the State Department between 8 and 8:30 a.m. in a chauffeur-driven car from a downtown club, and returned between 5 and 5:30 p.m. He still did his best work in the early morning. He still gave orders in military phraseology. Gradually, as the months passed, he came to adapt himself to the disorganized world of civilians, lost his military tartness of tongue and became human again. The process was painful and difficult, and in the further humanizing of Marshall the President played a part.

Marshall was intensely loyal and respectful to the man who had been elevated to the Presidency. He possessed an almost mystical belief in the integrity of the President; and if he revered the President, the reverence was returned in double measure. Truman's loyalty to Marshall was complete; he never questioned a decision made by Marshall or turned down one of Marshall's recommendations. The President was deeply interested in military history, and Marshall was an admitted authority on the history of the two world wars and the War between the States. Both the President and the Secretary of State had read deeply in Freeman's histories, and could discuss the minor details of battles with immense learning. As chairman of the Truman Committee, the President had read the reports of the Joint Committee on the Conduct of the War, a series of Congressional documents published nearly a hundred years before; he claimed that these studies enabled him to check the errors and malpractices in the production program of World War II. He knew his history; so did Marshall; and they fed each other with their knowledge of history, and on these levels they talked at ease. Marshall's admiration for the President was revealed a little later when he said: "The full stature of this man will only be proven by history, but I want to say here and now that there has never been a decision under this man's administration, affecting policies beyond our shores, that has not been in the best interest of this country. It is not the courage of these decisions that will live, but the integrity of them." The President, who saw Marshall nearly every day, usually at the end of the morning's work, stated his approval in simpler terms. "Watch

George Marshall," he said. "He will be steady as a rock."

If Marshall was steady—he had maintained an extraordinary rock-like steadiness all through the years with occasional outbursts of erratic temper—it was not so certain that he was always knowledgeable. He had almost no experience of dealing with the Russians, and he found himself baffled by Russian psychology. During most of the first month of his secretaryship he gave himself to the study of the Moscow Conference. Every morning, for two hours, he was briefed by the German and Austrian experts on the problems which would arise in the Conference. There were an immense number of problems concerning the destruction of German military matériel, land reform, trials of war criminals, the repatriation of prisoners of war, the transfers of whole populations, and the whole social and economic structure of Germany and Austria was to be placed under review. It was desperately necessary that there should be agreement between the four powers, for otherwise Germany and Austria would become plague spots capable of disseminating the plague once more over Europe. At Potsdam solutions had been roughed out; now they must be defined accurately under the terms of a general settlement. Those who attended the Moscow Conference were under no illusions about the possibility that no settlement would be reached, but they knew that in the history of the modern world the Moscow Conference, if agreement could be reached, would play the part of a new Congress of Vienna.

Marshall's airplane reached Berlin on March 8. Though Tom Connally had at one time promised to accompany him, he was finally dissuaded. Instead John Foster Dulles took his place as the ranking Republican adviser. The Republican party had regained control of the Congress; it was more than ever necessary that a Republican should be in attendance. John Foster Dulles was a little like a bulldog; lacking brilliance, he possessed tenacity and a missionary zeal, and he was an excellent committeeman, with an ever-watchful eye for the precise terms of an agreement and their interpretations. They stayed in Berlin for two days, discussing the prospects of the Conference with General Lucius D. Clay, the Commander of U.S. Forces in Europe, whose headquarters were at the German capital. General Clay gave an outline of the German situation as it existed in all its harsh and explosive detail. There was little encouragement in the picture. Germany had become the new battleground where ideologies would fight to a standstill or a new upheaval would result in the victory of one ideology over another. There was no emotion and no curiosity in the half-starved faces of the people who watched Marshall's staff car take him to a villa set aside for him on the Wannsee.

Two days later, on March 10, the Moscow Conference convened in an atmosphere of brutal suspicion, and Marshall, prepared to lock horns with any adversary on any battlefield, conscious that he could so dispose his forces that he would inevitably win the battle, found himself confronted by the same problems which confronted him in China: words, resolutions, memoranda, the wholly differing psychologies of East and West. Characteristically, almost his first action was to send for General Clay, as though he felt the need for another general to help him marshal his forces.

When talking with reporters in Washington, Marshall continually warned them that the world was in a critical situation: to achieve a military victory was comparatively easy, to win the peace immeasurably difficult. Now, as they sat about the conference table, Bevin, Bidault, Molotov and Marshall at their proper places with their advisers by their side, the crisis was physically represented by the four stern men, all exhausted and all wearied beyond endurance by reading innumerable papers and listening to the sometimes conflicting advice of their aides. There were quarrels between General Clay and John Foster Dulles. There were interminable preliminary conferences. There were conferences between Marshall and his assistants in the morning, and more conferences late at night. There were forty-four sterile sessions round the conference table between the representatives of the powers. Marshall labored to explain the precise connotation of American foreign policy; his precision was wasted on Molotov, who preferred invective and declamation. The Americans, like the French and British, favored a federal German government under a democratic constitution; the Russians favored a strong central government under a provisional constitution, and though they also desired a democratic government in Germany, it was clear that their definition of democracy differed profoundly from the American definition. The problem, then, was to define American democracy in a way which would be intelligible to the Russians. For days his aides worked on the problem. General Clay and John Foster Dulles each submitted a definition, but the final definition which Marshall submitted to the conferences bears the mark of Marshall's own style and his own deeply felt understanding of the nature of proper government. He said:

> The United States government understands democracy to mean the right of every individual to develop his mind and soul in ways of his choice, free of fear or coercion—provided only that he does not interfere with the rights of others. To us society is not democratic if men who respect the rights of their fellow men are not free to express their own beliefs and convictions without fear that they may be snatched away from their home and family. To us, a society is not free if law-abiding citizens live in fear of being denied the right to work or of being deprived of life, liberty and the pursuit of happiness.

This definition is not the best that could have been provided: significantly, it said more about what democracy was not than what it was. Significantly, too, it was designed to emphasize the essential differences between Russian Communism and Western Democracy; and Molotov, who could prepare barbed definitions as well as anyone, turned away to discuss other matters. There was, for example, the matter of German trade processes and patents. "As everyone knows"—the phrase which was usually employed to describe an event completely unknown or otherwise dubious was now coming into use—the United States had seized these industrial secrets for their exclusive use. By good fortune one of Marshall's aides had brought a letter from the Soviet commercial attaché in Washington which thanked the Secretary of Commerce for German patent specifications. Marshall read the letter into the record, and was not unpleased by the approving smiles of his aides. The victory, however, was a small one. Invisible, perpetually present, in huge solid ranks behind the foreign ministers at the conference table, were the armies of the former Allies. The conference, originally conceived to bring about agreement on the problem of Germany, was beginning to resemble one of those ancient councils of war in which the contending sides first parley and deliberate in the hope that they can thereby fathom each other's weak points. The conference, in fact, resembled the preliminary engagement of a new and more terrible war.

On the night of April 15 Marshall, accompanied by Charles E. Bohlen and the American Ambassador, General Walter Bedell Smith, were received by Stalin in the bare paneled conference room in the Kremlin where so many matters of prodigious importance had been decided. Bohlen acted as interpreter. Marshall was tired. He explained that he had come a long way only to discover that the situation had deteriorated in Europe. He spoke quietly of the differences which had arisen between East and West, which seemed no nearer solution. What could be done? Under what conditions could a real peace be achieved? There were no easy answers, and on the face of it there appeared to be no answers at all. Stalin doodled with a thick blue pencil, nodded, listened quietly. Once he interrupted to exchange a whispered word with Molotov. That was when Marshall spoke of the Soviet delay in answering enquiries about Lend-Lease. There was evidently a tragic undertone to Marshall's exploration of the situation, for Stalin said: "You are wrong to give so tragic an interpretation to our present disagreements," and then, employing the language which Marshall understood better than any other, Stalin continued with the frightening phrase: "Our present troubles are only the first skirmishes and brushes of reconnaissance forces." He thought that when people had exhausted themselves in dispute, they would recognize the necessity of compromise—a strange enough statement from a man who, during the course of a long revolutionary career, had never once recognized the necessity for compromise. Stalin kept on insisting that compromise was possible and desirable, and opened up promises of compromise on such subjects as the demilitarization of Germany, and reparations. "Above all," said Stalin, "it is necessary to have patience." The quiet friendly voice droned on, deceptively gentle, urgent and tolerant. The patient web was spun round the three visitors. Stalin acknowledged Soviet delays in answering the Lend-Lease enquiries, but he pointed out that the Soviets had also suffered from delays—there was, for example, the little matter of the financial credits. Immediately after the war the Soviet government had asked America for a loan; no answer was received; the document was pigeonholed, and it was not until a year later that Walter Bedell Smith was able to bring a late acknowledgment of the request. Somehow the incident was hurdled, with apologies and explanations. The interview, which lasted for nearly an hour and a half, was coming to an end, and nothing had been accomplished except the slow fashioning of a web into which Marshall had no intention of falling.

Just before Marshall left there was the usual banquet held in the great hall of Catherine the Great. There had been banquets before. There were banquets offered by each of the foreign ministers. At Molotov's banquet Marshall had worn the decoration of the Order of Suvorov, First Degree, on his dinner coat and toasted the health of the Russian Foreign Minister in vodka. But this final banquet was by far the most spendid of all. The Marshals of the Soviet Union came in their blue-green full dress uniform, their chests one solid gleam of medals. There were the uniformed officials of the Soviet Foreign Office with their gold epaulettes. Against the red velvet hangings the powerful members of the Politburo looked out of place in their civilian clothes. Marshall sat on Stalin's right. There were the inevitable speeches and the inevitable toasts. Afterwards the visitors were escorted to a large room where a cinema screen covered one wall. For the benefit of his guests Stalin had ordered the showing of the color film *The Stone Flower-*

The Stone Flower, filmed in Agfacolor with astonishingly successful trick work, tells the story of an enchanted princess who wanders through a forest and comes upon a crystal cave. She loses herself in the cave where the walls are thick with jewels, and monsters lurk within the glittering shadows. In the cave she would have died if the prince had not followed her. In the end the cave is split apart by a magic spell, the jeweled walls crumble and crash together and the prince and princess, having vanquished the demons, are allowed to return to the forest land. In this extraordinary film produced with an entirely new color process which made all colors so brilliant that they were almost blinding, there were overtones of stark tragedy. It was easy to see that the authors of the film were thinking in terms of the present, and everyone at the showing must have recognized the crystal cave and the earthquake which shattered it. But where was the magic flower of stone which would provide the key to the mystery, and where were the magic spells? *The Stone Flower,* though acted in Russian, was not made in the Soviet Union. Significantly, it had. been produced, acted and photographed in 1946 in Czechoslovakia.

The Moscow Conference, which lasted for more than a month, ended in failure. A few directives were issued to the Control Council in Germany. They were instructed to study the size of the occupation forces and to report their findings, but the Soviets refused to allow quadripartite inspections, with the result that the study was never completed. There were minor agreements, but the future of Germany was as unsettled before the conference as it was afterwards: no program was offered: there was agreement only to disagree. As he flew back from Moscow, Marshall could reflect that except for the decision to create a higher level of industry in Germany, the foreign ministers had wasted their time in endless circumambulatory discussions. There was only one real advantage arising from the conference: the Foreign Ministers of the three Western powers had been shown the full force of Soviet intransigence, their refusal to compromise even when they were talking of compromise, their determination to take the whole world under their wing. Marshall said in a radio talk on April 28, 1947, shortly after his return: "Agreement was made impossible at Moscow because, in our view, the Soviet Government insisted upon proposals which would have established in Germany a centralized government adapted to the seizure of absolute control." He was a little more hopeful a few days later when he addressed a White House gathering. "Despite the disagreements and difficulties encountered," he said, "possibly greater progress towards final settlement was made than is realized. The critical differences were for the first time brought into the light and now stand clearly defined, so that future negotiations can start with a knowledge of exactly what the issues are that must be settled." More succinctly he said: "The patient is sinking while the doctors deliberate."

At some time during the Moscow Conference a plan had begun to form in Marshall's mind. There was a desperate need to prevent the Communist advance across Europe, and this must be done even before the German problem was settled. The patient was sinking: there was need, not for surgery, but for oxygen.

At the little town of Cleveland, Mississippi, where President Truman had been invited to speak at the Delta Council in the Teachers'

College, the first stirrings of the Marshall Plan were heard. They were not announced by Marshall or by the President, but by Dean Acheson, who read the President's prepared statement. He said:

> Since world demand exceeds our ability to supply, we are going to have to concentrate our emergency assistance in areas where it will be most effective in building world political and economic stability, in promoting human freedom and democratic institutions, in fostering liberal trading policies, and in strengthening the authority of the United Nations. . . . Free people who are seeking to preserve their independence and democratic institutions and human freedoms against totalitarian pressure, either internal or external, will receive top priority for American reconstruction aid.

The issue was clear, though it was expressed in a curiously official form, as though a memorandum was being handed across the conference table. The importance of the speech was not observed at the time. It seemed to be, and perhaps was, no more than an effort to put some thoughts in order, and in the President's mind the awful responsibilities of America were not yet realized. The speech was made on May 8. A little less than a month later, when Marshall spoke at Harvard, the whole conception of the Plan had become clearer, less formal and more passionate, for there was no disguising the passion behind Marshall's words. He said:

> Our policy is directed not against any country or doctrine but against hunger, poverty, desperation and chaos. . . . At this critical point in history, we of the United States are deeply conscious of our responsibilities towards the world. We know that in this trying period, between a war that is over and a peace that is not yet secure, the destitute and oppressed of the earth look chiefly to us for sustenance and support until they can again face life with self-confidence and self-reliance.

They say that on that June day Marshall spoke, as he nearly always speaks, in a very soft and almost inaudible voice, gazing steadily at the notes before him, playing with his spectacles, and never for a moment looking at his audience. There have been times in American history when soft words have been uttered with all the apparent carelessness which heroic tradition demands: so Lincoln had spoken at Gettysburg, and Washington before him, with no hint in their manner of how they would affect the lives of millions. On that June day, for the first time in history, America through her Secretary of State stated that the cause of the destitute and oppressed of the earth was her cause and was part of the policy of her Government.

The Marshall Plan was now announced; and Marshall, who had returned from Moscow convinced that the Russians were basing their entire plan on the inertia and inaction of the United States and the Western powers, was determined that the Russians should not win the world by default. It was his custom to warn people against "fighting a problem" instead of applying themselves to the solution of it, and the Marshall Plan, by virtue of its immense scope, offered a real solution and not a piecemeal attempt to "solve the edges." A week later the American government announced that the Marshall plan applied to both Russia and Great Britain, and shortly afterwards Ernest Bevin in the Commons announced his country's wholehearted acceptance of the Plan. He declared:

> It is an idea which translates the problem from one of individual countries to one of a continent, and only a country that is a continent could look at another continent in that way. . . . When the Marshall proposals were announced, I grabbed them with both hands. I felt that it was the first chance we had ever been given since the end of the war to look at European economy as a whole. We used to use an old phrase: 'Whatever country you are born in, they croon over the baby in the same old way.' They have the same kind of dreams and aspirations. Why not let them live? Why set them at each other's throats?

The virtue of the Marshall Plan was that it was concerned with large wholes and possessed an immediate emotional appeal. Europe had been bled white. America was prepared to pour in the blood plasma. The responsibility for determining how much blood plasma should be poured naturally fell on the European countries involved: Marshall specifically asked the nations of Europe to declare their needs *jointly*—"The program should be a joint one agreed to by a number, if not all European nations." He also said that "the initiative should come from Europe," though in fact the initiative had come from the small policy-planning group around the President. Early in July the representatives of sixteen nations* assembled in Paris in a heat wave to work out the details of European needs, the American Government demanding the utmost speed. The speed was forthcoming, for by September, after some bickering, the report had been worked out, and on November 10 Marshall estimated the cost for the period April 1, 1948, to June 30, 1949, to be $7,500,000,000. The figure was later reduced to $6,800,000,000. These figures represented life or death for Europe. Eastern Europe was now being consolidated in Russian hands, and the menace of Russian foreign policy, working through the satellite states and the various Communist parties of the states still free of Russian domination, was daily increasing. The threat was real and urgent; and the Marshall Plan was a desperate effort to avert catastrophe.

While Europe wavered in the balance, the situation in China took a turn for the worse; and General Albert C. Wedemeyer, who had assumed the China command after the recall of General Stilwell, was ordered by the President to make a report on the situation in China and Korea. The Report, which was finally presented to the President on September 19, said very much what Marshall had said earlier in the year. The situation was desperate, and there was very little that America could do. Three days before General Wedemeyer had set out for China, on July 6, Marshall had sent a message to the Generalissimo which said bluntly that "the fundamental and lasting solution of China's problems must come from the Chinese themselves." The Chinese Communists had increased their hold on Manchuria, Shantung and Hopei, and though the Kuomintang armies had captured Yenan in March, the Chinese Communists had retained the initiative. The Wedemeyer Report, which was not published until it appeared in the American White Paper in August, 1949, recommended United States military and economic aid to the Nationalist Government for a period of five years; sketched out a plan for setting up a trusteeship over Manchuria; suggested that the

---

*These were Austria, Belgium, Denmark, Eire, France, Greece, Iceland, Italy, Luxemburg, The Netherlands, Norway, Portugal, Sweden, Switzerland, Turkey and the United Kingdom. A watching brief was kept for Western Germany. The Soviet Union, through Mr. Molotov, rejected the proposal outright on the grounds that it "infringed on national sovereignty." Czechoslovakia accepted the proposal on July 8, but withdrew two days later.

Nationalists reduce their military expenditure while increasing the effectiveness of their military establishment; and included provisions for the immediate transfer of ships to the Nationalists. It was an oddly inadequate report, and the political passages in particular suffered from a peculiar inability to come to conclusions. "Some sources say the Communist land reforms have benefitted the poor peasants," says the Report, "while other sources say that Communist terrorist tactics have alienated the vast majority of the peasants." Such arguments were not helpful, and Marshall deliberately banned the publication of the Report for a variety of reasons including its inadequacy and the complete inpracticality of some of its suggestions, the most impractical of all being the suggestion for a trusteeship over Manchuria.

Wedemeyer, who disliked the Kuomintang social system as much as Marshall disliked it, believed that the Nationalist army could still be saved. He was almost alone in that belief. The Kuomintang lines were over-extended; the Chinese Communists had infiltrated deep into Government territory; the Kuomintang generals were surrendering and taking vast supplies of American arms over to the enemy; and reported victories often did not occur. General Barr, the head of the American mission, heard that a battle was taking place at Kaifeng with millions of men involved. He flew over the city, saw no armies and no signs of war except the burning of a few cottages in the outskirts. It was that kind of war. When the Generalissimo suggested through intermediaries that the Americans should assume direct command of his armies, Marshall was forewarned and he wrote to Ambassador Stuart on November 27, 1947:

> I am however not willing that we should accept responsibility for Chinese strategic plans and operations.... Whatever the Generalissimo may feel moved to say with respect to his willingness to delegate necessary powers to Americans, I know from my own experience that advice is always listened to very politely but not infrequently ignored when deemed unpalatable.

A few days previously, speaking before a joint session of the Senate Committee on Foreign Relations and the House Committee on Foreign Affairs, Marshall announced a program of economic aid with the chief purpose of staying the inflation which had swept over

Nationalist China. He had no great hopes that the economic aid would be effective. He thought there would be a "70 per cent probability of effective use," and he was arranging that ammunition should be supplied to the Nationalists from America and from the Pacific islands; but the news from China was becoming increasingly menacing, and it seemed unlikely that anything except direct American participation in the war, with all its unfathomable consequences, could save the Generalissimo. In all Marshall's communications of this time concerning China the grammar becomes involved, and repetitive phrases are everywhere: they are the communications of a man who seems to have felt the uselessness of the Chinese adventure, and was so overwhelmed by the knowledge that nothing could be done effectively that his mind never grappled with the problem, never sought to get to the heart of it. He had reduced himself to the role of the agent responsible for pouring millions of dollars of equipment and hundreds of millions of dollars into China, while remaining a helpless spectator of the uses to which this aid was put. He had admitted defeat when he left China, and he continued to admit defeat during the following two years.

Defeat in China was one thing; defeat in Europe was another. Continuing to make gross mistakes in China because he was ignorant of the forces at work, he steeled himself to avoid errors in Europe. It was necessary to tread carefully. On all sides he was urged to "pour it on the Soviets and give them hell." Knowing, as he did, that the country had only one and a third infantry divisions ready to take the field, he was perfectly aware that America was as defenseless in safeguarding her European frontier as she was defenseless in China. He could only pray that as a result of the Marshall Plan, which had not yet become law, Europe would shortly be able to display her social and economic strength against Russia. The military defense of western Europe was problematical and depended almost exclusively on the threat of the atomic bomb.

At the fifth session of the Council of Foreign Ministers held in London, which began on November 25, Marshall, who had shown a cold contempt for the Generalissimo's military strategies, proceeded to show the same cold contempt for Molotov's political strategies. The Council of Foreign Ministers was transformed into a duel between these two formidable opponents. As usual, Marshall held open staff meetings and discussed the agenda with his advisers beforehand, but it was remarked that he paid little attention to the advice of his advisers and barely glanced at the notes and suggested replies which they handed to him at the conference table. When Molotov made sweeping charges against the Allies, accusing them of striving for an "imperialist peace" or plotting to ruin German industry as an undesirable competitor and using Germany as "a base for military adventures," Marshall replied that the charges were designed for another audience and another purpose; such procedures in the Council of Foreign Ministers did not inspire respect for the dignity of the Soviet Government. Molotov was seen to wince. Whenever Molotov advanced to the attack with accusations that the Allies were not fulfilling the Yalta and Potsdam agreements, there was always Marshall's quiet, urgent and ice-cold voice commanding the Soviet Foreign Minister to pay attention to his immediate audience, not the audience which read *Pravda* and *Izvestia*. Instead of "rehashing" old griefs, Molotov was told to study "the tragic delays of the last two years" and "eliminate misunderstandings." Finally, Marshall could bear the game no longer. He said: "I propose an adjournment, Mr. Chairman. I therefore do not think I have to express myself again. When we meet again I hope it will be in an atmosphere more conducive to the settlement of our differences." The Council, which came to an abrupt end on December 15, 1947, did not meet again until May, 1949, and by that time Marshall was no longer Secretary of State. He had closed the Council as arbitrarily and suddenly as he had left China, and he had successfully infuriated Molotov with the exhibition of his icy disdain. The consequences were serious, though perhaps no more serious than they would have been if Marshall had maintained an even temper. Molotov's hatred of America was passionate and inexhaustible; a little more fuel had been heaped into the fire. In September, in his famous "Little Assembly" speech before the United Nations, Marshall proposed the establishment of a special permanent committee within the General Assembly to circumvent Russian "frustration of the general will." Molotov was now more than ever determined that the "frustration of the general will" should continue.

As he surveyed the cards in his hand on his return from

London, Marshall could see that he possessed exactly one trump card, the Marshall Plan, now known as the European Recovery Program. On January 19, 1948, he addressed Congress and asked for $6.8 billion as the cost of the Program for the first fifteen months. He said: "An inadequate program would involve a wastage of our resources with an ineffective result. . . . Either undertake to meet the requirements of the problem or don't undertake it at all."

This was the old war horse at work, crying out his perpetual either/or, the same who wrote the curt directions on the memoranda passed over his desk, hot for deliberate action, forgetful that all political action outside an authoritarian state partakes of compromise. The ultimatum was received silently and uncomfortably. The need was urgent, and the Secretary of State had achieved enormous stature as the exponent of the Plan, but he had spoken to Congress like a general commanding his troops and Congress had rarely, in its long history, tolerated commands. Senator Walter George of Georgia remarked: "I don't think the State Department is justified in presenting these absolute alternatives. This is a method of propaganda that I don't appreciate. We're told here flatly that $6.8 billion is necessary and that we must do the whole thing or no part of it. That is not a proper statement to make before the legislative branch of the Government. Suppose we decide that $6 billion is enough. I don't believe it would prove absolutely fatal to the program." Marshall had, in fact, committed a grave tactical blunder, and was in danger of having the Plan rejected.

The danger in China was now more pressing than ever. On February 17, 1948, the American Embassy in Nanking sent an alarming report to Washington which indicated that the Chinese Communists had a foothold west of Hankow and were streaming into northern Kiangsu; the Nationalist troops in Manchuria were under siege, and they were faced with large Communist armies in south and central Hopei which were expected to coordinate their attacks with large-scale drives to the south by their armies in Manchuria. "The government which does not govern, or at most governs by inertia" seemed completely incapable of holding the enemy. On February 18 President Truman recommended that Congress authorize a program of aid to China to the amount of $570,000,000 for the period ending

June 30, 1949. Two days later Marshall introduced a statement which recognized the desperate need of the Nationalists, and then pointed out that they were no longer a fair risk:

> The conduct by the Government of the civil war now in progress, particularly in view of the geographic disadvantages—exposed and lengthy communications, and the inherent difficulties in dealing with guerrilla warfare—demands a high order of aggressive leadership in all major echelons of command, which is lacking. The civil war imposes a burden on the national budget of 70 per cent or more and the financing is now carried out by means of the issuance of paper money. Industrial production is low and transportation facilities are poor, the lack of adequate transportation particularly affecting the movement of foodstuffs. The results are an extreme, really a fantastic, inflation of currency, and the inevitable speculation in commodities as well as hoarding.

A few days later he read a long prepared statement to the Committees on Foreign Affairs and Foreign Relations, in which he reviewed the plight of the Nationalists and for the first time mentioned the possibility of their defeat. The Government failures had been worse than he anticipated. Their ineptness in battle, their determination to hold extended lines, the thousands of miles of communications bordered by mountains which gave the Chinese Communists advantages of easy retreat and sudden assault, the Nationalists' determination to cover all points with armies spread out thinly, all these were matters which had to be taken into consideration. To put China in proper shape to resist the Communists, the United States would have to take over the Chinese Government and administer its economic, military and governmental affairs, and this the United States was clearly not prepared to do, nor would the Chinese themselves assent to such an infringement of their sovereignty. "We must be prepared to face the possibility that the present Chinese Government may not be successful in maintaining itself against the Communist forces," he declared. As for economic aid to China, it must be considered as a gesture made necessary for psychological reasons. "It would be against United States interests to demonstrate a complete lack of confidence in the Chinese Government and to add to its difficulties by abruptly rejecting its request for assistance." Once more Marshall, like a squirrel in a revolving cage, found himself returning to the old familiar dilemma: why support the Kuomintang, which was unbelievably corrupt and seemed to be determined to do everything in its power to drag America down with it? Why help a diseased system? What exactly were the advantages of supporting the Kuomintang? He said:

> The issues in China are thoroughly confused. The Chinese Communists have succeeded to a considerable extent in identifying their movement with the popular demand for change in present conditions. On the other hand, there have been no indications that the present Chinese Government, with its traditions and methods, could satisfy this popular demand or create conditions which would satisfy the mass of Chinese people and prevent further violence and civil disobedience.
>
> I know from my own personal experience that large numbers of young Chinese, college graduates, have gone over to the Communist Party, not because they favored the ideology of the Party but because of their complete disgust with the corruption among the officials of the Chinese Government. In the opinion of these young men, the Communist Party was trying to do something for the common people, and no one accuses the Communist leaders or officials of personal graft. For this reason the Communist military forces are not all of the same way of thinking. I have recently been told by our representatives in Manchuria and other places that it is quite apparent that considerable groups are within the ranks of the Communist army because they are opposed to the iniquities of the political party in power, the Kuomintang, and its failure to do anything constructive for the common people and not because of any belief in Communist ideology.
>
> At present, the Chinese Government is not only weak but is lacking in self-discipline and inspiration. There is little evidence that these conditions can be basically corrected by foreign aid.

In this dilemma, Marshall could see the uselessness as well as the necessity of giving token aid. The Chinese Communists were already in a position to besiege Hsuchow, which would open up to them the road to Nanking and Shanghai, and though the seige of Hsuchow was inexplicably delayed until November, the signs of a

Nationalist collapse along the Lunghai railway were already evident. What should be done?

For a short period in March, 1948) Marshall seems to have thought there was still some hope of a broadening of the Chinese Government to include minority groups, though he never made clear which minority groups he had in mind, and the Democratic League had been outlawed by the Kuomintang the previous October. A number of conflicting press releases were issued, and finally on March 11 Marshall made a statement intended to put an end to the confusion. He referred to President Truman's statement of December 15, 1945, which expressed the belief of the United States that "peace, unity and democratic reform in China will be furthered if the basis of this Government is broadened to include other political elements in the country." The release continued:

> The Secretary said that the statement still stands. When asked specifically whether broadening the base of the Chinese Government meant we favored the inclusion of the Chinese Communist Party, he replied that the Communists were now in open rebellion against the Government and that this matter (the determination of whether the Communists should be included in the Chinese Government) was for the Chinese Government to decide, not for the United States Government to dictate.

This involved message was quite unusually unhelpful. It referred to a situation which had long since passed, implied hopefully and ineffectively that a broadening of the base of the Chinese Government would be regarded favorably, and showed that the Secretary refused to assume any responsibility whatsoever. On the same day President Truman was asked what kind of men he hoped would enter the Chinese Government, and he answered that he was in favor of the inclusion of liberals. By this time most of the liberals in China were in hiding, or under arrest, or dead.

The Marshall Plan had not yet become law; Europe was not yet out of danger and China was in a state of chaos; now more than ever Marshall found himself turning towards the one solution which had seemed for more than twenty years the most hopeful—Universal Military Training. On March 17 he spoke before the Armed Services Committee of the Senate. The previous week Czechoslovakia had become a full-fledged satellite state, and fateful elections were about to take place in Italy: no one could be certain of their outcome. Very shortly the situation in Europe might become as precarious as the situation in China. The Marshall Plan would soon be in operation, but was the Marshall Plan enough? He said:

> The Government of the United States has undertaken steps to meet this disintegrating trend in the heart of Europe. . . . But this economic program in the existing situation is not a complete answer. . . . The accelerating march of events in European areas has now made it clear that reliance for the future safety of those areas cannot be placed alone on the slow processes of reconstruction financed with our help. There is something more for the United States to do. We must show, conclusively, by decisive legislative action to all the nations of the world that the United States intends to be strong and to hold that strength ready to keep the European world both at peace and free. . . .
>
> I regard the present military policy of this Government as one based largely on meeting the problems of attrition, with the contrasting necessity for larger and larger appropriations to give us security. . . .
>
> The Nazis devoted all the resources of Germany to preparation for war on a given date, September 1, 1939. The purpose and procedure under universal military training is exactly the opposite. We would be striving to avoid such dates. We want peace, we want to be able to avoid war. Therefore, among other things, we want a system which will be bearable financially, which will not bankrupt the country, a system which, adjusted to world conditions, can be continued at a minimum of cost and personal contribution, a system in accordance with our traditions and strong desires.

It was one of the best of his many speeches on universal military training, but it did not notably advance the cause he was fighting for.

During the previous summer Marshall had attended the Inter-American Defense Parley in Rio de Janiero. This spring he attended the Ninth International Conference of American States held at Bogota, Colombia, as leader of the American delegation. When it was all over, the American delegation pronounced that it was "the culmination of the work of the previous conferences by effecting a major reorganization of the procedures, agencies, and institutions which make up the inter-American system." The stilted language followed a stilted Charter, signed on April 30, which said almost nothing in an intolerably high-flown language. The charter members agreed that "the true significance of American solidarity and good neighborliness can only mean the consolidation on this continent, within the framework of democratic institutions, of a system of individual liberty and social justice based on respect for the essential rights of man," and they were "resolved to persevere in the noble undertaking that humanity had conferred upon the United Nations, whose principles and purposes they solemnly reaffirm." The sentiments were beautiful, but there was no bite in the Charter; and the Communists took the opportunity to stage a brief and bloody show of force in Bogota. They were quelled, but they had successfully advertised their powers, the outbreak was well-timed and the charter-members were warned that there were Communists in the two American continents as well.

In April the Marshall Plan passed into law. In the two and a half years which followed, America gave aid valued at 8,231,000,000 dollars to 16 countries, and this prodigious treasure, which cost each American taxpayer $88, successfully laid the foundations for the reconstruction of Europe. The Plan is still being carried out, and seems likely to shade into economic cooperation dominated by the needs of mutual defense.

During the next months Russian intransigence in Germany increased. By July 1 the Soviet Government was announcing that it would no longer be represented at meetings of the Berlin Kommandatura; and as the tension increased in Europe, at the same time and at even greater tempo it increased in Asia, and about this time instructions were received by the Communist Parties in East Asia to take part in open revolt. In Indo-China, Malaya, the Philippines, India and Burma the full force of Soviet-led partisans was being felt. In China the Kuomintang was retreating on all fronts. On August 12, 1948, Marshall outlined the general policy of the United States towards the Nationalists in the simplest possible terms:

> 1. The United States Government must not directly or indirectly give any implication of support, encouragement

or acceptability of coalition government in China with Communist participation.

2. The United States Government has no intention of again offering its good offices as mediator in China.

The next day Marshall wrote to Ambassador Stuart: "Developments in China are obviously entering into a period of extreme flux and confusion in which it will be impossible with surety to perceive clearly far in advance the pattern of things to come and in which this Government plainly must preserve a maximum freedom of action." It was as though Marshall had at last come to the stage when he desired only the maximum freedom to do nothing whatsoever about China. Once again he was saying: "I wash my hands of the problem, which has passed altogether beyond by comprehension and my power to make judgments." When on October 23, Ambassador Stuart raised a number of extremely sensible hypothetic questions, such as whether the United States would regard the retirement of the Generalissimo as desirable and whether a coalition government would be favored, Marshall threw cold water on his Ambassador with the words: "It is not in the national interest to vouchsafe cut and dried answers to these oversimplified questions." Thereupon he repeated, in exactly the same words, the long and tortured phrase concerning "flux and confusion" which had appeared in his letter of August 13, as though there had been no change in the situation. The phrase, which was pontifical and largely meaningless—how could one preserve maximum of action in flux and confusion?—clearly impressed Marshall with its truth, and from this position he was not prepared to move. The "flux and confusion" came to an end the following month, with the beginning of the battle for Hsuchow, which lasted from November 9 until late in December. With their victory in this critical battle the Chinese Communists began their quick conquest of China, which thereafter was never more than a prolonged mopping-up campaign.

The pace was beginning to tell. Up to October 15, 1948, Marshall had spent 228 out of his 633 days in office in attending international conferences. In October Marshall went to his last conference in Paris. Though he was already ill, he still dominated the United States delegation, always arriving early at the dilapidated Hotel d'Iéna in order, as he told an astonished stenographer, to "get a better seat." As usual, the conference was inconclusive, but at one moment during his stay in Paris Marshall once again changed the course of United States policy. The elections were coming on, and President Truman was of the opinion that the time had come to make a deliberate peaceful gesture to the Soviet Union; he was thinking of sending the Vinson mission to Moscow. Before reaching a final decision the President telegraphed to Marshall and asked for his advice. Marshall, who felt that such a mission would be misunderstood and that his own work at the meeting of the Foreign Ministers would be made more difficult, said, "No," and the Vinson mission was never sent. There were more conferences with the Chinese Nationalists. The head of the Chinese delegation approached him, asking once again whether a high-ranking American officer could be placed in charge of Chinese armies. Marshall had no faith in the suggestion, and a few days later wrote to Under Secretary Lovett: "It would be foolhardy for the United States, at this stage of disintegration of the Chinese Government authority in civil as well as the military sphere, to embark upon such a quixotic adventure." It was Marshall's last communication on China before he retired temporarily from the scene. In December he underwent a major operation, and in the following month he resigned, worn out by illness and the long strain of guiding the foreign affairs of the United States.

There followed twenty months in which Marshall took no part in foreign policy though he served at intervals as an adviser on military planning. By March 1, 1949, he returned to active duty as General of the Army, but with no assignment, and on September 21, 1950, he was summoned back to duty as Secretary of Defense. In the interval the world had changed almost beyond recognition. Nationalist China had collapsed, its government driven out of the country to establish an insecure foothold in Formosa and for a period of ten and a half months Berlin had been under blockade. In the East and the West the threat of Communism had increased sharply; and the Korean war, fought on the periphery of Soviet power, seemed to promise a series of wars along the whole length of the Soviet frontiers. The situation could hardly be more dangerous. As Marshall observed in October, 1950: "The potential collective force of the United Nations was not enough to deter the aggressors in Korea. The actual collective forces of the North Atlantic states may not be enough to deter aggression in our North

Atlantic area, and definitely is not enough to resist attack without serious and critical initial losses."

To help him as Secretary of Defense, Marshall brought in Robert A. Lovett, who had been his Under Secretary when he was Secretary of State. He had full trust in Lovett's powers of judgment. "Lovett," he said, "is a man who is decisive, specific, frank." Lovett successfully relieved Marshall of the burden of administrative routine, and his quick mind, geared to Marshall's, could work unhurriedly in the whirlwind which now descended on the Pentagon. The old team which had won the war had broken up. There was a new Chief of Staff, General Joseph L. Collins, who received his appointment only a month before Marshall returned. Marshall had faith in Collins, who commanded the division which put an end to the campaign on Guadalcanal and later commanded a corps which landed on Utah Beach, and then went on to capture Cherbourg in the first large American assault following the North African victories. To his credit there was the capture of Mainz, Aachen, Dusseldorf and Cologne, and as Marshall remarked, "there is a great deal of experience in that."

The third Secretary of Defense—Forrestal and Johnson had preceded him—was faced with the same hard problems which had dogged him all his life. "The history of national defense in this country," he said in November, 1950, "has been a succession of feasts and famines." At the Congress of American Industry on December 8 he was equally explicit. He had addressed the Congress eight years before and asked for increased production; now he demanded the same, and he pointed out that the situation was now graver than it had ever been—the campaign against Germany and Japan was child's play compared with the remorseless and sometimes secret campaign which had to be fought against Russia on physical battlefields and on battlefields of the spirit. He said:

> Today the military situation is grave, more grave, I very much fear, than it was even in those most difficult days of eight years ago. We had then won our first strategic success by the landing in North Africa, but there were years of bitter fighting ahead.
> The American tendency to rush from pessimism to jubilant optimism, or the reverse, over the results of a single

> campaign and even the outcome of a single battle was then manifest and I remember cautioning you that the great struggle was still to come. Tonight I would caution you that this is a time for calm determination, a strong resolution to do what seems wise to protect the future security of the free world. It is no time for violent emotions.

As usual, Marshall was demanding that all problems should be seen in chastely cold outlines, but the Americans, faced with the sudden eruption of the Chinese Communists in Korea and the bewildering series of mistakes which had led General MacArthur to throw his forces against the Yalu river, were in no mood for such exhibitions of frigidity. "The Communist aggression," said Marshall about the same time, must be approached in the coldest, calmest, most calculating way." Such an attitude, admirable in a Secretary of Defense, was not calculated to appeal to the general public, who felt increasingly that the Communists were prepared to risk a full-scale war against an America hopelessly unprepared. They wanted words lit with the imagination; they received a douche of cold water.

The essential Marshall, frigid and austere, had remained unchanged. He dealt in figures, plans, replacements, man power; they were the counters on the chessboard. He wanted 2,714,000 men under arms by July 1, 1951, and he called upon Congress to approve a vast 6,561,262,000-dollar military building program which was, he said, "dictated by the current international tension." He wanted authority to draft all able-bodied youths for twenty-seven months of service when they reached the age of eighteen; afterwards they were to be enrolled for another three years' service in the organized reserves or for six years in the inactive reserves. Once again he saw the solution to all problems in universal military training, and continually in his speeches he quoted the words of Washington:

> It may be laid down as a primary position and the basis of our system that every citizen who enjoys the protection of a free government owes not only a proportion of his property, but even of his personal services, to the defense of it; and consequently, that the citizens of America (with a few legal exceptions) from 18 to 50 years of age should be borne on the militia rolls, provided with uniform and arms, and

so far accustomed to them that the total strength of the country might be called forth at short notice on any very interesting emergency.

The battle for universal military training had been fought step by step all the way; now at last he was coming near the fulfillment of his dream. Until this measure was brought about, he would continue to say that the United States was altogether too weak to fight a third world war.

He was now at the age of seventy in better health than he had ever been. An operation on his kidneys and a long rest had brought color to his cheeks, and there was less nervousness in his movements, and his voice was stronger. The errors he had made in China plagued him continually; the Korean war was evidence that he had failed decisively, and such a failure in any lesser man would have resulted in impeachment or abandonment into the oblivion which is sometimes offered to statesmen who have failed to accomplish their purpose. Instead, he was now at the height of his powers, possessing more influence than ever, and he was enjoying his task. He had never possessed a real understanding of political and social forces, but he understood the working of the Army perfectly, to the last remote detail. In June, 1950, when the Korean war broke out, the trained reserves of the Army were almost non-existent. By April, 1951, the strength of the military forces had been nearly doubled, and more men were obtained in those ten months than during the whole period which began with the mobilization of August, 1940, and ended three months after Pearl Harbor. For the first time Marshall felt the United States had leeway in trained men. He still talked in terms of "balanced forces," but his preference remained with the infantry; and he would remind those who came to see him that the burden of the battle was nearly always borne by infantrymen. It was the infantry which had taken Saipan, Guam, Tarawa and Kwa-jalein; they had captured the islands which eventually brought the United States in the position to drop the atomic bomb. It was useless, he declared, to rely on a push-button war. "War may start in the air, or maybe in the sea," he said," but pretty soon it will be in the mud. Whatever you win by air and naval action you must hold with ground troops." Korea was only one more example of the supremacy of the infantry, which Napoleon called "the queen of battles." As always, he was afraid that the Americans would relax, putting their trust in the atomic bomb (which the Russians already possessed in large numbers) or in tanks (which were always in danger of running too far in front of the infantry) or in paper agreements with the enemy. There was only one answer to the prevailing threat: preparedness. At whatever the cost he would see that America was prepared. To universal military service he added a demand for universal military training. "It is not a cheap solution," he said, "but it is one that can be borne financially as part of the reasonable price a resolute people will be willing to pay for their liberties."

While the Congress was debating universal military training and the war in Korea was still being fought with extraordinary bitterness, General Douglas MacArthur, like so many proconsuls in the past, was maneuvering himself into a position which would inevitably lead him to defy his superiors. Little by little, and perhaps unconsciously, he had come to view his directives as statements upon which he could exert his ingenuity; like a scholar deciphering a palimpsest, he would interpret them according to his own established theories. The defeat of his armies in northern Korea had rankled, for it had been brought about at a time when victory seemed near and almost tangible; he was not accustomed to defeat; he had no very great respect for Marshall's abilities, remembering always that he had been Chief of Staff when Marshall was a colonel; and in particular he was startled by the announcement received towards the end of 1950 that no further troops would be sent to Korea, and he perhaps suspected Marshall was responsible for the order. By a brilliant landing at Inchon he had retrieved the initiative, but in the early spring of 1951 the war in Korea was once more reaching the stage of a protracted stalemate, with each side claiming small and costly advances. In such an extremity MacArthur behaved as one might suspect he would behave, and his grandiose ambitions extended into fields of high politics, where he had little or no experience, and where he was always at a disadvantage because he was profoundly ignorant of the forces at work. He had decided that the time had come to extend the Korean war to the Chinese and Russian mainland. He would blockade Port Arthur and Dairen, bomb the railways in Manchuria and establish himself as Commander in Chief of the anti-Communist forces in Asia. In a letter written to Congressman Joseph Martin of Massachusetts on March 20, he wrote:

> It seems strangely difficult for some to realize that here in Asia is where the Communist conspirators have elected to make their play for global conquest, and that we have joined the issue thus raised on the battlefield; that here we fight Europe's war with arms while the diplomats there still fight it with words; that if we lose the war to Communism in Asia the fall of Europe is inevitable, win it and Europe most probably would avoid war and yet preserve freedom.

Except for one further passage expressing the belief that the Chinese Nationalist forces on Formosa should be used against the Chinese Communists in Korea, the letter was apparently innocuous, but implicit within the letter was a whole philosophy of direct action against the Communists on the Asiatic mainland and a studied disregard of the directive from the Joint Chiefs of Staff which he had received on December 6 and which counseled "extreme caution in public statements" by military commanders. The message was not cautious, and though the full extent of his lack of caution was not yet known, it could be guessed. On the day he wrote to Congressman Martin, he received a stern note from the Joint Chiefs of Staff reminding him of the December 6 directive. Five days later he announced that he was prepared to confer on the field with the enemy Commander in Chief "in an earnest effort to find any military means whereby the realization of the political objectives of the United Nations in Korea, to which no nation may justly take exceptions, might be accomplished without further bloodshed." What this meant was obscure, and the phrase: "to which no nations may justly take exception" was largely meaningless. He had been ordered to make no public statement without reference to Washington, and he had chosen to disobey the order. There were other straws in the wind. Asked for recommendations on how to provide security for the United Nations forces and maintain contact with the enemy during a period when diplomatic negotiations for the settlement of the Korean war might arise, he answered that security of command was adequate for his needs and he requested that no further limitations be imposed upon him in the conduct of his operations in Korea. The last phrase was perhaps the most ominous. Like the famous phrase, "Boundaries will not be considered as binding," it was a portent of disasters to come, and it was this phrase, more than any other, which was calculated to alarm the Joint Chiefs of Staff.

The letter to Congressman Martin was published on March 24, and on April 5 the President called a meeting of his advisers to discuss General MacArthur's attitude. These advisers were Marshall, Dean Acheson, General Bradley and the President's special assistant, Averell Harriman. No decisions were reached. On the following morning there was a further meeting, and Marshall was asked to secure the opinions of the Joint Chiefs of Staff. He met with them briefly, and all concurred that General MacArthur must be relieved from his four commands. On the night of April 10 the President issued his order to General MacArthur, relieving him of his commands. Marshall said later that the order in its final form was written partly by the Department of State and partly by the Department of Defense. The order was in two parts, one explanatory and the other a curt dismissal. One short paragraph is remarkably in the style of Marshall. It reads:

> You will turn over your commands, effective at once, to Lt. Gen. Matthew B. Ridgway. You are authorized to have issued such orders as are necessary to complete desired travel to such place as you select.

The fat was now in the fire and burning lustily. The manner of MacArthur's dismissal, the hatred and affection in which he was held, the glamour which attached to his name and his delight in the limelight made it certain that among the consequences of his dismissal would be a public examination of his actions. Ordered to political silence in Korea by the Joint Chiefs of Staff, he was offered the opportunity to state his views publicly before the Congress, and this he did in the manner of an old soldier making his farewell address to the nation he had served all his life. The speech was remarkable for its cautious and indirect approach (he referred to "the removal of restrictions on air reconnaissance" when he evidently meant the bombing of China and the Soviet Union), for its histrionics and for its occasional inaccuracies, as when he referred to the Chinese warlord Chang Tso-lin coming to power at the turn of the century, though in fact Chang Tso-lin did not achieve power until nearly a quarter of a century had passed. A regard for accuracy was not one of General MacArthur's strong points. But the impact of his speech, delivered with an extraordinary command of what actors call "projection," was exactly what he had intended it to be: the whole nation was immediately debating the issues arising out of the war in Korea.

The "great debate" was a duel fought between Marshall and MacArthur. Other actors in the drama took their seats—over a period of forty-two days thirteen witnesses appeared, and the record of their remarks and the remarks of their interlocutors reached a total of 2,450,000 words—but even when they were not present, Marshall and MacArthur dominated the scene. They represented two divergent streams of American policy. From the very beginning of American history these two streams had somehow coexisted, and sometimes they had given the appearance of being a single stream. One stream identified liberty with cautious responsibility; the other threw caution to the wind, and found excuses for irresponsibility. Both Marshall and MacArthur were accomplished actors, and both were utterly sincere, and for the most part they spoke, not with their own voices but with the voices of the traditions they represented. When, for example, MacArthur said: "I believe the major thing is to take off the inhibitions and let us use the maximum of peace we have," it was perfectly clear that he was speaking with one of the traditional voices, and when Marshall said: "We have sought in every possible way to avoid a third world war," it was clear that he was speaking in the other. The debate was crystallized around these two statements. Marshall desired collective action, the assurance that the Allies were in agreement, the cautious employment of existing gains; MacArthur was prepared to fight "alone, if necessary," he was contemptuous of the Allies and regarded existing gains as almost nonexistent. The Senators seemed to vie with one another in extracting military secrets from their witnesses, but few secrets were revealed. Marshall admitted that he was responsible for "killing" the Wedemeyer Report: his reasons were not altogether conclusive. He made mistakes about dates, and at one point spoke of a visit to General MacArthur's headquarters which did not occur until long after the date indicated. He spoke of how he had the feeling that he was continually being called upon to state facts which could be useful to the enemy, and he complained against the uses to which some of his statements were put. He resembled a busy schoolmaster attempting to educate his refractory pupils; MacArthur resembled a visiting lecturer determined to convince his audience by an appeal to sentiment. With deadly irony Marshall explained that MacArthur's long absence from Washington had put him in a position where it was unlikely that he would understand global strategies, and he added that his own prolonged residence in Washington was also dangerous. Neither of the protagonists asked for quarter, and neither gave it. MacArthur had hoped to breach the walls with dynamite; Marshall, with greater cunning and a deeper knowledge of his audience, breached the walls with the slow prodding of a battering-ram. In the end it was Marshall's view which prevailed.

At the height of the great debate, the Virginia Military Institute, where Marshall had graduated fifty years before, invited him to attend a reunion in his honor. It was May 15, the day which had been celebrated for eighty-six years as New Market Day, but now for the first time and for one year only the day had changed its name: it was Marshall Day, and Bernard Baruch came down to pay his tribute to the Secretary of Defense and the Governor of Virginia placed a medal round his neck and there were full dress parades in the sunlight as the cadets saluted the most distinguished of their graduates. Most of the men of his class were dead; few of the survivors were military men. Old civil engineers, wholesalers, executives, and artists came to dine with him on filet mignon in the officers' mess hall, and Marshall spoke of the hard days he had spent at the Institute, when the diet was slim and the winters bitterly cold, and sometimes he had to carry two upperclassmen's rifles as well as his own. "We were still paying off the Civil War debt in the mess hall," he said, and in a sense he had been paying it off all his life. Calm, serene, his hair silver in the candlelight, he talked to the old cadets, looking more than ever like someone who had stepped out of colonial Virginia, talking at length of past wars and more briefly of wars to come, while his audience listened agog, or gazed at the old class photograph which showed the cadets in their undress uniforms, stern and youthful, showing on their faces a kind of brazen innocence which seems to have been characteristic of people at the turn of the century. On that old photograph only one face was recognizable.

The other survivors had taken on flesh, grown bald, adopted entirely-new characteristics, possessed not even a fleeting resemblance to the persons they had been fifty years ago. Marshall had hardly changed. The photograph showed him with his long face tilted a little to one side, a hand dropped negligently on one knee, his hair parted in the middle and plastered to his skull. He had faced more storms than any of them and weathered better than all the rest.

On the second day of the reunion a barracks archway was dedicated in his honor. As long as archways last it would bear the name of George Catlett Marshall. It was the highest tribute the Institute could pay, for only two other men had archways named after them: they were Washington and Stonewall Jackson. Alone in his generation he could stand in their company.

For a few more months Marshall retained his position as Secretary of Defense, but already the reins were passing out of his hands, and he was satisfied that Lovett could do the job as well as he had ever done it. Lovett had advantages he had never possessed. The Assistant Secretary could "think from outside." He had not fought his way slowly to the top, in the long weary progress from rank to rank. To his friends Marshall said "There is iron in Lovett," and these words were taken as a hint that the general would resign as soon as an opportunity presented itself. To resign immediately after the uproar following the dismissal of MacArthur would be regarded as a sign of weakness; he would wait his time; then very quietly, with the least harm to anyone, he would slip away.

From his blue desk chair in the Pentagon, Marshall could now look out upon a world where the pieces of the jigsaw were fitting into place. The dykes were holding. The terrible days in the winter of 1947 when China was collapsing, when the Middle East was a tinder-box and there was danger of civil war in France and Italy, and no one knew whether Tito was still an obedient servant of the Kremlin—these days were over. Even then he had said that Communism had been stemmed, and the Russians were compelled to make a re-evaluation of their policy. Communism, of course, had not been stemmed. It was exploding over the whole of China and less than three years later it was to march down through Korea. But in the spring and summer of 1951 the hard outlines of the future could be discerned: a holding war that might last a hundred years, at the cost of unbelievable treasure and sacrifice of lives. Yet so it would have to be. It was a new age, and new men would have to take command. If the future was dark, he could tell himself that Universal Military Training was now working to make America stronger than it had ever been. "We were playing with fire while we had nothing with which to put it out," he had said in February 1948, and now at last there was a reasonable assurance that the fire-fighters were ready.

Meanwhile the mysterious and murderous war in Korea was still being fought, and at the beginning of June he decided to see for himself how the ground lay. He visited the battlefields and talked to the soldiers, and then went on to General Ridgeway's headquarters at Tokyo in a mood of restrained optimism. When reporters talked about stalemate he answered: "They called Greece a stalemate, and General Van Fleet had an answer to that. They called the Berlin blockade a stalemate—the airlift stopped that. Practically everything we do that is not completed that afternoon is a stalemate in our country." He talked of the high morale of the Eighth Army, the way they had struck a classic blow against the enemy lines, the cheerfulness of the soldiers, and how the rotation of troops was working; and in the intervals of conferences with the United Nations High Command he may have remembered wryly that he had fought bitterly for a while in the Spring of 1947 against the removal of American troops from Korea, but by the autumn he was already working on plans for removing them. There were many who believed that the removal of American troops was a kind of invitation to the Communists to launch an attack against the south.

Wearing civilian clothes, speaking quietly, the blue eyes flashing with indignation only once (and that was when someone mentioned MacArthur's recent telegram to the joint Congressional Committee saying that Marshall's Far Eastern Mission was a failure for which the world was paying in blood), Marshall puzzled the reporters gathered in the Dai Ichi building, who could not understand why he had flown across the Pacific. Had he brought directives for General Ridgeway? Had he come to discuss a ceasefire? Was he arranging a truce? He was doing none of these things, and the reporters, accustomed to regard Marshall as a legend whose every move was portentous with significance, shook their heads incredulously. "I am here to see the whole service problem, but nobody believes me," Marshall complained, thinking of all the telegrams which said "He is evidently here on a secret mission," or "In spite of what the Secretary has said. . . ." There was always to be this aura about the legend, and to the very end it was assumed that he had come to Korea on some dark purpose of his own. Asked to comment on MacArthur's ungracious telegram, he replied that he had said all that needed to be said at the Congressional enquiry, and it was noticed that his lips shut tight, and there was an air of finality in his tone.

The legend remained: it could be broken up into little pieces, and each piece could be minutely examined, but when they were put together again, there was still the legend, the taut straight soldier who had wielded such immense powers that one could never quite regard him as human. For three months after his return from Korea he retained his seat in power. Then on September 12, shortly before eleven o'clock in the morning, he summoned reporters to his office in the Pentagon and announced almost casually: "My resignation as Secretary of Defense takes effect at eleven o'clock Eastern Standard Time this morning." That was all, or nearly all. He explained that he had originally agreed to remain as Secretary until the end of June, but there was some important military legislation before Congress and he had remained behind until his desk was clear. From now on, Lovett would take over the command.

There remained a brief ceremony of farewell with President Truman. Then it was all over. The wars, the longing, the hardships, the stern discipline he had worn as solemnly as he had worn his clothes, all this was over; and so was the sense of power and command, and the futility of power and command, and the deep need to serve and the comradeship. For more than fifty years he had been part of a close brotherhood, and was no longer. The cameras photographed him as he sat between Truman and Lovett, his hands folded on his lap, his face a mask. It was a good mask. At the age of seventy he looked more than ever as though he had stepped out of a canvas painted during the age of Charles I or the age of Washington. He did not nod to the cameras, nor wave with his hands, nor smile, nor gesture, nor show in any way whether he was moved. Tight-lipped, he was the prince who served his queen to the end.

CHAPTER SIXTEEN

Portrait

The old gaunt features still look down from the walls of the Pentagon and a hundred other places, and now more than ever we see the two Marshalls at war with one another—the stern forehead and eyes at war with the gentleness of the mouth. Tall and blue-eyed, he looks out at a world he increasingly distrusts, a world perpetually removed from the ordered habits of his ancient Virginia. The once-powerful shoulders have lost their power, age marks the fine patrician features, the handwriting is no longer so firm, but there is still the look of youth on him. All that will power and intelligence and natural ability could achieve he has attained, high position and honors have been showered on him, and he knows clearly enough that these are valueless in themselves. As old age settles on him, what remains?

We shall not know the final answers until long after his death; even then they may escape us. But it can be said of him, as it can be said of few others, that he lived for an idea, and the idea was America. For this he strained the muscles of his heart and mind with an unrelenting desire to serve, like a medieval knight content to serve his mistress at a distance. For this he lived his apparently passionless and austere life, concealing his passion under a mask of austerity, attempting always by a kind of sleight of hand to show himself in disguise, deliberately surrounding himself with a cold shell to ward off from his neighbors the raging fires inside. The coldness was real—too many soldiers have felt that ice-cold wind. Yet it was probably essential, and without it he could hardly have breathed. His nerves were more fine-spun than he knew; somewhere he was wounded. This soldier, who never fired a shot in anger and who very rarely presented himself in a dangerous place on the battlefield, showed the marks of an indelible wound.

What was the name of the wound? Probably there is no name for it. It may have begun at the time of the famous hazing incident, but it is more likely to have deeper roots. It is significant that he chose to marry a beautiful woman who was doomed to die of heart disease and who miraculously survived under his care longer than any doctors anticipated. With her he lived close to the edge of death. It was not that he desired to live close to death: it was simply that inevitably he found himself in this position until, when he became Chief of Staff, the knowledge of death became ever-present. He was the man who had "killed the marionette," and knew exactly where he was going, and went there, and made mistakes, and seemed not to belong to our own time: a man possessed of Roman gravity and an unusually accurate understanding of the forces at work in the world, and at the same time he was a man who was perpetually grief-stricken, because death was in the air around him. The mask of the grand inquisitor concealed a man who was so conscious of death that there were occasions when he could barely trust himself to speak aloud.

Given an extreme sensitivity and at the same time a purely logical mind, which thought in terms of visual symbols; given his reluctance to form friendships and his constant attempts to influence people by example and by force of logic; given his origins in the small corner of Virginia which had been the birthplace of the greatest American generals and legislators; given habits so orderly that timepieces could be checked by his comings and goings; given the terrible hazing during which he had avoided death by a hair-breadth; given a natural ability to think in terms of lines of force; given fabulous powers of concentration; given all these he could hardly avoid becoming what he became—an enigma and a prodigious symbol of the best of his age.

Though he thinks in terms of America, there is very little in his character which is markedly American. He lacks the *brio* and romanticism which is the mark of the great Americans of the past; he has invented no resonant phrases; he has none of Lincoln's gregariousness, none of Roosevelt's insatiable thirst for experience.

His characteristics are English and aristocratic. He dislikes, and perhaps despises the crowd. Living on a perpetual pedestal, incapable of expansiveness, aware of his own formidable powers, he carries himself with the air of one dedicated to a remote purpose, closer perhaps to Lord Curzon than anyone else who has achieved a comparable position in recent history. Lord Curzon was physically crippled; Marshall was hurt; and very probably neither would have come to high position without their sufferings and their hurts. Once when Lord Curzon saw some English soldiers bathing, he remarked on the whiteness of their flesh and said it had never occurred to him that the lower orders possessed such physical beauty when they were naked. It would never have occurred to Marshall that there was any difference between the physical appearance of the higher and lower orders; but he was supremely aware of the existence of these orders. It is not only that he is a natural aristocrat, but he follows the aristocratic tradition of Virginia, with the Virginian's courtly devotion to honor and to women—during the war he wrote thousands of letters to grief-stricken wives and mothers, and he was a little surprised to discover that they were forgiving and generous in their understanding. No other Chief of Staff had written such letters. Engrained in him is the knowledge of an aristocracy of birth which has been maintained on American soil for three hundred years. He has the aristocrat's disdain for details; he must think in large outlines, huge concepts, the immutable laws of chivalry and honor and power, though chivalry is nearly dead within the tremendous modern war machine, and honor has become a propagandist's plaything, and only naked power gives hope of survival.

One should not underestimate the aristocrat, who fulfills in the modern world many conflicting functions. Baudelaire was perhaps the first to observe that, as the machine age evolved, the aristocrat in the disguise of the dandy offered a curious similarity to the machine he detested, because it removed his power from him. The aristocrat is impersonal like the machine; is indeed haunted by impersonality, not only because he conceals himself under his titles, but because he knows that power springs from an attitude of impersonality, and in the modern world power can be employed effectively only by those who are prepared to assume the impersonal mask. The modern aristocrat disdains titles. He is content to exert his power mysteriously and silently, and it pleases him that no one knows who he is. With Marshall the sense of ingrained aristocracy and remoteness was inescapable; so was his impersonality. He could not unbend. He had to study, especially in wartime, his least gesture, remembering that at a critical moment in the last war he went riding with General Pershing to headquarters in Chaumont, and suddenly the old general leaned back to rest, and immediately it was assumed he was exhausted by the war and discouraged by the news from the battlefields. If Pershing was discouraged, who had a right to feel encouraged?

Impersonal by instinct or tradition, Marshall made a virtue out of necessity. Driving one day from Capitol Hill after a grilling of several hours by Congressional members, he closed his eyes and said: "If I can only keep all personal feelings out of my system, I may be able to get through with this job." He was more explicit in a long conversation which Mrs. Marshall has recorded in her admirable book, *Together*. While he was talking to her, she had a feeling that he was really talking to himself. "It was as though he lived outside of himself and George Marshall was someone he was constantly appraising, advising and training to meet a situation. He would say, 'I cannot afford the luxury of sentiment, mine must be cold logic. Sentiment is for others. . . . It is not easy to tell men they have failed. . . . I cannot allow myself to get angry, that would be fatal—it is too exhausting. My brain must be kept clear.'"

But the anger remained, burning fitfully underneath, inescapable because it was a part of the man, however much he attempted by an act of will to bury it; and some of his strength came from that explosive reserve of hidden anger, and some of his weakness, for the anger would well up and take unrecognizable shapes, so that sometimes his verdicts on men were capricious and at other times his judgment was clouded. One does not reduce oneself to a machine without paying the penalty.

Yet the character he made of himself, that cold, accurate and formal machine devoted to the highest purposes of duty, was part of an already existing pattern which began to emerge towards the end of the nineteenth century. Walter Bagehot speaks of the great soldier of his day who is "a quiet, grave man, busied in charts, exact in sums, master of the art of tactics, occupied in trivial detail; thinking, as the

Duke of Wellington was said to do, *most* of the shoes of the soldiers; despising all manner of éclat and eloquence; perhaps, like Count Moltke, silent in seven languages." Bagehot's portrait is perhaps as close to Marshall as we shall ever get, but it leaves out the desperate passions, the fierce and monkish devotions which can be observed playing beneath the surface of Marshall's mind, as he castigates himself mercilessly, sharpening the senses that will become useful in war and deadening the rest, drilling his body until it becomes an athletic machine and drilling his mind until it becomes responsive only to the problems of war. "The line he must draw is a hair-breadth," said Emerson of another hero. But those who walk along a hair-breadth line sometimes go berserk under the strain, and when they fall off the line, they fall with a wild flaying of the arms and a prodigious capacity for making mistakes. Marshall's mistakes were mistakes of cold temper, sudden spiritual alterations, momentary in-quacies. They did not happen often, but when they did happen they were fatal, and they arose from the manner of man he was. He was like the man who prepares immense calculations and comprehensive studies with unfaltering intelligence. Everything, to the last remote unit, is accounted for, every permutation and combination of forces is foreseen, and all that is now necessary is to press the button and the attack can be launched. So it happened at St. Mihiel and the Meuse-Argonne. But in the next war, though all the preparations were made as brilliantly as human intelligence could make them, the one decisive factor—the place and time of the battle—was mislaid at the last moment. To reply, as he did, that the place and time of the battle were not of his own choosing and he was inescapably on the defensive is to avoid the issue, since there was sufficient information in the War Department to show that an attack on Pearl Harbor was mathematically certain once the Japanese attacked America. He refused until the last moment to believe that the Japanese would take the hazards which he would have himself cheerfully assumed. Carelessness, the blind spot, the inability to understand the psychology of other nations, these, too, had their part in the tragic failure.

There is no way of proving cause and effect in matters of the mind. We can only guess sometimes why Marshall behaved as did. There were so many triumphs and failures in his life coming quick after one another that the miracle is that he remained in character for so long, the core of his mind as inflexible as ever, while he dealt flexibly with the varying problems of the hour. He sometimes thought he knew more than he knew. His memory, more often than he recognized it, failed him. The superb machine sometimes broke down. It never occurred to him that the fools were sometimes right, that there was something odd in the fact that G.I.'s were known to face him with considerably more fear than they were known to face the Japanese or the Germans, and that the violence of his passions, so carefully guarded, so secret that sometimes they may have been unknown to himself, were plainly visible to others. He chose his own truth and followed it; and if it led him down byways of error and remoteness from ordinary human interests, into a proud and aristocratic isolation, he was not entirely to blame: the times demanded a man of this character, and he was as much a child of his time as any other. He will always be respected and acclaimed; he will not be loved; nor would he have desired it.

To understand a military commander, it is necessary above all to know his attitude towards killing, which is his trade. It is an ugly trade, and Marshall was aware of its ugliness. While General MacArthur went out of his way in the Congressional hearings to deny that he rejoiced in war, all his gestures and the tone of his voice spoke of how much joy he derived from soldiering. Marshall's attitude was considerably more complex, as he was himself far more complex than MacArthur. Intensely ambitious, he enjoyed the uses of power. Intensely conscientious, he enjoyed the application of his mind to details. Intensely devoted to his country, he enjoyed the exercise of his devotion. The physical details of a battlefield horrified him, as they must horrify everyone who is civilized, and when he speaks of battlefields, he does so almost abstractly, talking about lines of fire and positions, all the mechanical details of war to which his mind was particularly attuned, and he rarely speaks of the individual engagements. He had known war intimately in France; he had seen the breaking of bodies and heard the inhuman screaming of the wounded, and he loathed war with a bitter loathing. If war could have been fought on a chessboard, he would have been happier. It is inconceivable that he would ever, like MacArthur, have gazed down at dead Japanese or Korean bodies and said: "This is a good sight for my weary eyes."

In nearly everything except their voices Marshall and MacArthur are poles apart. Though Marshall retains his Southern accent, both voices are quiet, muffled and dignified, and touched by the courtesy of real power, perhaps inescapably, for both have been conscious over long periods of their lives that they wield great powers to command. Such men have no need to raise their tones. They are conscious that their merest whispers are enough, and they know only too well that if they raise their voices they might disturb the atmospheric conditions.

Marshall, rising from obscurity to command the greatest mechanized military power that had ever been created, was continually aware of his obscure origins. MacArthur, plagued by his father's fame, fundamentally uncertain of himself, given to displays of childish showmanship, saw himself as a legend even before he became a legend, and had no need to disturb himself about his origins. His dazzling talents led him from one dizzy height to another. Standing on the invasion beach at Leyte, he exclaimed: "I have returned. By the grace of Almighty God, our forces stand again on Philippine soil. The hour of your redemption is at hand. Rally to me!" These words, spoken against the background of a raging battle and announced with dramatic intensity, were characteristic of his pride in his own accomplishments: the infantrymen who fought his campaigns were not always so admiring. They detected the note of irresponsibility which lay concealed within the Victorian fustian, and sometimes wished he would bridle his romantic tongue.

If MacArthur was Victorian, Marshall was Elizabethan, and more particularly he was like the Elizabethans in Ireland, exiles from their own land, men who were generous in intrigue and accomplished in war and without scruples except the scruple of gentlemanliness, with a taste for social restraint and a certain dryness, determined to show excellence in all things, not because excellence was desirable in itself, but because excellence was a sign of man's utmost accomplishment. They insisted—or rather Spenser insisted—that the Elizabethan knight should show no outward signs of strain, and his greatest accomplishments should be performed quietly. The *Faerie Queene* was widely read in colonial Virginia, but by the time Marshall was learning to read the heroic tradition of the Elizabethan age was more widely known through *The Three Musketeers,* a book which Marshall has continued to read at intervals throughout his life. In the portrait of D'Artagnan he saw himself magnified.

There is a geography of the mind. The mind of an Englishman remains English wherever he is, becoming the more English the more he removes himself from English shores, and so it was with Marshall. He retained the peculiar qualities of a Virginian and never ceased proclaiming, even when he was silent, that he was a Virginian to the core. Like the colonial Virginians he could be abrupt and terrifying in his anger. There is a legend in the Army that when Eisenhower was toying with the idea of becoming the Republican candidate for the Presidency, Marshall wrote him a stern note which said that if Eisenhower persisted in his candidacy on the Republican side, then he, Marshall, would be compelled to assume the candidacy on the Democratic side, "and," said Marshall, "I shall beat you." The story, of which there are a number of variants, is almost certainly untrue, but it is significant that the story is widely believed. The legends which derived from Marshall are concerned for the most part with his calm assumption of his own powers and his extraordinary capacity to assume the greatest burdens without any noticeable sagging of the shoulders. The legends however tended to obscure the man; the tenderness was real, and far too often for his own comfort the inquisitor inquired into his own moral purposes. If pride raged, he would deaden it with deliberate strategems; and his sternness was only another facet of his high conception of duty.

"He who tries to rule over men, who are by nature equal to him, acts with intolerable pride," wrote St. Augustine in the first book of his *Christian Doctrine.* These words were constantly repeated by Pope Gregory VII, the Hildebrand, who not only ruled over men with an iron hand but abused kings and princes with a savage delight in his sacerdotal powers. Marshall, too, had desired to rule over men, and he suffered some of the consequences. He never concealed his pride. He had, in Stonewall Jackson's phrase, "no gift for seeming." His pride was easily discerned: his face could not conceal his complexity, his quiet manner did not conceal the overriding ambition to master himself and others. Like Benjamin Franklin, whom he revered, he wanted to display his powers in all the fields of attainment, and because he was a man of single-minded genius he failed in the subjects he had never mastered. He was not a deep or an original military thinker: he added nothing new to strategy. In a sense he was a self-educated man, and self-educated men rarely learn by experience and they tend to stereotype their mistakes: most of his mistakes sprang from his failure to think in anything but military terms. Yet if he did not possess "the sleepless tact, unmoveable calmness, and the patience which no folly, no provocation, no blunders can shake"—these were the qualities which Franklin demanded of the diplomat—he possessed what was more important for the immediate purpose of his country: he could win battles. A failure as Ambassador to China and an unimpressive Secretary of State except in the role of harbinger of the Marshall Plan, he was magnificent as Secretary of Defense and the greatest Chief of Staff the country has ever possessed. In these last his powers were in perfect equilibrium. In the landscape where all things are measured, condemned or praised, he could walk at ease, with the certain knowledge that he had filled these two roles more than handsomely.

In any age, in any place, Marshall would have been remarkable. He came to birth at a time when the forces of the modern world were being shaped. He dedicated himself to thinking in terms of lines of force, those invisible and wavering boundaries set with knives which are thrown out by armies and by nations. His triumph was to come to maturity at a time when such knowledge had become precious; but there was another triumph even greater than this. To hold any kind of power is to commit a crime, which can only be expiated by a sense of the utmost responsibility: and it follows that the expiation must be as great as the crime. He assumed burdens of responsibility as great, and perhaps greater, than any man of his time, and he did this willingly, with unyielding loyalty, and so expiated his crime to the uttermost.

For the rest he moved through the world in a strange mastery of it, singing its praises, content to be himself, delighting in his accomplishments and in the supple strength of his body, good beyond the ordinary measure of goodness, but always lonely and hurt, though he rarely showed either the hurt or the loneliness. It was his fate to be almost unbearably sensitive in a brutally insensitive profession. It was also his fate to encounter antagonists worthy of his steel—among them, on their various levels, were Mao Tse-tung and Douglas MacArthur, whose sensibilities were as explosive as his own. He was a man who delighted in common things, and his favorite picture was a photograph of a ruined church at Vaux in Picardy, where the soldiers are singing hymns around a battered organ: this too was a measure of the man and his truth.

So, in the end he became a legend. There are disadvantages in becoming a legend: it is already too late to prevent them from continuing their independent existence. But of him it may be said that not only did he live for America, but America was his point of departure and the circumference of his dreams and ambitions. Because of him and the plan which is indissolubly connected with his name, Americans can reach out to new frontiers of the spirit, and Melville's dream of "a future which shall see the estranged children of Adam restored to the old hearth-stone in Eden" is brought appreciably nearer.

Select Bibliography

American Armies and Battlefields in Europe, prepared by the American Battle Monuments Commission. Washington, U.S. Government Printing Office, 1938.

Arnold H. H., *Global Mission.* New York, Harper and Brothers, 1949.

Beard, Charles ., *President Roosevelt and the Coming of the War.* New Haven, Yale University Press, 1948.

Beveridge, Alfred J., *Life of John Marshall.* New York, Houghton Mifflin Company, 1916.

Bradley, Omar N., *A Soldier's Story.* New York, Henry Holt and Company, 1951.

Brace, Philip Alexander, *Social Life of Virginia in the Seventeenth Century.* Lynchburg, J. P. Bell and Company, 1927.

Butcher, Harry C., *My Three Years with Eisenhower.* New York, Simon and Schuster, 1947.

Byrnes, James F., *Speaking Frankly.* New York, Harper and Brothers, 1947.

Churchill, Winston S., *The Grand Alliance.* Boston, Houghton Mifflin Company, 1950.

_____ *The Hinge of Fate.* Boston, Houghton Mifflin Company, 1950.

Clark, Mark, *Calculated Risk.* New York, Harper and Brothers, 1950.

Clay, Lucius D., *Decision in Germany.* New York, Doubleday and Company, 1950.

Couper, William, *One Hundred Years at V.M.I.* Richmond, Garrett and Massie, n.d.

Daniels, Jonathan, *The Man of Independence.* Philadelphia, J. B.

Lippincott Co., 1950.

Dennett, Tyler, *Americans in Eastern Asia.* New York, Barnes and Noble, 1941.

Department of Defense, mimeographed copies of speeches by General Marshall.

Department of State, *United States Relations with China.* Washington, Office of Public Affairs, 1949.

DeWeerd, . ., "Selected Speeches and Statements of General of the Army George C. Marshall." *Infantry Journal,* Washington, 1945.

Dulles, John Foster, *War or Peace.* New York, The Macmillan Company, 1950.

Eisenhower, Dwight D., *Crusade in Europe.* New York, Doubleday and Company, 1950.

First Division, Summary of Operations in the World War, prepared by the American Battle Monuments Commission. Washington, U.S. Government Printing Office, 1944.

Forman, Henry Chandlee, *Jamestown and St. Mary's.* Baltimore, John Hopkins Press, 1938.

The Forrestal Diaries, edited by Walter Millis, New York, Viking Press, 1951.

Frye, William, *Marshall: Citizen Soldier.* Indianapolis, The Bobbs-Merrill Company, 1947.

Personal Memoirs of U. S. Grant. New York, Charles L. Webster and Co., 1894.

Grew, Joseph C., *Ten Years in Japan.* New York, Simon and Schuster, 1944.

Gunther, John, *Roosevelt in Retrospect.* New York, Harper and Brothers, 1950.

Hagood, Johnson, *The Services of Supply.* Boston, Houghton Mifflin, 1927.

Harbord, James G., *The American Army in France, 1917-1919.* Boston, Little, Brown and Company, 1936.

History of the First Division during the World War. Philadelphia, The John C. Winston Company, 1922.

Hull, Cordell, *The Memoirs of Cordell Hull.* New York, The Macmillan Company, 1948.

Johnson, Thomas M., *Without Censor.* Indianapolis, The Bobbs-

Merrill Company, 1928.

Lauterbach, Richard E., *Danger from the East.* New York, Harper and Brothers, 1947.

Leahy, William D., *I Was There.* New York, Whittlesey House, 1950.

Lee, Robert E., *Recollections and Letters of General Robert E. Lee.* New York, Garden City Publishing Company, 1924.

Liebling, A. J., "A Profile of General Marshall," *The New Yorker,* October 26, 1940.

Liggett, General Hunter, *A.E.F. Ten Years Ago in France.* New York, Dodd, Mead and Company, 1928.

Marshall, George C., Jr., with Captain C. O. Sherrill, *Notes on Cordage and Tackle.* Fort Leavenworth, Army Service Schools, 1909.

Marshall, George C., "Infantry in Battle," *Infantry Journal.* Washington, 1939.

General of the Army George C. Marshall, General of the Army . H. Arnold, Fleet Admiral Ernest J. King: War Reports. Philadelphia, J. B. Lippincott Co., 1947.

Marshall, George C., *The Winning of the War in Europe and the Pacific.* New York, War Department 8c Simon and Schuster, 1945.

Marshall, Katharine Tupper, *Together: Annals of an Army Wife.* New York, Tupper and Love Inc., 1946.

Maurice, Sir Frederick, *The Last Four Months.* Boston, Little, Brown and Company, 1919.

Millis, Walter, *These are the Generals.* New York, Alfred A. Knopf, 1943.

_____ *This is Pearl.* New York, William Morrow and Co., 1947.

Morgenstern, George, *Pearl Harbor: The Story of a Secret War.* New York, The Devin Adair Co., 1947.

Mott, A. Bentley, *Twenty Years as Military Attaché.* New York, Oxford University Press, 1937.

Mowrer, Edgar Ansel, *The Nightmare of American Foreign Policy.* New York, Alfred A. Knopf, 1948.

The National Archive: Franklin D. Roosevelt Library, Hyde Park, . Y. Photostats of correspondence between President Roosevelt and General Marshall.

The National Encyclopedia of American Biography. New York, James T. White and Company, 1893.

Palmer, Frederick, *John J. Pershing, General of the Armies.* Harrisburg, The Military Service Publishing Company, 1948.

_____ *Our Greatest Battle (The Meuse-Argonne).* New York, Dodd, Mead and Company, 1919.

Paxson, Frederick L., *America at War 1917-1918.* Boston, Houghton Mifflin Co., 1939.

Pershing, J. J., *My Experiences in the World War.* New York, Frederick A. Stokes Co., 1931.

Phillips, Cabell, *Dateline: Washington.* New York, Doubleday and Company, 1949.

Record of Service in the World War of V.M.I, compiled by the Historiographer of the V.M.I., 1920.

Report of the Joint Congressional Committee on the Investigation of Pearl Harbor.

Sherwood, Robert E., *Roosevelt and Hopkins, An Intimate History.* New York, Harper and Brothers, 1950.

Stettinius, Edward R., Jr., *Lend-Lease: Weapon for Victory.* New York, The Macmillan Company, 1944.

_____ *Roosevelt and the Russians.* New York, Doubleday and Company, 1949.

Stilwell, Joseph, *The Stilwell Papers,* edited by Theodore White. New York, William Sloane Associates, 1948.

Stimson, Henry L., and McGeorge Bundy, *On Active Service in Peace and War.* New York, Harper and Brothers, 1948.

Tully, Grace, *F.D.R. My Boss.* New York, Charles Scribner's, 1949.

United States Army in the World War 1917-1919. Military Operations of the American Expeditionary Forces. Washington, Historical Division, Departaient of the Army, 1948. (Volumes 8 and 9 give details of the operations of the St. Mihiel and Meuse-Argonne battles.)

Wertenbaker, Thomas J., *The Planters of Colonial Virginia.* Princeton, Princeton University Press, 1927.

Winant, John G., *Letter from Grosvenor Square.* Boston, Houghton Mifflin Company, 1947.

Woollcott, Alexander, *The Command is Forward.* New York,

The Century Company, 1919.

World War Records: First Division A.E.F. (Mimeographed copy in New York Public Library.)

World's Work, vols. 37, 38. Articles by Arthur W. Page on the battles of Cantigny, St. Mihiel and Meuse-Argonne.

Also files of the *Infantry Journal,* the *New York Times, Newsweek, Time* and the *Virginia Magazine of History and Biography.*

Index

A
Acheson, Dean, 123, 299
Adams, John, 9
African campaign, beginning of, 187-188
Afrika Korps, 187
defeat, 197
Agricultural and Mechanical College of Texas, 17
Aguinaldo, Emilio, 29
Air force, expansion of, 111
Air war, problems of, 145
Alaska, operations in, 200
Alexander, Sir Harold, 212
Allen, Major General Henry T., 92
Allen, Major General Terry, 197
American Manganese Manufacturing Co., 15
American White Paper, 266
ANAKIM, 194, 198
Arcadia Conference, 163-164
Argonne Forest, 82
Army and Navy Register, 207, 208
Army reorganization, 143-146, 169-170
Arnim, General von, 197
Arnold, General Henry H., 132, 169
Atlantic Charter, 132
Attack, Marshall's theory of, 247-248
Attu, battle of, 201
Aurelio de Goes Monteiro, Pedro, 116
Australia, vulnerability of, 164

B
Baker, Newton D., 54, 130
Bard, Ralph ., 243
Baruch, Bernard, 320
Beardall, Captain John, 154, 161
Bell, J. Franklin, 30, 34, 206
recognition of Marshall, 36-37
Bellinger, Admiral, 138
Bevin, Ernest, 300
Biennial Report, 127-129
Second, 203-204
Third, 244-253
Bismarck, Prince Otto von, 82
Bismarck Sea, battle of, 196
Bohlen, Charles E., 292
BOLERO, 176, 183
delay in, 187
Bomb, atomic, 242
first use of, 243
Booth, Major . E., 35
Bordeaux, General, 48
Bradley, General Omar N., x, 105
opposition to capture of Berlin, 238
Brazil, Marshall mission to, 116-117
Brook, Sir Alan, 168, 176, 178
at Teheran Conference, 215
Brown, Katherine Tupper, 107
Bryan, William Jennings, 96
Bugge, Captain Jens, 35
Bullard, General Robert L., 49, 68
at Cantigny, 60
Commander in France, 51
influence on Marshall, 59
Bundy, Colonel Charles W., 149
Burma Road, 194
Bush, Vannevar, 242
Byrnes, James F., 119

C
Cairo Conference, 213-214
Cantigny, battle of, 60-70
Marshall's report on, 64-67
plan of attack, 62-63
Carnegie, Andrew, 14
Casablanca Conference, 193-194
Cassino, 222
Catlett, Elizabeth, 10
Catlett, John, 10
Chang Chih-chung, General, 265
Chang Chun, General, 261

Chang Tso-lin, 318
Charles I, King of England, 11
Chastelux, Marquis de, 10
Chen Kuo-fu, 270
Chen Li-fu, 258
Chennault, General Claire, 198
Chiang Kai-shek, 167, 185
  character, 259, 282
  opposition to truce, 274
  plan for governmental reform, 264
China, civil war in, 269
  economic aid to, 302-303
  hatred of America in, 285
  National Assembly, 281-282
Chou En-lai, 258
Chu Teh, 265
Churchill, Winston, 18, 132
  at Arcadia Conference, 163-165
  at Casablanca, 194
  inspection of U.S. troops by, 183
  opposition to invasion of Europe, 178
  relations with Marshall, 135
Citadel, Charleston, 17
Civilian Conservation Corps, 108
  in Washington, 110
Clark, General Mark, 179
  training schools established by, 198
Clay, General Lucius D., 293
Clayton, William L., 243
Clemenceau, Georges, 45
Coles, Elizabeth Carter, 23
Collins, General Joseph L., 105
  Chief of Staff, 313
Communist party, Chinese, 101
  connection with Soviet Union, 265
  triumph of, 311
  East Asian, 310
Compton, Karl T., 243
Conant, James B., 242
Conference, Arcadia, 163-164
  Cairo, 213-214
  Casablanca, 193-194
  Moscow, 293-298
  OCTAGON, 225-226
  off-record, 188
  Paris, 311-312
  Quebec, 204-206
  Teheran, 214-217
  TRIDENT, 198
  Yalta, 232-237
Conference of State Governors, 201
Confidential Letter to the Fleet, 151
Conger, A. L., 77
Congressional hearings, pressure of, 144-145
Connally, Tom, 291
Conner, General Fox, 69, 86, 94
Cordelier, General, 107
Council of Foreign Ministers, 303-304
Craig, Lewis, 7
Craig, General Malin, 29, 110, 111, 206
  retirement, 117
Cripps mission, 178
Cromwell, Oliver, 11
Cunningham, Admiral, 195

D

Dakar, 134
Darlan, Admiral, 188
Davis, Jefferson, 16
De Gaulle, General, 187
De Lattre de Tassigny, General, 230
Debeney, General Marie-Eugène, 68
Declaration of Independence, 4
Defense, preparations for, 164-165
Department of State, unification of, 290
Dern, George, 109
Devers, General Jacob, 241
Dewey, Thomas, 230
DeWitt, General John L., 30, 74
Dickman, General, 89
Dill, Sir John, 133
  appointment to Washington, 168
  death, 231
  inspection of U.S. troops by, 179
  pessimism of, 141

Dodona Manor, 203
Doolittle raid, 179
Douglas, Ephraim, 9
Drum, General Hugh ., 74
  action on Sedan order, 87
  aversion to air service, 78
  quarrel with Marshall, 167
Duffy, Father, 88
Duke, Basil, 8
Dulles, John Foster, 293
Dunbar Furnace Company, 15

E

Eaker, General Ira C., 224
East Asia Co-prosperity Sphere, 140
Edison, Thomas ., 12
Eisenhower, Dwight D., xi, 119, 187
  in charge of African campaign, 186
  Chief of Staff, 253
  dispute with British Command, 233
  first trip to Europe, 189
  involvement with Darlan, 188
  Supreme Commander, 217, 218
El Alamein, 184
Ely, Colonel Hanson E., 68
Embick, Major Gereral Stanley D., 206
Emerson, Ralph Waldo, 126
Enright, Thomas F., 47
Erskine, John, 94
European invasion, plan for, 176
European Recovery Plan, 305

F

Feng Yu-hsiang, 101, 104
Five-Man Committee, 277, 278
Flying Tigers, 146
Foch, Marshal Ferdinand, 54
  in command of American troops, 72-73
Forrestal, James V., 313
Fort Leavenworth, 30
Frankfurter, Felix, 208
Franklin, Benjamin, 262
Freya Stellung, 184
Frick, H. C., 12
Fuqua, Colonel Stephen O., 30, 51, 74, 90

G

Gallahn, Albert, 9
Gas attack, first, 52
Generals, modern, ix-x
George, Walter, 305
Germany, surrender of, 239
Gerow, Brigadier General, 148
Ghost writers, 245
Gibraltar, inspection of, 199
Gillem, Lieutenant General Alvin C., Jr., 267, 271
Giraud, General, 188
  visit to Washington, 202
Gordon, General (Chinese), 256
Grant, Ulysses S., 8, 20
Grant, Colonel Walter S., 74
Greece, problem of, 291
Green, William, 218
Gresham, Corporal James B., 47
Grew, Joseph, 147
Guadalcanal, 187
GYMNAST, 178, 183-185
  preparations for, 187

H

Hagood, Lieutenant Colonel Johnson, 17, 35, 36, 50
  recommendation of Marshall, 109
Haig, Sir Douglas, 55
Halsey, Admiral Forrest, 226
Harriman, Averell, 318
Harrison, George L., 242
Hanvood, Admiral, 182
Hay, Merle D., 47
Hertling, Chancellor Georg von, 71
Hemisphere Defense Plan No. 1, 124
Henry, Patrick, 4
Hindenburg Line, 75
Hinge of Fate, 182
Hirohito, Emperor of Japan, 144
Hirschauer, General, 74
Historians, task of, xi
Hitler, Adolf, 108
  invasion of Austria, 111
  invasion of Russia, 126

meeting with Mussolini, 124
HOBGOBLIN, 200
Hodges, General Courtney H., 241
Hodges, John R., 107
Hopkins, Harry, 112, 134
illness, 177
influence on invasion plans, 176
opposition to, 208
House, Edward, 49
Howard, Roy W., 91
Hsueh Yueh, General, 168
Hudson's Bay Company, 110
Hull, Cordell, 123
opinion of Japan, 141
warning of attack, 147
Hurley, General Patrick, 253
HUSKY, 194

I
Infantry Journal, 31-32, 96, 97
Infantry in Battle, 97, 106
Inönü, Ismet, 217
Inter-American Defense Parley, 309
International Conference of American States, 309

J
Jackson, Thomas J. (Stonewall), 16, 21-22, 91
Jamestown, Virginia, 3
Japan, aggression by, 136
plans for invasion of, 242
surrender, 243
Jefferson, Thomas, 4, 126
Johnson, Louis, 313
Johnson, Thomas M., 64
Joint Board Estimate of U.S. Over-all Production Requirements, 140
Joint Chiefs of Staff, 168-169

K
Kalgan, capture of, 279-280
Kasserine Pass, 196, 197
Keith, Mary Randolph, 6
Kennan, George, 291
Kenney, Lieutenant General, 196
Kimmel, Admiral . E., 136

King, Admiral Ernest S., 132
Knights of Labor, 12
Knollys, Lord, 176
Knox, Frank, 119
Konoye, Prince, 144
Korea, war in, 314, 316
Kramer, Commander, 156
Kriemhilde Stellung, 84
Kuomintang, 101
aggression by, 270
rise of, 101

L
Lafayette, Marquis de, 9
Laiguelot, General, 88-8g Lanham, Colonel Charles T., 105, 232
Lawrence, T. E., 98
Leahy, Admiral William D., 186
opposition to invasion of Japan, 242
Lederer, John, 10
Lee, Robert E., 8
opinion of Stonewall Jackson, 180
Lend-Lease, 146
Lewis, Major Robert, 69-70
Leyte, 226-227
Liggett, General Hunter, 37, 59, 89
Commander of Second Army, 84-85
Lind, Jenny, 9-10
Lo Lung-chi, 258
Lovett, Robert ., 291
Assistant Secretary of Defense, 313
Secretary of Defense, 323

M
MacArthur, General Douglas, 88, 108, 110, 173
defeat in Philippines, 174
defiance of authority by, 317
dismissal, 318
letter to Joseph Martin, 317
mistakes in Korea, 314
recall to duty, 138
victory in Bismarck Sea, 196
Madison, James, 4
Malvar, Miguel, 25
Manchuria, Russian gains in, 236

Mangin, General Charles M. E., 71
Manpower Bill, 196
Mao Tse-tung, 258
March, General Peyton C., 33
Mareschal, William le, 4
Marines, Chinese ambush of, 275
Markham, Elizabeth, 5
Marshall, Charles, 8
Marshall, George Catlett, 8-9, 12-13
Marshall, George Catlett, Jr., 5
 aide-de-camp to Pershing, 94-95
 appointment to army, 23-24
 appointment to China, 100
 appointment to General Headquarters, 70
 appointment to Infantry School, 105
 attack on labor leaders, 218
 as author, 244-245
 belief in invasion of Europe, 175
 birth, 10
 boyhood, 13-14
 Chief of Operations, Second Army, 84
 Chief of Staff, 117
 Chinese opinion of, 260
 commencement speech at VMI, 118
 Deputy Chief of Staff, 112
 duel with MacArthur, 319-320
 envoy to China, 254-284
 errors in European policy, 238
 estimate of Chinese communism, 265
 failure in China, 284-285
 failure to prepare Hawaii, 150
 fear of a divided country, 160
 first command, 25
 fixed habits, 154
 as football player, 22-23
 interview with Stalin, 296
 lecture tour, 94
 limitations, 219
 marriage, 24
 marriage, second, 107
 meeting with British Chiefs of Staff, 177
 mission to Brazil, 116
 misunderstanding of Japan, 138
 North China tour, 265-266
 Pacific journey, 217-218
 plan for European invasion, 176
 promotion denied, 68
 promotion to General, 109
 quarrel with MacArthur, 196
 reaction to China, 103
 relations with Eisenhower, 195
 relations with press, 219
 relations with Roosevelt, 172
 report on Cantigny, 64-67
 routine as Chief of Staff, 171-172
 schooldays, 17-23
 Secretary of Defense, 312-323
 Secretary of State, 289-312
 service in Philippines, 25-29
 thyroid operation, 110
 on united command, 165-166
 visit to Korea, 322
Marshall, Humphrey, 100
 opinions on China, 255-256
Marshall, Captain John, 4-5
Marshall, Chief Justice John, 4, 6
Marshall, John, of the Forest, 5
Marshall, Louis, 7-8
Marshall, Marie, 13, 14
Marshall, Martin, 7
Marshall, Robert, 5
Marshall, Stuart Bradford, 12, 13-14
Marshall, Thomas, 5, 6
Marshall, Thomas Alexander, 7
Marshall, William, 5-7
Marshall, William Champe, 7-8
Marshall family, 4-9
Marshall Islands, capture of, 221
Marshall Plan, 299-301, 305, 310
Martin, Charles, 111
Martin, General, 137, 138
Martin, Joseph, 317
Marwitz, General George K. von der, 83
McCleare, Colonel Robert, 74
McGuire, Hunter, 16

McNair, General Lesley J., 169, 175
death, 225
McNarney, General Joseph T., 169
Memorandum on Quartermaster Supplies 44-45
Miles, General Sherman, 138
"Molly Maguires," 9
Molotov, Vyachislav, 181
at Moscow Conference, 294-295
Moltke, Helmut von, 41
Montfaucon, 83
Montgomery, Field Marshal Bernard, 194
Morgan, John H., 269
Morgan, Wilfred, 147
Morgenthau, Henry, 208
Morrison, John F., 30
Moscow Conference, 293-298
Mountbatten, Lord Louis, 166, 178
inspection of U.S. troops by, 179
Munitions Assignment Board, 172
Murmansk, 73
Mussolini, Benito, 124

N

Napoleon I, Emperor of France, 316
Napoleon III, Emperor of France, 86
National Assembly, Chinese, 281-282
National Guard, 108
National Rifle Matches, 34
Negroes, in U.S. Army, 162
New Market, battle of, 20-21
Nicholson, Leonard K., 18
Nimitz, Admiral Chester, 225, 226
Normandy, invasion of, 223-224
North Ireland, expedition to, 170
Northcliffe, Lord, 49

O

OCTAGON, 225
Okinawa campaign, 241-242
OVERLORD, 200

P

Palmer, John M., 33, 102
Panama Canal, closing to Japanese shipping of, 137

Paris Conference, 311-312
Parker, General Frank, 87, 90
Patterson, Robert P., 253
Patton, General George S., 187
quarrel with Marshall, 196-197
Pearl Harbor, defense of, 121-124
Japanese raid on, 161
Marshall's report on, 122-123
Navy Court of Enquiry on, 254
warning of attack, 136
Pershing, General John J., 45, 81, 102, 108-109
at Cantigny, 61
creation of Second Army, 84
dispute with Foch, 72
illness, 111
memoirs, 98
opposition to Marshall's transfer, 207
at VMI, 95
Pétain, Marshal Henri, 54, 186
Philippine Islands, defeat in, 173
military aid for, 146
Pickett, Mary Anne, 6
Placentia Bay meeting, 132-134
Plog, William, 18
Pope, Thomas, 5
Portal, Sir Charles, 176
Pound, Admiral Sir Dudley, 176
Preparedness, Marshall's advocacy of, 113
PWA, 112

Q

Quebec Conference, 204
Quezon, Manuel, 25
appeal for Philippine neutrality, 173

R

Rabaul, 194
Rainbow Division, 88-8g
Randolph, John, 3
Richmond, Virginia, 3
Ridgeway, Lieutenant General Matthew B., 116

Commander in Korea, 318
Rifle Training Association, 114
Rome, fall of, 222-223
Rommel, General Erwin, 184
Roosevelt, Eleanor, 239
Roosevelt, Franklin D., 18, 109, 124
action against Japan, 136
air force program, 111
attempts to maintain peace with Japan, 153
influence on military decisions, 183
Roosevelt, Theodore, Jr., 88
Roosevelt and Hopkins, 205
Root, Elihu, 169
Runyon, Damon, 91
Russell, General Henry D., 150
Russia, difficulties with, 216
German invasion of, 126
Marshall's opinion of, 142-143
problem of, 205
Russia's Position, 205
S
St. Mihiel, battle of, 76-79
School of the Line, 30
Second front, 181
Sedan, 86-87
Selective Service, 127
extension of, 135
Sheridan, Philip, 118
Sherrill, Captain C. O., 32
Sherwood, Robert E., 205
Shihpingchieh, battle of, 272
Shipping, Japanese, 137
Short, General Walter C., 159
failure to prepare Hawaii, 150
resignation, 172
Shuttle bombing, 216
Sibert, General William M., 48
Sicily, attack on, 194
Singapore, 124
Smith, General Walter Bedell, 107, 234
Smuts, General Jan C., 217
Somervell, General Brehon B., 112, 169
Soong, T. V., 167
Spaatz, General Carl, 241
Stalin, Josef, 181
advocacy of OVERLORD, 215
victory at Yalta, 235-236
Standard Oil Company, 12
Stark, Admiral Harold R., 132, 136, 139
failure to warn Hawaii, 157
shortcomings of, 142
Stettinius, Edward, 233
Stillwell, General Joseph W., 105
appointment to China command, 167
recall, 229
Stimson, Henry, 94, 119, 149
tribute to Marshall, 239-240
Stone Flower, 297
Strong, General Robert W., 218
Stuart, Leighton, 275, 311
Summerall, General Charles P., 87, 90
Sun Yat-sen, 101, 104, 146
Surrender, unconditional, 194-195
T
Taliaferro, Matilda, 7
Tanks, Sherman, 182-183
Taylor, Major M. J. R., 29
Teheran Conference, 214
Third Party, Chinese, 281
Tidewater of Virginia, 3
Tientsin, 100-101
Tito, Marshal, 321
Tobruk, fall of, 182
Together, 227
Togo, Hideki, 147
message to Nomura, 152
Tolstoy, Leo, 98
TORCH, 185
Training schools, in Tunisia, 198
TRIDENT, 198
Truman, President Harry S., 239
relations with Marshall, 292

Turner, Admiral Richmond K., 154

U

Uniontown, Pennsylvania, 9
United command, Marshall's declaration for, 165-166
  in Pacific area, 166
United States Army in the World War, 1917-1919, 82
United Verde Copper Company, 15
Universal military training, 308, 314
Unpreparedness, American, 96-97

V

Vandenberg, Arthur, 291
Veterans of Foreign Wars, 102
Vichy, 186
Vincent, John C., 259
Virginia, founding of, 3
Virginia Military Institute, 14, 16
Virginia Polytechnic Institute, 17
Voroshilov, Andrei, 215

W

Wainwright, General Jonathan, 174
Wallace, Henry B., 242
War, twentieth century, 247-248
Ward, Frederick T., 256
Ward, Major Ralph, 74
Washington, George, 4, 6
Washington, John, 5
Watkins, Major Lewis H., 74
Wavell, Sir Archibald, 166
Wedemeyer, General Albert C., 192
  report on China, 301-303
Wheeler, Burton K., 129, 210
White Russians, 101
Whitman, Walt, 9
Wilkinson, Admiral T. S., 154
Willkie, Wendell, 186
Wilson, Sir Henry M., 224
Wilson, Woodrow, 38
Winning of the War in Europe and the Pacific, 244
Woodring, Harry H., 117
World War I, armistice, 90
  beginning, 40-41
  early problems of, 41-42
  failure of American troops, 49
  first engagement with enemy, 46-47
  food shortages, 44
  German offensive, 54
  transportation, 43
World War II, Marshall's summary of, 246-248
  preparedness for, 164
WPA, 112
Wu P'ei-fu, 101

Y

Yalta Conference, 232-237

For sales, editorial information, subsidiary rights information
or a catalog, please write or
phone or email:

Brick Tower Press
Manhanset House
Dering Harbor, New York 11965-0342
Sales: 1-800-68-BRICK
Tel: 212-427-7139
www.ibooksinc.com
email: bricktower@aol.com

www.Ingram.com

www.ingramcontent.com/pod-product-compliance
Lightning Source LLC
Chambersburg PA
CBHW050550170426
43201CB00011B/1641